ISBN 978-0-282-37511-9
PIBN 10849389

1 MONTH OF
FREE
READING

at

www.ForgottenBooks.com

By purchasing this book you are eligible for one month membership to ForgottenBooks.com, giving you unlimited access to our entire collection of over 1,000,000 titles via our web site and mobile apps.

To claim your free month visit:

www.forgottenbooks.com/free849389

English
Français
Deutsche
Italiano
Español
Português

www.forgottenbooks.com

Mythology Photography **Fiction**
Fishing Christianity **Art** Cooking
Essays Buddhism Freemasonry
Medicine **Biology** Music **Ancient
Egypt** Evolution Carpentry Physics
Dance Geology **Mathematics** Fitness
Shakespeare **Folklore** Yoga Marketing
Confidence Immortality Biographies
Poetry **Psychology** Witchcraft
Electronics Chemistry History **Law**
Accounting **Philosophy** Anthropology
Alchemy Drama Quantum Mechanics
Atheism Sexual Health **Ancient History**
Entrepreneurship Languages Sport
Paleontology Needlework Islam
Metaphysics Investment Archaeology
Parenting Statistics Criminology
Motivational

LIEUTENANT-GENERAL

IR THOMAS PICTON,

G.C.B. &c.

INCLUDING HIS CORRESPONDENCE,

FROM ORIGINALS IN POSSESSION OF HIS FAMILY, &c.

BY H. B. ROBINSON.

SECOND EDITION REVISED, WITH ADDITIONS.

IN TWO VOLUMES.

VOL. I.

LONDON:

RICHARD BENTLEY, NEW BURLINGTON STREET,

𝔓𝔲𝔟𝔩𝔦𝔰𝔥𝔢𝔯 𝔦𝔫 𝔒𝔯𝔡𝔦𝔫𝔞𝔯𝔶 𝔱𝔬 𝔥𝔦𝔰 𝔐𝔞𝔧𝔢𝔰𝔱𝔶.

1836.

HENRY MORSE STEPHENS

TO HIS GRACE

THE DUKE OF WELLINGTON,

&c. &c.

Sir Thomas Picton fought and fell under your Grace's command—England never lost a more devoted soldier, nor your Grace a more zealous officer.

This Memoir is dedicated to your Grace in Sir Thomas Picton's own words, when, in reply to the House of Commons, upon receiving the thanks of that honourable assembly for his services, he observed

" It would be unfortunate indeed if we failed entirely to reflect some of the rays of the great luminary that directed us."

London, 1835.

VOL. I.   *b*

PREFACE

TO THE SECOND EDITION.

In publishing the second edition of the Memoirs of Sir Thomas Picton, the Author has endeavoured, by a careful revision of the text, and by the introduction of much new and valuable matter, to render the Work more worthy of the personage whose memorable life he has attempted to depict. Numerous additional letters are now added. For these he is indebted to the liberality and kindness of Capt. Marryat, R. N. whose biographical sketch of Sir Thomas Picton in a recent number of the Metropolitan (for the writer presumes to attribute to him the authorship of that article) is alike honourable to his head and to his heart.

To numerous other friends of Sir Thomas Picton, the biographer is indebted for valuable assistance, more particularly to Major General Sir Charles Colville, and to Sir Frederick Maitland, of whose information he has carefully availed himself.

London,
December, 1835.

INTRODUCTION.

OF the numerous distinguished officers whose
brilliant services were familiar to their countrymen at the close of the late war, many have already found biographers. Such memoirs, when
drawn from authentic sources, are a valuable
addition to our annals : they contribute to that
mass of materials from which hereafter, when
all inducement to partial praise or censure shall
have ceased, an adequate history will be drawn
of that eventful period.

Of these companions of the one great chief,
none was more illustrious than Picton. Always
engaged in important commands — present at
the most daring and successful movements, the
history of his life includes the most prominent

events in the Peninsular War. A more zealous or a braver soldier there was not in our army.

Some brief memoirs of Sir Thomas Picton have been published; but these are devoid of authority, and are generally incorrect. It was a consideration of these circumstances which induced the author, who had, access to entirely new and authentic materials, to undertake the present work.

Some years since, when he was in South Wales, accident gave him an introduction to the brother of the late gallant general, the Reverend Edward Picton, of Iscoed, near Ferryside, Carmarthenshire. This beautiful spot had long been the property of the general, and by him it was bequeathed to its present possessor. In almost every corner of the mansion a bust, a painting, or some other memorial, reminded the visitor of Sir Thomas. On these records the author dwelt with a deep interest. After many years, it recurred to the memory of the author, that whilst at Iscoed he had heard Mr. Picton speak of letters and manuscripts in his possession relating to his brother. Having conceived the idea of writing a life of the general, the author applied to be permitted the use of these valuable papers in the composition of his intended Memoir; and in a short time afterwards he was gratified by the receipt of a box containing the whole of the documents in Mr. Picton's possession which related to the public career of his gallant brother.*

From these manuscripts, the recollections of his family and friends, together with the valuable communications of officers who served with him throughout the whole of his distinguished career, the present Work has been composed. It was not, however, possible that a life of Sir Thomas Picton could be written without embracing a general outline of the operations of the British army in the Peninsula. This was the scene of his principal services, and we must necessarily follow him into the field where his renown was acquired.

One subject connected with the early life of Sir Thomas Picton possesses a painful interest:

* Frequent applications had been made to Mr. Picton for the use of these papers in preparing a Memoir of the general, but to all, his constant answer was, that he would not allow them to be published during his life-time. By a remarkable coincidence, this worthy gentleman died in September last, just as this Work was about to be published.

—the protracted prosecution to which he was subjected. The grave has, however, closed over nearly all who took an active part in those proceedings ; and his brilliant career and glorious death have wholly removed the stigma which upon that occasion was attempted to be inflicted on his name.*.

The letters of Sir Thomas Picton introduced into this work are full of interest. The majority of them were written within a few days after the different occurrences to which they relate. This gives them a value to which more elaborate compositions cannot lay claim ; for the unpremeditated conceptions of a strong and comprehensive mind possess a truth and freshness which no after consideration can improve.

---

* A circumstance relating to this disgraceful prosecution ought to be recorded, as highly honourable to both the parties concerned. I nt he course of the narrative it is stated that excessive bail, amounting to the enormous sum of twenty thousand pounds, was required for the appearance of the gallant general to meet the charge, but it has not hitherto been made public to whose generosity Sir Thomas Picton was indebted upon this extremely trying occasion. To the late Joseph Marryat, Esq., M.P. for Sandwich, this act of public spirit, to which he was unsolicited, is to be ascribed.

In some instances the excitement of battle had scarcely passed away when the general sat down to calm the apprehension of fraternal affection or friendly solicitude. The soldier can be traced in every line. He seldom speaks of his own dangers and escapes, but confines himself to a relation of the proceedings of " his division"—the brave "fighting division;" how his soldiers conducted themselves; the part they bore in the struggles of the day, their heroism, and their losses: but of himself, who was ever at their head, and who shared with them every danger and privation, he says little. Once, and only once, does he allude to his own danger: this occurs in a letter to his brother just after the battle of Vittoria, in which he observes, " I was very fortunate, having escaped with only one shot-hole in my great-coat."

In consequence of this total absence of personal details in his correspondence, the author has been happy to avail himself of the information communicated by officers who served with him. Many of these are still living, and to them he is indebted for many particulars of Sir Thomas Picton's actions, his judgment, decision, and heroism. The author regrets that he is not allowed to strengthen the authority of these communications by publishing the names of the distinguished officers to whom he is indebted for them.

London, Sept. 1835.

CONTENTS

THE FIRST VOLUME.

CHAPTER I.

CHAPTER II.

CHAPTER III.

CHAPTER VII.

CHAPTER VIII.

CHAPTER IX.

CHAPTER XIX.

TO THE BINDER.

The Plan of Operations at the Sierra de Busacos to be
placed opposite page 317.

THE LIFE

OF

LIEUTENANT-GENERAL

SIR THOMAS PICTON,

G.C.B.

CHAPTER I.

Parentage.— Education.— Enters the Army.— Repairs to Gibraltar.—Made Lieutenant.—Captain of the Seventy-fifth Foot.— Leaves Gibraltar.— Siege.— His Regiment Disbanded. — Serious Mutiny in consequence. — His Spirited Conduct.—Receives the Royal Approbation.—Placed upon Half-pay.—Pursuits.—Personal Appearance.—Martial Disposition.

THOMAS PICTON, the subject of the present memoir, was born in the month of August 1758, at the residence of his father, Thomas Picton, Esq. of Poyston, in the county of Pembroke. Thomas was a younger brother; but, unlike the majority of young men so circumstanced, he was not entirely dependent

upon his own exertions for future fortune:
on the contrary, young Picton was entitled
upon the death of his mother to considerable
property; an event which, on its occurrence,
rendered him independent of any profession.

But this in his early youth was only a distant expectation; and it was then necessary
that he should attach himself to some profession. His earliest thoughts and inclinations
led him to select that of arms; and, according
to the words of his reverend brother, "he would
not hear of any other."

The prospects in a soldier's life are certainly
not such as would induce a sober preference;
but to the young, the army has irresistible
charms. Its constant excitement, occasional
successes, and the hope of fame, possess at-
tractions; although the many who have fought
and fallen without their names being known
beyond the circle of their private friends,
prove this hope to be as vain as it is dazzling.

With an ardour for all military studies,
young Picton particularly directed his attention to those sciences which make the rising

soldier an ornament to his profession; and the proficiency he soon acquired in these, gave him at once a superiority over his companions, who had contented themselves with the inapplicable course of education prescribed at our public and private schools. Latin and Greek are there made the groundwork for the soldier and the sailor, as well as for the lawyer and the divine; whereas the mathematics are the great requisite to the aspirant for military fame, and a knowledge of Euclid will be of more professional utility to him in after-life than an acquaintance with all the Greek and Roman classics. Fortunate in the advice of a sensible parent, and having a natural taste for the studies connected with his profession, Picton was permitted to follow the bent of his inclinations: but it must not thence be inferred that the young soldier was allowed entirely to neglect the acquirement of those branches of education which are indispensable to the character of a gentleman. Before he commenced his military education, his friends had taken care to instil into him some little, although of course, at his tender age, not a very extensive, knowledge of the classics, and of the literature of his own country.

After leaving school he was sent, previously to entering upon his professional career, to a military academy kept by a Frenchman named Lachée, where he obtained a great addition to his knowledge of mathematics and the art of war.

In December 1771, being then thirteen years of age, he obtained an ensigncy in the Twelfth regiment of foot, then commanded by his uncle, Lieutenant-colonel William Picton, Lord Cornwallis being colonel. The name of Thomas Picton appears in the Gazette for February 1772, as appointed ensign in that regiment; the date of his first commission being January the 22nd in that year.

The present age would condemn the admission of so young a soldier into our army as unnatural and dangerous: for it is surely unnatural to expose to all the perils and privations of war those who still require maternal care; and dangerous, to place in a probable situation of responsibility one who can possess neither judgment nor resolution, qualities so

absolutely necessary in the performance of
every military duty. When Ensign Picton entered the army it was no uncommon occurrence
for the captain of a company to be a boy at
school, while many of equally tender years were
already employed in active service : and yet it
cannot be denied that the English army, during
the late struggle with continental Europe, produced officers who in courage and military excellence might rival those of any nation in the
world; although nearly the whole of these entered the army at the same time of life as the
subject of this memoir.

Nearly two years elapsed after obtaining his
commission before young Picton joined his
regiment ; but during this period, and, in fact,
during the first six years of his holding this
rank, he had no pay, in consequence of the
peculiar circumstances under which he received his ensigncy. A captain in the regiment,
who had rendered himself obnoxious to the
rest of the officers, had been allowed to retire
upon full pay; and in consequence of this
arrangement, the youngest ensign without
purchase received no pay, the youngest lieu-

tenant without purchase received that of an
ensign, and the youngest captain that of a lieutenant.

Our young soldier left the military academy
of Monsieur Lachée to join his regiment at
Gibraltar, there to undergo the unvarying, and,
in general, uninteresting, routine of garrison
duty. Those, and they are but few, who survive, and remember that early period of his
career, speak of him as manifesting even then
that strongly marked character for firmness
and decision which distinguished him through
life.

From the boyish ensign he soon became the
steady but inquisitive soldier; his principal
delight, whilst upon duty in this fortress,
(which presents every feature of the engineer's art,) was to wander through the mazes
of fortification, trace the operation and design of the numerous works, observe the choice
of position, formation, and support of the endless batteries; while he would frequently be
arranging plans of attack, with additional defences which the garrison might erect in case
of being driven from some of their positions.
With these plans, and a host of inquiries,

young Picton was in the habit of almost persecuting the officers of the garrison; and they are recorded here as an illustration of the decided taste which he thus early betrayed for the military profession.

It was another occasional source of amusement to him, whilst stationed at Gibraltar, to make excursions into Spain; and during these expeditions he obtained such knowledge of the language as enabled him in after-years to fill that important situation which produced so great an influence both over his fortunes and his happiness. It was not only the Spanish language, however, that he acquired during this period of inaction ; his leisure hours, which were by far too many for his active disposition, were devoted to the study of such books as were calculated to advance him in the knowledge of his professional duties : in addition to which, he was greatly indebted to his uncle for many practical hints drawn from his own observations during a long life of constant and distinguished service.*

* The estimation in which this meritorious officer was held by his Sovereign, cannot be better expressed than by the following extract from a manuscript in his own hand-

In March 1777, Ensign Picton was promoted to the rank of lieutenant in the same
regiment. He was, however, now weary of
the monotony of garrison duty, and anxiously
looked forward to an appointment to some
active service. During the five years he had
been at Gibraltar, he had served under Generals Sir Robert Boyd and Lord Heathfield;
but the merits of one in so humble a rank as
that held by Lieutenant Picton seldom call
forth the particular notice of their superiors;

writing, in reference to his being appointed lieutenant-
colonel of the Twelfth regiment, which is worthy of record as exhibiting the tenacious recollection, and the pleasure in rewarding merit, which marked the character of
George the Third. " When Lieutenant-colonel Picton went
to court to kiss hands on his appointment, having had the
honour after the levee of being admitted to an audience in
the King's closet, he addressed his Majesty with profound
respect, expressing his most dutiful and grateful acknowledgments for the honour that had been conferred upon
him. The Sovereign, with the utmost complacency, was
pleased to say: ' You are solely obliged to Captain Picton,
who in Germany commanded the grenadier company of the
Twelfth regiment during the last war;' alluding in particular
to the colonel's having had the honour of being thanked, as
captain of the grenadiers, by Prince Ferdinand, in the public orders of the army, in consequence of the report made
by the then Hereditary Prince of Brunswick of his behaviour under his Serene Highness's command at the affair of
Zierenberg."

and he requested his uncle to obtain for him
an exchange into some regiment which had an
earlier prospect of taking the field. This, in
times when officers were more in request and
vacancies more frequent, was not a very difficult task; and in January 1778 he was gazetted captain in the Seventy-fifth, or Prince of
Wales' regiment of foot; in consequence of
which he returned to England, and thus, by
a singular fatality, was debarred from participating in one of the most memorable and important sieges recorded in modern history.

Within a few months from the period of
his leaving Gibraltar, the Spaniards fitted out
their grand expedition for the investment and
attack of this key to the Mediterranean. The
history of this siege is one of unparalleled
interest. Every contrivance of modern warfare was resorted to by the besiegers, directed
by the ablest engineers of France and Spain:
the eyes of all Europe were fixed upon the
struggle. The English nation, confident in
the courage and skill of its defenders, watched
with anxious hope the progress of the operations. The Twelfth regiment, commanded by
Captain Picton's uncle, who was in 1779 ap-

pointed colonel, bore a distinguished part in
the defence ; and it was always with a feeling
of deep regret that the subject of this memoir
spoke of the circumstance of his leaving Gibraltar at that particular period, by which he
lost the opportunity of participating in the defence of that fortress.

The details of this memorable siege are well
known ; and it is only necessary to state that,
after almost incessant operations for three years
in erecting batteries, making assaults, and in
unsuccessful endeavours to prevent our fleets
from affording relief to the garrison, the besiegers made one last and desperate effort on
the 13th September 1782. The garrison were
however prepared at all points; an incessant
fire of red-hot shot destroyed the Spanish ship-
ping, dismounted their guns, and burnt their
batteries; at the same time, the British troops
repulsed every assault, drove the assailants from
their works, and, after an immense slaughter,
compelled them to abandon the siege, leaving
Gibraltar from that day in the undisputed possession of the English.

Captain Picton had indeed much reason to
regret his impatience in quitting the Twelfth

regiment. In the pursuit of active employment he was particularly unfortunate, as he was now doomed to undergo the still more irksome and monotonous routine of doing duty in provincial towns and home garrisons; during the whole of which time he was continually reading in the public prints the spirit-stirring accounts of the progress of the siege of Gibraltar. Another five years of his life was thus passed without calling forth any of those brilliant talents which even at this period were apparent to those who knew him intimately. Even after this period of unprofitable service, it was his fate to be thrown still farther from the sphere to which his inclinations led him, and for which he was so admirably calculated.

The sudden reduction which took place in the military force of Great Britain in the year 1783, occasioned much disappointment among those aspirants for distinctions who had recent-ly obtained commissions in the new regiments which had been raised the preceding year. These were almost without any exception re-duced or totally disbanded; and a great num-ber of individuals in humble life were thus thrown back upon their own resources, the exhaustion of which had in most instances been their only inducement for entering the army. It will readily be believed that this measure, however necessary, was exceedingly obnoxious to those whom it thus affected, and on several occasions these feelings were expressed to an alarming extent.

The Seventy-fifth was at this period quartered in Bristol, Captain Picton being at the time senior, and consequently commanding, officer. In accordance with the general order calling upon the commanders of regiments to make the necessary preparations for disbanding their corps, Captain Picton assembled the men in College Green Square, and read to them the instructions which he had received; requiring them at the same time to conform quietly and with readiness to the necessity of the case. Only a slight murmur of discontent was at first audible after the order to disembody the regiment had been read, the soldiers being probably awed by the presence of their officers; but no sooner had they retired than the men were guilty of the most mutinous and turbulent conduct, assembling together in a body, and entering into a general compact upon oath not to give up their arms or obey the commands of their officers. Several other regiments were at this time in the city, and the most fearful apprehensions were entertained by the inhabitants lest the contagion should spread, and a disorderly soldiery be let loose upon them. Some officers of the Seventy-fifth were quickly upon the spot, who in vain exhorted the rioters to return to their duty, and submit to the commands of their superiors; telling them that their opposition must be useless, and that it was disgraceful to the character of British soldiers. But their efforts were vain, clamour drowned their voices, and their attempts to reason with the mutineers only drew upon themselves threats of personal violence.

Affairs were in this alarming state when information was brought to Captain Picton of the disorder. He immediately hastened to the scene of confusion and tumult; and, singling out in an instant the most active of the mutineers, he drew his sword, and without a moment's hesitation rushed into the midst of them, seized him, and dragged him forth from amongst his comrades. He was immediately taken by some non-commissioned officers who had followed their captain, and placed under arrest. This decisive step daunted the other mutineers, and they saw the leader in silence led off to the guard-house. A few words from their captain, spoken in a tone which did not seem to admit of reply, now sent them at once to their barracks. By this intrepidity and resolution, which in moments of emergency distinguish a superior mind, the danger was at once averted, and the regiment was forthwith disbanded without another murmur.

Upon the report of these proceedings being made at the War Office, the spirited conduct of Captain Picton became known to the King, who directed that the royal approbation should be communicated to him for " the courage and true military spirit which he displayed in quelling the mutiny in the Seventy-fifth regiment." This was conveyed to Captain Picton through the then Commander-in-chief, Field-marshal Conway, with a promise from that officer of the first vacant majority ; but, as the sequel will prove, this message was the only reward which Captain Picton ever received for this important service.

Upon the disbanding of his regiment, Captain Picton was placed upon half-pay, and retired into Pembrokeshire, where he enjoyed the affection and esteem of a numerous circle of relations and friends; and although it was much against his inclination that he thus early left his professional duties, and retired into private life, still he readily adapted himself to the novelty of his situation; for it must be remembered, that from the age of thirteen he had been a soldier, and consequently his recollections of home were only those of a boy. Thus far his career had been successful, but not very eventful. A captain at five-and-twenty is now considered in a fair way to the highest military rank which interest or merit can obtain for him. But Captain Picton was doomed to lose all the advantages which he had already gained in his early and rapid promotion. Fortune had never yet given him an opportunity of displaying those talents which he so unquestionably possessed; and those who were in authority naturally estimated the merits of an individual by the

services he had performed. After his regiment
was disbanded, Sir Thomas Picton remained
for the long period of twelve years on the half-
pay list of captains!

We shall pass over this interval briefly: few
events occur in the domestic circle of a country town worthy of being recorded. Had there
been any active hostilities in which Captain
Picton could have taken a part, it is more
than probable that the natural bent of his disposition would have induced him to volunteer
his services; but during nearly the whole of
this time Europe was at peace. He was therefore more reconciled to the necessity of his
situation, although he was unremitting in his
applications to be placed on full-pay in some
regiment ordered on foreign service. The unvarying reply of the gentlemen of the War
Office was, that he would be appointed to the
"earliest vacancy." But repeated disappointments convinced him that an official promise
is not always to be depended upon; and, after
a few more unsuccessful efforts, he gave up
the attempt.

His time was passed during this period of

inactivity, according to the statement of his brother, the Rev. Edward Picton, in "the enjoyment of the sports of the field, in studying the classics, but more particularly in perfecting himself in the art of war." He was now preparing for that career which was afterwards so well known, and which was destined to be productive of so much honour to himself and advantage to his country. Few biographies offer a better or more elevated example to the young soldier, of the advantages which he may obtain by improving his mind in the knowledge of his profession, than this of Sir Thomas Picton's domestic life. Some writer says, " that to feel great is to be great." Without admitting the truth of this assertion in its full extent, it cannot be denied that men seldom become elevated above the level of their ambition. Captain Picton was no doubt at this time conscious that the abilities he possessed required only an opportunity to display themselves, in order to be appreciated; and while labouring to qualify himself to improve any such opportunity to the utmost, he was looking forward to the attainment of the highest honours of his profession.

In person Captain Picton was at this time tall and well-proportioned, approaching the athletic; his height about six feet one inch, and his features large but well formed. The natural expression of his face was stern and dignified; but his smile dispelled at once a repulsive expression which sometimes hung upon his brow. None who ever saw that smile could deny that it betokened a warm and generous heart. His eyes were brilliant and expressive; his voice sharp, and his manner of speaking quick and animated. He always commanded respect and attention; the earnestness of his delivery and the power of his language impressed the hearer with conviction. But in the field, his tone of voice was totally altered; it was there full and deep; every word was calm and impressive, and its effect upon his soldiers was apparent in the increased confidence of their charge.

Picton, thus resolved to prepare himself for any rank in his profession to which Fortune might elevate him, applied with ardour to every pursuit which could possibly assist him

various duties he might be called
perform; and it was during this long
f privacy that he laid the foundation
fter fame, and qualified himself to
for a place among the heroes of his

CHAPTER II.

Unsuccessful attempts to obtain employment.—Embarks
for the West Indies.—Joins Sir John Vaughan.—Made
Deputy Quarter-Master-General.—Superseded by Gene-
ral Knox.—Introduction to Sir Ralph Abercromby.—
Assists in the Capture of St. Lucia and St. Vincent.—
Voyage to England and return to Martinique with Sir
Ralph Abercromby.—Capture of Trinidad.—Made Com-
mandant.—Instructions from Sir Ralph Abercromby.

In February 1793, France commenced that
extraordinary struggle against the nations of
Europe, which, notwithstanding her internal
discord, and the depopulating activity of the
guillotine, she carried on with as much vigour
and success as in her best and brightest days.
The preparations for hostilities, and his strong
desire for active service, induced Captain
Picton to renew his applications to the Commander-in-chief for employment: but they
were still unavailing; the same polite replies
and general assurances were made to his letters
as formerly, and he was soon convinced that

interest, and nothing but interest, would obtain for him his wishes. Of this he had not much; and no one could have been surprised had he turned with disgust from a profession in which he had such slender prospects of · success. Fortunately, however, Captain Picton rightly considered that *his* past services gave him no particular claim for preferment; and this reconciled him in some degree to the disappointment which he had constantly to endure.

One whole year of hostilities was passed by Captain Picton in endeavours to obtain employment; when, tired of making applications, and hopeless of success, he resolved upon trying to procure for himself that which he had been so long seeking from others. Accordingly, towards the end of the year 1794, he embarked, without any appointment, for the West Indies, having no better prospect than a slight acquaintance with Sir John Vaughan, who had just been appointed commander-in-chief in that part of the globe. This step was probably the remote cause of Sir Thomas Picton's after fame; and to Sir John Vaughan England is probably indebted for the important services afterwards rendered by the

man whose abilities he discovered and employed. Sir John Vaughan at once appointed Captain Picton to the Seventeenth foot, making
him at the same time his confidential aid-de-
camp, by which he had a closer and more constant opportunity of discerning the activity of
his disposition and the strength of his judgment. Captain Picton was now for the first
time, in active service, and so well pleased
was his general with the manner in which he
fulfilled the duties of his situation, that he
quickly promoted him to a majority in the
Sixty-eighth regiment, together with the appointment of deputy quarter-master-general,
which entitled him to the brevet rank of lieutenant-colonel.

Fortune seemed thus inclined to recompense
him for the length of time he had lost;
and it will be perceived that when once Sir
Thomas Picton had an opportunity of displaying the powers of his mind, his abilities were
so highly appreciated, that he was never afterwards exposed to neglect; but, on the contrary,
his life was passed in active and meritorious
services. Sir John Vaughan held his important command for little more than one year,

when ill health compelled him to resign, and Major Picton had, a short time after this event, to regret the loss of his friend. He died at Martinique, in the month of August 1795.

Major Picton was continued at the head of the quarter-master-general's department until superseded by General Knox, when he resolved to return to Europe, having little expectation of promotion or employment now that his patron was no more. Before, however, he could put his plans in execution, he was called upon by General Leigh, (who was at this period senior officer in the West Indies,) to assist him in receiving Sir Ralph Abercromby, upon the arrival of that gallant veteran at Barbadoes, to take the command in the place of the late Sir John Vaughan.

This was the first occasion upon which Major Picton had been personally introduced to Sir Ralph: the name was familiar to the general, through the knowledge which he possessed of his uncle; the merits of Major Picton were, however, totally unknown to Sir Ralph previously to this meeting; but it is probable that that discerning officer discovered, at this

interview the superior powers and attainments
of his new acquaintance. He received him
in the most warm and friendly manner; and
when, after Major Picton had in few words
related his services, the situations he had
held, and that, apprehensive of not being enabled to continue in active employment in the
West Indies, he intended to return immediately to England; Sir Ralph took his hand,
and in language as gratifying as it was unexpected, requested that he would continue with
him during the ensuing campaign, hoping, as
he observed, " to give him an opportunity of
returning in a way more agreeable." This
invitation was so flattering, and so much
in accordance with Picton's desires, that he
did not hesitate to accept it; and from this
period until the death of Sir Ralph Abercromby, a mutual regard and esteem existed
between these illustrious men, which no petty
intrigue or professional jealousy could for a
moment impair.

Immediately upon the arrival of Sir Ralph
in the West Indies, he made every arrangement for active hostilities against such colonies
as still remained in possession of the French.

The first place against which he directed his forces was St. Lucia, whither he was accompanied by Major Picton, as one of his suite, but not holding any command. Major Picton could not, however, remain an inactive spectator during the progress of the attack, and accordingly volunteered to occupy any post to which Sir Ralph might appoint him. In the attack upon this island he acted a zealous, although not a very distinguished part. His rank at this period was only major, for with the situation of deputy quarter-master-general he lost the brevet rank of lieutenant-colonel, and fell back into that which he actually held in the army. He had no recognised appointment in the force under Sir Ralph Abercromby : his services therefore, however individually meritorious, were not performed under circumstances which would warrant any specific mention of him by Sir Ralph in his public despatches. During the whole of the proceedings he acted as a volunteer aid-de-camp to Sir Ralph, and, as was strongly testified by that able chief, obtained from him his warmest approbation for judgment and intrepidity.

On the 22nd of April, the troops destined for

the attack upon St. Lucia sailed from Carlisle
Bay, in the fleet commanded by Admiral Sir
John Laforey, and arrived off Longville Bay
the evening of the 26th, when Major-general
Campbell was ordered immediately to disem-
bark with seventeen hundred men; this he
succeeded in doing, and took up a position for
the night, without any further opposition than
a few guns fired from the batteries on Pigeon
Island. Early on the following morning he
advanced upon Choc Bay, where the fleet had
anchored during the night with the remainder
of the troops; the moment the head of this
column was perceived, the centre division of
the army disembarked near the village of Choc,
when a force of about five hundred men,
which had been faintly and vainly resisting
the advance of Major-general Campbell's corps,
retired with precipitation to a spot called
Morne Chabot, one of the strongest and most
commanding situations in the neighbourhood.

As it was absolutely necessary to obtain
possession of this fort before investing Morne
Fortune, Sir Ralph Abercromby ordered an assault to be made during the night by two de-

tachments; the one commanded by Brigadier-general Hope, and the other by Brigadier-general Moore.* This attack was intended to be made upon two opposite sides at the same moment; and accordingly Brigadier-general Moore, having to proceed by the most circuitous route, commenced his march with about five hundred men precisely at midnight; while Brigadier-general Hope, who had to follow a more direct path, delayed his departure for a short time longer, when he also, with about the same number of men, moved forward.

The information upon which this expedition was planned had unfortunately been drawn from ignorant or treacherous guides; and the calculation of time necessary for the two corps to perform the distance was consequently erroneous. Brigadier-general Moore's leading column suddenly fell in with an advanced picquet of the enemy at least an hour and a half earlier than was expected. Upon this occasion, the promptitude and decision of that distinguished officer were particularly conspicuous. Finding that his march was dis-

* Afterwards Sir John Moore.

covered, and that it was impossible to halt
the troops, as from the narrowness of the path
they were marching in single file, he at once
resolved upon making the attack, without
waiting for the co-operation of Brigadier-general Hope's division. The spirit of his men
ably seconded his determination. Forming
with as much expedition and regularity as
the nature of the ground would admit, they
pushed on with a resolution that was irresistible, and in a very short time carried the post at the point of the bayonet.
Sir Ralph Abercromby observed in his despatch, that " Brigadier-general Hope's division
marched with so much precision, that they
arrived exactly at the time appointed; and,
if fortunately the attack could have been executed as was directed, the whole force of the
enemy would have fallen." The loss sustained by the French during this short but
brilliant affair was between forty and fifty men
killed, and two hundred stand of arms, with
some ammunition.

Active preparations were now made for the
investment of Morne Fortune, where the
enemy had established himself in some force,

having a garrison of about two thousand well-disciplined and well-affected coloured troops, several hundred whites, besides a number of black people who had flown thither for refuge. The difficulty of communication in this country rendered the proceedings more tedious than was at first imagined, while the operation of erecting batteries for the reduction of this fortress was a work of constant labour and much danger.

During the progress of the siege, the enemy made several desperate sorties, but were invariably repulsed with considerable loss ; although not without doing much injury to the besiegers. The rugged and mountainous character of the country rendered the progress of the siege slow, and its event doubtful ; but the persevering disposition and endless resources of the English general overcame every obstacle. Every inch of ground was disputed by the defenders with courage and skill, and nothing but the most indefatigable exertion and constant preparation for attack enabled the assailants to erect a battery on the mountainous ridge of Duchasseux, which in a great measure commands the fortress. During this laborious operation, the

officers and seamen of the fleet (which, Sir
John Laforey having resigned the command,
was now under the orders of Rear-admiral Sir
Hugh Christian,) rendered the most important
services in dragging up the guns, and transporting the ammunition up the steep and
rugged ground over which it was of necessity
conveyed.

By incessant efforts day and night the besiegers were enabled to open a battery of eighteen guns on the 16th of May; but this being
only on the first parallel, the further approaches
were continued until the morning of the 24th,
when three regiments were ordered to gain
possession of a more advanced post. In this
they were opposed in the most vigorous and
resolute manner by the enemy; but the contest was not of long duration. Brigadier-general Moore led the assault with an energy which
soon overcame all opposition; and the assailants
succeeded in establishing themselves within
about five hundred yards of the fort. Two
batteries of eight guns were immediately
commenced, and were to have been opened on
the following morning; when, towards night,

the enemy, perceiving that further resistance would be futile, sent a flag of truce, demanding a suspension of hostilities until noon the following day. A truce was granted until eight o'clock the next morning, when the capitulation of the whole island ensued; and the garrison, to the number of two thousand, marched out and laid down their arms. The loss of the English during this short but laborious siege was five hundred and sixty-six killed, wounded, and missing, including several valuable and promising officers.

It would be impossible at this time to follow Major Picton through the different situations in which he was placed, and the services which he performed during this siege; but for a striking proof of the estimation in which his conduct was held by the general, it is only necessary to quote the following passage from the public orders issued by Sir Ralph Abercromby immediately after the subjugation of the island. In this he says, "that all orders coming through Lieutenant-colonel Picton shall be considered as the orders of the commander-in-chief." So decided a mark of approbation thus universally expressed to the whole army must be interpreted as a strong testimony of the high opinion entertained of his merits; but, not contented with paying him this distinguished compliment, Sir Ralph, without solicitation upon his part, recommended him for the lieutenant-colonelcy of the Fifty-sixth regiment.

After having arranged with Major-general Nicholls an expedition against Grenada, Sir Ralph Abercromby proceeded in person with the rest of the troops, accompanied by Lieutenant-colonel Picton, to attack the island of St. Vincent's. On the 7th of June, the fleet arrived off the island; but the soldiers were not disembarked until the evening of the 8th. Early the following morning they marched in one column by their right as far as Stubbs, about eight miles from Kingston, where they were formed into three divisions, and bivouacked for the night opposite to their places of attack. At daylight the next day the assault on the forts was commenced, and continued with various success and but little intermission until the afternoon; the garrison still making a determined resistance. The resolution of British troops at length, however, prevailed : they were successful in every direction, and before four o'clock the English colours waved upon every position lately occupied by the enemy. In this well-contested struggle, of the English, one hundred and seventy-nine rank and file, besides officers, were killed or wounded.

Upon the termination of this short but brilliant campaign, Colonel Picton accompanied Sir Ralph Abercromby to Martinique, whence, after remaining a short period, he sailed with him for Europe, in the Arethusa. During the whole of this voyage, and the short stay Sir Ralph made in England, Colonel Picton and he were on the most friendly and intimate terms; and he was often in after years heard to speak of this period of his life as one of unalloyed pleasure. It was not only the great strength of mind and general information possessed by Sir Ralph Abercromby which made Colonel Picton recall with so much satisfaction the hours he had passed in his society, but he always expressed himself to be deeply indebted to that experienced soldier for some lessons upon military tactics, which he never forgot, and which he was afterwards enabled to apply. He was therefore justly called one of Sir Ralph Abercromby's pupils, and he was proud of the appellation. There never was a better master, while few scholars ever attained so near to the perfection of their tutor.

After a stay in England of not more than two months, during which time Colonel Picton was constantly with his kind patron, he again sailed with Sir Ralph for the West Indies, and without any incident worthy of remark arrived, near the end of January 1797, at Martinique. An expedition against Trinidad had for some time been determined on; and shortly after the return of the commander-in-chief to the West Indies, he made the necessary arrangements with Admiral Harvey to proceed at once to the capture of that valuable island. The Spaniards had long been in expectation of an attack; and had collected four ships of the line and several frigates for their defence, which were moored in a bay under the protection of some batteries of considerable strength.

On the evening of the 16th of February the English squadron arrived off this bay;

when the admiral, having observed the position of the Spanish fleet, ordered preparations to be made for an early attack on the following morning. During the night, however, flames were perceived bursting from one of their ships, which spread with so much rapidity, that in a short time the whole were consumed, with the exception of one line-of-battle ship, which contrived to escape the conflagration, but which was captured by the boats of the British fleet. After this disaster, which was said to have been produced by accident, the enemy was not in a condition to make any effectual resistance; and when Sir Ralph Abercromby landed his troops in the morning, he was permitted to march into Puerto de Espagna, the principal town, almost unopposed. The governor requested permission to treat; which being granted, and the terms agreed to, the whole island was surrendered to Great Britain without any further resistance.

The reduction of Trinidad was one of the most important events in the life of Picton, since in its consequences it threw a shadow not only over his living fortunes, but even over his memory.

In our relation of the circumstances out of which the accusations afterwards brought against him arose, we shall adhere strictly to the facts of the case; a simple statement of these will be his best and his sufficient vindication. Almost the first act of Sir Ralph Abercromby after obtaining possession of Trinidad, was to appoint Colonel Picton governor and commandant of his new conquest; a mark of approbation which he had never ventured to solicit, and which was therefore quite unexpected.

Sir Ralph Abercromby made but a brief stay at this island; but during the short time he was there, he saw enough to convince him that the duties which Colonel Picton would have to perform were very arduous. He was constantly beset by a crowd of complainants against the corruption and cupidity of the administrators of justice; and a few days before his departure from the island, while giving Colonel Picton some additional instructions, he observed: " I have placed you in a trying and delicate situation,—nor, to give you any chance of overcoming the difficulties opposed to you, can I leave you a strong garrison; but I shall give you ample powers : *execute Spanish law as well*

as you can ; do justice according to your conscience, and that is all that can be expected
from you. His Majesty's government will be
minutely informed of your situation, and, no
doubt, will make all due allowances."

On the 25th of February, Sir Ralph Abercromby sailed from Trinidad, having previously
drawn up with his own hand the following
code of " instructions" for the guidance of
Colonel Picton and Chief-Justice Nicholl in
administering the laws of the colony.

" INSTRUCTIONS.

" General SIR RALPH ABERCROMBY, K.B.

" Commander-in-chief of His Majesty's Forces in the Windward and Leeward Charibbee Islands, &c. &c.

" The island of Trinidad having submitted
to his Majesty's arms, by the power and authority vested in me, by these presents I no-
minate you, John Nicholl, Esq. to be chief
judge and auditor (during his Majesty's pleasure) over all and every part of the said island ;
and you are hereby required and commanded
to perform and execute all manner of things
appertaining to the aforesaid offices, conformably to the instructions and powers you shall

receive from me through the Lieutenant-colonel Picton, whom I have appointed governor
of the said island; and whose instructions and
powers are to be considered of equal force as
if given under my hand.   And as there was
no stipulation (in the capitulation) in favour
of the Spanish laws in the administration of
justice, and as they were merely continued by
my circular letter to the commandants of quarters, magistrates, &c. in order to avoid the
confusion which might result from too strict
an adherence to the forms of the jurisprudence
under an English government, you will receive particular instructions from Lieutenant-
colonel Picton explanatory of my intentions.
And as I have judged it expedient to suspend
from his employment the assessor-general, and
not to name any one to fill that office in his
stead, you are ordered to proceed in all causes,
whether civil or criminal, without any assessor,
although it may be contrary to the form and
spirit of the Spanish laws.   And I hereby
declare that all sentences given and signed
by you without the accompaniment of an
assessor, shall have the same force and validity
as if they were so accompanied, and shall be

executed in the same common and ordinary
form.

" And as I have received serious complaints
of the extortions practised by the exactions
of excessive fees, and the mal-applications of
useless and unnecessary proceedings in the administration of justice, by the escrivanos, attor-
neys, &c. you are hereby required to shorten
and simplify the proceedings, and to terminate
all causes in the most expeditious and least
expensive manner that the circumstances of
them will admit, according to the dictates of
your conscience, the best of your abilities,
and conformably to the instructions you shall
receive from Lieutenant-colonel Picton, although it should be contrary to the usual practice of the Spanish government. And I also
give you full power and authority to suspend
from their employments all escrivanos, attor-
neys, or other officers, who shall be guilty of
extortions, contumacy, or contravention of your
decrees.

" In all civil causes, the parties are to be
allowed an appeal from your tribunal to the
King in council, when the matter in litigation
exceeds 500*l.* sterling; and in all criminal

have been as flattering to the individual, as they ought to have been convincing to the world, of the propriety of the person selected for the important duties which he had to perform. No language could possibly have been more flattering, as it must have conveyed a pleasing conviction to the mind of Colonel Picton that it was his own merit alone, and no friendly intervention, which obtained for him the distinguished preference; and after so strong a pledge of confidence it is but reasonable to suppose that he would endeavour still to merit that high estimation which Sir Ralph had thus strikingly expressed, by every exertion in his power to fulfil the duties of the trust to his satisfaction.

The enemies of Picton, when they afterwards inveighed against him as "*un homme antique en scélératesse,*"—and when, speaking of his actions, they declared that, " excepting Danton and some of his coadjutors under Robespierre, there are no instances in modern times of similar atrocity,"—made as direct a charge against the discernment of Sir Ralph, as they did against the character of the man he had honoured with his confidence. But Abercromby's character was too well known to bear such an imputation. To give colour to their calumnies, they were obliged to deny that the general had given Colonel Picton the appointment upon his own judgment; they insisted that it had been bestowed upon him at the earnest solicitation of Brigadier-general Maitland. But the degree of truth with which this statement was made cannot be more satisfactorily shown than by the following letter from that officer to Colonel Picton.

"Barbadoes, August 24th, 1804.

" DEAR PICTON,

" I have seen it asserted in a late publication, that I obtained the government of Trinidad for you: it appears also that you have publicly said that it was offered to you. On my part I declare, that you were not indebted for that appointment to any interest which I made with Sir Ralph Abercromby, for I made none to that end.

" The observation that your knowledge of the Spanish language was a peculiar advantage to you in that situation, I certainly have frequently made, and I believe did make about the time of your appointment; but whether I made this remark to Sir Ralph or not, (which at this distance of time I can neither affirm nor deny,) of this I am clear, that I made no interest to obtain the government for you.

"When it is known that you were in Sir Ralph's suite (though you held no situation, you lived in his family,) from January 1796 until your appointment at Trinidad, within which period you made two voyages with him in his Majesty's ship Arethusa, Captain Wolley, the one from the West Indies to England, and the other from England to the West Indies; that during these voyages you (I may say we) lived, and even slept, in the same cabin with the general; I am persuaded that no person will hesitate to acknowledge that the general had a thorough opportunity to form his own judgment of you, and that from his opinion, thence formed, is evidently traced the cause which led him to appoint you to be commandant at Trinidad: for if this be not just, then it follows, either that he had formed *no* opinion of you at all, or that he appointed you *contrary* to his own opinion; which, when applied to the actions of Sir Ralph Abercromby, I believe everybody will say, in the language of geometricians, is absurd.

    " I am always, my dear Picton,

        " Yours, with the greatest regard,

           " FREDERICK MAITLAND."

" Colonel Thomas Picton."

This letter declares at once the honest reasons which induced Sir Ralph Abercromby to select Colonel Picton for this important post. He had had a long-continued opportunity of seeing and judging his character; the impression on his mind was favourable, and therefore he gave him the appointment. It was unnecessary after the production of this letter to adduce further argument that Sir Ralph Abercromby nominated Colonel Picton commandant of Trinidad *for no other reason and from no other motive* than that he considered him qualified in every respect for the duties of the situation. The accusers of Colonel Picton were therefore driven to assert that he had by a long course of duplicity deceived Sir Ralph into the belief of his efficiency, and thereby abused the generous confidence of the general : but even this position is untenable ; for it does not appear that, to the hour of his death, Sir Ralph ever expressed himself in any degree disappointed or deceived in the opinion which he had formed of Colonel Picton; neither was he ever heard to censure any of his acts as governor of Trinidad. On the contrary, after having revisited the colony in the month of June, he expressed his "entire and complete approbation of Colonel Picton's conduct," and in consequence recommended him strongly in his subsequent despatches as "an officer in every respect qualified to fill the important situation of governor of the island." Any further evidence to show the estimation in which Sir Ralph Abercromby held the character and abilities of Colonel Picton, would be superfluous.

In the instructions from his Majesty's government to Sir Ralph Abercromby, relative to the attack on the island of Trinidad is the following remark:

"The island of Trinidad is pointed out as the source of great mischief to the British islands, being a shelter for privateers who annoy their trade, and affords an asylum for bad people of every description, who man the privateers and row-boats, which make depredations upon the coasts, carrying 'off slaves and property : it is therefore recommended to Sir Ralph Abercromby, if he can collect a sufficient force without exposing the British islands, to make an attack upon Trinidad, and if 'the force he can spare should not be sufficient to keep possession after he has taken it, to make the attack notwithstanding, for the purpose of destroying or carrying away all military stores and arms that he may find there, and to seize upon and to send to England the brigands and mischievous people who have made that island their home."

This at one view displays the nature of the trust reposed in Colonel Picton. After Sir Ralph had taken possession of the island, he, with that kind feeling and consideration which ever distinguished him, granted to the inhabitants the exercise of their own laws, and the institutions which subsisted previously to the capitulation.

When Colonel Picton first entered upon the duties of his appointment, the amount of the population was 17,718; and it will be shown in reply to the accusations brought against him, whether the administration of the laws

under his government tended to give confidence to settlers, or, as his accusers strongly
and pertinaciously asserted, compelled those
who were already located to fly from his "*oppressive domination, machinations, and delin-
quencies.*"

The first act of Colonel Picton was to discover the actual condition of the island, and
to ascertain how far the extract already given
from Sir Ralph Abercromby's instructions was
borne out by the character of the people. He
was greatly assisted in these inquiries by the
respectable part of the population, who volun-
tarily came forward to give such information
as they were enabled to impart; and a short
time after he had been appointed to the governorship, he received the following address from
the inhabitants.

"ADDRESS.

"To his Excellency THOMAS PICTON, Esq.
Governor and Commander-in-chief of the
Island of Trinidad, &c. &c.

" May it please your Excellency,

"The last governor of this colony for his
Catholic Majesty, perhaps too much occupied

in the last moments of the reduction of the
island, obtained from the conqueror, by the
capitulation, the ratification of all the acts previously passed under the Spanish government,
but forgot to demand the continuation of our
laws; a thing the more necessary, as the establishment of new ones, however good they
might be, might occasion the greatest disorder. This inconvenience could not escape the
penetration of his Excellency Sir Ralph Abercromby, (whose humanity and disinterestedness
cannot be sufficiently praised,) and in the
course of a few days after the capitulation he
was pleased to issue a proclamation, declaring
this favourable resolution ;—which increased,
if possible, the gratitude of the inhabitants
of this island, already so much indebted to
him for the wise measures he adopted at the
conquest, to preserve them from the horrors
attendant on war.

" The zeal which your excellency has invariably displayed for the preservation of the colony,
and the welfare of its inhabitants, has insured
you for ever their confidence, and induces them
to take the liberty of laying before you some
observations, which they think of consequence

towards securing to them, until the peace, the possession of their property, for the preservation of which you have proved your anxiety.

" That assemblage of men of justice, the majority of whom ·no doubt presented instances of corruption of which no other colony could furnish examples, and whose iniquities and horrors have exceeded those of every government known to us, have brought all but ruin on the inhabitants : those shameful and permanent violations of all the laws of the Indies, and others of the kingdom, by which his Catholic Majesty intended that we should be governed, (laws full of wisdom and foresight,) and which would undoubtedly have ensured our happiness, if their administrators had been men of ordinary honesty, were wholly perverted. Murders and robberies were committed with impunity ; widows and orphans despoiled ; inheritances plundered ; creditors and debtors equally ruined in affairs of the most simple nature ; unfortunate colonists, scarcely arrived at the moment of enjoying the fruits of long and painful labours, which would have afforded the means of existence to their families, were devoured without pity on the most trifling discussion, like victims fattened only for that purpose! In short, who can deny that these disorders had increased to such a degree, that a man destitute of employment or property might attempt anything against a proprietor; because the latter, convinced beforehand of the usurpation of part of his property, and of the loss of the remainder by the excessive costs of justice, would have rather submitted to the most violent assaults in his house and on his person, than have offered any resistance to them?

"Such was the dismal but faithful picture of the colony at the period of its conquest; and that peace which it enjoyed, (which alone had contributed to attract that multitude of exiles who had been forced to fly from the civil wars which raged in the neighbouring islands,) that peace of which they so highly applauded the advantages, was sold to us at the price of being devoured in the den of chicanery, if any difficulty obliged us to have recourse to justice; whilst our administrators, in their despatches to the court of Madrid, attributed the rapid and unexpected increase of population to the effects of a wise and virtuous administration. We have not thought necessary to give your excellency a detail of the numerous acts just mentioned. You were not long at the head of this government without obtaining a perfect knowledge of them; in consequence of the necessity imposed upon you to pursue the affairs of justice already commenced. What was your astonishment on beholding such infamy, and how often have you expressed your indignation thereon! Yes, sir, we will say, that penetrated with the misfortunes of several persons who could not escape the claws of these vultures, your excellency wished to relieve them; but how could it be effected, if with that intent you are obliged to have recourse to several of the same men of whom we complain, whose interest it is to support each other, and to bury in darkness what we are desirous of making known to the world?

"The zeal and anxiety which your excellency has manifested for the good of this colony can only meet with the success you so well deserve by assenting to the request that we now presume to make, for the establishment of a superior tribunal, erected in the following manner, or in any other that your excellency may judge most expedient.

"Signed by a great majority of the respectable inhabitants, natives of all countries."*

Having ascertained that the opinion expressed by the government at home as to the character of the inhabitants of this island was not undeserved, Colonel Picton felt himself in a position which might have intimidated a man of less resolution; but, with that energy by which he was distinguished, he immediately applied himself to discover the root of the existing evil, and the most effective means for its extermination. Amongst those who had been recommended to him as intimately acquainted with the internal state of the country was Don Christoval de Robles, who had for nearly half a century held important situations in the administration of the colony. Colonel Picton readily availed himself of the advice of this gentleman; and, in a short time, he sent to the governor the

* The mixed character of these memorialists, and their ignorance of the English language, account for the whimsical manner in which this document is worded.

following document, which was so perfectly in accordance with his own observations, and the statements of the other respectable inha-' bitants to whom he was referred, that Colonel Picton enclosed the original paper in his despatches, to show at one view the actual state of the island.

" DON CHRISTOVAL DE ROBLES' RECOMMENDA-
TION TO COLONEL PICTON.

" As you have done me the honour of consulting me, I will give you my honest and candid sentiments on the situation of this colony.

" The population is mostly composed of refugees and desperate characters, who have been implicated in the rebellions and massacres of all the neighbouring islands; their principles are incompatible with all regular government, and their inveteracy to your nation is irreconcilable. The timidity of the former government suffered their crimes to pass unpunished ; and at your arrival they were actually masters of the island. You may judge of the numbers capable of bearing arms, by the application of the French consul to the governor, on the ap-

pearance of the British fleet, when he offered
him the assistance of three thousand repub-
licans, which, not being inclined to make any
resistance, he thought proper to decline.

" To those you may add the Spanish peons,
or people of colour,—a set of vagabonds, who
casually come over from the continent, and
who are ready to join in any disorder that
affords a prospect of plunder; and a great
proportion of the slaves, who have been sent
here from the other islands for crimes dangerous to their safety. These people are now
apparently quiet; but they are the more dangerous, as they are only waiting for a favourable opportunity to show themselves. They
are studying you and your garrison.

" A considerable portion of your troops, if
one may draw a conclusion from their conversation and conduct, are not well affected,
and may be easily seduced; and those people
will leave no means untried to effect it. If
you do not give an imposing character to your
government before the climate diminishes the
number of your soldiers, your situation will
become alarming. If. those men do not fear
you, they will despise you ; and you may

easily foresee the consequences. They have been accustomed to a timid and temporising government; a few acts of vigour may disconcert their projects. But, perhaps, you expect some co-operation from the magistrates and tribunals :—allow yourself no longer to be deceived ; there is not a sufficient confidence in the duration of your government to induce any one to commit himself by a vigorous application to the law. They are all apprehensive of returning under the dominion of their old masters, and will be careful not to expose themselves. They are, besides, people of weak and timid characters, from whom no energy can be expected. There is but one line of conduct by which you can extricate yourself from all these difficulties.

" The circumstances of the conquest have virtually combined in you the whole power of the government. You are supreme political, criminal, civil, and military judge. You unite in your own person the separate powers of the governor, tribunals, and royal audience of Caraccas; our laws enable you to judge summarily, without recusation or appeal. Circumstances like the present have been foreseen by our lawyers, who have provided remedies equal to the occasion. You are not shackled by forms or modes of prosecution. If you do substantial justice, you are only answerable to God and your conscience."

The following extract from the laws of Grenada proves that De Robles was not singular in his estimation of the character of the people of Trinidad.

"And whereas some persons have come from Trinidad, and lurked in these islands for the purpose of seducing and carrying off slaves; and other persons residing in Trinidad have sent artful negro or mulatto slaves for the like purpose; and it is but just and reasonable to proceed against those who reside on the very spot *which holds out a retreat for fraudulent debtors and stealers of slaves, and where no redress or justice can be· had.".* This act then goes on to enact, "That all persons *coming from Trinidad* shall give bond on their arrival in one thousand pounds sterling, to be of good behaviour; and if such bond is not given, such person to be declared a *vagabond, and, without any other proof than that of usual or* *frequent residence in Trinidad, to be committed to gaol."**

Such was the state of Trinidad when Colonel Picton was appointed to the government. It must be evident, from the preceding extracts, that severe measures only could enable him to keep possession of a place, the inhabitants of which were composed of such heterogeneous and lawless materials. The means at his disposal for this purpose were, however, but very inadequate to the difficulty of the object. The following statement of the military establishment at this period is from a return made by Colonel Picton to the commander-in-chief :—

" The Fifty-seventh regiment cannot bring into the field above 300
" Hompesch's detachment (composed entirely of foreigners, and possessing very little of my confidence) 100
" Soter's French negroes (chiefly picked up in the island) 100
" Artillery . . 20

" Total effectives . 520

Inadequate as this force was, even for the protection of the most vulnerable points round

* Laws of Grenada, vol. iii. page 232, clause 8.

the island, it was not to be supposed that any
reduction could be made from the military
posts in order to perform the duties of police.
Still, had these troops been well affected and
well disciplined, or had they been all British
soldiers, the activity and resolution of Colonel
Picton might have compensated for the deficiency in their numbers; but, according to the
remarks made in his despatches, it appears that
the foreigners were "constantly deserting, or
bordering on mutiny, through the insidious representations of disaffected persons, employed,
it was supposed, by the Spanish government
for that purpose."

In one of his earliest letters to Sir Ralph
Abercromby, a short time subsequently to his
appointment, he says: "The only inquietude
we have experienced, has been occasioned by
the deserters, most of them Germans." Again,
he adds; "I have been under the necessity
of calling Hompesch's into town, to be immediately under my own inspection. A very
great spirit of insubordination prevails in that
corps; and, I am sorry to say, the officers (with
the exception of the major, who is unfortunately ill) use no endeavours to repress it. They

report ten deserted with their arms, &c.; but,
I very much fear, they exceed that number.
However, I believe it is put an end to for the
present; for in consequence of a circular letter
I addressed to the different commandants of
quarters, publishing a reward of sixteen dollars
for each one apprehended or killed, five have
been brought in, and one, who had written
a letter to his comrades, saying he was at
the head of five hundred men, has already
suffered."

The powers vested in Colonel Picton by
the commander-in-chief prove the high opinion
which that distinguished individual entertained of his discretion and judgment.   Chief
Justice Nicholl was directed *" to consider his
instructions and powers as of equal force as if
given under Sir Ralph's own hand;* while, " in
all criminal causes," the appeal was directed
to be made " to the governor," and no sentence was to be executed until approved of
by him."

It will thus be seen that Colonel Picton was
invested with authority to execute the most
summary and extreme civil and military punishments, without reference to any other tribunal.

The necessity for this, however, cannot be doubted; nor can the use which he in this instance made of that authority be condemned. In the British army, desertion in time of war is always punished with death. Colonel Picton made an early example of the mutinous ringleaders; by which, and placing the detachment under his own immediate inspection, he succeeded in bringing the men back to a sense of duty and subordination.

As soon as the first impulse to desertion had been subdued, Colonel Picton endeavoured by more gentle measures to convince the disaffected, that the way to obtain redress for either real or imaginary wrongs, was not by subverting military discipline, or opposing the laws; and in a letter addressed to Sir Ralph Abercromby, only thirteen days after his appointment to the government, he says, " By his Majesty's ship Pelican, I send to head-quarters five deserters from Brigadier-general Hompesch's regiment. It was not my intention to have troubled your excellency with any of them; but as they complain of a want of justice, and say that their never having been accounted with has been the reason of their desertion, I could not think of proceeding against them in a summary manner."

While this mutinous spirit was manifested by the troops, and while disaffection pervaded the island, constant preparations were made by the Spanish government, from without, to regain possession of their colony. Colonel Picton was not, however, intimidated by the critical situation in which he was placed; and perhaps at no period of his after life did he display more discretion, fortitude, and activity, than while fulfilling the duties of this important post. With extraordinary tact he contrived to obtain the co-operation, and cement the confidence, of the respectable and well-affected portion of the inhabitants, who were at once embodied in the form of militia; by which his own inadequate force of British troops was made disposable for the protection of the island from external foes; and in a subsequent letter to Sir Ralph Abercromby, dated April 4th, he observes: " A very exact police has been established in the town, and is gradually extending itself over the whole island. We are getting through the press of undecided processes as fast as we can. The colony is everywhere quiet, and the inhabitants pay prompt obedience to the orders of government."

It will thus be seen that, in little more than one month from his appointment, he had overcome many of the existing dangers, and succeeded in placing the captured island, if not in a position of security, at least in one of great improvement.. Constant anxiety and indefatigable exertion were the means by which this was effected.

In every letter to the commander-in-chief, Colonel Picton reminds him of the totally unprotected state of the coast for want of a small naval force ; and in one of these communications he remarks, " The north-east coast, from Toque to Mayero and Greaya, continues to be much annoyed by French privateers. A twelve-gun schooner, and another of a smaller class, continue to hover about these parts ; and there is little doubt but that they communicate with the disaffected, and probably supply them with arms. The respectable inhabitants make very serious representations of their unprotected and exposed situation; and say they shall be under the necessity of abandoning their homes, unless some naval protection be afforded them."

Colonel Picton did not relax in his endeavours to regulate the affairs of the island; and his efforts were gradually successful, for when he had been only six months in possession of the government, he was enabled to report an improvement in the aspect of affairs which must have been far beyond the expectation of all who knew the condition of the island when entrusted to his care. The following is a copy of his letter to the authorities at home.

" Port of Spain, 26th July, 1797.
" SIR,

" His Majesty's ship Dictator being ordered to Martinique, I profit by the occasion (the intercourse with England being more direct) to acquaint you with the situation of this island. The most perfect tranquillity and good-humour prevail throughout the colony; and the inhabitants of all classes acknowledge that their situation has been much ameliorated under the influence and protection of his Majesty's government.

" Since his Excellency Sir Ralph Abercromby

has authorized me to arm launches for the protection of the intercourse with the neighbouring Spanish provinces, that trade has experienced a very great increase; and the market for British manufactures has become very considerable, and is daily increasing. Plantation provisions of all kinds are so plentiful as to enable me to permit the exportation of them to Grenada and St. Vincent's, which have lately suffered great distress from a discontinuance of the usual small supplies from America," &c.

" To the Right Hon. H. Dundas."

CHAPTER IV.

Fatal Effects of the Rainy Season. — Frustration of a
Conspiracy. — Estimation by his Majesty's Government
of Colonel Picton's exertions. — His Views as to further
Conquests on the Continent adjacent to Trinidad. —
Curious passage in Picton's Correspondence relative to the
Battle of the Nile.—Cruisers sent to protect the Trade
of Trinidad. — Proposed Reward for Colonel Picton's
Head.—His amusing Letters on this subject.—Spanish
Inhabitants of Trinidad averse to the Restoration of
the Colony to the Mother Country. — Correspondence on
the subject.

THE first rainy season proved alarmingly
fatal to the small force under the command of
Colonel Picton; and he says, in a letter dated
October 25th, " The number of rank and file
sick in hospital and quarters amount to five
hundred and thirty-seven:" while at this and
subsequent periods, demonstrations of attack
were being constantly made by the Governor
of Caraccas; but which the disturbed state of
that city fortunately averted. About November, however, an attempt of a desperate and ex-

tensive nature was made by the coloured inhabitants of Trinidad (who were mostly French, and had ever been disaffected,) to bring about a revolution. This conspiracy had been long suspected by Colonel Picton, and he had taken every precaution to render it abortive. A number of refugees had collected on the opposite coast of Paria, who were to pass over and join their friends in the island with arms and ammunition; these were dispersed, and their stores and habitations destroyed, by a force sent against them, at the same time that the ringleaders of the insurgents on the island were seized and brought to trial; when, in the words of Colonel Picton, " by the immediate execution of one of the principals, and the imprisonment of several others, the remainder were overawed, and led to see the futility of their designs."

As a strong proof of the high sense in which his exertions were held by his Majesty's government, he received in March 1798 a letter from the Right Hon. H. Dundas, informing him, that " his Majesty had been graciously pleased, in consideration of the extraordinary expense attending the civil and military command of

the island, to order that an allowance of one
thousand two hundred pounds per annum
should be made to the commandant, with
authority to charge that sum against the
revenues of the island."

Colonel Picton, in one of his despatches,
seems to acknowledge another and more formal
testimony by the government of its approbation of his services. He writes—

" His Majesty's gracious approbation of my
humble endeavours to promote the interest
and honour of his government in this island,
which you have so handsomely conveyed to
me in your despatch of the 14th of January,
is particularly flattering; and I am highly sensible of the honour, which I shall endeavour
to merit by continuing to pursue similar measures with increased zeal."

Such testimonies were, it will readily be believed, highly gratifying to Colonel Picton;
and he continued by unremitting exertions to
advance still further the interests of the colony.
In a subsequent letter he remarks, " The roads,
though nearly impracticable when his Majesty's
arms took possession of the island, are now the
finest in the West Indies; and, upon the whole,

the face of the country is undergoing a very flattering change."

But his attention was not confined exclusively to Trinidad: he was for a long time studying the character and political security of the neighbouring continent, which, as one of the richest and most fertile countries in the world, held out an alluring prospect. The result of his inquiries was so perfectly in accordance with the general report, that he was constantly urging both his Majesty's government and the various commanders of the forces in the West Indies, to attempt to annex these fertile provinces to the British dominions; but although he was convinced that the conquest of the whole country might be effected with but little difficulty or expense, his applications were unavailing.

One letter in particular, addressed to Lieutenant-general Cuyler, the then commander in-chief in the West Indies, sets forth so clearly, and in such glowing terms, the value of this conquest, and the facility with which it might be effected, that it is inserted in the Appendix for the perusal of the reader. Regardless, however, of his constant representations to this effect, the government were either too supine, or too much occupied elsewhere, to undertake any enterprise in this quarter of the world : the opportunity was allowed to pass ; and these provinces remained undisturbed in the possession of Spain until the peace which was shortly afterwards concluded.

There is a curious passage in Colonel Picton's correspondence of this time. He had just heard the first rumour of the battle of the Nile, and observes,—

" A vessel, which left Glasgow on the 3rd of October, brings provincial papers of the 2nd, by which it appears that there is great reason to believe that Sir Horatio Nelson had at length discovered the retreat of Bonaparte's fleet on the coast of Egypt, but not at Alexandria ; and that an attack had been made upon it, which terminated highly favourably to his Majesty's arms. If so, the hero of Italy will appear more like a refugee than a conqueror ; and probably terminate his golden dreams amongst the sands of Asia."

Colonel Picton was no prophet ; but although he was mistaken in deducing its consequences, he felt all an Englishman's exultation when he received the news of Nelson's brilliant achievement. He writes again,—

"The victory gained by Sir Horatio Nelson, whether considered singly, or with respect to the events it will probably produce, must be regarded as the most brilliant and important that has ever graced our naval annals. England is yet in a proud situation, with the eyes and hopes of the whole world upon her; and she may now look forward to a period when her voice will be heard and respected."

In the beginning of the year 1799, Admiral Harvey, who was then in command of the fleet in the West Indies, sent some small cruisers to protect the trade which Colonel Picton had established with the continent. With these, under the command of Captain Dixon, of his Majesty's sloop Victorieux, he destroyed the batteries which had been erected to intercept the traffic of some of the smaller rivers. The removal of these obstructions, and the confidence which traders now reposed in his power and willingness to protect them, directed much of the commerce of the neighbouring continent to this island; and rendered it so

formidable a rival to the Spanish possessions on
the main, that the Governors of Caraccas and
Guayana offered a reward of twenty thousand
dollars for the English Governor's head.

Colonel Picton had for some time before
this been in friendly communication with these
officers, respecting the exchange of prisoners.
Mutual efforts were made to ameliorate the horrors of war, and to afford protection to private
individuals. In a letter to the Governor of Caraccas he remarks, " I shall have great pleasure
in facilitating your excellency's benevolent intentions respecting the unfortunate individuals
whom the fortune of war has separated from
their homes, their families, and their friends ;
and will most sincerely co-operate in every measure that may conduce to an event not less
interesting to my humanity than to your excellency's." While, in a similar communication to the Governor of Guayana, he adds,
" The nations which we represent are not
naturally inimical ; but the pressure of imperious circumstances and extraordinary events
have produced a war, the asperities to individuals resulting from which, I shall have great
happiness in co-operating with your excellency to soften and alleviate."

Of course this liberal offer for the head of Colonel Picton could not be interpreted as a proof of increased good feeling on the part of these gentlemen; but, as he was not desirous of giving them any additional offence, or appearing at all hurt by this public announcement of the value in which he was held, he returned for answer the following piquant and amusing notes.

"Trinidad, 25th January 1799.

" Sir,

" Your excellency has highly flattered my vanity by the very handsome value which you have been pleased to fix upon my head. Twenty thousand dollars is an offer which would not discredit your royal master's munificence !

" As the trifle has had the good fortune to recommend itself to your excellency's attention, come and take it, and it will be much at your service: in expectation of which, I have the honour to be, &c. &c. &c.

(Signed) " THOMAS PICTON."

" His Excellency, Don Pedro Carbonelli,

" Governor-general, Caraccas."

And to the Governor of Guayana, the following : —

" Sir,   " Port of Spain, 25th January 1799.

" I understand your excellency has done me
the honour of valuing my head at twenty
thousand dollars. I am sorry it is not in my
power to return the compliment.   Modesty
obliges me to remark that your excellency
has far over-rated the trifle ; but, as it has
found means to recommend itself to your excellency's attention, if you will give yourself
the trouble of coming to take it, it will be
much at your service.

 "Your excellency's very devoted
    " humble servant,
  (Signed)   " THOMAS PICTON."
"The Governor of Guayana."

But Colonel Picton's personal strength and
courage were too well known : even this
tempting offer was not sufficient to induce
any of the bad characters who at this time
infested the island to undertake the desperate
task of gaining possession of his head. The
interpretation which was afterwards put upon
this uncivilized proclamation is a singular in-

stance of the facility with which the most
atrocious acts will be defended by men who
are prejudiced against the subject of them.
This very proceeding of the two governors of
the Spanish provinces was afterwards held up
to the British nation as a laudable measure,
provoked by the gross exactions and cruelties
perpetrated by Colonel Picton on their subjects
who traded to Trinidad. No conduct on Colonel Picton's part could remove the infamy of
this transaction : but, so far from the excuse
given being founded in fact, at this very period
he was known amongst the South American
Spaniards by the familiar appellation of " El
Tio," *the uncle or friend.*

In consequence of the brilliant successes of
the British arms towards the end of the year
1799, the Spanish inhabitants of Trinidad became apprehensive of a peace, and that the
island would be again restored to the mother
country in exchange for Porto Rico or some
other equivalent. Alarmed at this probability,
an address was presented to Colonel Picton by
the most respectable inhabitants, calling upon
him to make a strong representation to the
British government of the frightful situation

in which the colony would be placed if again
put under the dominion of the Spanish crown.
Colonel Picton was at the same time requested
to address Sir Ralph Abercromby, to whom
the whole colony still looked up as their conqueror and patron, calling upon him to protect
them from the sanguinary persecution which
those who had shown the least favour to the
conquerors had every reason to expect if again
in the power of "the most *vindictive* and *revenge-
ful* government in the world." Conformably to
the wishes of the inhabitants, he immediately
addressed the Right Honourable H. Dundas
and Sir Ralph Abercromby upon the subject;
and as these communications show in a very
eminent degree his strong powers of discernment, and admirably illustrate the still unchanged character of the Spanish nation, they
will be perused with interest. To Mr. Dundas
he says—

("*Private.*)

"Port of Spain, Trinidad,
"Sir,   24th October 1799.

"Some very strong and earnest representations, made by the most respectable inhabitants
of this colony respecting the unjustifiable and
alarming conduct of the government of Carac-

cas, occasion this letter. If the island of Trinidad should be restored to Spain at a peace, we must resign all hope of ever being well received by the natives of South America. Those inhabitants of this island who have expressed any satisfaction with his Majesty's government, or have paid any personal attention to his representative, are known to be already prejudged and marked out as victims for the vengeance of the Spanish government whenever chance or circumstances may subject them to its jealous tyranny.

" The Spaniards who recollect the conduct of their government subsequent to the peace of 1763, upon the restoration of the Havannah, when common acts of civility and attention to his Majesty's governor were punished as criminal actions, are convinced that the menaces secretly circulated by the emissaries of Caraccas are to be regarded as the predeterminations of a government whose politics know no restraint from morality, and with which loose suspicion entails certain ruin.

" The present extraordinary conduct of the council (Junta del gobierno) of Caraccas sufficiently evinces the government has not changed its principles. Amongst a number of other instances, an old gentleman, (Don Christoval de Robles,) the most respectable Spaniard I have ever known, in whom alone the high sense of honour the nation pretends to is not fabulous, who had held the principal civil employment of the island for a number of years with honour and unimpeached integrity; because he has unguardedly expressed himself pleased with the justice of his Majesty's government, and has been ready on all occasions of difficulty to assist me with his advice and experience, has been proceeded against privately by the Junta del gobierno of Caraccas, and adjudged a traitor to his king and country. This decree has actually been acted upon; and property, which he casually possessed upon the continent, has in consequence been confiscated.

"This island being either exchanged or restored at a peace, will produce in the minds of the South Americans a lasting distrust of the English nation; they are naturally favourably disposed to his Majesty's government, but the apprehension of again falling under the dominion of Spain keeps them at a fearful distance. They say: 'You take possession of our country, at which we rejoice as an event most favourable to our happiness and conducive to our prosperity; but we have scarcely tasted the advantages of an equitable and just government, when you make a sacrifice of us as a peace-offering to a jealous and vindictive government, whose spies have registered all our good offices, which will not fail to be construed into crimes for which our persons and property will answer.'

"You conceive, perhaps, that I am overcharging the picture; but, I regret to say, too many facts can be adduced to attest its truth.

"I hope his Majesty's ministers will never be brought either to restore or exchange this valuable island; for, besides the certain ruin and misery which it will occasion to all those who have shown any attachment to his Majesty's government, it will leave a lasting, indelible impression on the minds of the South Americans. Though a valuable equivalent might be proposed, I humbly conceive it would be highly impolitic to accept it. The inhabitants of all the neighbouring provinces have their eyes fixed upon Trinidad: if retained, it will exalt their estimation of the power and energy of his Majesty's government, and determine them upon the first favourable occasion to seek its protection ; if restored, it will leave an opinion of weakness, unfavourable and destructive to any future views on this quarter of the world.

"I have the honour to be, &c.

(Signed) "THOMAS PICTON."

"The Right Honourable

"H. Dundas."

At the same time he addressed Sir Ralph Abercromby to the following effect :—

"Trinidad, October 30th, 1799.

"SIR,

"Every one here looks forward to your excellency's protection and patronage, and you must expect to be troubled upon all occasions of consequence to the prosperity and well-being of this colony.

"The late brilliant and important successes of the allied armies, and other favourable circumstances, holding out the probability of an approaching peace, the most respectable planters and settlers of Trinidad begin to entertain serious apprehensions of their future situation; and express great alarm and uneasiness lest his Majesty's ministers might be induced to exchange this island for Porto Rico, or any other proposed equivalent. They are well aware of the high degree of importance attached by the Spanish government to this settlement on account of its situation, which will render it at all times dangerous and formidable to the neighbouring provinces of South America; the inhabitants of which have their eyes continually fixed upon Trinidad, and cannot fail to be affected by its newly-acquired opulence and flourishing situation.

"I have taken the liberty of enclosing the copy of a letter I have just written to Mr. Secretary Dundas on the occasion, by which your excellency will see the ruin which menaces the English and other inhabitants who have shown any marks of attachment to his Majesty's government, upon the event of the island being restored. The great object of the Spanish government in wishing to repossess itself of this island, is to show their subjects in these countries the little reliance they can place upon the protection and promises of the

British government, which so easily sacrifices
them for a supposed advantage; and, above
all, by the vengeance they will not fail to
execute upon all those who have shown themselves pleased with the new order of things,
to deter their subjects on the continent from
all thoughts of ameliorating their miserable
situation by having recourse to the protection
of Great Britain.

" It requires considerable practical knowledge
of the Spanish government to be enabled to
form anything like a just idea of its politics.
The individual is superstitious without religion
and punctilious without honour; the government, with all the formality and mask of integrity, and the most extravagant pretensions to
good faith, pursues the object of its ambition,
avarice, or revenge, without any restraint from
morality or respect for engagements.

" No stipulation on the part of Great Britain
will be effectual to secure the inhabitants from
its unrelenting resentment. Its mode is to
promise everything; but the public instructions to their governors, &c. which they refer
to upon all occasions, are always accompanied
by others, *via reservada*, of an opposite import.

Those who possessed situations under the Spanish government, who were permitted by your excellency to retain them and remain upon this island, accepted of your indulgence by the advice of M. Chacon, for the purpose of remaining as spies upon the conduct of the inhabitants. These people kept a minute register, in which all the inhabitants who had at any time expressed themselves pleased with his Majesty's government were calumniated in the most scandalous manner, and represented as traitors to the King of Spain. This was carried on with great secrecy; but at length a disagreement amongst the parties led to a discovery, and I was enabled to get possession of it. The false and infamous representations it contained were calculated to render all the most respectable inhabitants objects of resentment to the Spanish government.

" I beg leave to refer your excellency to the enclosed copy of a letter to Mr. Secretary Dundas, wherein I have urged the reasons why I am of opinion that it would be extremely impolitic to restore Trinidad on any terms, or for any equivalent. I shall not now intrude any further upon your time than to

claim a continuance of your patronage in favour of a large body of planters, who, having through your means experienced the advantages of his Majesty's government, conceive they have a claim upon your future good offices.

" I have the honour to be, &c.

(Signed)   " TH. PICTON."

" His Excellency
" Sir Ralph Abercromby."

It would appear that the strength of these representations had their due weight with his Majesty's ministers: for, in the peace which ensued about two years after this period; Trinidad was retained amongst the British possessions.

CHAPTER V

Character of Colonel Picton's Administration. — Reward of his services. — Attempt to injure his reputation. — Formally appointed Governor of Trinidad. — Change of Ministry at home. — Trinidad put in commission. — Insulting treatment of Governor Picton. — His feelings in consequence.—He determines to resign.

EACH act of Colonel Picton's administration appeared the result of a well-matured judgment and an honest zeal. Every record of his life is an honourable memorial of services rendered. From the first moment of his being placed in that situation which enabled him to show the great powers of his mind, his career ensured a continued series of advantages to his country; esteemed and respected by all men of worth to whom he was known, he received from them the kindly attentions and regards of private life; while his public services were constantly obtaining for him the approbation of his sovereign and the warm commendations of his ministers. Nor did his services pass unrewarded : in a letter dated January 4th, 1800, we find him again requesting Mr. Dundas to lay his grateful acknowledgments at his Majesty's feet for his further munificence in adding the sum of one thousand two hundred pounds to his annual salary.

It was, however, about this period that an attempt was made to injure his reputation. Some person in England, who had obtained the ear of the minister, made a charge against him of having exported the produce of the colony in foreign vessels, to the injury of the British ship-owner; and it was implied that he did this for his own advantage. But this charge was discovered to proceed from private ill-will and personal disappointment; and it was so clearly disproved by documentary evidence sent to England from Trinidad, that Mr. Dundas wrote a highly complimentary letter to Colonel Picton, containing an assurance " that he and his colleagues were perfectly satisfied with his explanation, and convinced that the charges brought against him were without the least foundation."

But a more distinguished and gratifying mark of the estimation in which he was still held by his royal master and his government was conveyed to him within a few months after he had refuted these unfounded imputations. He was now formally appointed governor of the island: hitherto he had only held the situation under the instructions of Sir Ralph Abercromby — being, in point of fact, military commandant; but he now received his Majesty's commission appointing him "civil and military governor." A letter from Lord Hobart, dated June 29th, 1801, announcing his Majesty's determination, accompanied the despatch containing his appointment to the governorship; and the following short extract from this letter contains a flattering testimony of the value in which his services were held: "The ability and zeal which you have shown in administering the affairs of the island of Trinidad, and the honourable testimony borne to your conduct by the commander-in-chief of his Majesty's forces in the Leeward and Windward Charibbee Islands on every occasion, have induced his Majesty to appoint you to the civil government of that island; and I have the satisfaction of enclosing herewith your commission, and the instructions, under his Majesty's sign manual, for your guidance in executing the duties of that office."

This unequivocal mark of confidence bestowed upon him by his own government was to Colonel Picton a great source of consolation under the difficulties which beset him, and a spur to further exertion: to use his own words, " it could not fail to animate his zeal and humble endeavours to merit a continuance of his Majesty's favour."

Appended to the commission was a mass of instructions, headed " Instructions to our trusty and well-beloved Thomas Picton, Esq. our Governor and Commander-in-chief in and over our island of Trinidad. Given at our Court at Saint James's, the first day of June eighteen hundred and one, in the forty-first year of our reign."

We have subjoined an extract from these instructions, because it is necessary that the reader should understand the extent of Colonel Picton's powers before we enter into a detail of the charges which were afterwards preférred against him for his conduct in the government of this island.

" It is our will and pleasure, that for the present, and until our further pleasure shall be signified therein, the same courts of judicature which subsisted in the said island previous to the surrender thereof to us, shall, for the present, be continued in the exercise of all the judicial powers belonging to them in all criminal and civil cases, and that they shall proceed according to the laws by which the said island was then governed; and that such judicial powers as, previous to the surrender of the said island to us, were exercised by the Spanish governor, shall be exercised by you our governor in like manner as the same were exercised previous to the surrender of the said island."

So decisive are these "instructions" in pointing out the course to be pursued by Governor Picton in the administration of the laws, that all responsibility seemed at once taken from him in regard to their operation. But it will be perceived, on reference to the instructions left by Sir Ralph Abercromby upon appointing Colonel Picton to the command of the island, that *they* formed the basis upon which those now sent by his Majesty's government were established; and by this ratification of Governor Picton's former powers and instructions, it was evident that the antecedent operation had given satisfaction, and that every act which Colonel Picton had committed up to this period was thus justified and approved by his Majesty's ministers.

Towards the close of this year he received a further instance of his Majesty's favour, in being promoted to the rank of Brigadier-general; the Gazette appointment being dated October the 22nd, 1801. Unfortunately, at this period a change took place in the affairs at home: Mr. Pitt, who had for nearly eighteen years been at the head of the administration, resigned his situation. With a change of ministers came, as usual, a change of measures; and Lord Sidmouth, who then came into office, conceived that the condition of the West India colonies might be improved by what he denominated " putting the islands in commission;" or, in other language, taking the government out of the hands of the present governors, and placing it under the control of three or more individuals, called commissioners, who were, in their united capacity, to administer the laws and have command over the troops in the separate islands. It is difficult to say upon what grounds this change was projected; but we offer the following extracts from Lord Hobart's letter to Governor Picton, in the hope that the reader may be able to glean from them some satisfactory explanation.

This letter is dated July the 9th, 1802. After the usual preamble to introduce the subject of the communication, his lordship explains its object by observing, " His Majesty has thought it expedient to place the government of the island in commission ; judging that, from the union of civil, military, and naval talents, combined in the persons selected for this service, advantages must arise which cannot be expected from the labours of any one individual."

Now, from the tenor of this passage, it might be imagined that some of Governor Picton's measures had been of evil tendency to the interests of the colony. If, however,

it is proved that this conclusion is without
foundation, the only interpretation which can
be put upon this proceeding is, that "advantages *may* arise" under this experimental
change which had not been produced under
the old system. The following passage from
the same letter from Lord Hobart will prove
the first conclusion groundless; and we are in
consequence left to trace the operations of this
new government.

His lordship adds, immediately after the last
extract, "The experience of your conduct from
the time the island was first placed under your
charge has induced his Majesty to select you
as one of the persons to whom this important trust (that of commissioner) shall be con-
fided." And then comes a recital of the names
of the other two commissioners;—the first on
the list being William Fullarton, Esq. colonel
in the Indian army, F.R.S.; after him, Samuel
Hood, Esq. a captain in his Majesty's navy;
and last of all, Brigadier-general Picton, the
late governor, whose good conduct in that capacity, as above stated, had obtained for him
the high opinion of his Majesty's government,
together with the subordinate and inferior ap-

pointment of junior commissioner! The argument, in point of fact, was what logicians would call " *ad absurdum*," viz. that Colonel Picton's conduct as governor had given so much satisfaction to his Majesty's ministers that they had superseded him in his situation, and conferred upon him an appointment inferior both in rank, respectability, and remuneration!—Perhaps as novel a mode of rewarding five years' approved and meritorious services as could possibly have suggested itself to the mind of a minister.

It would be difficult to say what were the feelings of Governor Picton upon being exposed to this insulting treatment, just as he had by the greatest good management and exertion succeeded in bringing the colony to a degree of tranquillity and prosperity which the most sanguine could hardly have anticipated. To say he was indignant at this treatment, would be only attributing to him the common resentment of an ordinary mind : he was more, much more; he experienced all that a noble and high-spirited man must feel when exposed to unmerited insult—an insult rendered more galling by being disguised in the garb of

compliment; and for this he was expected to
be grateful, — was told it was an honour and
a proof of the high estimation in which he was
held.

From his private correspondence, in which he
adverts to the receipt of this intelligence, it appears that he considered himself not only " ill-
treated," but " insulted." He observes : " Never,
I am certain, did the actions of men so totally
contradict their protestations as in the treatment which I have received. After the continued assurances of the satisfaction which I
have given by the active, and, as they say,
' judicious,' discharge of my duty, together
with their reiterated assertions that the government of this island should undergo no
alteration, I the next month receive a letter
announcing that I am to consider myself as no
longer the governor; but, in consideration of
my ' good conduct,' I am told that I am appointed to the important trust of *junior commissioner.*"

Had Governor Picton refused the unworthy
situation which he was now offered, the colony
must have suffered materially for want of his
assistance ; for it was not to be supposed that

either of the other commissioners, Colonel Fullarton or Commodore Hood, could possess any
knowledge of the affairs of the island. It was
this consideration alone which induced him to
hold for a short period the appointment to
which he was nominated ; it being, however,
his full determination to tender his resignation
so soon after his coadjutors' arrival in Trinidad
as he could furnish them with such information
as would assist them in administering the affairs
of the government, without producing those injurious consequences usually attendant upon a
change of rulers.

CHAPTER VI.

Statement relative to Dr. Lynch and the Under Secretary of
State. — Conflicting affidavits of those gentlemen. — Colonel Draper and Mr. Sullivan.—General Picton's reception
of Colonel Fullarton in Trinidad. — Extraordinary motion
in Council. — General Picton resigns his office of Commissioner.—His letter to the Attorney-general of Trinidad.
— Difficulties which General Picton had to encounter in
assuming the government of Trinidad. — Colonel Pullar-
ton's pamphlet.—Charges brought against General Picton.
— Colonel Fullarton publicly rebuked by Sir Samuel
Hood. — Extracts from Colonel Fullarton's pamphlet.

PAUSING for a while in tracing the operation of this experimental scheme of government and its results, together with the influence which it had upon the life and character
of the subject of this memoir, we will notice
a transaction which seems to throw some light
upon the intentions of government in institut-
ing this commission. The facts are these ;—

Dr. Frederic Thaddeus Lynch was prac-
tising in the town of Galway, as a physician, when his wife's brother, Nicholas Lynch,

a resident in the island of Trinidad, came
to Ireland on a visit to his relations. This gentleman represented to Dr. Lynch in glowing
terms the success which would be sure to
attend him if he would go to the West Indies, and there practise as a physician; which,
together with similar statements in the public
prints at the same period, induced Dr. Lynch
to leave Galway and come to London, to embark for Trinidad. In London he saw several
accounts in the papers, purporting that government would give large tracts of land to any
white persons desirous of settling in Trinidad;
and accordingly Dr. Lynch called at the secretary of state's office, in order to have an interview with Lord Hobart, the principal secretary of state, or Mr. Sullivan, the under-
secretary. He had an interview with Mr.
Sullivan, to whom he mentioned the object of
his application. Mr. Sullivan, however, informed him, that the grants of land alluded to
were very trifling, and intended for mechanics
or labouring men, and not for those in his
sphere of life. Satisfied with this information,
Dr. Lynch was about to depart, when Mr.
Sullivan asked him whether he had any letters

of introduction to his Majesty's commissioners
in Trinidad; upon which Dr. Lynch replied,
that he had only two, which were addressed to
Governor Picton. In reply to this Mr. Sullivan remarked, "You had better procure some,
if possible, to the first commissioner, Colonel
Fullarton:" the reason which he gave for this
recommendation being, "*That Colonel Fullarton
would have it in his power to be of more service to
Dr. Lynch, as in all probability Colonel Picton
would be ordered to return to England before the
expiration of six months; as Colonel Fullarton was
instructed to investigate the conduct of Colonel
Picton whilst in the Island of Trinidad.*"

Thus far the affidavit of Dr. Lynch; after
having perused which, it is startling to read
the following extract from that made by Mr.
Sullivan:

"The Right Honourable John Sullivan, one
of his Majesty's most Honourable Privy Council, &c. *maketh oath and saith, that he did not,
at the time referred to in the affidavit of Dr. Lynch,
or at any time since, know, nor had he any reason
to suspect or believe, that Colonel Fullarton had
any instructions whatever, either of a public or
private nature, to investigate the conduct of General*

Picton in Trinidad, or to procure his removal from the government of that island, or his being ordered to return to England;" while in the same affidavit he goes on to state, that " This deponent now positively and solemnly upon his oath declares that he never did, either directly or indirectly, inform Dr. Lynch or any other person, either in conversation or otherwise, before the month of December one thousand eight hundred and two, or at any other time, that in all probability General Picton' would be ordered to return to England in six months, as Colonel Fullarton was instructed to investigate the past conduct of General Picton at Trinidad ; nor use any words to that or the like effect," &c.

There is something painful in the perusal of these contradictory statements, made upon oath, and coming from two individuals filling respectable situations in society. It is obvious that either Mr. Sullivan or Dr. Lynch must have been guilty of a wilful and deliberate perjury ; which, we shall not pretend to decide : but Colonel Draper, who so nobly defended General Picton during his protracted persecution of eight years, was so fully convinced of the truth

of Dr. Lynch's statement, that in his " Address
to the British Public," he undisguisedly charges
Mr. Sullivan with the crime of perjury, and
calls upon him to vindicate himself before the
people of England.   Mr. Sullivan contented
himself, however, by filing a criminal information against Lieutenant-colonel Draper for the
libel.   The result was not entirely satisfactory
to the Right Honourable Secretary ; for, after
proceedings which lasted nearly three years, Colonel Draper, when found guilty, was required
merely to give two sureties in five hundred
pounds each, and to be bound himself in one
thousand pounds, to appear when called upon to
receive judgment, and to be of good behaviour.
No judgment was ever afterwards given.

It is now necessary to continue the history
of General Picton's career ; as every reader will
form his own conclusion with regard to the
comparative veracity of the two affidavits.

Colonel Fullarton, the first commissioner,
arrived in Trinidad about the 4th of January 1803, when he was received by General
Picton with every mark of respect and hospi-
tality ; nay, even a friendly intercourse seemed
to exist between them ; and in a letter from

the first commissioner to Mr. Sullivan, he remarks: " I was received by General Picton
with great politeness, and with all the attention which Lord Hobart had been pleased to
direct :" while in a subsequent communication, he adds, "General Picton and I have
carefully read Lord Hobart's instructions to the
commissioners, and we shall not lose a moment in preparing to carry his lordship's intentions into effect."

Colonel Fullarton, after availing himself of
the information which the late governor was so
able and ready to impart, commenced making
himself extremely active in the affairs of the
island; in fact, as General Picton afterwards
observed, when speaking of the first commissioner's arrival at Trinidad, " I began to think,
after a short time, that Colonel Fullarton was
sent out to supersede me as governor of the
island; for, long before the arrival of Commodore Hood, he would have taken the management of both myself and the government
under his sole control." But still there was no
positive misunderstanding between the two
commissioners until the 12th of February,
about ten days previously to the arrival of

Commodore Hood, when General Picton was
astonished by Colonel Fullarton making the
following motion in council :—" That there be
produced certified statements of all the criminal proceedings which have taken place since
the commencement of the late government;
together with a list, specifying every individual, of whatever country, colour, or condition,
who has been imprisoned, banished, fettered,
flogged, burned, or otherwise punished; also
specifying the dates of their respective commit-
ments, trials, sentence, period of confinement,
punishments; and of all those who have died in
prison."

It could not for one moment be doubted
that this was a preliminary step towards an
inquiry into the conduct of the late governor,
under whose sanction, and by whose directions,
these little *désagrémens* were supposed to have
been inflicted. This was the first hostile act
of Colonel Fullarton against General Picton,
who might now foresee what was to follow.
General Picton doubtless did so, but he was
not to be daunted. His conduct throughout
this unhappy business was worthy of himself.
Conscious of his own integrity, he endured the

ignominy attempted to be thrown upon his name with patience, because he knew it to be undeserved. When he perceived the dishonourable grounds upon which Colonel Fullarton had commenced his attack, having no taste for that species of warfare, and feeling at the same time that he could not hope to cooperate with him for the benefit of the colony, he resolved no longer to delay the resolution which he had previously formed of relinquishing the office of commissioner; and accordingly, upon the arrival of Sir Samuel Hood, on the 22nd of February, he tendered his resignation to his Majesty.

Nothing can more strongly evince the opinion which General Picton entertained of Colonel Fullarton and his actions at this period than the following letter to Mr. Gloster, the attorney-general of Trinidad, written for the purpose of obtaining the before-mentioned affidavit from Dr. Lynch.

"London, May 20th, 1805.

" MY DEAR SIR,

" Having laid your letter, and its enclosure from Dr. Lynch, before the Right Hon. Board of Privy Council, Mr. Sullivan, at his own

request, was examined upon oath, and to my
great astonishment denied *in toto* the conversation stated in Dr. Lynch's letter; neither, however, denying nor acknowledging that he had
an interview with him. Under such circumstances, and in the particularly delicate situation in which I was placed, it would have been
the height of imprudence in me to have pursued the business any further upon the single
evidence of a letter; I was therefore under the
necessity of appearing satisfied with the explanation, and declined asking Mr. Sullivan any
questions: but retiring from the board, I immediately expressed my doubts to Mr. Fawkener,
the clerk in waiting, and communicated to him
my determination of immediately applying to
Dr. Lynch for a confirmation of his statement
upon oath. I have, in consequence, to request
that you will have the goodness to assure Dr.
Lynch that I am very remote from entertaining
suspicion of his veracity; but as his statement
to you has been wholly denied upon oath by
Mr. Sullivan, I would recommend that he
should maturely reconsider the business, and
after recalling all the circumstances to his recollection, if he should then be convinced of the

correctness of his former statement, in that case I wish that he would re-state it upon oath before the chief justice, and transmit certified copies of such affidavit to the Right Honourable Earl Camden, Secretary of State for the Colonial Department, and to the Right Honourable Lord Viscount Sidmouth, President of the Council, which will enable me at a future period to bring the business again forward in a less questionable shape.

" If the statement be really true, no expression can sufficiently characterise the conduct it relates to; and if not, it is most extraordinary that Dr. Lynch should have had so circumstantial, and, I might almost say, prophetic a dream. As to there being any separate private instructions to Mr. Fullarton from the secretary of state's office, that is entirely out of the question ; but if there really was any secret understanding, it must have been wholly between Mr. Fullarton and Mr. Sullivan. They might, like *true Indian politicians*, have prepared two strings to their bow ; and, if the insult of degrading me from the high situation of governor-in-chief to that of a junior commissioner did not excite my resentment, and occasion my immediate resignation, the other mode might have been reserved as an ultimatum to get rid of me at áll events.

"Do not, my dear sir, delay attending to this business, which is of considerable import-ance to,

"Your faithful humble servant, &c.

"THOMAS PICTON."

But before entering into the charges which were brought against General Picton, within six months after the appointment of Colonel Fullarton to the office of first commissioner, it may not be considered superfluous briefly to recapitulate from the public documents the difficulties which he had to encounter from the period of his first assuming the government of Trinidad. These documents represent the population as composed of bad people of every description, — brigands, refugees, and desperate characters, who had been implicated in the rebellions and mas-sacres of all the neighbouring islands, — long accustomed to a timid and temporizing go-vernment with no regular police, and living in an island situated only a few leagues from a populous continent inhabited by the enemy, and presenting an immense extent of unprotected coast, which enabled them to keep up an almost uninterrupted communication with the numerous disaffected in the colony. To subdue this mass of disaffection, and mould it into something like a stable government, Colonel Picton had, in the early and most perilous period of his arduous duties, a force which would have been held contemptible even if the island had been one of our oldest and most loyal possessions.

By the monthly return, dated September 1st, 1797, the number of British troops fit for duty in the garrisons of Trinidad amounted to only three hundred and fifteen rank and file ; while, to protect the coast, there were only two guard-ships, one of these being totally unfit for service. In a letter to Sir Ralph Abercromby, dated May 29th, 1797, General Picton observes, " I receive repeated expresses from the commanders of the windward and remote quarters of the island, representing that the enemy's privateers are continually hovering about the coasts, and keep up a constant communication with their friends on shore: this they accomplish without the least risk or danger, as we have not seen or heard of an English cruiser off the coast for nearly two months."

In addition to these means, Governor Picton had one great difficulty within himself, in being entirely ignorant of the laws which he had to administer; for although he was perfectly well acquainted with the French and Spanish languages, and had obtained a great insight into the characters and habits of the people, still he was not acquainted with the laws of Spain, although he was to be made amenable to his country for this omission in his education; and he was actually tried by the laws of England for being ignorant of the laws of Spain: —a species of knowledge with which even the judge by whom he was tried was probably not very conversant, and which was at least a very pardonable omission in the education of a soldier.

When we reflect for a moment upon these accumulated difficulties and abuses which Governor Picton had to overcome and correct, and compare them with the inadequate means at his disposal, we may wonder that the most sanguine disposition could under such circumstances anticipate success : but Picton not only dared to hope for, but even achieved it. Colonel Fullarton shall himself bear testimony to the qualities which enabled him to do so. During the time that the public attention was engrossed by this affair, several pamphlets appeared on both sides. Amongst others, Colonel Fullarton himself assumed the pen, and in his second pamphlet the following passage occurs : "On the departure of Sir Ralph Abercromby, in March 1797, Colonel Picton remained as commandant ; several circumstances, as before mentioned, concurred to qualify him for the appointment,— great natural sagacity, address, activity, and acquaintance with the French and Spanish languages, without which it is impossible for any one to be an efficient ruler of Trinidad."

But Colonel Fullarton accords him this meed of praise only that he may afterwards more unreservedly riot in abuse. We shall continue our quotations from this pamphlet.

" At that time the ungovernable violence and the systematic tyranny of Colonel Picton were probably restrained by the respected character and virtues of Sir Ralph Abercromby · from displaying anything like the rigour and extent which they afterwards exhibited, and which he now describes as the 'energies of his nature.' From the first month subsequent to Sir Ralph Abercromby's departure, Colonel Picton, in his capacity as commandant, and afterwards governor of Trinidad, commenced a career marked with atrocities, which, though I am precluded at present from detailing, must in some form or other come before the world, and at all events, I am warranted in asserting, 'must be registered in the records of eternal justice."

Whether this last sentence is merely a silly attempt at fine writing, or whether it is intended to convey a grossly impious hope, we leave to the reader. But let us hear the Colonel again.

" Colonel Picton contrived very soon to outrage and expel the assessor for the Spanish laws, Don Jurado, and almost every Spanish and English lawyer, from the settlement, stating in a letter to a confidential correspondent, that lawyers were like carrion-crows, who flocked around carcasses and corruption.

" A continued series of severities occasioned the flight of many hundred Spanish peons or labourers.

* * * * * *

" The suspension and imprisonment of Don Francisco de Castro, Dr. Timbrell, and others, were only continuations of the same persecuting spirit. All these collective cases, however, to which I have now referred, convey but a mutilated and imperfect notion of the connected series of oppressive acts by which Colonel Picton so powerfully enforced the reign of terror, shut all mouths that dared to speak against him, and, by the influence of fear, decep_ tion, corruption, and incredible artifice, extorted addresses praising his vigilance, his vigour, and his measures, from which he was denominated by his partisans ' the saviour of the island.' "

These are but a few of the charges brought against General Picton by Colonel Fullarton in this pamphlet. The reader would, however, be tired and disgusted by a detail of its tedious contents. It would be almost impossible, and it is quite unnecessary, to enumerate all the charges it contained, and the assertions it put forward; the majority were merely the inventions of a malignant spirit, and the rest were the highly-coloured and exaggerated descriptions of an enemy. There was,

however, one statement made by Colonel Fullarton, which, as it comes within the range of
proof, may serve to show upon what basis he
rested his facts. At p. 40 of this pamphlet
he says—

"A continued series of severities occasioned
the flight of many hundred Spanish peons or
labourers;" and at p. 41, "A great body of
Spanish inhabitants and *other foreigners* in
Trinidad abandoned the colony."

This is a tangible assertion, which may be
proved or disproved from official documents. If
true, it certainly raises a strong presumption
against General Picton's administration; but, if
false, it furnishes a yet stronger ground for
rejecting the rest of Colonel Fullarton's testimony; for we can hardly suppose that a man
who would venture upon a falsehood capable
of immediate disproof, would hesitate at others
which could be examined with difficulty, and
only at a distant period.

General Picton's friends met it thus:—From
the official return of the population made by
Mr. Mallet, the government surveyor, it appears that in the year 1797 (when Colonel
Picton commenced his administration) the

number of inhabitants was 17,718. In 1802 it amounted to 28,427. This was certainly an increase of 10,709 inhabitants in five years;—an unhappy piece of evidence, because its authority was indisputable. But General Picton's friends could assume the offensive against his accuser: they reminded Colonel Fullarton of the public rebuke he received from his brother commissioner, Sir Samuel Hood,—a name no less celebrated in our naval, than that of Picton in our military annals. That straightforward sailor was ashamed of the dissembling practices of his colleague. Having in vain tried to co-operate with Colonel Fullarton, at length he could restrain his indignation no longer, but addressed him, (in consequence of Colonel Fullarton having caused a proclamation of the commission to be made and posted up unknown to his coadjutors,) in the presence of the whole council of Trinidad, in the following words:

" I was never consulted respecting the proclamation; and I am sorry, sir, that you have so bad a memory. Do you already forget having assured me that the proclamation was torn down by General Picton's partisans? I am ashamed of you; ashamed to be seen in the same company.   Not with you, General Picton —I shall be.proud to act with you on all occasions; you have never attempted to impose upon me; you have allowed. me to see my own way. I have never had any conversation with General Picton respecting the disagreements; but as for you, sir, (turning to Mr. Fullarton,) your behaviour has been such, that nothing but the paramount obligation of his Majesty's commission could seat us at the same board. I shall, however, request to be relieved as soon as possible from so disagreeable a situation, with a colleague with whom I can have no further confidence. I was in hopes you had been occupied in carrying his Majesty's orders into effect, by forwarding the objects of the commission; but I find, on the contrary, that every step you have taken has tended to protract them. You have, in the most arbitrary, indecent manner, taken advantage of my absence to suspend the public secretary, contrary to the opinion of the council and of your colleague, who protested against the measure, and advised that the consideration should be postponed until my arrival.

Instead of cordially co-operating with General
Picton, you seem to have done everything in
your power to inspire him with disgust. The
general dissatisfaction which your proceedings
have given to the public bodies, magistrates,
and respectable people of the colony, is but
too apparent. You are doing everything you
can to ruin the country; but you shall not
effect it—we will not allow you."

General Picton, in his letter to Lord Hobart,
remarks, that "Mr. Fullarton was so confounded by these truths, urged with the manly
and forcible eloquence with which a noble mind
is naturally transported on the discovery of
falsehood and treachery, that he could not utter
a syllable in reply." Colonel Fullarton, nevertheless, ventured to express himself upon a future occasion, when further removed from the
indignant commodore: then he denied that Sir
Samuel Hood had ever made use of such language, although he acknowledged that he had
" uttered many improper and inadmissible expressions; but," he adds, " even if this ha-
rangue had been uttered in my presence, with
all the forcible and manly eloquence so inge-
niously discovered in the enunciations of the

commodore, it would be the first instance upon which any sort of eloquence, from the bellowing of a boatswain to the superior emanations of the most distinguished orators, had ever silenced or confounded me."

Sir Samuél Hood never, however, contradicted one word of the report given of his speech, and was even known to remark the correctness with which it was recorded. Colonel Fullarton was evidently unwilling to admit, and would not readily believe, that Sir Samuel Hood entertained so unfavourable an opinion of him; and in several passages of his second pamphlet he endeavours to show that Commodore Hood did not look upon him in so culpable a light as, from that officer's remarks, both verbal and in writing, the world would have been induced to suppose. In one paragraph he says, " The names of Hood, Grinfiéld, and Maitland are undoubtedly familiar to the public mind for important naval and military services on which they have been employed: it is unfortunate for the two former of those characters that they have suffered their well-earned reputations to be tarnished by a man whose superior sagacity and artifice, aided by the machinations of numerous adherents implicated with him, acquired an ascendency over their inferior penetration."

This sentence seems to admit that those officers had expressed themselves in a decided manner as inimical to Colonel Fullarton and his measures: and the world knows what to think of opprobrium thrown upon such names as these.*

* The following letter from Sir Samuel Hood to Earl Camden, Secretary of State for the Colonial Department, expresses in still more distinct terms the opinion which he entertained of the first commissioner.

"Centaur, Carlisle Bay, Barbadoes, Sept. 1, 1804.
" MY LORD,

" I should do great injustice to myself and my late colleague, Brigadier-general Picton, if I did not (after reading a publication of Mr. Fullarton's respecting the commission at Trinidad last year) inform your lordship at an early period, of the fabrication in various passages of words said to have been spoken by me. The very harsh expressions and the acrimony with which Mr. Fullarton brings forward this epistle, false almost in every page, are such, that I trust your lordship and others of his Majesty's ministers will view it as it deserves. Mr. Fullarton asserts that I consulted the brigadier, before the council was assembled, respecting the matteis we were to enter upon ; *I declare upon my honour no such communication ever took place;* neither did ever the brigadier make use of one expression out of the commission that could tend to lead me on his side: but I was guided by honourable sentiments, and not by such duplicity and in-

Perhaps it may be useful to subjoin a few
more extracts from Colonel Fullarton's pamphlet: they will discover the feelings which
actuated the author in his accusations. We
print them without remark.

" A gentleman of great reputation in the
literary world found several quires of Colonel
Picton's printed libel on the counter of a shop,

triguing as was exhibited in every part of Mr. Fullarton's
transactions.   But Mr. Fullarton used every art even to
get *his lady* to aid in leading me into a track that must have
soon destroyed the tranquillity of the colony. This false
philanthropy must now be sufficiently brought to light, so
as to need no comment. He interprets words spoken in
council, in my house, as not agreeing with my colleague:
I give the most perfect contradiction thereto; and I cannot
allow this to pass over without remarking on the means
adopted by persons whom he calls gentlemen, who would
listen to any conversation where their presence was not required; and it was not probable my servants should listen,
and carry any conversation to the house of the first commissioner. I conceive such allegations can only tend to
prove how ready Mr. Fullarton has been to catch at subjects
which I should shudder to repeat, had I made use of such
ignoble means to gain the information stated. I will not
trespass longer on your lordship's time; and I shall conclude
this in saying, the upright and just measures adopted by the
late governor saved the island: and I rest assured his character cannot be spoken of too highly, or traduced by the
artful measures of an old intriguing politician.

" I have the honour to be, &c.

" Earl Camden, K.B. &c."   " SAMUEL HOOD."

where they were used to wrap up the com-
modities. sold to customers, and circulated in
that manner."

" The charges against Colonel Picton were
referred to in my letter to General Grinfield,
dated the 23rd of May 1803: they involve a
mass of criminality such as has never been
brought against any British ruler. If they
were unfounded in point of fact, then the fa-
bricator of them would have deserved to be
consigned to everlasting infamy and condign
punishment."

" Those who read the charges, cases, and
statements I have brought forward, will perceive that anything of quarrel on personal
grounds was entirely *out of the question.* I
must again repeat, that Colonel Picton went to
war with me because I would not sanction and
adopt a system of government in Trinidad
which, on his part, exhibits a more extended
course of power abused, of good talents applied
to evil purposes, and of more numerous atrocities by one person, than can be equalled in all
the folio volumes of the State Trials, which I
have carefully searched on this occasion."

" These preliminary explanations appear in-

dispensable to the comprehension of the means
by which Colonel Picton enforced his system
of oppression, hermetically sealed up all sources
of complaint, and extorted a mass of false and
counterfeit applause; harassing with obloquy
and persecution every one who impeded any
object beneficial to his pecuniary concerns, or
who otherwise fell under his ungovernable re-
sentments."

" Colonel Picton affords the strongest illustration of the character, so admirably portrayed in Dr. Moore's Zeluco, of an officer who
could always restrain his temper in perfect forbearance and submission on the parade, under
the reprehension of a commanding officer of
such vociferating tendencies as General Grinfield; but could never put the rein on his impetuous nature when in command, or uncon-
strained by the presence of a superior; and
still less could curb his violence when a poor
soldier or helpless victim was at the mercy of
his resentment."

CHAPTER VII.

Testimonials in favour of General Picton's abilities and conduct.—Flattering Address from the Inhabitants of Trinidad to the King.—Realization of Dr. Lynch's " Prophetic Dream."—General Picton's resignation accepted.—Leaves Trinidad.—Arrival at Barbadoes.—Joins General Grinfield in an Expedition against St. Lucia and Tobago.—Capture of the former.—General Orders. —The Fleet sails for Tobago. — Its Capitulation. — Despatch from the Commander-in-chief.—General Picton appointed Commandant. —Excitement in England against him. — Its effects.— Leaves Tobago.—Arrives in London.—Artful devices to inflame the British Public.—Their success.

THE reader would doubtless be happy to turn from the painful narrative of an individual endeavouring by every means in his power to˙ destroy the good name of a man whose character had hitherto been without stain, and whose after-life was marked by the most distinguished services. But much still remains untold, ˙and the biographer of Picton unwillingly recalls these now forgotten calumnies.

We will first see what was thought of these statements at the time by those who possessed the most ample means of correctly estimating them.

A few extracts from the correspondence of the parties are merely necessary to show in what degree . of esteem General Picton was held, and the light in which the charges brought against him were viewed by the officers under whose immediate observation both the general and Colonel Fullarton were · placed. These distinguished men, without a single exception, expressed, both verbally and in print, their unqualified approbation of the conduct of General Picton; while, on the other hand, they spoke in decided censure of his accuser.

Amongst those who may be mentioned as the warmest supporters and friends of General Picton, were Sir Ralph Abercromby; Vice-admiral, Sir Samuel Hood; Lord Hobart, at that time secretary for the colonial department; Generals Grinfield and Maitland; Lieutenant-governor Hislop; Colonels Mosheim, Grant, and Draper; together with Captains Champain, Dickson, and Western, of

the Royal Navy. Many of these names are so
well known, and their characters are so highly
appreciated, that it is only necessary to give
a few brief extracts from their correspondence,
to prove that General Picton must either
have been the most deceitful, artful, and corrupt private friend or public servant that ever
(in the language of his accuser) " disgraced
the British name and character :" or that the
blackest malice, falsehood, and treachery were
employed to stigmatize his reputation, and
brand his memory with infamy. It is needless
to give the whole contents of the letters from.
which the following extracts are drawn ; for,
as direct testimonies of the opinion entertained
of General Picton by their writers, these por-
tions are alone valuable.

In a letter from Lord Hobart, dated July
19th, 1802, he says :—

" The first official notification I have received of any dissatisfaction at your government has been *from yourself;* and I can only
observe, that the zeal and ability you have
uniformly shown in maintaining the security and tranquillity of the Island during the
very critical period of your command, would

alone call upon me to receive any accounts of that kind with the *greatest circumspec-tion.*   (Signed)   " HOBART."
" To Brigadier-general Picton,
&c. &c."

Lieutenant-general W. Grinfield, the com-mander-in-chief in the West Indies, in his public despatches, dated the 11th and 13th of August 1803, expresses himself in these strong and decided terms:—

" Circumstances, unexpected by Colonel Pic-ton, or by any other person, have placed him for a little time in a disagreeable situation ; but I am fully persuaded that his general conduct has been such as will convince the world of his merit, and his fame will rise the higher for the unmerited persecution under which he now labours.   (Signed)   " W. GRINFIELD,
                                    " Lieutenant-general."
" Right Honourable Lord Hobart,
&c. &c."

At the same time, in his despatches to his Royal Highness the Duke of York, this officer observes :—

" The disagreeable situation in which he (General Picton) has unfortunately, unintentionally, and disagreeably been placed, through the extraordinary conduct of Colonel Fullarton, requires me to desire you particularly to express my entire satisfaction of Brigadier-general Picton, both as a soldier and a gentleman.

(Signed)   " W. GRINFIELD,
" Lieutenant-general."

" Colonel Churton,
" Secretary to H. R. H. the Commander-in-chief."

Brigadier-general Maitland, who was ordered to take the military command of the colony in June 1803, after General Picton had resigned the office of junior commissioner, thus spoke of him, in reply to the magistrates and council, when they waited upon him with an address upon his being relieved in the command by Lieutenant-governor Hislop :—

" Gentlemen, I am most grateful for this public testimony of your approbation of my conduct, for which I return you my warmest thanks. It rises in my esteem for this reason, that as I replaced a most distinguished and meritorious officer, it was more difficult to gain applause. I will not throw away this opportunity of expressing, in unison with you, that I

greatly honour and esteem Brigadier-general
Picton. In a period of public danger, when
the colony was beset with traitors, and shaken
by the unruly behaviour of a disorderly soldiery, (for such was the major part of the garrison in May 1797,) his undisturbed mind awed
the factious, subdued the danger, and saved the
colony.   (Signed)   " F. R. MAITLAND."

After these gratifying testimonials of the
high estimation in which General Picton was
held by those distinguished men who had an
immediate opportunity of observing his character and actions, we are prepared to view the
persecution which he had so long to endure
with less pain, because we feel that they were
unable to deprive him of the esteem of those
of his friends whose approbation was most
valuable.

We have deviated somewhat from strict
chronological order in canvassing in this place
charges which were not made public until
eighteen months afterwards. But it has been
deemed more convenient to introduce them
here; and to dispose of their credibility whilst
reviewing the conduct upon which they pur-

ported to be founded. Their evidence we
have thus examined : their influence upon the
fortunes of the subject of our memoir must
occur again in our narrative. It is now, however, necessary to trace the career of General
Picton until his return to England.

. It has already been observed, that, feeling
insulted by the appointment which he now
held, General Picton tendered his resignation;
While the accumulated insults of the first
commissioner made him particularly desirous of
being released from his disagreeable situation,
he was at the same time apprehensive lest an
address which the inhabitants (hearing of his
intention) had sent to the King, praying his Majesty not to accept the resignation of their governor, might be the means of compelling him
to remain. Every succeeding day convinced him
that Colonel Fullarton was either appointed to,
or had taken upon himself, the duty of investi-
gator into his past conduct; and General Picton,
upon more than one occasion, expressed his entire conviction that the first commissioner was
privately instructed to make out a case against
him sufficiently strong to procure his removal.
If this were true, as indeed there seems but

too much reason to believe, it was mean
and pitiful conduct on the part of the government to intrude a mere spy into the confidence of a man whom it dared not openly attack, in order to work his ruin, and to
use a mere tool for the accomplishment of
an object so disgraceful to its members personally. It is but reasonable to suppose
that Governor Picton was deemed guilty
of something censurable : how absurd, then,
that in order to disguise or qualify the inquiry, he was complimented upon his conduct, and appointed (doubtless as a reward)
one of the commission to inquire into his
own culpability ! It is curious to observe how
accurately the facts of this affair coincided
with what General Picton called " Dr. Lynch's
prophetic dream."

It will be remembered, that on the 4th
of January, Mr. Commissioner Fullarton arrived in Trinidad, and according to the words
of Dr. Lynch's affidavit Mr. Sullivan informed
him, " that in all probability General Picton
would be ordered to return to England before
six months." On the 31st of May, being four
days within the six months, General Picton

received a communication from Lord Hobart, stating that "his Majesty had been pleased to accept his resignation:" and a few days after this announcement he was superseded in the military command of the Island by the following general order of the commander-in-chief, Lieutenant-general Grinfield.

"GENERAL ORDERS.

"Head-quarters, Barbadoes, June 11th, 1803.

"Brigadier-general Maitland is to relieve Brigadier-general Picton in the command of the troops in the Island of Trinidad.

"Brigadier-general Maitland is to proceed to Trinidad with as little delay as possible; and Brigadier-general Picton, on his being relieved, has the leave of the commander of the forces to remain any time he thinks necessary at Trinidad to settle his affairs, and he may then proceed to Barbadoes or to Europe, as he pleases, specifying his intention as soon as possible to the commander of the forces.

(Signed)   "Geo. B. Morden,

"Lieut.-colonel, Dep. Adj.-general.

"Alex. Pitman, Brigadier-major."

Thus Colonel Fullarton did investigate the conduct of the late governor, and General Picton did resign within six months.

In judging between the contradictory affidavits of Dr. Lynch and Mr. Sullivan, we may certainly, therefore, remember that the coincidence of facts strongly corroborates that of the former gentleman.

General Picton had little to detain him at Trinidad, and accordingly, on the 14th of June, he embarked for Barbadoes. According to Colonel Fullarton, "he embarked in the dark, on board the Nelly, armed schooner, for Barbadoes; not daring, as it appeared, to face an injured and exasperated people, after he was divested of the support arising from the civil and military power with which he had been formerly invested."

The following brief extract from a modern and authentic work upon the West Indies gives, however, a somewhat different impression with regard to the estimation in which General Picton was held by those who were so lately subject to his authority. "On the 23rd of April 1803," says Mr. Southey, in his Chronological History of the West Indies,

"the inhabitants of Trinidad presented their
governor, Brigadier-general Picton, with a
sword, upon his resigning the government of
that Island. They also sent an address to the
King, praying him not to accept of their governor's resignation."

Brigadier-general Picton arrived in Carlisle
Bay, Barbadoes, at the moment when the expedition was about to sail for the purpose of
retaking the islands of St. Lucia and Tobago
from the French. General Grinfield readily
availed himself of Brigadier-general Picton's
offer to join the expedition, and expressed
much satisfaction in employing the services of
so meritorious an officer. Colonel Fullarton,
in his second pamphlet, seems to consider it
necessary to offer an apology for General Grinfield, for this "improper deviation from principles of military duty;" and accordingly ven-
tures to "avow the belief that General Grinfield was induced to employ Brigadier-general
Picton at St. Lucia and Tobago, by a strong
desire to conciliate Commodore Hood, with
whom it was most essential for the public service that he should continue to act on terms of
cordiality and co-operation; which, it is per-

fectly evident, could not have been the case
had General Grinfield refused to gratify the
commodore in protecting Brigadier Picton."
That General Grinfield could have done without this officious apology will readily be believed, upon a recollection of the observations
already quoted, which were made upon Brigadier-general Picton by his commander in his
despatches after the successful issue of this expedition; of the operations of which a brief
account is subjoined.

"At daylight, on the 21st of June, the
expedition for the attack of St. Lucia, under
the command of Commodore Hood and General Grinfield, was off the north end of that
Island. In the course of the day, the greater
part of the troops were disembarked in Choc
Bay. About half-past five the out-posts of the
enemy were driven in, the town of Costries
was taken, and a summons sent to the French
commandant, Brigadier Nogues. Upon the receipt of his refusal, it was determined upon by
the British commanders that the Morne Fortune should be stormed the following morning
at four o'clock; which was accordingly done,
and the place carried in about half an hour."*

* Southey.

General Grinfield, in his despatches, states, "that notwithstanding the spirited resistance of the French, yet no sooner were the works carried by assault, and the opposition no longer existed, than every idea of animosity seemed to cease, and not a French soldier was either killed or wounded." The Island was, in consequence, unconditionally restored to the British government.

In the "general orders" issued upon this occasion by the commander of the forces, after remarking upon the gallant behaviour of the second battalion of the Royals, and the Sixty-fourth regiment, he concludes by saying, "he is very sorry that the Sixty-eighth regiment, by its being in reserve under Brigadier-general Picton, was not in the action; otherwise there can be no doubt but they would have merited an equal report, as was evinced by a small detachment of that regiment in a feint attack under the command of Lieutenant-colonel Shipley."

After having secured the possession of this conquest, the troops were again embarked, and the fleet got under weigh for the Island of Tobago, where it arrived on the 30th of

June. General Grinfield immediately sent to demand the surrender of the place to his Britannic Majesty, at the same time proceeding to land his troops; the advanced column of which, headed by Brigadier-general Picton, pushed on without delay, in order to urge the reply to the summons. The French general (Berthier) being, however, apprised of the force of the British, and of the taking of St. Lucia, agreed to capitulate the same day; and according to the despatch of General Grinfield, "the French garrison marched out with the honours of war, laying down their arms after passing the guard of honour under the command of Brigadier-general Picton."

In the general orders the following remark occurs:—"The advance march of the first column, consisting of two companies of the Sixty-fourth regiment and five companies of the Third West India regiment, under Brigadier-general Picton, which was in all probability the cause of the speedy surrender, is entitled to military commendation."

To express in a most convincing manner the unshaken confidence which the commander of the forces reposed in General Picton he appointed him, without any solicitation, commandant of the Island of Tobago; this situation, however, he was enabled to hold for a very short period, as he was within a few weeks informed that Colonel Fullarton and his associates had left Trinidad for England, with a series of charges affecting his honour and humanity.

The reader will not have forgotten the highly flattering testimony in General Picton's favour, which we recently extracted from General Grinfield's correspondence with Lord Hobart and the Duke of York. At this time Colonel Fullarton had preferred no less than thirty-six criminal processes against his predecessor before the council of Trinidad. What General Grinfield thought of these accusations, his acts and his correspondence alike testify; and so far was his view of the circumstances concurred with by all who knew anything of Trinidad, that in the West Indies, where it may be supposed there was a better opportunity of judging of the facts, it was pretty generally thought that Colonel Fullarton had much more need of an apology for his behaviour towards Governor Picton, than

General Grinfield for employing that officer's services.

During the short period that General Picton held the appointment of commandant of Tobago, he received every flattering attention from the local authorities, and upon his departure, many complimentary letters of regret. But no time was to be lost: he received several communications from his friends in England, informing him of the horrible tales of cruelty that were current concerning him, and that the public were becoming exasperated against the "cruel governor who had been guilty of such excesses."

Upon receiving these statements, he felt that indignation which every honourable man must experience when he knows himself to be charged with crimes of which his conscience tells him he is innocent. His only anxiety was to be upon the field with his enemies; for with that idea so common to a noble mind, he thought that to be innocent was enough to enable him to prove it. Few are aware how difficult is the task of disproving any accusation, however unfounded or gross, so as to leave the individual free from the insinuations of envy or malice. The world always gives the accuser credit for some authority to support the charge; and, unless the individual against whom it be brought can disprove the fact by sufficient evidence, believes him guilty : so that the accusation is received upon presumed authority, while the vindication is not admitted unless confirmed by clear and acknowledged testimonies.

Let us imagine the situation of Governor Picton, when Colonel Fullarton, shortly after his arrival in Trinidad, preferred against him the six-and-thirty processes before alluded to: what ingenuity or exertion could procure sufficient evidence to disprove these imputations to the satisfaction of the world? A life passed in acts of constant benevolence and virtue would not have obtained for him an unsullied reputation. He might be acquitted by those in possession of just or liberal sentiments ; but the world would still say, " He never got well out of all those charges."

General Picton arrived in London in the month of October, and soon discovered the truth of the statements of his friends. The daily prints were occasionally reminding the

public, (doubtless at the instigation of his
enemies,) that " the blood-stained Governor of
Trinidad was in England, and that the friends
of humanity were preparing to bring him
before the bar of offended justice, there to
expiate his crimes;" while, in more indirect
terms, the prejudice of the British people was
enlisted on the side of the prosecutors by certain hints, such as, " His Majesty's Government
is to institute an inquiry into the conduct of
a late governor, whose unheard-of cruelties will
harrow up the feelings, and call forth the indignation, of every sensitive and virtuous mind."

Neither exertion nor expense was spared
in order to ensure the ends of the prosecutors;
their only wish was to prove him guilty; his
acquittal would bring disgrace upon themselves,
and be the means of clearing him from the
many calumnies with which they had attempted to overwhelm him. Corruption and perjury were even employed, in order to mislead
the judges, and stir up the vindictive feelings
of the public against " one of those men whose
unprecedented cruelties, according to the statement of Lord Walsingham, " had deluged our
colonies with human blood."

In addition to these exciting and unjust means, the press, that guide to popular opinion, with too much credulity lent its powerful aid in support of "injured innocence" and "outraged humanity;" while, fearful that even these auxiliaries would not be sufficient, coloured drawings were paraded through the streets, calling forth the public commiseration, by exhibiting the "*picture of the girl, pulley, spike, and the grillos.*"

In fact, every species of deception and artifice was employed to work upon the senses and blind the judgments of the public, so that Governor Picton should be made to fall at the feet of his accusers; whether as the victim of justice, treachery, or persecution, was of little importance to them.

CHAPTER VIII.

General Picton's patriotism. — Threatened Invasion of England by Napoleon. — Picton's Letter to Mr. Addington. — His plan for the defence of the country. — Its reception. — Prosecution continued. — Interview with Lord Hobart. — Arrested by order of the Privy Council. — Enormous bail. — Indicted upon a criminal information. — Observations upon the Indictment. — Mandamus to obtain Evidence at Trinidad.—Trial.

DEEPLY wounded in spirit by the acts of an individual; unjustly held up to the British nation as an object of reproach, and on the point of being involved in all the expense and ignominy of a prosecution by the Government; which, at the same time that it was intended to convince the world of his guilt, would justify the vindictiveness of his accusers; and this after the very same government had for years, both by rewards and correspondence, lauded his conduct to their sovereign, and given their unanimous sanction and approbation to every act of his administration whilst governing the Island of Trinidad : overwhelmed at once by private persecution and public injustice, it will hardly be believed that he was even at this period employed in devising a plan for the protection and defence of his country.

Napoleon, who had clipped the wings of the Austrian eagle, destroyed that of Prussia, and seized the smaller states of Europe, at this period meditated an invasion of England. The French army was collected at Boulogne, with a flotilla for their transport to the shores of England ; Napoleon's design being to bring the war to the very homes of the English.

A miserable remnant of disaffection, it is true, existed at this moment in Great Britain ; but its efforts were directed against the Government, not against the country ; and even had Napoleon succeeded in landing his troops, it is very doubtful whether the most clamorous in the cry of political dissent would not have been among the most zealous in resisting the invaders. Numerous plans and suggestions for the defence of the country were constantly sent to the ministers ; advice, money, and personal services were incessantly tendered ; and as the

danger appeared to increase, so the means to
meet it were accumulated. Amongst the earliest to offer service was General Picton ; and
there is no doubt that had his abilities been
called into action in the defence of the kingdom, they would have placed him in an elevated
position, alike honourable to himself and valuable to his country. The following is a letter
addressed by him to Mr. Addington, at this
period of general excitement and apprehension.

"SIR,   "20th October, 1803.

"From the ambitious views and preponde-
rating power of the French republic, there will
be an absolute necessity, whether in peace or
war, for placing this country in a permanent
situation, so as to be at all times in readiness
to resist sudden enterprises. An appearance
of weakness will not fail to invite an attack,
whilst an adequate state of preparation will
show the impossibility of its succeeding. The
country should not only be in a situation to
oppose a successful resistance to an invading
enemy, however numerous its armies or formidable its preparations, but so organized and
arranged as to inspire a general sentiment of

security and safety, without which she cannot long be able to preserve her independence and high rank in the political scale.

" The volunteers are the overflowing of the national spirit, and probably the happiest expedient which could have been employed to meet the immediate exigency of the times : but the spirit is kept up by fermentation, which, I apprehend, it will be neither possible nor politic to continue as a permanent means of defence : it is supported by alarm and apprehension; and the mind which is kept in continual agitation by those sentiments relaxes gradually, and at length yields to their destructive influence.

" There are many other insurmountable objections to it, as a permanent national system, which will render its continuance precarious, inadequate, and even dangerous; for it is of a democratic construction, destructive of all discipline, without which armed bodies are but mobs, more formidable to their friends than to their enemies.

" The grand desideratum is, a broad effectual system of defence upon an economical plan; and the greatest possible force provided at the lowest expense. Prudence must go hand in hand with preparation, or the remedy will produce a crisis equally ruinous with the disease.

" I shall leave the army and the militia where they are, considering them as easily augmentable to any extent circumstances may require. But first of all I must make some preliminary observations on the situation of a hostile army landing in this country.

" They must unavoidably come deficient in two of the most important departments of an army, cannon and cavalry ; and their great object must be to force us to general and decisive actions, by way of remedying as soon as possible, the serious inconveniences resulting from the want of those essential arms. What is advantageous to the enemy will, of course, be disadvantageous to us ; and it cannot be dissembled, considering their experience and practical discipline, that they would at first have considerable advantage over new troops ; besides, the fate of battles is frequently dependent upon the caprice of fortune, and on causes not under the influence of human direction. We have inappreciable advantages, if we know how to make use of them, which it would be wanton

and impolitic to hazard at once on the throw
of a die. But it may be remarked, ' if the
enemy is determined to bring you to action,
you must fight:' yes, you must fight, but you
fight on your own terms.

"According to the plan I mean to propose,
you must greatly out-number the enemy in
light troops, cavalry, and cannon. The moment he puts his columns in motion, they
should be harassed in every direction by the
irregulars, who, under protection of the cavalry
and cannon judiciously posted, may approach
them on all points, and distress them by an incessant fire. If they make detachments to dislodge your light troops, they can easily avoid
them; and if they disperse in the pursuit, they
must fall an easy prey to your cavalry. They
must make up their minds either to perish gradually by this harassing warfare, or have recourse to the expedient of detaching, which
would be little less destructive. Your regular
troops should dispute advantageous posts and
favourable grounds, but never hazard a general
affair; the principal efforts should be made on
the rear and the flanks, which arrest the enemy's
movements, and render his progress slow and

difficult, if not impossible. His confidence will necessarily abate as he sees no period to his labours; whilst you gradually increase in military experience and courage, and prepare yourselves for the day which will crown your patient efforts with success.

" In this kind of war you cannot have too many light troops. An active man, who knows how to load and fire at a mark, will immediately become a useful soldier : with a very little instruction, and a few days' practical experience, he will acquire a sufficient expertness in the few simple necessary movements, and in the mode of concealing himself so as to annoy the enemy. My plan is not to arm the country generally, but that every man from fifteen to fifty should be made sufficiently acquainted with arms to be useful on an emergency,—that they should be divided into five or more classes, so that you may call them out by degrees : arrange the young and unmarried men in the first, and those who are more advanced in life, and have families, in the more remote classes. The means of instruction should be placed within their reach, and every man should be compelled by law to conform. From these you may at all times augment your regulars and militia to any extent, and call out as great a number of irregulars as circumstances might require. If an enemy should effect a landing in force, and a campaign take place on British ground, the troops of the line and militia will require a continual infusion of recruits to supply their unavoidable losses; it would therefore be advisable to establish depôts for each corps, where a supplement of one-fourth its number should be kept in constant training for that purpose.

"I am of opinion that the arms for the irregulars should be brown, except the bayonet, and that the calibre should take a ball of twenty-five to the pound; for, independently of freeing the soldier from an unnecessary encumbering weight, which greatly impedes his movements in the desultory kind of warfare he is to carry on, there will be a saving in ammunition of nearly thirty-five per cent.—an object of no small importance on an extensive scale.

"These troops should be clothed in a grey jacket and round hat, with accoutrements equally simple; a pouch to contain twenty-four rounds, powder-horn and bullet-bag, suspended by a strong black or tan leather belt, when called out upon active service. They should be divided into corps not exceeding five hundred men, with an active officer of the line to command each ; and they may eventually be formed into brigades, with irregular cavalry attached, and be placed under the command of partisans of superior rank. This system once made a part of the law of the land, you may call out the proportion of the population which the public safety and the circumstances of the times require without any alarming exertion, which unavoidably elevates the public mind only to let it down lower.

"These are but rough hints, which I have hastily thrown together, as suggested to me by the situation of the country. If any one of them should prove useful, I shall esteem myself overpaid for the trouble I have taken.

"I have the honour to be,

"Your very faithful, humble servant,

"TH. PICTON."*

"To the Right Hon. Henry Addington."

* Appended to this letter is the following plan, in Sir Thomas Picton's own hand, for a new organization of the public force :

It must be remembered, while perusing this
letter, that General Picton was as yet an inexperienced soldier, having served thus far more
in a civil than a military career; but, with a disposition which led him to follow with interest
every professional study and pursuit, he had

" First,— The defence of the United Kingdom, and of our
political existence as an independent nation, requires a large
regular force, to be constantly supplied from unperishing
sources, and to be supported upon the most economical plan.

" Second,—That two hundred and fifty thousand men,
cavalry and infantry, and ten thousand artillery, under the
existing circumstances and relative situation of the country,
will be necessary for that purpose.

" Third,—That the militia, though a most respectable body,
and admirably calculated for the object of its original institution, from a total change in the state of Europe, is become
wholly inadequate, and ought to be blended and assimilated
with the regular force.

" Fourth,—That the old as well as new system of recruiting,
having proved ineffectual for the purpose of raising or supporting the necessary public force, ought to be given up,
except for colonial service.

" Fifth,—That the public force consist of a certain number
of first and second battalions, with a reserve, in case of invasion or actual necessity, consisting of one-fourth the establishment of the two battalions, from which they are constantly to be supplied.

" Sixth,—The militia to be in the first instance incorpo-
rated into the establishment, and the population at large to
make up the deficiency by conscription.

" Seventh,—During peace the second battalion to be always quartered in the counties to which they are attached,

made himself master of every theory connected with field movements and fortification, so that whenever required to enter upon active service he had only to add experience to knowledge to become great. Still this letter, as coming from the pen of Sir Thomas Picton, will be read

---

and only two fifths of the establishment kept actually embodied.

" Eighth,—The head-quarters of every second battalion to be a depôt of arms for the use of the country.

" Ninth,—The second battalions to be commanded by general officers or colonels, with an allowance of six hundred pounds per annum, free of all taxes, &c. in lieu of pay and other emoluments.

" Tenth,—Permanent head-quarters at Exeter and York ; the assembly of these central armies of reserve to be established at Salisbury, Bristol, and Worcester.

" Eleventh,—Depôts of ordnance stores to be established at each of the head-quarters.

" Twelfth,—Powder-mills and manufactories of artillery, arms, and ammunition, to be established at Worcester and its neighbourhood.

"Thirteenth,—The first battalion to be always completed from the second, except in case of actual invasion, when both are to be supplied from the reserve.

" Fourteenth,—First class of conscription from eighteen to twenty-four, unmarried.

" Second, from twenty-four to thirty, unmarried.

" Third, from eighteen to twenty-four, married.

" Fourth, from twenty-four to thirty, married.

" Fifth, from thirty to forty, unmarried.

" Sixth, from thirty to forty, married, respect being paid to the fathers of children.

with interest, as the production of a man who afterwards attained a celebrity which would have gained for his suggestions both attention and respect.

In tracing the histories of all who have dis= tinguished themselves in any particular path of life, it is strange to observe the little esteem in which their early thoughts or actions were held; we are almost invariably indebted to the indi- vidual himself for pointing out his own supe- riority.

General Picton had at this period done no act which entitled his suggestions to particular attention, and in consequence he merely re- ceived from Mr. Addington's secretary an ac- knowledgment of his letter, together with the information that it added another to the many which had been addressed to the minister upon the same subject.

———

Fifteenth,—The period of service limited during peace to two years in the second battalion, and five in the first.

"Sixteenth,—Young men who volunteer for the cavalry, and attend at their own expense at the periods of exercise, until called upon actual service, to be excused the con- scription.

"Seventeenth,—During peace one-fifth of the first batta- lion to be occasionally discharged, and to be filled up by the second battalion, and lastly by conscription.

But returning to General Picton's career, it is now necessary to turn our attention to the particular charge upon which Governor Picton was tried, and upon which he was condemned by the public, in spite of the judgment of a court of justice, and the decision of his Majesty's Privy Council. It was this charge upon which his future prospects were to depend, and by which the numerous accusations brought against him were to be supported.

In consequence of the sinister proceedings of his enemies, which every day assumed a new and more aggravated form, General Picton felt himself placed in the situation of a man who, without trial, is convicted. An investigation into his conduct he could demand, but the privacy of an inquiry in the Privy Council would avail him little with the public, while the secrecy of the engines, and the low artifices which were employed, in order to shield the authors and instigators of these calumnies, rendered General Picton uncertain how to act, so as to clear his own character from the charges with which it was stained, and at the same time bring to account those who had thus aspersed him. He could not stoop to their low cunning, or trace them through the tortuous paths through which they attacked him : his noble and candid nature led him to seek his enemies in the open field. With all ."the world" opposed to him, he felt that he must struggle for himself; and accordingly he waited on Lord Hobart ; when it is to be presumed he demanded from that minister an explanation of the situation in which he was placed, and to know whether he was to consider that he had incurred the censure of his Majesty's government, as well as that. of his subjects. The particulars of this interview, however, are not known, as for some reason General Picton never afterwards alluded to it even to his most intimate friends.

In the beginning of December, he was arrested by a King's messenger, by order of his Majesty's Privy Council, and was confined in the house of Mr. Sparrow, upon the oaths and depositions of Luise Calderon, Raphael Sbando, Pedro Vargas, and Juan Montes.* This was

* The characters of these individuals may. be thus summed up in a few words, from the evidence returned upon the mandamus :—

the first decisive step taken by the Government in this prosecution; and General Picton was now called upon to exert himself in order to meet the accusations which were brought against him, and to convince the world that he was innocent. His enemies had taken a strong position: they had appealed to the feelings of the public to avenge the cause of innocence and outraged humanity. The " blood-stained tyrant" was now before them; these friends of justice had brought him to the bar of retribution, and the people of England were called upon to pronounce him guilty. These exciting announcements were received as they were intended; and the public voice at length became so loud, that the Government were compelled, in order to stop the clamour, to enter

---

Luise Calderon, living with a man to whom she was inconstant, and of whom she ultimately became an accomplice in robbing. Raphael Shando, once convicted of stealing, and sent to the galleys, "and not to be believed upon his oath." Pedro Vargas swore that he was a Spanish lawyer, and was accordingly brought forward to explain the Spanish laws; but his evidence was so full of prevarication and falsehood, that the judge was upon the point of committing him for wilful and corrupt perjury. Juan Montes, a deserter from the Havannah, and generally believed in Trinidad to be a spy to the Spanish government.

into the inquiry. A short time after his arrest he was allowed to put in bail; but this was required to the enormous sum of forty thousand pounds!

Still he was not permitted to rest: a criminal indictment was laid against him, founded upon one of the before-mentioned charges, preferred by Colonel Fullarton in the Council of Trinidad,—"For the application of torture to extort confession from Luise Calderon, a girl under fourteen years of age, respecting a robbery supposed to have been committed by Carlos Gonzales against Pedro Ruiz, stated to have been frequently employed as an agent by General Picton. The torture is stated to have been applied with such severity that the girl fell down in appearance dead, and there was no physician or surgeon to assist."

The indictment found by the grand jury was, however, framed in the accustomed style of exaggeration, and apparently wilful misstatement; in fact, the perusal of this inflammatory document was, to use the words of another distinguished victim of persecution, enough to make General Picton doubt "whether he was not as guilty as he was represented."

Amongst a variety of ingenious devices which had their origin solely in the head of the attorney who modelled this document, he is accused of " having affixed a rope to the wrists of Luise Calderon, which certain rope was made to pass through a certain pulley attached to the ceiling of the prison;" and then the said Thomas is charged with " having caused her to be alternately raised up and down upon a certain sharp spike affixed to the floor, so that the feet of the said Luise fell every time upon the said spike, to the great injury and oppression of the said Luise;" and he the said Thomas is then accused of " unlawfully and *maliciously intending to injure and oppress* the said Luise;" and "that he did make an assault, and then and there unmercifully and cruelly did bruise, beat, wound, and ill-treat the said Luise, so that her life was greatly despaired of," &c.

Upon this indictment, which was found in Hilary Term 1804, a mandamus was granted, calling upon the lieutenant-governor of Trinidad, General Hislop, " to receive proofs and examine witnesses in reference to the prosecution pending against the late governor, General

Picton."* These writs of mandamus were re-
turnable in Michaelmas Term 1805 ; and the
cause came on for trial in the Court of King's
Bench, before Lord Ellenborough and a special
jury; on the 24th of February 1806.

* To avoid recurring again to the affairs of Trinidad, it is
only necessary to remark that the " *commissioner government*" was, after a few months' trial, found to be totally
incompetent to carry on the administration of the Island.
The short reign of this discordant and heterogeneous
government had proved highly injurious to the peace
of the colony ; and the order and subordination which
Governor Picton had, after so long a period, and with so
much difficulty, succeeded in establishing, were in one month
nearly destroyed. Lieutenant-general Hislop was appointed lieutenant-governor upon the recall of the commissioners, and he was compelled by the severest measures
again to reduce to subjection the turbulent population : but
it would appear that he had either more difficulties to overcome, or less firmness for the task; for by the following
letter from Trinidad, nearly eighteen months after he had
been appointed to the government, it will be seen that much
apprehension still existed, and that he had not entirely succeeded in rooting out the seeds of discontent and rebellion.

"Trinidad, Dec. 19th, 1805.

"We had nearly experienced a rebellion of the negroes
here, and a general massacre of the whites, which, had it
taken place, would have involved all the Windward Islands
in general devastation. The explosion of such a volcano
here, as well as at St. Domingo, would have completely overwhelmed not only the British, but all the other colonies.

It would be both uninteresting and unnecessary to give the whole proceedings of this unprecedented trial.   Mr. Garrow was employed on
behalf of the crown, or, more properly on that
of Colonel Fullarton and Company ; while Mr.
Dallas had to conduct the defence for General
Picton.   The usual eloquence, sophistry, and
ingenuity were displayed by both those distinguished lawyers.   The witnesses were, as
usual, made to contradict each other and themselves ; forgetting, whilst under the bewilder-

One of the kings -or emperors, a negro slave of Shand's
estate, has this day been executed in the square of the town ;
to-morrow six others of the royal dynasty take .their leave
of this world ; and the severest scrutiny is making as to
the intentions of these nefarious conspirators.   Colonel J.
Gloster discovered the plot, in the valley where he is commandant, and made immediate communication of it to the
governor, who sent a strong detachment of regulars in the
dead of night, and took all the conspirators into custody.
Their uniforms and standards were found concealed.   The
council has had a permanent sitting of eight days.   The
unwearied solicitude and precautions of our excellent governor, Lieutenant-general Hislop, are above all praise.   The
projects of these scoundrels were, to get possession of all the
white men, and grind them in Mr. Shand's new windmill,
and they were to cast lots for the white ladies.   Not a
child was to have escaped their fury.   The plans of these
monsters have fortunately been completely frustrated, and
no injurious consequences are now apprehended.

ing influence of the learned gentlemen, every fact connected with their existence, and being made to admit or deny everything they knew, according as it answered the intentions of their ingenious examiners.

To heighten the effect, a coloured drawing was produced in court and shown to the jury, just, as Mr. Garrow *innocently* remarked, "by way of explaining the instrument of torture, and to show how and in what manner the girl was placed upon it;" while he observed to the noble and learned lord on the bench, PRIVATELY,—that is to say, in a whisper which was intended to be heard by no one else in court, *excepting the jury*,—"I wish your lordship could have seen the *involuntary* expression of the witnesses' sensations upon looking at the drawing." Then this admirable pleader, upon being charged by the counsel for the defence with making use of unfair means in the prosecution of his case, afterwards said in his address to the jury, "Gentlemen, with respect to the picture which has been stated to have inflamed your minds, I ask nothing of your passions;"—precisely like knocking a man down, and then, finding the offended party not strong

enough to resist the injury, saying, " I ask
nothing of your forbearance." In justice,
however, to the able and learned lord on the
bench, it must be admitted that he signified in
strong language his disapprobation of " such
tricks" as the introduction of the obnoxious
drawing into court, at the same time that he
expressed a hope that "no use would be made
of it out of doors,"— with what effect has already been shown.

Another little *jeu d'esprit* of this " garrulous"
Mr. Garrow, as Colonel Draper facetiously calls
him, was the witticism already alluded to of
changing the appellation of picketing for the
more appropriate and elegant one, as he observed, of *Pictoning.* In fact, every artifice that
could amuse, harrow up the feelings, or impose
upon the understandings of the jury, was by
turns employed to obtain from them a verdict
which should convince the British public that
Governor Picton was guilty of every enormity
which was laid to his charge, and that his accusers were actuated solely by feelings of humanity and a love of justice.

CHAPTER IX.

Summary of facts extracted from the evidence. — Perjured Witness.—Malicious insinuation.—Strong evidence against the truth of the Charges. — Mr. Garrow's ingenuity. — Verdict.

BUT it is now time to give a brief outline of the proceedings up to this period; and as all the statements here made are from the authenticated documents brought forward in evidence, it is unnecessary to re-state the authorities and precise words in which they are expressed. First then—

Colonel Picton was directed by Sir Ralph Abercromby and his Majesty's commission to govern the island according to the laws in force at the time of its capitulation, with certain discretionary powers to simplify and accelerate the proceedings. On the 7th of December 1801, (nearly four years after Colonel Picton's appointment,) one Pedro Ruiz, an industrious man, who sold tobacco, appeared in the government court at Trinidad, and complained that the lock of one of his trunks had been broken, and that he had been robbed of two thousand hard dollars (four hundred pounds sterling). Luise Calderon, the interesting subject of the philanthropy of the people of England, and of this prosecution, was his mistress and house-keeper; having lived with him, according to her own statement on oath, *"between two years and a half and three years at the time of the robbery."*

A young married man, named Carlos Gon-zales, was at the time in habits of intimacy with this Luise Calderon, and had been seen to enter the house during the absence of Pedro Ruiz the day upon which the money was stolen. In consequence of the deposition thus made, his excellency the governor directed Señor Hilariot Begorrat, the alcalde in ordi-nary, *"to prosecute"* this case, in order to discover the offender or offenders, that he or they might be brought to justice; in the same manner as any English magistrate is instructed to trace out and apprehend the guilty parties concerned in any offence against the laws. Luise Calderon and Carlos were immediately taken into custody, and examined separately;

but both denied the whole charge, or that they had ever had an intrigue : and the female prisoner, upon being again interrogated, disclaimed all knowledge as to the perpetrators of the robbery.

In consequence of this obstinate denial, added to the strong suspicions existing against both the prisoners, the alcalde was desirous of proceeding according to the Spanish laws to extort confession by means of a slight torture ; but, finding that he had not power to inflict this punishment without the sanction of the governor, he caused to be prepared by a notary the following document.

" Official communication of his honour the Alcalde of the first election, to his excellency Governor Picton, December the 23rd, 1801.

" In consequence of the strong suspicions his honour entertains of the mulatto Luise Calderon, a domestic of Pedro Ruiz, concealing the truth relative to the aforesaid robbery expressed in these proceedings, and his honour being persuaded that she will discover the truth of the matter by means of a slight torture inflicted on

the said Calderon; and whereas his honour is
not invested with power to execute the same,
his excellency the Governor and Captain-general
of this island must be made acquainted hereof,
with the summary of this process, by virtue of
this document, to the intent that his excellency
may determine as may appear to him justice.
The usual and requisite forms to be adopted
and observed by the notary in this cause, and
in pursuance hereof, his honour thus decreed
and ordered; and he signed hereto, which I the
under-written notary attest this day, the 22nd
of the aforesaid month and year.

" Before me, FRANCISCO DE CASTRO.

(Signed)   " BEGORRAT."

Upon this representation, and after Governor
Picton had been made acquainted by the above-
mentioned notary with the usual mode of proceeding upon such occasions according to the
laws of the island,* he inquired of the notary

---

* Extracted from the *Recopilacion of Castile* and the
Purtidas.

" The question of torment is to be applied for confirmation and proof, there not being sufficient.".

Curia Philipica, No. 2, fol. 229.

" In the same crimes for which the question is applicable

in what manner he should word the sentence which was applied for by the alcalde; upon which the notary wrote the following for the governor to sign,—

"Appliquez là question à Luise Calderon.

"Th. Picton."

(In English)

"Apply the question (or torture) to Luise Calderon.

"Th. Picton."

In order, however, if possible, to save the prisoner from this infliction, the notary, in the presence of the alcalde, caused her to be brought into a private room, where she was made acquainted with the above order, and told that it would immediately be put in force unless she

to the delinquent, in the same it is applicable to the witness who varies or prevaricates in his evidence, or who denies the truth, or who refuses to declare it, there being a presumption that he knows it; not being of those persons to whom the torment cannot be applied according to the law of Partida and its Gregorian glossary."

Curia Philipica, No. 4, fol. 229.

"And in the same crimes for which the torment is applicable to the delinquent, in case an evidence of low vile character and bad morals is admitted, he is to testify under torment; otherwise his evidence is of no validity."

Law de Partida.

confessed what she knew respecting the offence ; but she again said *" that she did not know who had committed the robbery on Pedro Ruiz;"* when, upon her still persisting in a denial, the picket was resorted to. This operation is effected by making the prisoner stand upon a piece of wood about five or six inches long, and one inch, or one inch and a quarter square, with a flat top. By the laws of the island, a strongly suspected person might be made to remain upon this for any time not exceeding an hour, unless willing to make confession.

At first the prisoner appeared resolute in her determination to be silent ; but after a little time she acknowledged that she had submitted to the wishes of Carlos Gonzales, and that it was he who had stolen the money from the house of Ruiz ; but she denied knowing where he had deposited it, or having received any portion thereof. She was then confronted with Gonzales, when she charged him with being the person who had committed the robbery ; but he contradicted the accusation, and said that it was false testimony. He nevertheless fell upon his knees before all the witnesses, and acknowledged having been intimate with Luisé

Calderon for about four months, and that he
had visited her upon the day on which the
robbery had been perpetrated, having before
sworn that such had never been the case.

It is well known that few countries enjoy
the inestimable advantages of "*trial by jury:*"
some, it is true, aim at our boasted privilege, but
so imperfectly that it can hardly be recognised
as the same principle. In Spain, however, the
course of justice is totally different. The deposition on oath of witnesses in private, or confronted one with another, and even the extorted confession of the accused, are the only
testimonies which are sought for; these, with
certain forms and solemnities, are laid before
the " superior tribunal," the power of which in
this instance was concentrated in the governor,
who, upon a strict examination of the different
affidavits, decreed that Carlos Gonzales was
guilty of the robbery. He was in consequence
condemned, according to the laws of Spain en-
acted for the punishment of the like description
of offence; his sentence being as follows:—

" Perpetual banishment from the island; to
pay a fine of one thousand eight hundred dollars; to pay all the costs of the process, and to

labour on the public works until the term of
this his sentence shall be fulfilled : which said
fine to indemnify the said Pedro Ruiz. And
the mulatto Luise Calderon shall be set at liberty, and considered to have expiated the offence
by the long imprisonment she has suffered.

(Signed)   " TH. PICTON."

This is a brief but faithful outline of the
facts upon which Governor Picton was accused
and found guilty ; and natural enough it was
that such should be the verdict of the jury.
General Picton was charged with " *unlawfully
inflicting the torture on Luise Calderon.*" Mr.
Garrow and his witness proved to the satisfaction of the court that there was no law in the
island which warranted such a punishment, and
the verdict could not therefore be otherwise.
But if the reader has patience to follow the
proceedings a little further, he will perceive
that an entire acquittal from the only portion
of the charge upon which General Picton was
found guilty was inevitable. Before, however,
entering upon this final point of the proceedings, it may be advisable to show briefly in
how far the charges made by Mr. Commis-

sioner Fullarton were borne out by the witnesses for the prosecution. ·

In the first place, just to evince how ready the accuser was to distort facts for the cause of *justice* and *humanity,* Luise Calderon *was not under fourteen years of age.** A reverend and holy curate of the Roman Catholic church, by name Josef Maria Angeles, was examined respecting the registry of baptism: he produced a certificate, which, according to his testimony, was extracted from the registry-book, and which set forth that Luise Calderon was born the 25th of August 1788; but as he first stated that the entry was made by himself "*three months after the baptism of the child,*" and then upon the same question being again asked, when he had forgotten his former answer, he said he "*believed it was a year or more,*" the court very properly determined he was not to be believed upon his oath: and the end of this

---

* By the laws of Spain, no person under the age of fourteen can be made subject to the " question;" consequently, the indictment being thus framed, compelled the defendant to bring evidence to prove the exact age of the girl, or submit to be found guilty upon this count; which would, in fact, alone have been sufficient for the judge to direct a verdict of guilty.

respectable witness was, that he was removed from his sacerdotal office by the vicar-general, and ultimately found guilty of forgery and perjury.

Another certificate was however obtained from the Vicar-general Alvarado, which specified that the aforesaid Luise was an infant and baptised by him " on the 6th day of September 1786 :" the truth of this was confirmed by witnesses who had seen her in her mother's arms at the latter end of the year 1786, by the evidence of the mother herself, by her own confession, and that of Pedro Ruiz, her late master. Luise Calderon was therefore proved to have been *above fifteen* when the " question" was applied ; and *this* the court believed.

The insidious remark that " *Pedro Ruiz was stated to have been frequently employed as an agent by General Picton*" was another proof of the vindictive feeling which induced Mr. Fullarton to come forward as the champion of outraged humanity. It had no bearing upon the case whatever, and was employed only as an aggravation, or rather indirect aspersion on the character of the defendant. One witness was however examined respecting the implied sinister agency of Pedro Ruiz; but nothing further could be elicited than that General Picton had occasionally bought mules and cattle from the said Ruiz, which had been paid for immediately upon delivery.

After this mischievous insinuation, comes the following false and iniquitous statement, or rather report; for all through the charge much caution is employed by Mr. Fullarton not to commit himself by a direct assertion, and the words "*stated to have been*" are constantly recurring:—" The torture is '*stated to have been*' applied two successive times with so much severity, that the girl fell down in appearance dead, and there was no physician or surgeon to assist."

In reply to this gross and palpable misstatement, let the reader for one moment turn to the evidence, and then ask himself whether the motive for this prosecution was *solely humanity?* The picket has already been described, and the manner of its use; but observe its effects upon the prisoner as proved by the evidence: " Her feet were not swollen." " No surgeon or medical man was called for by her or others; neither was the attendance of one necessary." " She

did not cry out at all." "After the punishment
and confession, *she walked from the gaol to the
house of Pedro Ruiz, a distance of fifteen hundred
paces,* when she showed how Carlos had taken
the trunk, brought it to the door, broken the
padlock, and taken away the money; she all
the while smoking a cigar; after which she
walked back to the gaol as if she had suffered
no pain whatever:" while, as a conclusion, the
chief alcalde stated, "that, as he considered
the picket in gaol a very slight torture compared with those employed in Spain, he ordered it, in preference, to Luise Calderon." But
this, be it remembered, was in answer to Mr.
Garrow's ingenious but outrageously impudent
assertion, that, "so far from Governor Picton
having found torture in daily use under former
governors—so far from his being bound by
any circumstances of necessity to inflict it, he
has all the merit of the invention."

The evidence now stood thus: that General
Picton, being governor of Trinidad, and being
charged to administer the Spanish laws, had
caused something that may be termed a torture
to be inflicted upon a girl above fifteen years
old. That this act was in perfect accordance

with those laws, we have already shown. Any attempt to extort a confession is so abhorrent to our English ideas of justice, that the mere mention of an instrument of torture is sufficient to draw a cry of indignation from any assembly of our countrymen; and rightly so, for such an attempt is as absurd as it is cruel. But General Picton was not administering justice in a peaceful state; his task was to keep a conquered island. The population was turbulent and disaffected, and General Picton's force was small. In such a case every mitigation of severity is interpreted as an admission of weakness; and although we must regret, as General Picton undoubtedly also regretted, that his duty forced upon him the infliction of severities, unknown in England because unnecessary, yet we must admit that he was morally justified by the exigencies of his situation, and certainly legally justified by the letter of his instructions.

The case being in this dilemma, nothing but the ingenuity or effrontery of Mr. Garrow could have obtained for the prosecutors a verdict. The jury were bewildered; they came into court with strong feelings against the

accused, as juries often do : in fact, they were
to pass judgment in the name of the people of
England upon " a bloody and inhuman governor," who, according to the opening address of
Mr. Garrow, " without the least pretence of law,
without the least moral justification, but solely
to gratify his tyrannical disposition by the oppression of the unfortunate and defenceless
victim of his cruelty," did all that he had been
trying to make them believe; but the fact was,
these twelve honest but incredulous men COULD
NOT believe both him and the witnesses, so they
confined their belief solely to the latter; and
had they decided solely upon " the merits" of
the case, they would beyond a doubt have
given their unhesitating verdict in favour of
justice.

But that able advocate Mr. Garrow was not so
easily to be defeated : what was justice to him ?
—he wanted to gain his cause.   Still, what was
to be done? the obstinate jury would not believe
his reiterated asseverations that " Governor Picton had maliciously, wantonly, and to gratify a
tyrannical disposition, subjected an interesting
young Spanish girl under fourteen years of age
to torture until she fell down in appearance

dead."* Not a word of all this' could Mr. Garrow persuade the jury to believe; but, happy thought!—law!—they must believe his law; and accordingly he asserted, and brought a witness named Vargas, alias Smith, to swear, that the old Castilian Spanish laws were not in force at the time of the conquest of the

* The following fact is rather an amusing illustration of the overdone efforts of General Picton's accusers. It is contained in a letter from a gentleman in Trinidad, who had just returned from Scotland.

"A few weeks before I last left Scotland, Mr. Fullarton arrived with his family from Trinidad; at that moment I was in Ayrshire, and mixed with several of his friends; and dining one day at the lord provost's (mayor's) house in Ayr, mark my astonishment when I was told that, along with Colonel Fullarton, there had arrived with his lady a 'Mademoiselle Luise Calderon,' whom the Colonel and Mrs. Fullarton paraded about with them in their carriage, introducing her *wherever* they went as the ' *blessed innocent*' who was the devoted victim of Colonel Picton's tyranny, &c.   (Signed)   "JOHN DOWNIE."

"Trinidad, September 8th 1805."

The introduction of Miss Luise into such good society might have been exceedingly agreeable to all parties; but as the ladies of Scotland are rather famous for their uncompromising sense of decorum, it seems strange that they should have exposed themselves to the contaminating influence of a young lady who, by her voluntary statement, was a very improper person to associate with modest ladies; while, by her extorted confession, she acknowledged herself to be, if not a thief, at least an accomplice.

island by Sir Ralph Abercromby, and, consequently, that punishing an offender according to that code was unlawful. This he told the judge, who could not contradict him, or his respectable witness; the defendant's counsel was unprepared for so barefaced an assertion, and Colonel Draper says: "I sat near Mr. Garrow. He astonished me! The noble and learned judge heard him, — what shall I say? he believed him! — the jury of course believed him, and they found accordingly — a general verdict of guilty."

CHAPTER X.

Effects of the Verdict upon the Friends of each party.—
General Picton's Letter to Sir Samuel Hood.

THUS far, then, Colonel Fullarton, his friends,
and the majority of the public, were victorious; justice was appeased; the measure of
punishment was left to the discretion of the
judges; and to this day many of those who
remember Governor Picton being tried and
found guilty of " *unlawfully picketing an interesting Spanish girl under fourteen years of age*,"
do not know that any further proceedings
were taken for his vindication.   One reason
for this strange ignorance is, that they never
took the trouble to inquire; but, with a laudable love of justice but too general, remained
contented, not to say pleased, with the knowledge that an individual holding a high and
respectable situation had been reduced to a level
something below that of the party making him
the subject of his reflections.

General Picton was thus found guilty of permitting an "unlawful punishment" to be inflicted on Luise Calderon : as an English judge might so far outstretch, or be ignorant of the laws which he had to administer, as to order a prisoner convicted of a capital crime to be decapitated instead of hanged,—*that* would be unlawful punishment.

The enemies of General Picton were not, however, quite contented with the manner in which this verdict had been obtained, as it was too evident that nothing but the unexpected assertion of Mr. Garrow could have succeeded in getting any. Colonel Fullarton, indeed, anticipated that the termination of this prosecution would confirm or give probability to the calumnious accusations with which he had charged the defendant.

But General Picton and his friends were even less pleased than his accusers with the result of this trial; an entire acquittal was confidently anticipated; and as the simple verdict of "guilty" embraced the whole of the charges, although it was evident to all who chose to take the trouble to inquire, that none of them were proved, still it involved the defendant in all the disastrous results attendant upon a similar verdict founded upon the most perfect and comprehensive evidence. " Humanity is satisfied ;" so said Colonel Fullarton, when informed that the jury had found his victim " guilty." " But I am not," he might have added: for his actions proved that nothing but the total ruin of both General Picton's name and fortune would satisfy him. The subject was not allowed to drop, although humanity *was* satisfied : pamphlets, caricatures, and newspaper-insinuations were industriously circulated ; all that the legal inquiry had failed to prove, it was attempted to wind around the senses of men by artful and repeated mis-statements; while to those whose judgments were too strong to be thus imposed upon, falsehood was had recourse to, assisted by appeals to their passions, to join in the universal outcry against this " inhuman oppressor of youth and innocence." *

* Lieutenant-colonel Draper, in his spirited and able Address to the British Public, published in 1806, says, with almost prophetic truth, "The zeal, abilities, and acknowledged integrity of Colonel Picton will survive these unworthy and unjust aspersions; and he will live, I trust, to add still more to the fame, wealth, and honour of a just and generous nation."

From this picture of artifice trying to impose upon justice by assuming the garb of humanity, let the reader turn to the following letter, written at this period by General Picton to Commodore Sir Samuel Hood.

"London, March 1, 1806.

"MY DEAR SIR,

"I doubt not but you will do me the justice to believe that the inventions of malice and the credulity of ignorance are equally unable to affect my mind or influence my conduct in any situation or circumstances of life; or that the indecent caricatures exhibited everywhere in the streets and windows, and the malignant, scandalous libels which have inundated the metropolis, to outrage truth, and to corrupt the sources of public justice, will neither succeed in alarming my apprehensions, nor irritating my disposition. Yet I am very far from despising the judgment of the public; on the contrary, no one possesses a higher veneration for it, when calmly and coolly exercised; but, to have any value in my mind, it must proceed from the operation of reason, and be the result of temperate investigation.

" The reputation which rests upon the solid foundation of honourable services and zealous devotion to the cause of our country, is an object of virtuous ambition to which no well-ordered mind can ever be insensible; it is the shadow which accompanies the solid substance of meritorious actions, and the evidence of their existence, — it is the only genuine source of popularity; and the public opinion which rests upon any other foundation, or is derived from any other cause, though it may for a time serve the purposes of faction and intrigue, will ever be esteemed by prudent and deserving persons as a counterfeit coin, and spurious imitation of the more precious metal.

" The inhabitants of this country possess, perhaps, more of the milk of human kindness than those of any other nation in the world; they are more feelingly alive to every tale of woe or oppression; and these amiable qualities are, in a great measure, the cause of their being so open to the impositions and *canting hypocrisy of pretended philanthropists:* but they have invariably a fund of sound sense at bottom, which will never allow any delusion to be of long duration. Such a public, when the first impréssion begins to subside, will naturally inquire into the causes and motives of appeals to their passions; and when an apparently public object is pursued and pressed upon them with all the rancour and animosity of private interest and resentment, they will not be slow in suspecting some concealed selfish motive lurking beneath the specious patriotic pretext.

"This hypocrisy of patriotism, like that of religion, has always been most successful in its impositions upon people of ingenuous and candid dispositions. But, even with them, the age of delusion is nearly over; and extravagant pretensions, either to the one or the other, have fallen everywhere into merited suspicion. It is, however, much to be lamented that the great principles upon which the well-being of all civil as well as political societies rest, have been much weakened in the estimation of the world from the interested and selfish motives by which their appearances have been urged, and the still more interested objects to which those unprincipled and designing impostors have directed them.

"These reflections naturally lead to a consideration of the indefensible means employed to impose upon the credulity of the public in my case, and to make them the tools and instruments of private passion and resentment. You are too well acquainted with the corrupt sources from which they emanate to feel any astonishment at the impudence with which they have been employed: the puppet-show men may conceal themselves behind the curtain, but no one is ignorant of the hand which touches the strings and the wires, and sets the men of straw in motion. I need not here recall to your mind the circumstances which led to our resignation as two of his Majesty's commissioners for the government of Trinidad: they are of too extraordinary a nature not to be permanently fixed in your recollection without any effort of mine to renew the impression. My resignation, you well remember, was readily and easily admitted; and whatever the pretext might be, I believe you had no difficulty in penetrating the reasons why *yours*, though urged with more strength, met with a different reception.

"The disagreements amongst the commissioners produced at least one good consequence, as they led to the abolition of a chimerical system of government, which has realized

the apprehensions of every practical statesman,,
by producing an infinity of evil, and no one
advantage, except a convincing proof of its im-
practicability, which may deter future theore-
tical politicians from attempting a similar in-
congruity.

" Amongst a variety of means, equally honourable to the heads and hearts of the contrivers,
a specious appeal has been made to the humanity and passions of the public in favour of a
common mulatto girl, of the vilest class, and
most corrupt morals, who, living in the confidence and under the protection of an industrious tradesman, formed an illicit connexion
with a negro, who robbed him, with her concurrence, of the whole earnings of a life of
industrious parsimony, amounting to nearly
five hundred pounds sterling.

" *This respectable personage,* who was guilty
of the most flagrant perjury upon her exami-
nations, was proceeded against before the ordinary magistrates of the colony according to
due course of law, and nothing but mistaken
lenity saved her from an ignominious death
upon the gallows.   Such is the person who has
been selected to act the part of a most virtuous,

interesting *young lady,* whose sufferings have been painted in such glowing colours to the public; and who, at the very time she was fixed upon as the heroine of this mountebank exhibition, was living under the impression that she had been treated with peculiar mildness by the remission of the punishment ordained by the laws for a crime of such complicated villany.

" In consequence of circumstances connected with the above transaction, an indictment having been preferred against me in the Court of King's Bench, I was under the necessity of applying for a mandamus to examine evidence in Trinidad, the result of which I now lay before the public (faithfully copied from the official returns), in order that they may have the means of detecting the artifices which have been practised upon their passions to mislead their judgments ; and I have chosen to address it to you, sir, as a testimony of the high veneration and esteem which I entertain for your character, public and private, and as a mark of the inappreciable value I place upon a friendship which commenced under circumstances of a most trying nature, and grew up amongst

difficulties. You, sir, had opportunities of becoming acquainted with the sentiments and
opinions of all the respectable inhabitants and
proprietors of a colony I had governed for so
many years, without instructions, advice, or
assistance.

" Did you ever learn any circumstances,
during your official residence in that country,
which could lead you to suspect anything dis-
creditable to my character as a public or private
man, in my civil or military capacities? I may
boldly venture to say, no; or I never should
have been honoured with your confidence and
friendship.

" In my public situation, as chief of the civil
and military departments in a newly-conquered
country, possessing great discretionary power
without any accurate limit or definition, I am
conscious that I at all times and on all occasions
faithfully performed my public duty to the
full extent of my abilities. Whether I am
entitled to any degree of credit or not, is
scarcely worth inquiry; I am not asking for
any rewards, therefore it will be superfluous to
ascertain the value of my claims: all that I am
solicitous of establishing is, that I have, on all

occasions, ɔdone what I considered most con-
formable to my public obligations, without any
respect to private passion or individual interest:
a position which I confidently trust *no man of
truth and honour,* who had an opportunity of
witnessing and examining my conduct, will be
inclined to contest or dispute with me.

" You see, sir, my claims upon the public
are not extravagant or unreasonable: I neither
claim rewards for my past services, nor challenge
credit for great talents and extraordinary moral
powers to operate wonders in their cause for
the future. I make no such pretensions; but I
have a right to demand a presumption that the
moderate share or portion of talents which they
are willing to allow me was employed zealously
and honestly, to the best of my judgment.
Such is the extent of my claims upon the
public, and to which the strongest testimony
has been borne by every one of the high authorities I acted under during the whole of my
civil and military employments.

" You well know, sir, that I was placed,
without any solicitation, as a matter of professional duty, in a most extraordinary situation; at the head of a new conquest, without

any legal adviser to guide me in the administration of an intricate system of foreign laws,
written in a foreign language ; without any magistrate legally constituted or acquainted with
the jurisprudence of the country to execute
them; without any law-books, except such as
I could casually pick up upon the spot; without any council with whom I could share the
responsibility, and without any detailed instructions to supply the deficiency ; and that,
so situated, I was left, nearly six years, solely to
my own judgment and discretion, to carry on
the business of the colony in the best manner
I could.   Thus circumstanced, what more could
reasonably be expected of me than that I
should act honestly, to the extent of my abilities, with the best advice I could procure in
the place?   How is it possible that I could
become acquainted with the laws, or the practice of them, except from the books within my
reach, and the magistrates who were most accustomed to their application?   I did guide
myself on this, as well as on every other occasion,
by the advice of the magistrates and other law-
officers, the only sources of legal information or
practice; and if more was required of me, I am

ready to confess I am not capable of impossibilities.

"However, sir, if I were to estimate my merits in so novel a situation by the assurances of confidence and approbation which I continued officially to receive from the high authorities under which I acted up to the very moment of my resignation, I might allow myself to indulge in very considerable claims and pretensions, without incurring a charge of extravagance : but I have learned to estimate such assurances by the consequences which have followed them, and which it is not within the bounds of probability that I shall early or easily forget.

"I trust that the English people are too reasonable to require of me more than they would of any other person of moderate abilities under similar circumstances. Let any one of them suppose himself posted where I was, without any solicitation or intrigue on his part ; would he be satisfied to be placed in the midst of darkness, and then punished for not seeing clearly ? I am ordered to administer an intricate system of laws, of which I am totally ignorant, and then I am made accountable for the

errors I involuntarily committed; and crimi-
nally prosecuted for what I could not possibly
avoid.

" If my deviations, indeed, proceeded from
corrupt or malicious motives, the people of
England would have a right to exact a severe
and rigid account of them : they would not do
justice to themselves, and to the character of
the British nation, if they did not; and I am
ready to acknowledge that, in such a case, I
should have nothing to plead in my defence.

" The simple fact is, there were great difficulties in making any arrangements for the administration of a conquest, the circumstances and
population of which they were not sufficiently
acquainted with : and the only expedient they
could have recourse to in order to get rid of the
embarrassment was by throwing it upon me;
confiding the remedy to my judgment and discretion.   I did not shrink from the task, however difficult; and my obedience was at least
a strong proof of my zeal for his Majesty's service, and my confidence in the authorities I
acted under; if not of my prudence and discretion.   It is true, I took a great responsibility upon myself.   I could not move a step in

the public service without incurring serious responsibility, which was imperiously forced on
me by circumstances; and it was incurred honestly, honourably, and disinterestedly, in the
service of the public, without any possible advantage to myself. It was a sacrifice I made
of personal interest and personal safety, which
entitles me to some consideration, both from
the public and the departments of government
with which I was connected, though I never
made any claim upon either.

"I never made any claim: but my forbearance does not exonerate *them* from a performance of their public duty; it rather increases
the obligation. Those authorities know that I
did my best, and probably as well as any man
could have done in my situation. In the face
of the people of England, I confidently say,
that they know, from every source of credible
information, from all the distinguished public
characters with whom I was in relation, civil or
military, in the different confidential situations
I was employed in, that I invariably sacrificed
every private consideration and personal interest
to my high, perhaps Quixotic, idea of public
duty. They know that agriculture, that com-

merce, that the public revenues, increased and
flourished under my administration to an extent scarcely to be expected, considering the
unfavourable circumstances under which the
colony was placed ; that the public expenses
were narrowed within the bounds of the most
rigid economy ; and *that the whole disbursements
of the colony were not only provided for without a
single call upon the Treasury, but that a large sum
had been economised, and laid up in the colonial
chest, as a resource for any extraordinary emergency.*

" Neither you, sir, nor his Majesty's ministers
are ignorant of what has become of that *large
sum,* nor what extraordinary calls have been
made upon the treasury of this country in
consequence of its sudden dissipation.   They
know that I applied the revenues and administered the laws of the country honestly and im-
partially, to the best of my abilities ; and they
are not ignorant that I sacrificed all fees and
emoluments, to a large annual amount, (and to
which I had an unquestionable right,) to promote the interests of commerce, and of his
Majesty's government.   And yet, what have I
not been exposed to ? To every species of in-

dignity; to expenses ruinous to any officer in his Majesty's service, whatever his rank might be; and to circumstances, the effects of which are calculated to damp the ardour and cool the zeal of every public servant who may be similarly situated.

" I am not of a contentious spirit either in public or private life; and there are few who have been more disposed to make sacrifices to concord than I, on all occasions when the essential duties of my public situations would allow me to follow the natural bent of my inclination. With such a disposition, during my long service I had the happiness to steer clear of all misunderstandings and contentions, as well with the chiefs under whose immediate orders I acted, as with all those with whom it was my duty to co-operate in promoting the public service ; and I had a fair prospect of being enabled to end my public career without a single serious disagreement, when an event, which it was impossible to expect or foresee, exposed me to circumstances which rendered all prudence nugatory.

" His Majesty had been graciously pleased, without any solicitation on my part, as a spon-

taneous act of royal favour, to appoint me to
the high and confidential situation of Governor
and Commander-in-chief of Trinidad, expressly
as a reward for my former services as military
commandant of that important colony. Amidst
the strongest official assurances of the fullest
confidence and approbation of the measures
which I had pursued in this high station, without any previous communication, I was suddenly superseded, and appointed to a subordinate
situation in the same government, without my
consent or even knowledge. Humiliating as
my position became, thus degraded in the eyes
of the world, it being signified to me as the
express command of my sovereign, I did not
hesitate a moment to obey, and in so doing I
gave the strongest proof of my devotion to his
royal will, by a sacrifice of every feeling; in
consequence of which I have been exposed to a
series of wicked machinations, such as no man
ever before experienced.

"But to return to the subject from which I
have insensibly strayed. The most wicked and
indefensible means have been made use of to
pre-occupy the public mind with opinions unfavourable to me, at a time when a cause of

the utmost importance to my character is pending in the Court of King's Bench; a conduct the more atrocious, as it is manifestly calculated to deprive me of a fair, impartial trial, by influencing the passions of those who eventually are to be my judges; an attempt which, I trust confidently, the people of this country will not see without indignation.

" All I ask of them is, what religion and morality equally require as indispensable duties; that they abstain from rash, premature judgment, and wait until they fairly and fully hear both sides of the question, before they give their verdict against an officer who has been serving them with zeal and fidelity for nearly thirty-seven years. I solicit no rewards, I ask no favours; but I demand as a right, what they cannot refuse me without injustice, — an impartial hearing, and a suspension of judgment until the final issue of the new trial for which I am about to move.

" With many apologies for the length of my intrusion, " I am, &c. &c.

" THOMAS PICTON."

" Sir Samuel Hood, K.B.'"

CHAPTER XI.

Motion for a new trial " made absolute." — Investigation in
the Privy Council brought to a conclusion. — Their Report. — Remarks upon. — A second issued. — Sir Samuel
Hood offers himself as a Candidate for ·Westminster. —
Colonel Fullarton's attack. — " The Picton Veil, or, The
Hood of Westminster," a poem.—The Duke of Queensberry. — His munificent offer to General Picton.

THE calm and elevated tone of this letter
forms a striking contrast to the vindictive and
low-minded expressions of General Picton's
enemies ; it breathes throughout a noble contempt for the senseless outcry of the mob, and
a laudable desire for the good opinion of the
more intelligent portion of the public.   Such
sentiments would have done honour to a Roman
patriot; and if we were called upon to portray
the character of Sir Thomas Picton by any
single act of his life, we would turn to this
letter, in the confident assurance that the expressions which it contains are the sincere ema-

nations of a dignified and virtuous mind. The efforts of General Picton's accusers were, however, unfortunately too successful; the public attention was so constantly directed to the " *guilty* and *blood-stained governor*," that, by the frequency of the accusations, the minds of even the most just gradually fell into a tacit belief that they were all true.

When once conviction of another's guilt has taken possession of the mind, all attempts at vindication are unavailing: the individual is contented with having arrived at a conclusion, and if that opinion be unfavourable, he will never take the trouble to be convinced to the contrary. So, in the present instance, the jury found Governor Picton guilty; pamphlets and the newspapers assured the public that he was so,—and in consequence he has ever since been spoken of as " *cruel*" and " *remorseless.*" But let posterity do him justice. Men will now read to judge for themselves: and it is hoped that his memory will no longer be tarnished by even a whisper of reproach.

On the 26th of April 1806, Mr. Dallas, in an elaborate and powerful speech before Lord Ellenborough and three judges, moved for a

rule to show cause why there should not be a
new trial in the case of the King *versus* Picton.

It is unnecessary to recapitulate the whole of
the arguments employed by this able advocate,
more especially as they are already in print.
He grounded the application upon two points :
the first, "That in the evidence on which the
verdict was founded, there was a gross misrepresentation of a most material fact," (in allusion
to the non-existence of the old Castilian laws, as
asserted by Mr. Garrow,) — "a fact so material
as to constitute in one respect the very ground
and foundation of the charge; and that this
misrepresentation took place under such circumstances as rendered it impossible for General Picton, or those who had to conduct his
defence, to have foreseen, or to have been
guarded against it by the exertion of any care
or diligence on their part." The second ground
was thus stated :—"Supposing your lordships
should be of opinion (even now) that the only
fact found by the jury was correctly found,
still on this indictment the defendant is and
ought to have been acquitted, inasmuch as the
act complained of was done in the course of his
judicial duty—not maliciously, but erroneously

done, and therefore not the subject of any civil suit, and still less of a criminal prosecution."

Mr. Dallas proved, to the entire satisfaction of the judges, " that what the witness Vargas, *alias* Smith, swore, was *literally* true, but substantially and *virtually* false ;" that " the law of Old Spain, which is the law of Castile, *was* in force in the island of Trinidad at the time of its capitulation ;" that " Colonel Picton was instructed both by Sir Ralph Abercromby and his Majesty's government to administer the laws which he found in the island ;" and that " the punishment inflicted on Luise Calderon was in perfect accordance with those laws."

Upon these statements, which were drawn from the most able authorities and supported by the clearest evidence, and as the very argument by which the verdict had been obtained was negatived, the rule for a new trial " was made absolute."

It was during these legal proceedings that the Privy Council was engaged in investigating an endless list of enormities said to have been committed by Governor Picton during his administration in Trinidad. The result of this judicial inquiry was of more vital importance to the future prospects of the general than the decision of the law-court ; for, if one tenth part of the charges brought by Colonel Fullarton before that honourable assembly were established, the loss of his military rank, and the infliction of some heavy fine or punishment, would destroy at once both his fortune and character. Long and patient was this investigation: every kind of evidence was suborned in support of the accusations ; affidavits and witnesses being obtained at any expense, to show that the persecuted object of Colonel Fullarton's hatred was guilty.

The defence which General Picton was enabled to advance would not have sufficed in a court of law: the variety of the charges defied the utmost assiduity to procure evidence to rebut them in detail; though to the impartial and liberal feelings of gentlemen, where no professional sophistry was hired to mislead their judgments, such evidence as could be brought forward in time was sufficient. Upon the affidavits of individuals of the highest respectability in the island of Trinidad, who distinctly swore to the injustice of many of the principal charges, and considering the exalted character borne by

General Picton, with perhaps a feeling amongst the members of the Privy Council that Colonel Fullarton was not actuated solely " by a love of justice," they acquitted his victim of the accusations.

In January 1807, nearly four years from the commencement of the inquiry, they at length made a report, the substance of which was, that "there was no foundation whatever for further proceedings on any of the numerous charges brought forward by Colonel Fullarton against General Picton."

A publication of the day observes upon this report,—" When we recollect that more than three years have elapsed since these charges were first submitted to the Privy Council ; that they were pursued under three successive administrations ; that they have of course undergone the fullest and most rigid investigation ; and that the late sittings were attended by the different members who had marked the whole progress of the business ;—we cannot, we confess, but feel for the deep humiliation of the rash accuser, who has thus been foiled in every attempt, and who has reaped nothing but defeat and disappointment from his strenuous and un-

exampled efforts in the cause of *virtue, justice,*
and *truth.*"*

Shortly after this first report of the Privy

* " No man was better qualified than Picton to rule a newly-
acquired conquest, inundated as it was by all that was deprav-
ed and savage in society. Let the reader bear in mind that he
was enjoined, most strictly enjoined by his orders, and by the
very wording of his appointment, in all civil matters, to enforce
the law then existing, that is to say, the Castilian code. By
his vigour he regenerated the island. He brought commerce
to her shores, and plenty and happiness followed in her train.
Every respectable inhabitant looked upon him as a friend and
as a father. The Trinidadians feared nothing so much as being
compelled to return under the sway of their ancient authorities ; yet, for all these benefits, he experienced, not from those
whom he governed, and whose happiness he consolidated, but
from a mean party in England, the blackest persecution and
the vilest ingratitude ;—a persecution that ever after rankled
in his heart—an ingratitude that he was too noble not to
forgive, but too sensitive ever to forget.

 " All the invidious calumnies launched so vindictively
against him amount simply to this :—that he implicitly obeyed his instructions ; and had he not done so, would have
subjected himself, not only to reprimand but to removal. He
was bound to administer the old Castilian law—he did so,
and was persecuted.

 " These are the simple facts.—A woman of loose morals
had conspired with her paramour to rob, and actually did rob,
her master of more than a thousand dollars. Her evidence
was wanted to ensure conviction : she was contumacious :
there was no moral doubt of her guilt and that of her confe-
derate. The alcalde, or magistrate, by whom those offences
were cognizable, merely as a *matter of course,* and in the
routine of his office, applied to the Governor Picton, in con-
formity to the Spanish law then in force, for his signature to

Council, a second was published, in which the name of Sir Samuel Hood was introduced, in conjunction with that of General Picton, as

apply to her the inconvenience, torture we cannot call it, of the picket. The signature was given as a *matter of course;* the picket was applied, the whole truth displayed ; the guilty punished, and the defrauded man righted. Substantive justice was administered to all parties.

" But let not our generous and kindly-hearted countrymen run away with a false notion of the severity of the punishment of this picket. It was of an infinitely shorter duration and hardly more severe than what every English drunkard, in every English village, is liable to receive—the stocks. The punishment of the picket was the compelling the offender to stand upon a surface of one square inch upon one leg, whilst one arm was suspended by a rope above her head. This was formerly the punishment resorted to in the English cavalry for minor offences. We grant that it is not an enviable position, but by no means an infliction deserving the epithet of torture.

" But had this infliction been breaking upon the wheel, it would not have been the fault of Picton. He made not the law : he was only there to administer it, and he only administered it upon the demand of the proper officer.

" How often is it the case that naval and military men, who know no other party than that of the country for which they are recklessly staking their lives, are made a sacrifice to the caprice, the pique, or the vindictiveness of faction ! No one ever suffered from this injustice more than Picton. They not only attempted insult, but inflicted injury. We have neither space nor patience to dwell upon this persecution' which brought him before a British jury, enlisted against him the vilest popular passions, and thus wheedled them by administering to their prejudices, into giving a verdict of *guilty* against him, and which originated in ministerial revenge.

having been charged with committing certain'
misdemeanours whilst commissioner of Trinidad.   This report was, however, even more
honourable to the accused than the former.
The characters of both General Picton and Sir
Samuel Hood came forth from this long and'
minute inquiry without a stain.

It was after this report had been issued by
the Privy Council, that Sir Samuel Hood, the
friend and companion of Picton, offered himself
as a candidate to represent the city of Westminster in Parliament.   Upon this occasion Colonel
Fullarton, not from any desire to serve the
cause of the opposing parties, but solely to
avenge himself on the hustings for the castigation which he had received from Sir Samuel
Hood in the Council at Trinidad, printed and
published three folio pages, calling on the gallant commodore to answer him two-and-twenty
queries, most of them extracted from his charges
against General Picton ; such as, the " list of
persons fettered, flogged, burned, &c. ;" * and
numerous others, in equally inflammatory and
exciting language.   But, as a conclusion to the
chain of abuse and machination concocted by

* Vide page 102.

the friends and admirers of Colonel Fullarton, (we would not willingly believe that it was the production of the colonel's own pen,) a poem was published, called " The Picton Veil, or, the Hood of Westminster," which is unrivalled for malice and rancour.

This tissue of falsehoods was widely circulated amongst the nobility, and friends of both Sir Samuel Hood and General Picton. The best and noblest of the land are here vilified in the most foul and scurrilous language : the principal objects of the assassin's venom were the leading members of the Privy Council, and upon them he has lavished it with an unsparing hand. But as the writer is convinced that no adequate idea can be conveyed of this production by mere extracts, he has thought it advisable to give this precious *morceau* entire.

THE PICTON VEIL;

OR,

THE HOOD OF WESTMINSTER.

See Grenville head the mighty troop
Of legal statesmen in a group;
Dimly he views them through his glass,*
And drills his followers as they pass.

* Lord Grenville wore spectacles.

The outward vision, true, 'tis dark ;
But had great justice' vital spark
Clear'd from dull mist the mental sight,
His conduct then had stood the light.
　　It bodes our country little good,
When murder's cover'd by a Hood.

　　And lo ! where, humbled in the dust,
Sits him who holds the sacred trust,
Keeper of conscience to his king !
His own seems lost, no power to sting ;
Or it had whisper'd in his ear :
Wilt thou a murd'rer dare to clear,
And plead to the Great Judge of all,
That, to obey proud Grenville's call,
Justice and mercy both must fall ?
　　It bodes our country little good,
When murder's cover'd by a Hood.

　　Next Eldon comes, of palsied mind,
But half to good or ill inclined.
Still, not like Erskine did he yield ;
For three whole years he kept the field,
Feebly held justice with a straw,
Nor sanction'd murder by a law.
　　It bodes our country little good,
When crimes are cover'd by a Hood.

　　Sidmouth, who at the board presides,
By Grenville's fiat he abides :
The Doctor's conscience feels no qualm,
An opiate has procured a calm.
'Tis Grenville must the risk endure,
Should too much blood require a cure.

It bodes our country little good,
When murder's cover'd by a Hood.

Anstruther also must attend
As Grenville's and Lord Wellesley's friend,
His part to shelter Eastern crimes;
Guilt he won't see in Western climes,
His principles must meet the times.
It bodes our country little good,
When murder's cover'd by a Hood.

Here follows a stiff legal plant,
Master of Rolls, Sir William Grant.
In politics though quite ajar,
He hopes to heal the recent scar,
If, yielding now to the great flood,
He helps to screen a man of blood.
In measured words and accents slow,
He sets at nought sad scenes of woe.
It bodes our country little good,
When murder's cover'd by a Hood.

See Castlereagh, with dauntless front,
Who in Hibernia bore the brunt
Of flogging, torturing without end,
In soul allied as Picton's friend:
No wonder he his voice should raise
To sound aloud a murd'rer's praise.
It bodes our country little good,
When crimes are cover'd by a Hood.

Recorded on the list of fame,
Spencer! high stood thy honour'd name;
Brought now to hide a culprit's shame,

Grenville has got thee join'd with knaves,
To turn free Britons into slaves,
Who under thee once ruled the waves.
  It bodes our country little good,
When murder's cover'd by a Hood.

  Say, Moira, by what ordinance
Dost thou with visage black advance?
'Tis fear has bound thee fast in chains,
Leads thee to shroud the ghost of Haynes,*
And with fresh guilt renew thy stains.
  It bodes our country little good,
When murder's cover'd by a Hood.

  Windham, thy metaphysic mind,
That turns and twists, excuse can find
For baiting bulls, or human-kind;
Though great they call'd thee—yes, 'tis fact,
Now thou art dwindled down t' enact
Proud Grenville's purpose, or the Training Act.
  It bodes our country little good,
When murder's cover'd by a Hood.

  Oh! Fullarton, the brave and good,
With noble firmness you withstood
Torture and waste of human blood:
Long may a God of mercy spare
Thy life unto thy country's prayer,
'Gainst tyrant foes to prove her shield,
Either in council or the field!

So fearful was the writer of this infamous
production of the odium and punishment

* Colonel Isaac Haynes, executed by Lord Rawdon, without trial, in America.

which were his due, that not even the printer's name was attached to the libel, nor did he ever acknowledge the authorship.

A circumstance occurred about this time, which is well worthy of record, as a happy illustration of the character of that eccentric nobleman—the last Duke of Queensberry. The prosecution against General Picton was proceeding with all the rancour of party spirit, and the voice of the country was raised against him in an universal outcry. A few staunch friends, however, still clung to him; some of whom had had opportunities of witnessing his conduct in the West Indies, and others who knew him too well to believe for one moment the charges which were brought against him. These friends were yet unchanged, although assailed with reproach for holding communion with a man whom the world condemned.

General Picton was one day dining at the Grosvenor Coffee-house, in company with some of these friends, when Colonel Darling, who highly honoured General Picton, and was intimate with the Duke of Queensberry, joined the party. After some general conversation, Colonel Darling said, " Picton, I have just left the Duke of Queensberry, and he has charged me with a message for you."— "Indeed!" replied Picton; "I am certainly much honoured, more especially as I never had the pleasure of being introduced to his grace."—"I know it," said the colonel; "but he has often spoken of you and your affairs in the most friendly and liberal manner."

General Picton expressed his sense of the honour conferred upon him by the duke. "And now," continued the colonel, "he wishes to show you his feelings with regard to the proceedings instituted against you, by a 'more decided mark of his consideration."

"What do you mean, Darling?" inquired the general with some surprise.

"Simply this," rejoined the colonel. "The duke has watched the whole course of your prosecution with much interest, and he has now desired me to express to you his entire conviction of your innocence, together with the high sense which he entertains of your character." General Picton bowed in acknowledgment of this compliment.

"But that is not all," continued the colonel. "I have just parted with him; and, to be brief,

he has desired me to say, that as he is aware of
the great expenses which you must incur in
defending yourself against a Government prosecution, and as he is uncertain whether your
fortune can support the heavy demands upon
you, he is desirous that you should make him
your banker during the remainder of the proceedings... He offers you the use of any sum
under ten thousand pounds."

Picton was for a moment silent; this mark
of consideration from a stranger overcame him.
He could not immediately express his feelings; but at length expatiated with much earnestness on the munificent generosity of the
duke, to whom he immediately wrote a brief
note, which he handed to Colonel Darling
for perusal. In this, he stated how highly
flattered he was by the opinion which his
grace had expressed of him; while, in reference to his proffered munificence, he added,
" Had it not been for the kindness and generosity of a near relation," (his uncle,) "who has
lent me his fortune to defend my character,
I should most readily have availed myself
of your disinterested liberality. At present, I
am in no want of pecuniary aid; but shall

ever feel grateful for the considerate manner in which you offered me your assistance."

Until two days before the departure of the general for the Peninsula, he had no further communication with this eccentric but generous nobleman. Picton was again at the Grosvenor Coffee-house, making preparations for his journey, when the Duke of Queensberry's card was brought in, with a request from his grace that he would oblige him by coming to his carriage at the door for one moment. The general immediately complied with his wish; when the duke, shaking him warmly by the hand, after having apologised on the ground of his infirmity for not leaving his carriage, observed :—

" General Picton, I have ventured out expressly to shake you by the hand, and bid you farewell before you leave the country; and there is one request which I have to make, and which I hope you will oblige me in."

The general expressed in warm terms the satisfaction which he should experience in obliging his grace in any possible manner.

" Well, then," observed the duke, " it is this: you know what vague and contradictory accounts we get in the newspapers about the proceedings of our army; — now, I want you to write me a letter occasionally — that is, whenever you can find leisure — just that I may know the truth."

General Picton promised to comply with his wishes, by sending him the particulars of every affair of importance. This he did punctually; and whenever a letter arrived from the general, the duke used always to observe, "Ah! this is a letter from Picton; now we shall have the truth." But he was not long one of General Picton's correspondents, as he died in December 1810, when, as a mark of the esteem in which he held the general, he left him a legacy of five thousand pounds.

CHAPTER XII.

Second trial of General Picton.—Testimonials to his character and abilities.— Inhabitants of Trinidad present him
with a sword.—Their magnificent subscription to defray
the expenses of his trial.—The above sum generously returned by Picton.—Argument on a special verdict.

THE second trial of General Picton for the
same offence was now approaching. He had
borne, in the intervening time, all the odium of
being considered guilty, and, in addition to the
enormous costs of his defence, all the injury
arising from the necessary neglect of his profession which that defence occasioned.

The sole cause and originator of this extraordinary and tedious prosecution was, however,
doomed not to see its termination, or the tardy
justice which was at length rendered to the
object of his persecution.

Early in February 1808, Colonel Fullarton
was attacked by an inflammatory cold, which

settled on his lungs, and on the 13th he expired. The outcry which had so long existed against General Picton, and which had been kept alive during the life of Colonel Fullarton, died with him. The public mind, no longer excited by slanderous accusations, at once subsided into calm judgment; and as the period for the second trial approached, not a remark was made which could in any way predispose the minds of his judges.

It must be remembered, that as this prosecution was instituted at the suit of the King, the death of Colonel Fullarton did not at all interfere with the course of justice. It is true, that there no longer existed any strong feeling of personal animosity; but still the proceedings were conducted in the same form; the whole of the depositions of Colonel Fullarton were on record, and consequently justice lost nothing by the removal of this witness. There were still, however, some spirits malignant enough to desire another verdict of guilty, and to triumph in such an anticipation. The witnesses engaged on a trial generally make the cause so much their own, that they often give their evidence with the rancour of personal enmity, apparently considering that to gain the verdict is to obtain a victory.

One incident, however, occurred to General Picton about this period, which for a while dispelled the gloom which his continued persecution, and the consciousness of existing under the undeserved execration of the public, had thrown over his character. This was his promotion to the rank of Major-General, which appeared in the Gazette of the 25th of April 1808. Professional fame and promotion were always the highest sources of personal gratification to him; and this testimony of approbation was particularly seasonable.

On the 11th of June his new trial came on before Lord Ellenborough and a special jury, when the evidence was again gone through at even a greater length. The testimonials to General Picton's character and abilities as governor given upon this occasion are so strong that a brief recital of them is but justice to him. These testimonials were all given on oath in answer to the question — "Did you know Governor Picton, and what was his general character?"

The first witness was Don Hilario Begorrat, ordinary judge. His answer to the latter part of the question was—"Great integrity and disinterestedness; a man of knowledge and firmness, who saved the colony by his talents."

Colonel de Soter answered—"A character full of dignity, justice, activity, and generosity; beloved by the inhabitants, feared by all the disturbers of tranquillity, and generally considered as the founder of the colony."

Don Francisco de Farfan, a planter.—"He was a man just, disinterested, and capable by his talents to govern all men."

Baron de Montalembert.—"I knew him intimately, and his character was the most honourable and most respected that a chief could desire to possess in his government. I wish to declare that I came to the island to settle in consequence of the honourable report of character and reputation that was made to me of Governor Picton by his Majesty's ministers, his Grace the Duke of Portland, and the Right Honourable H. Dundas."

Alexander Williams, Esq. a proprietor in the island seventeen years. — "I knew him. His general character was that of an upright and just governor; and generally esteemed in the colony, particularly by the foreigners."

John Lynch, Esq. a proprietor for twelve years.—" I knew him from his first arrival as governor; and his general character was that of a very honest, upright man, esteemed by all good men of every country."

Chevalier de la Sauvager, formerly governor of Tobago.—" I knew him. His character was that of a man calculated to govern a colony, and knowing how to keep every man in his proper situation, and to render justice to all."

Benois Dert, Esq. a proprietor for twenty years. —" I knew Brigadier-general Picton. His character was that of a man who made himself feared and beloved by all."

Chevalier de Gannes, a proprietor for ten years.—" I knew him intimately. When I arrived in this colony, there were a number of very bad subjects in it, and it was threatened with a general subversion of good order. Brigadier-general Picton restored order, maintained the police, protected commerce and the importation of provisions, and tripled the value of land in cultivation: I always knew him to be extremely just towards all the inhabitants of the colony, without any prejudice to any of the various foreigners in it."

Vincent Patrice, Esq. commandant of La Ventille.—" I knew General Picton. I consider that the capture of the island has restored tranquillity, and caused commerce and agriculture to flourish."

Count de Soppinott, proprietor for ten years. —" I knew Brigadier-general Picton as governor-in-chief of this island: I saw him govern with all dignity, loyalty, and perfect justice; with a firmness which secured the tranquillity of the colony, to the satisfaction of every honest man, and which repressed all the evil-minded persons in it."

Lazar Achard, Esq. proprietor for eighteen years.—" I knew Brigadier-general Picton as a just man, and of integrity; and I shall owe to him eternal gratitude for having preserved my life and fortune by his courage, activity, and abilities, in times when we were threatened with fire, and the malevolence of the negroes and other vagabonds, who only waited for a favourable moment to cut our throats."

The Honourable John Nihell, member of council, and judge of the court of Consulado.

—" To the firmness of his government, and his apparent determination to suffer no persons of revolutionary principles to remain in the colony, I attribute the order and tranquillity in the island after its capture; and I ascribe the present flourishing state of this colony to the firmness and uniform good conduct of General Picton, in giving ample protection to all good and peaceable subjects, and driving out all of a contrary character."

Mich. St. Pè, alcalde of the second election. —" I knew Governor Picton since 1798; and he was a man of good morals and practice, frank, impartial, disinterested; zealous for his Majesty's service, and for the preservation of the colony. There are very few inhabitants, of those who were here before the capture of the colony, who do not believe they owe to his vigilance their whole families."

The Honourable Philip Langton, Esquire, alcalde of the first election.—" I had the honour of being intimately acquainted with General Picton; and all the respectable characters that I ever heard speak of him in the colony join me in considering him as an active, intelligent, humane, and disinterested magistrate, warmly attached to the interests of his sovereign and of this colony."

Such testimonials,* from individuals of un-impeachable respectability, were enough to make men of that station in life whence a spe-

---

* The feelings of the inhabitants of Trinidad, and the impression which General Picton's conduct as governor had left upon their minds, cannot be more strikingly shown than by the two following instances :—the first, that within a short time previously, and subsequently to his departure from Trinidad, the inhabitants of the island subscribed a sum of money for the purpose of presenting him with a handsome sword, as an evidence of the high estimation in which they held his character, both in his public and private capacities. This money was remitted to England, with an humble address from the subscribers to his royal highness the Duke of York, requesting him to present to their late governor this testimonial of their esteem and respect. In compliance with this address, his royal highness was graciously pleased to present the sword to General Picton, accompanying this act of condescension with some highly flattering remarks upon his judicious conduct whilst governor.

The second instance was even more soothing to the feelings of General Picton, especially as it was the means of enabling him to indulge in that noble generosity which formed so prominent and admirable a portion of his character. Whilst the prosecution was proceeding with the most vindictive activity—when the government and people of England seemed arrayed against him in a body—at that moment the inhabitants of Trinidad came forward with a spirit and feeling which made General Picton ever remember them with unfeigned gratitude. Confident that the expenses to

cial jury is drawn, reject any prejudice which
public clamour might have raised; the whole
course of the present proceedings was marked
by a milder and less excited feeling ; and even
the ingenuity and eloquence of Mr. Garrow
seemed deficient. During the first trial he had

which he must necessarily be exposed were enough to ruin
one in his then moderate circumstances, they in the most
liberal and considerate manner subscribed amongst themselves a sum amounting to nearly four thousand pounds,
which was remitted to England, with a respectful but friendly
address, praying him to accept it, that it might be employed
in obtaining justice and refuting the many libellous charges
which had been brought against him. It will readily be believed that this proof of the continued esteem of those whom
he had governed for so long a period must have been most
gratifying to him. General Picton *was* deeply impressed by
this mark of consideration, and returned to the inhabitants
his warmest and sincerest thanks.

A short time after the receipt of this money, a dreadful
fire broke out in the principal town of Trinidad, destroying
a great deal of property, and doing much injury to the poorer
inhabitants, many of whom were left utterly destitute. . The
moment General Picton was made acquainted with this distressing calamity, he took the most expeditious means of
remitting the whole amount back to the island for the relief
of those who had suffered. This act requires no comment,
and it might have been supposed that so eloquent an appeal
would at least have mitigated the rancour of his enemies.
But the cry of popular reproach had been raised against
him; it was kept alive by private enmity; and it was not a
single act of virtue that could wipe away the stain.

exhausted all his expedients, and he now came into court with, as he well knew, no argument which was likely to benefit his cause: his only hope was, that in the course of the evidence he might be enabled to catch at some legal point and again succeed in obtaining a verdict. But his opponent was too wary: he was prepared with witnesses for every probable contingency; and consequently, after a protracted hearing, the jury returned the following special verdict:—

" That by the law of Spain torture existed in the Island of Trinidad at the time of the cession to Great Britain, and that no malice existed in the mind of the defendant against Luise Calderon independent of the illegality of the act."

The reader will at once perceive that this decision completely destroyed the foundation upon which the former verdict had been obtained, viz. Mr. Garrow's assertion that the law of Spain did not exist in the island of Trinidad at the time of the cession to Great Britain. Consequently, it is only reasonable to presume that, had General Picton's counsel been prepared in the first instance with the requisite evidence (which he afterwards obtained for the special jury) to disprove Mr. Garrow's statement, the jury would then have acquitted General Picton, and he would have been spared the accumulation of expense, anxiety, and opprobrium which he had in consequence to endure.

The words at the termination of the special verdict, " independent of the illegality of the act," refer to the question (which was left to the decision of the judges,) whether, as a British governor, he should have allowed such a punishment to be inflicted ?   But the vindication which he pleaded in answer to this was :—" I was desired to administer the laws of the island as they existed at the capitulation.   Of these I knew nothing ; but my knowledge of the language enabled me to learn them.   A judge was appointed under me, with the same instructions, to administer Spanish law ; and he *was* acquainted with the laws of Spain : to him therefore I was obliged to look ; and, however contrary to my opinion of justice and humanity, which was founded upon our own admirable institution, I was compelled to sanction his proceedings.   Had I been told to administer English law, I should have done so to the best of my ability ; but I was instructed to administer justice according to a code of which I was totally ignorant ; and the disturbed state of the colony left me little time for study. In the case for which I am now being tried, if I was guilty of anything culpable, it was ignorance ; but the notary cited the law to me,* and I then thought I had no alternative but to administer the Spanish laws as they were, instead of, as I have since learned, modelling them to the forms prescribed by our own legislature, and to the feelings of the British public. By the laws of England, which it appears ought to have been put in force instead of those of Spain, I think the girl Luise Calderon as an accessory before the fact, and Gonzales as the principal, would have been hanged for stealing in a dwelling-house above the value of forty shillings, while Pedro Ruiz would have lost his money ; and I leave impartial minds to determine whether in this instance Spanish law was not more satisfactory and merciful to all parties."

These remarks are contained in a letter from

* Vide page 164.

General.Picton to a friend, and form an admirable summing up of the whole proceedings. That we may not be called from the contemplation of General Picton's brilliant career, which has obtained for him a lasting fame, the concluding proceedings of this prosecution are here briefly detailed.

An argument on the special verdict was heard on the 10th of February 1810, when the Court ordered " the defendant's recognizance to be respited until they should further order ;" which may be said to have terminated this disgraceful prosecution. But as no judgment was ever given, we subjoin the following note which concludes the report of this case in " Howell's State Trials:"—" It was thought by, the bar, that had the opinion of the Court been delivered, judgment would have been given against General Picton ; but that, upon a consideration of the merits, it would have been followed by a punishment so slight, and so little commensurate with the magnitude of the questions embraced by the case, as to have reflected but little credit upon the prosecution : and I have been informed, that it was by the advice of one of the learned counsel, who greatly distinguished himself in arguing the questions which arose in this case, that it was not again agitated."

And thus, in the language of a contemporary, " after a trial which seemed to have no end ; after an expense of seven thousand pounds, which must have completed his ruin, had not his venerable uncle, General W. Picton, defrayed the whole costs of the suit, while *the expenses of his prosecutors were all paid by the Government ;* his honour and justice were established on the firmest basis, and to the perfect satisfaction of every upright mind."

CHAPTER XIII.

Expedition to Walcheren. — Attack on and surrender of
Flushing.—General Picton's letter relative to this event.
— Appointed Governor of Flushing. — The Walcheren
fever.—Return of General Picton to England.—Sir John
Moore's retreat from Corunna, and its consequences.—
Movements of the British Army under Lord Wellington.

GENERAL PICTON had long sighed over the
apparent destruction of all his professional
prospects; and to those with whom he was
intimate, he frequently expressed his impatience at being detained in England while
his old companions in arms were engaged in
active service upon the Continent. Still, it
was impossible for him to leave his enemies at
home even for the purpose of fighting against
those of his country abroad; for no services
which he might there perform would clear his
reputation from the stigma which would await
him on his return. From the tedious processes of the law he was almost in despair of

ever being released; and more than once during the proceedings he would have left his cause and character to the justice of the nation, and have sought a more active and congenial pursuit, had not his friends dissuaded him from this wild notion, and succeeded in convincing him of the importance of his presence to his defence.

For nearly six years he was, therefore, compelled to be an inactive but anxious observer of the proceedings of our troops. He perused with feverish excitement the various accounts from Spain, and watched the movements of Sir John Moore with all the military ardour so conspicuous in his character. The disastrous retreat upon Corunna, and the death of that unfortunate general, combined to raise the true spirit of General Picton's character above every other consideration; and early in 1809 he made application for some active employment.

The abilities of General Picton were highly appreciated by his royal highness the Duke of York. The estimation in which he was held, and the flattering language in which he was spoken of, by Sir Ralph Abercromby, had obtained for him the duke's favour; and

one distinguishing feature of his royal highness's official character whilst holding the situation of Commander-in-chief was, with very
few exceptions, always to employ those officers
whose abilities he considered would be most
conducive to the success of his Majesty's arms.

It will be remembered, that about the end
of July 1809 an expedition was fitted out by
the British Government, of which at that time
the Duke of Portland was premier. The preparations were commenced early in May. Towards the end of July a fleet assembled in the
Downs, consisting of thirty-nine sail of the
line and thirty-six frigates, together with a
considerable number of gun-boats, bombs, and
small craft; the troops, amounting to about
forty thousand men, assembled at the neighbouring sea-ports; making the whole force,
including seamen and marines, nearly one hundred thousand men. The curiosity and expectation of the country were excited; the
spectacle was grateful to the pride and flattering to the hopes of the nation; and Dover,
Deal, Ramsgate, and Margate were full of
visitors, anxious to witness the sailing of this
imposing armament.

Its destination was not long a mystery. To take possession of Flushing, and destroy the French fleet, arsenals, and dockyards up the Scheldt, was universally known to be the object of this *secret* expedition ; and it is even stated that so little precaution was taken to prevent this fact from being made public, that the French were actually acquainted with it in April, and then ordered Flushing and the Scheldt to be put in the best state of defence. Still, so powerful was this armament, and so confident of success were its projectors, that they appointed to the command " a man whose very name," in the words of a writer upon this expedition, " was proverbial for inactivity." This was Lord Chatham, the brother of Wil. liam Pitt.* The reason for his being selected in preference to the many more able and dis- tinguished officers was unfortunately too ap- parent : his fortune was embarrassed, and this lucrative command would improve it. But the country had to pay largely both in riches and honour for this sacrifice of national interest to private emolument.

* He was, during his life, known by the nick-name of " The *late* Lord Chatham."

It was to this expedition that Major-general Picton was appointed, being on the staff of the commander-in-chief.   He did not entertain any great opinion of the plan of this undertaking, and frequently expressed to Colonel Pleydel the doubts which he had of its success; and the result proved these to have been well founded.   He joined the army towards the end of July; and on the 28th and 29th, the fleet, under the command of Sir Richard Strachán, got under weigh in two divisions.

On arriving at Walcheren and South Beveland, the enemy showed no disposition to make any resistance.   At Flushing, however, it appeared that they intended to concentrate all their force, and, if possible, check the British advance.   This place was accordingly invested, and by the 13th of August the batteries were completed; at which period the frigates and smaller vessels having taken their respective stations, the bombardment commenced with considerable effect.   The town suffered dreadfully, both from the shells and Congreve rockets; and, on the following day, the line-of-battle ships cannonaded the forts for several hours, until the enemy's fire was silenced.

Early the next morning, General Monnet, who commanded in Flushing, demanded a suspension of hostilities for a few hours; after the expiration of which the town was surrendered to the British, when the garrison, consisting of about six thousand men, were made prisoners of war.

Although the expedition was thus far successful, still the mode of conducting the attack was the subject of much animadversion amongst the military men of the day. It was observed that a total want of skill and energy marked the whole of the proceedings. The batteries and trenches were formed one after another without method or arrangement; and much confusion existed in consequence of neither the officers nor soldiers attached to the engineer department knowing their proper situations, by which the works were carried on very slowly. The troops were placed within the range of the enemy's guns before any of the necessary stores for attack were landed; while no precautions were taken to confine the enemy to his fortifications. The men in the trenches seldom had any covering party in their front; and the enemy's advanced picquets were frequently on their flanks. It was further observed that the island of Cadsand, the only place whence the enemy could possibly receive supplies or reinforcements, was left unoccupied; and as the naval force had not interrupted the communication, advantage was taken of this omission to pass three thousand men over from Cadsand to Flushing.

It is not our province to enter into the justice of these remarks; but the known misconduct of this futile expedition certainly favours them. The following letter, written five days after the surrender of Flushing, to Colonel Pleydel, discovers General Picton's sentiments upon the occasion.

"Flushing, 20th August 1809.

" MY DEAR COLONEL,

" I have to acknowledge your very kind letter of the 15th, which was particularly agreeable, as it contained such satisfactory information of the general's health. The letter which you allude to as having appeared in *The Times* I never heard a word of before; nor have I received a line from either of those gentlemen since I left England.

" I perfectly agree with you in opinion, that

the obstacles to our further advance towards
Antwerp are nearly insurmountable ;. and I
may with very little qualification say, wholly
so. In my opinion, we shall not attempt anything further; although we make great demonstrations, as if we were determined to proceed
immediately. According to the accounts we
have here, a very respectable force has been
collected at Antwerp; and all the country
through which we must unavoidably pass has
been completely flooded. Under such circumstances, I trust we are too wise to commit the
safety of the fleet and army ; and that we shall
prudently content ourselves with *the laurels*
which we have already gathered.

" Marshal Bernadotte has arrived on the
opposite shores of Cadsand, and is now busily
employed in erecting mortar batteries, for the
annoyance of Flushing, and of our squadron
which rides at anchor in its vicinity. The distance between the two islands is barely three
miles, and it is apprehended that their large
mortars will range that distance.

" I have the command in Flushing, and the
neighbouring country, with four regiments.
The town is a perfect heap of ruins, exhibiting

a state of misery not easily conceivable. Every
house has been materially damaged, and not
one in twenty is in any degree habitable, or capable of affording protection against either the
rain or climate. The best thing we can do will
be to destroy the military defences, naval ar-
senal, and basin, and then withdraw our army
and squadron as soon as possible.

" I have fallen in with an excellent manuscript plan of Flushing, which will give you a
good idea of the place and our proceedings,
when I have the pleasure of meeting you : and
I rather think that period is at no great distance.

" With my best wishes for your health,

" Believe me, &c.

" THOMAS PICTON."

The opinion expressed by General Picton of
the wisdom of the directors of this expedition
did them no more than justice. A large force
was collected at Antwerp, composed of the
national guards of the Belgic provinces and
those from the nearest points of France; while
the forts on the Scheldt were well manned, and
every preparation made to oppose the advance
of our fleet and army. The immense quantity

of stores at Antwerp was partly removed, and the remainder kept ready for immediate transportation; and preparations had been made for carrying the French ships higher up the river, in case the British troops had succeeded in their attempt to force the passage. All idea of pushing up the Scheldt was therefore abandoned, and, on the 14th of September, Lord Chatham, with the greater portion of the troops, returned to England; leaving, however, a considerable body to keep possession of the island of Walcheren, while a part of the fleet blockaded the river so as to enable our merchants to introduce their goods into Holland.

The havoc which this pestilential spot caused amongst our troops is too well known. By the official returns it would appear that, trifling as were our losses from fire and sword, this was the most fatal contest in which our army was ever engaged; nearly one half of the troops were carried off by the fever, while the majority of the others bore with them to the grave the effects of this dreadful disease. Amongst the latter was General Picton, who, shortly after the occupation of Flushing, was himself attacked, in the performance of his arduous duties as governor, and while rendering every assistance which humanity could dictate to the sick and wounded.

A strong constitution and medical skill enabled him to survive the shock; but its rapid progress and deadly violence in a few hours reduced him to the brink of the grave. He never, indeed, entirely recovered from the effects of the malady. So soon as the immediate danger was past, he was ordered to return to England; and in a ship like a lazar-house he was brought home.

But a brief allusion to the termination of this expedition may not be uninteresting to the reader. In the month of September, at which period the fever made the most dreadful ravages, the average number of deaths in the army was from two hundred and fifty to three hundred a week. Still the British Government could not determine either upon giving it up or retaining it.

Applications were constantly made for leave to employ the peasants in the island in thickening the parapets and strengthening the dilapidated ramparts of Flushing, but without effect, until near the end of October, when large quantities of brick and lime, together with some artificers, were sent from England. But after their arrival, the plans of the Government were changed, and in the middle of November they commenced demolishing the works and basin; and as soon as this was accomplished, the island of Walcheren was evacuated by the remains of the British troops: being, in fact, the only termination which could have been anticipated. The enemy was justly elated, while the British people saw with indignation the imbecility of those who planned and conducted this expensive and fatal expedition.

Upon his arrival in England, General Picton was advised to visit Cheltenham, the waters of which place were recommended as the only means of recovering from that prostration of strength which the Walcheren fever had left. Thence he removed to Bath. But he was not long allowed to remain inactive; the affairs of Europe presented an appearance anything but gratifying, and England found herself compelled to employ not only her wealth and arms to stop the progress of Napoleon, but even to have recourse to defensive preparations, which presented quite a novel feature in her history.

The unfortunate evacuation of Spain, consequent on the retreat of Sir John Moore, and
the inability of the small force in Portugal to
offer an effectual resistance to the advance of
Soult, and afterwards of Massena, gave confidence to the enemies of England ; while her
allies, who were watching anxiously for some
proof of her military prowess, began to doubt
her power to co-operate with them.

The people of Spain were making brave but
hopeless struggles against the king who had
been placed upon their throne by Napoleon,
and who was sustained in that position solely
by the presence of a French army. Austria
had been beaten down in the unequal conflict ;
and it appeared that, unless England could animate some of the vanquished states to a fresh
struggle, the whole of continental Europe must
fall beneath the power of Napoleon, who would
then have but one, and that his dearest hope,
to realize,—the conquest of Great Britain.

The master-mind of Wellington was, however, embracing the whole position and resources of the situation in which he was placed.
To rescue Spain at this moment was impossible :
too much dissension existed in that country to

hope for that unanimous co-operation which alone could render her struggles successful; and it cannot be doubted that Lord Wellesley had now to feel the effects of Sir John Moore's want of success in co-operating with the naturally indolent Spaniards, when the first effervescence of patriotism stimulated them to exertions foreign to their character. Sir John Moore seems to have doubted when he might perhaps have had confidence: but if he had stirred up and kept alive the spirit of the moment, he would probably have rescued Spain, instead of leaving her to be overrun by an army far inferior, at least in numbers, to that which the English general might have headed. It is true the Spanish army was at this moment ill organized and worse armed; but they were numerous and brave, and possessed a hatred for their invaders, which would have excited them to an obstinate defence. Fighting by the side of British troops, whose cool resolution and steady discipline would have been a check upon their intemperate impetuosity, their efforts would have been directed by experienced judgment to the most vulnerable and therefore most advantageous points of attack.

Sir John Moore could not have suffered more either in privations, losses, or fame, by risking a battle in the interior of Spain, than he did in his retreat to Corunna; and the same heroism and skill which there enabled this miserable and disorganized remnant of the British army, not only to check, but even to obtain a victory over their pursuers, might have spared them the necessity of a retreat. But it was too late, — they fought for safety, and not victory.

It has been asserted in vindication of Sir John Moore, that, from the inspections which he had been enabled to make of the Spanish forces, he was convinced that to depend upon them to the same extent as upon regular troops, or even to operate at all with them, would be to expose his army to almost certain defeat. He accordingly waited until the Spaniards were sufficiently organized to be effective; but, by some extraordinary mismanagement or inactivity amongst those whose duty it was to drill the recruits, many months were occupied in accomplishing badly what any sergeant in our service would be ashamed of not doing well in the same number of weeks; and, in consequence, every officer sent by the British general to watch the state of the Spanish levies returned with the same report, that they were in a miserable state as to discipline, although the public and official documents of the supreme Junta assured him that it was quite the reverse. But as the information received by the Junta itself was no less imperfect than that which was forwarded to Sir John Moore, it ceases to be a matter of surprise that it should condemn the English general, and accuse the British nation of having deserted the Spanish cause, when every assistance had been rendered in co-operating with it.

According to these reports, Sir John Moore had at one period of the campaign no less than one hundred and twenty thousand men ready to act under his command. These were, however, spread over a great extent, and possessed in some instances a very imperfect line of communication. Still, no effort was made to concentrate this force, and thus to form any effectual opposition to the advance of Napoleon and Soult. The consequences are well known; the Spanish armies were beaten in detail: first, that of General Blake, at Espinosa; then that of the Conde de Belvidere, who commanded the army of Estremadura. Castaños, at the head of the armies of Andalusia and Arragon, now alone remained of the three " large Spanish armies" which had tempted the British Government to send a force to Spain. Castaños would have retreated upon the defeat of the other two generals; but he was deceived into an action, and met the French near Tudela. The result was certain; his young soldiers fought bravely, but were beaten.

Napoleon having thus removed those impediments to his grand operations, which would otherwise have divided his force, next moved towards Madrid, with the intention of driving the English out of Spain. The success of his plans, the disastrous retreat of our army, the compulsory though gallant defence of its embarkation at Corunna, together with the death of Sir John Moore, are all too well known to need recapitulation.

We have been tempted to digress from our subject thus far in order to show the position of affairs at the time when General Picton joined Lord Wellington, and we cannot better conclude this part of our narrative than in the words of a gallant officer who served under the command of Sir John Moore in this memorable campaign.

" Perhaps the British army has produced some abler men than Sir John Moore; it has certainly produced many who, in point of military talent, were and are quite his equals; but it cannot, and perhaps never could, boast of one more beloved, not by his own personal friends alone, but by every individual that served under him. It would be affectation to deny that Sir John Moore, during his disastrous retreat, issued many orders in the highest degree painful to the feelings of honourable men, who felt that their conduct had not merited them. His warmest admirers have acknowledged this, and his best friends have lamented it. But, in all probability, no one would have lamented it more heartily than himself, had he lived to review in a moment of calmness the general conduct of this campaign; because there never lived a man possessed of a better heart, nor, in ordinary cases, of a clearer judgment."*

* Marquis of Londonderry's Narrative.

·· Returning.to.the period when Lord Wellington was. compelled,· in order. to avoid being
placed in the same. situation: as ·his predecessor,
to move his army into Portugal, and there to
assume a defensive position, it will be·perceived
that all attempts:made·by the English general
to·obtain ·the co-operation. of the .Spaniards in
an efficient degree proved unavailing.

. The recollection of .Sir .John ,Moore's inde-
cision, and his 'retreat when (according to the
opinion and belief of the :Junta) everything
had. been done, by Spain which'· Spain could
do, doubtless rendered .them cautious. of confiding·in: British aid, and even. uncertain of our
abilities. By·such a man as Lord Wellington,
want of decision in military operations. must
have been considered a crime;· and unwilling to. be made responsible 'for .the vacillating conduct of the Spanish leaders and government, he resolved by one. determined step
to make ·himself .independent of .their move-
ments, and, after having gathered strength, to
rescue them and their country from the despotism of France, even· without relying upon
any assistance from themselves.

Another strong inducement on the part of

Lord Wellington for quitting Spain, was the total neglect of his army by those whose duty it was to supply it with provisions and forage. In a letter to the Marquis of Wellesley, dated the 18th of August, upon this subject, he says: " Since the 22nd of last month, the horses have not received their regular deliveries of barley, and the infantry not ten days' bread.

* . * * * * *

" Fifty thousand men are collected upon a spot which cannot afford subsistence for ten thousand, and there are no means of sending to a distance to make good the deficiency: the Junta have issued orders, which, for want of arrangement; there are no persons to obey; and the army would perish here, if I were to remain, before the supplies could arrive."

CHAPTER XIV.

Retreat of the British army upon Torres Vedras.—General
Picton receives orders to join the army in Spain.—His
anxiety to reach the field of operation.—Appointed to the
command of the Third Division.—Skirmishes and manœuvres of General Crawfurd.

W.HEN the British general announced his
intention of falling back upon Portugal, the
Spanish government pretended great astonishment. The sincerity of their surprise might
however be doubted, from the simple fact
that they had long since been prepared for
such a measure, not only by circumstances
but even by public announcements. Still
they were determined to be surprised; and
when the reality of Lord Wellington's designs
could no longer be misunderstood, they offered to supply him with everything which he
demanded; but as their promises were not to
be relied on, he turned a deaf ear to their fears

as well as their remonstrances, and on the 4th of August 1809, crossed the Tagus by the bridge of Arzobispo, and established his head-quarters at Deleytoza.

The force of the enemy at this time in Spain was supposed to be little short of one hundred and thirty thousand men; of these, thirty-five thousand were employed in Arragon and Catalonia, and the remainder in the two Castiles and Estremadura ; while, to oppose them, Lord Wellington had only twenty-three thousand British capable of bearing arms, together with about seventy thousand Spanish troops dispersed in different parts of the country, badly armed and worse disciplined. Still their numbers, and the dearth of information under which the French generals laboured, owing to the ill-will of the inhabitants, gave to these armies a formidable appearance, which prevented Soult from concentrating his force against the British, and overwhelming them before they could reach the lines of Torres Vedras ; and even when Lord Wellington was established in that extraordinary position, the apprehension of being attacked in the rear by the whole Spanish nation, compelled Soult to

leave ʼ a ' large army to watch their movements.

. It might have been supposed that the many
victories which the French had obtained over
the Spaniards would have. made .them despise
their attacks. Soult had, in fact, learned to look
with contempt upon them :as regular soldiers,
and in consequence directed his personal efforts
against the British forces. But Joseph Bonaparte, placed upon the throne of Spain by Napoleon, without any of the abilities necessary to
support the crown of an usurper, felt that his
only security was in his brother's arms ; whenever Soult, therefore, wanted any reinforcements to carry on his operations, Joseph always
had some remarkably good reason for refusing
them. Had it not been for this confliction of
interests and plans amongst the French commanders, Soult would doubtless have run any
hazard to bring Lord Wellington to a battle
before he was enabled to fall back upon Lisbon;
nay, had he known the exact numbers of the
British, it is more than probable that he would
have made the attempt with the army which
he commanded : but, fortunately for the fate of
Europe, the numbers of the British were greatly

exaggerated; while those of the enemy were
proportionably underrated. Lord Wellington
did not therefore hurry his retreat, because he
did not know the strength of his opponent;
while Soult did not push on his advance to
cut him off from Lisbon for the same reason.

On the morning of the 11th the army resumed its march, and arrived at Jaraicejo on
the same day; from thence, on the 20th, it continued its route by Truxillo, Maejador, Mede-
lin, and Merida. While the head-quarters of the
army were at this latter place, a despatch came
from Lord Wellesley, who had long been at
Madrid trying to model the Junta into something like a consistent body. In this letter he
informed Lord Wellington of the terror of the
Junta, and the general alarm and confusion of
the people, at being left to the defence of their
own troops; for such was in point of fact the
only interpretation which could be put upon
their fears. Lord Wellesley, wishing to give
them confidence, then proposed to Lord Wellington that he should endeavour to cover Andalusia by taking up a position behind the Guadiana, so that his left should rest upon the frontier of Portugal; adding, however, this remark,

" I am fully sensible not only of the *indelicacy*, but of the inutility, of attempting to offer you any opinion of mine in a situation where your own judgment must be the best guide."

Upon receiving this despatch, Lord Wellington halted at Merida for a few days, but he was ultimately obliged to refuse all further co-operation with the Spanish Junta. Being, however, unwilling entirely to abandon the seat of war, and at the same time being desirous of giving his troops a little rest and confidence from the dispiriting effects of constant retreat, he put the army in cantonments on the banks of the Guadiana, occupying Badajoz, Elvas, Campo-mayor, &c. This position ensured to him either an uninterrupted retreat upon Lisbon, or advance into Spain, as circumstances might render advisable; while, at the same time, abundance of forage and provisions could be obtained from the surrounding country.

The sickness in the army at this period was of a most alarming nature; it had prevailed amongst the troops to a considerable extent; but with inactivity it appeared to gain additional violence, and during the stay of the allies

in these cantonments there were frequently
from eight to nine thousand men in the hospitals at one time. Still, however, they remained at this place until December.

It was now that the Spaniards were made
to suffer the consequences of their vacillating and treacherous conduct. Their armies
were beaten in nearly all directions. The fatal
battle of Ocana, with the unprofitable success and afterwards disastrous defeat on the
heights of Tormes, destroyed the remnants
of the Spanish armies; while the French were
left unmolested to advance into the south of
Spain, and threaten Portugal by entering the
province of Beira. To effect the first object,
Joseph Bonaparte at once put himself at the
head of a large army, having under him Soult
as his major-general, with Victor, Mortier, and
Sebastiani each in command of his own corps.
Napoleon had just conquered Germany; the
fatal battle of Wagram having, according to
many, decided the fate of Europe; and the
Peninsula, it was supposed, must ere long submit to the united forces of the French generals.

It is said that Napoleon expressed dissatisfaction at the inactivity and imperfect success of Joseph: to beat the Spaniards was, in the opinion of the conqueror at Wagram, hardly deserving of praise; the expulsion of the British forces was his ambition 'and his hope. While an English soldier was in the field against him; he felt that he had to contend with an enemy that he respected; and he now resolved to turn the whole of his strength against Wellington and his little band. Spain was almost entirely subdued; Albuquerque, the only Spanish general who deserved the gratitude of his country, in opposition to the supreme Junta, and entirely on his own responsibility; flew to defend Cadiz, the only place of strength that still held out in the cause of patriotism.

Joseph, who had again established his authority in the capital, pushed on Soult to invest Cadiz before the arrival of the Spanish general; but Albuquerque, despising the warning instructions of the Junta, by great exertions contrived to reach that city just two days before the French army: by which decided measure the fortress was put in such a state of defence, that a large French army was occupied in its investment: for nearly two years, thus weakening the force employed against the allies in Portugal. Lord Wellington now became apprehensive for the fate of Lisbon. The French had received large levies, and were evidently preparing to attack Portugal by the most vulnerable points, Ciudad Rodrigo and Almeida; and they were only waiting until the winter was over to commence their march. The English general had not, however, sufficient men to study convenience or seasons, and was compelled to make up by diligence and activity for the inadequacy of the force with which he had to contend against a numerous and victorious enemy.

It should here be observed, that during the cantonment of the troops on the banks of the Guadiana, Lord Wellington was forwarding the construction of those stupendous lines of defence which he now looked forward to as the only present means of keeping a British force in Portugal. At the same time that he was forming the lines of Torres Vedras, he was organising the troops to defend them; and Portugal was preparing an army under his direction, which he hoped would be worthy of fighting by the side of English soldiers. He had apparently resolved in his own mind, that upon the defence of Lisbon depended the fate of Europe, and the result certainly confirmed both his judgment and abilities.

The cantonment around Badajoz was broken up on the 15th of December, when, with as little delay as possible, the army was marched in twenty-one days into the valley of the Mondego, in the very centre of the province of Beira. The advance, under General Craw-furd, took up a position in front of Almeida, his patrols extending as far as Ciudad Rodrigo; General Hill was in the mean time posted with about ten thousand men at Abrantes, to protect Lisbon on the south, the right flank of the army, and watch Badajoz; the head-quarters being at Viseu, while that of the Portuguese was at Thomar, in which place and its neighbouring villages the troops were quartered.

The improvement in the health of the allied army was the first beneficial result apparent from this change of position: in addition to which, both provisions and forage were much more abundant. The British army was so posted as to form a line of defence from the

Tagus to the Douro, with General Hill, as before mentioned, on the extreme right; his right
being again protected by Elvas and Badajoz,
which latter was then held by Romana, both
places having a respectable garrison. Still, it
could not be supposed that either of these fortresses could arrest the march of Mortier and
Regnier, (who were then at Merida with about
twenty thousand men,) provided those generals
should advance by this route upon Lisbon.
General Hill's position consequently gave perfect security to our army in its retreat upon
the lines of Torres Vedras, as the force under
his command could at all events defend the
passage of the Tagus until Lord Wellington's
army was enabled to fall back to his assistance.

Much manœuvring took place between these
generals; whenever Mortier advanced towards
Badajoz, Hill pushed his army on in the same
direction to its relief, which was no sooner perceived than the French general again fell back
to his former position; but it afterwards became evident that this was done only for the
purpose of diverting the attention of the British commander-in-chief from the vast preparations which were being made in the interior,

and the immense levies of troops which were marching in from France, and proceeding to the frontier of Portugal, in order to overwhelm the British force at one blow upon the commencement of the ensuing campaign.

Our subject does not impose upon us a detailed account of the events of this war; but a general outline of the proceedings of the allied armies is necessary, inasmuch as those proceedings are connected with the military career of General Picton.

The letters of the general describe more particularly the different engagements in which he was concerned; and it is therefore necessary to follow the progress of the army, and more especially that of the third division, in order to give connexion to the narrative. With this design, we have recapitulated the proceedings of the allies up to the period when General Picton first held a command, in order that their situation may be clearly understood.

It was the good fortune of Sir Thomas Picton to join the British army at the precise moment when the reverses and disappointments to which it had hitherto been exposed had ceased. But, perhaps, the real state of the resources of Great Britain, and the position of our affairs, cannot be better expressed than by the following remarks.

" Never at any period had the cloud which lowered on the cause of Spanish liberty shed a darker or more impenetrable gloom. Those whose confidence in the zeal, the devotion, the native and untamed energy of the Spanish people, had led them to predict a successful termination to the contest, now wavered in their hope. The British government, urged by the enthusiasm of the people, had at first rushed blindfold into the contest: the vast resources of England had been inefficiently wasted, her utmost efforts had been found unequal to arrest the progress of the French arms, and the lamentable expedition to the Scheldt had exposed the counsels of her rulers to the ridicule of Europe." *

This was unfortunately not an exaggerated picture, and there was not a much more flattering prospect in the perspective. A defensive war is never gratifying to the pride of a nation; and the desertion of Spain, and

* Annals of the Peninsular Campaign.

subsequent retreat towards Lisbon, were considered by the majority of the people of England as only a preliminary to the total evacuation of Portugal, either at the point of the
enemy's bayonets, or by a more speedy. but
even yet more disgraceful retreat before their
approach.   Lord Wellington did not assure
the government of success in his attempt to
defend Lisbon; but he remarked, that if he
were supported, he had every reason to expect it.   He wanted arms, soldiers, money,
and officers. The government could not promise him much; dissatisfaction was naturally
excited at its wavering and imbecile policy
in entering into one enterprise without reflection, and then, instead of pursuing it with
vigour, plunging into another where no hope
of success could exist.   Ministers now, however,
resolved to direct the whole resources of the
country to assist Lord Wellington in keeping
a footing on the Peninsula : but these were
now so few, that the British general had much
difficulty in obtaining sufficient means to support his army ; while reinforcements of men
arrived so slowly, that Lord Wellington soon
discovered that he could place little depen-

dence upon any promised succours from England. Some valuable officers were, however, added to his staff, and amongst them, early in 1810, may be enumerated General Picton.

It has already been observed that he had been suffering for some time from the remains of the Walcheren fever : he was now remaining at Bath in order to recruit his impaired constitution. While at this place, he received orders to join the army in Portugal immediately : and, although far from being restored to perfect health, he obeyed with the greatest alacrity, and made preparations to embark.

The service in which he was now about to engage was, according to his own words, " one in which a man could not fail to gain honour, if he only did his duty ; while, if he wished to distinguish himself, there was plenty of room." And he used frequently to remark, previously to his joining the army, " that to fight against the arms of Napoleon was more worthy a British soldier, than to war against the troops of any other nation in the world."

General Picton's anxiety to reach the field of operation made him facilitate his arrange-

ments at home, with a noble desire, as he
wrote to an old and esteemed friend, to convince the people of England, that if ever he
was guilty of an act injurious to the interests
or honour of his country, it was the fault
of his judgment, and not in accordance with
the dearest wishes of his heart. " I will," he
adds, " show them that my only desire for
fame is, that by deserving it I may benefit
my country ; that if I obtain honour, it may
be to her glory ; and if my life is shed in her
service, that she will do my memory justice."
The remains of the deadly complaint which he
had imbibed at Walcheren still lurked about
his system ; but his was not a spirit to be
restrained by bodily infirmity. Regardless of
every selfish consideration, he embarked with
feelings certainly soured by the persecution
and injustice to which he had been exposed,
but still ardent in the cause for which he was
about to fight, and ambitious to distinguish
himself in the coming struggle.

The head-quarters of the army of Wellington were at Viseu when General Picton arrived in Portugal, and he was immediately
appointed to the commaind of the third divi-

sion of the army. This division was composed
of the following regiments :—

BRIGADES.

Colonel Mackinnon, $\begin{cases} \text{45th Reg. 1st bat.} \\ \text{74th Reg. ; 88th, 1st bat.} \end{cases}$

Major-Gen. Lightburne, $\begin{cases} \text{5th Reg.; 2nd bat. 58th ;} \\ \text{ditto 83rd ; ditto 1st comp. 5th} \\ \text{bat. of 60th Reg.} \end{cases}$

These forces, thus placed under the command of General Picton, were quartered in
the neighbourhood of Celerico. The first division, under General Spencer, was at Viseu ; the
second, under General Hill, at Abrantes ; the
fourth, under General Cole, at Guarda ; and
the light division, under General Crawfurd,
at Pinhel ; while the cavalry, commanded by
General Cotton, was stationed along the banks
of the river Mondego: the total amount of
British troops at this moment in the field
being twenty-three thousand four hundred
men.

The English general was now awaiting the
advance of the French ; his design being to re-
tard their progress, so that they should exhaust
their resources before he drew them into the
snare which he had been so long and skilfully
preparing. He therefore caused the fortresses

of Ciudad Rodrigo and Almeida to be put in
as efficient a state of defence as they would
admit of, and reinforced the garrisons. The
lines of Torres Vedras were already in an advanced state of preparation to receive the army,
and all was anxiety for the opening of the
campaign. But little was, however, expected
from this small army. In England, the affairs
of Portugal were the subject of continual ridicule; the very idea that so small a force
as twenty-four thousand men would be able
to resist the whole French army, was looked
upon as so absurd, that those who had ha-
zarded their reputation upon the result were
afterwards at a loss how to account for their
want of foresight; while in France there was
but one opinion, and this amounted to a certainty, that "the miserable few composing
the remnant of the British army would be
driven into the sea, and Massena would have
possession of Portugal within *seventeen* days
after his army was put in motion." Lord
Wellington was not ignorant that these opinions were generally expressed, and that himself and his army were objects of ridicule not
only in France but to his own countrymen:

nevertheless he had confidence in himself and in his soldiers ; he estimated at their due value the fears of his countrymen and the hopes of his enemies ; looked back upon his lines, and with unwavering resolution determined to disregard both.

During this period of apparent inactivity, the confidence of the troops was kept up by the skirmishes and manœuvres of the light division, under General Crawfurd. With this division, which had served under Sir John Moore, and which was in the most perfect state of discipline, General Crawfurd commenced a series of daring, although not very profitable, manœuvres, which were for a time the wonder and admiration of the whole army. Crawfurd's original proposition to Lord Wellington was, that he should advance to the river Agueda, while General Cole should move his division from Guarda to protect the line of the Coa.

Colonel Napier* says, " But that general (Cole) would not quit his own position at Guarda, and Lord Wellington approving, and yet desirous to secure the line of the Coa, with

* In his able " History of the Peninsular War."

a view to succour Ciudad Rodrigo, brought up
the third division to Pinhel." The singular
wording of this sentence admits of rather an
extraordinary interpretation, and would even
imply that General Crawfurd planned and executed these manœuvres without orders from,
or the authority of, Lord Wellington: for
Crawfurd's proposition was of course made to
him; and General Cole telling the commander
of the forces that he *would not quit his position,*
would be rather an unprecedented measure, and
certainly not one at all suited to the determined
and uncompromising character of Wellington.
If, on the contrary, Crawfurd made the proposition to General Cole, and that officer had
then said he would not move, Crawfurd must
have acted, if not without the concurrence, at
least without the support, of Lord Wellington.
Instead of General Cole having refused to move
his division to the Coa, it is much more probable that Lord Wellington, considering Crawfurd's proposition as likely to involve the security of his line, made the alteration which
Colonel Napier states. For it cannot be denied, that if the fourth division had been removed from Guarda to Pinhel, the rear and

right of the British position would have been exposed; whereas, by the advance of Picton's division, the centre was only thrown more forward: and doubtless it was this consideration, and not the opposition of General Cole, which gave rise to the rejection of this part of General Crawfurd's proposition.

General Picton was accordingly ordered to move his division to Pinhel, with instructions to support Crawfurd in case it should be necessary; but, at the same time, strictly to avoid an action with the enemy, unless compelled by imperative circumstances. The French army under Massena (now Prince of Essling, and whom Napoleon used to call "the favourite child of Victory,") was now placed in extended divisions between San Felizes, Ledesma, and Salamanca, making active preparations for opening the campaign by the attack of Ciudad Rodrigo. The principal object of General Crawfurd's operations was to give confidence to that garrison, protect some villages between the Azava and Coa from the depredations of the French, and to enable the British army to draw such resources from the protected country as would otherwise have been drained by the enemy.

The position of Crawfurd and his division was, however, one of extreme danger, and required all that activity for which he was so much distinguished. His troops were at the same time in so perfect a state of command, that the whole division could upon any occasion, whether of surprise or otherwise, be in order of battle, with the baggage packed and in the rear, in less than a quarter of an hour. The war which he carried on was of a marauding and desultory nature. The French were too deeply engaged in preparing to drive the British army into the sea, to pay much attention to the bold movements of so small a force; and only an occasional skirmish between the hostile foraging parties enabled Crawfurd's troops to convince themselves that the French cavalry were not invincible; for in these little affairs the British cavalry were generally victorious.

It is, however, quite evident that Lord Wellington could never, in accordance with the plans which he had marked out for the defence of Portugal, have intended for one moment that Crawfurd should risk a general engagement; and knowing the fiery and determined spirit of that officer, it is a matter of surprise that he should have entrusted him with so momentous a command. Picton, cool and immovable, of a character totally opposed to that of Crawfurd, was, it is true, ordered to support him in case of his involving himself, which it would appear the commander of the forces thought probable: but Picton knew the delicacy of that duty;—he knew that if, through the rashness of Crawfurd, he should be under the necessity of bringing his division to rescue him from the enemy, and in his turn should require to be supported by General Cole with the fourth division, that consequences might ensue which all the skill and foresight of Lord Wellington would not be able to repair or guard against. How he acted when called upon by General Crawfurd for his assistance, together with the remarks made upon his conduct by Colonel Napier, will presently be developed.

CHAPTER XV.

Investment of Ciudad Rodrigo. — Picton's opinion of the
situation of the Army.—Operations of General Crawfurd.
— Fall of Ciudad Rodrigo, and advance of the French
army.— Death of Colonel Talbot.— Affair of the Coa.—
Colonel Napier's account, and remarks thereon.—Charge
against General Picton refuted.

ABOUT the end of April, upon the French
general making a movement towards Ciudad
Rodrigo by advancing the sixth corps, Lord
Wellington changed his head-quarters to Celerico ; the corps of Sir Rowland Hill still remaining in the vicinity of Abrantes, to protect
Lisbon and the rear of the British position
from the attack of Regnier by the way of
Alentejo.

On the 26th of April, the French invested Ciudad Rodrigo, having about twenty-
five thousand men beneath the walls. The
position of Lord Wellington and the English
army was at this moment one of great interest.

The Spanish garrison naturally looked for relief from their allies,—nay, it had almost been promised to them; but, excepting that the British general moved his head-quarters a little nearer to the frontier, no demonstration was made even to co-operate with the besieged. The army was anxious to be led to the attack; but those officers who knew the magnitude of Lord Wellington's plans, saw the necessity for restraining its ardour; and the remark of General Picton upon this trying and peculiar situation is still remembered by a friend who cherishes his memory. " If," he observed, "we attempt to relieve the place, the French will drive us out of Portugal; while, if they get possession of it, they will lose time, which is more important to them than Ciudad Rodrigo; but they have got to find this out." The event proved that this check to the advance of the French, by wasting their resources, and giving the British nation time to recover from the effects of the unfortunate expedition to the Scheldt, saved the Peninsula.

The opinion of General Picton may here again be given from the same authority, to the effect that, " had the French, instead of

wasting their time in the attack on Ciudad
Rodrigo and Almeida, pushed boldly on, Massena in front and Regnier in flank, by the way
of Alentejo, the result would have been much
more doubtful. Hill's division," he observed,
" many of which were Portuguese, could not
have resisted the French army of Estremadura;
while, although it would have cost Massena a
considerable number of men to force the different positions which the allied army could take
up to check the enemy, still, as the French
were at this period nearly three to one, the
majority of them old soldiers, and all well disciplined, he must have ultimately succeeded
against the allied army, one-half of which was
composed of Portuguese, upon whom entire de-
pendance could not be placed. In addition to
this," he observed, " that if the French had
moved upon Alentejo with anything like determination or force, Lord Wellington must
have at once retreated into the lines, or at
least to the support of Hill; when little could
have been done to stop the advance of Massena
until the British army was behind the lines of
Torres Vedras."

General Picton, nevertheless, had a favour-

able opinion of the position selected by Lord
Wellington, and always spoke of his operations
in Portugal with the most unqualified approbation. The Marquis of Londonderry, in his
" Narrative," referring to the same period to
which these remarks apply, observes; " There
were indeed many persons in the army who
saw something of risk in our advanced situation ;" and it is therefore to be presumed that
others had their apprehensions of the success
of Lord Wellington's plans. Picton, however,
penetrated the designs of his illustrious commander, and did homage to his consummate
skill.

But it is necessary to return to the proceedings of General Crawfurd, whose rashness
might have involved the whole army of Wellington, by compelling him either to come to
a general engagement with the enemy, or to
make a hurried retreat within the first line of
defence. The result of the former would have
been too doubtful for Lord Wellington to risk,
with his disparity of force; while the latter
would have caused the immediate surrender
of Ciudad Rodrigo, and afterwards that of Almeida.

The details of the latter part of these operations are here more particularly entered into, as
the conduct and character of General Picton are
called in question by a modern writer, upon
perhaps as serious an accusation as could be
brought against a British officer, namely—that
of neglecting his professional duty for the indulgence of personal animosity.

General Crawfurd maintained his position
upon the Agueda river and the stream of
Azava, even after the French had commenced
their operations against Ciudad Rodrigo; but
in the beginning of June, about four thousand
of their cavalry crossed the Agueda, when
Crawfurd fell back to the neighbourhood of
Gallegos, being still sufficiently near the besieged fortress to continue the confidence of
the garrison and its hope of assistance in case
of a favourable opportunity; while, further to
produce this impression upon the defenders of
Ciudad Rodrigo, Lord Wellington about this
period moved his head-quarters to a village
about half-way between Celerico and Almeida,
sending Crawfurd at the same time the Fourteenth and Sixteenth Light Dragoons to assist
him in maintaining his present position.

The Spaniards naturally concluded that these advance movements were preparatory to an attempt to relieve the besieged fortress; but such does not appear to have been the intention of Lord Wellington. Had Massena been improvident enough (which the English general could hardly have expected) to detach many troops from the army before Rodrigo, Lord Wellington, by his situation, was enabled quickly to concentrate his force upon the besiegers, and probably compel them to raise the siege. Crawfurd, with his two additional regiments of cavalry and some Spaniards, became more daring in his movements, and ventured upon several skirmishes with the enemy. The hostile force was, however, too overwhelming to allow him more than a momentary advantage: nevertheless, he determined to contest the ground.

Massena, having now fully invested and nearly reduced Ciudad Rodrigo, commenced his advance upon the allied position. After having in vain tried to provoke Lord Wellington to an attempt to relieve the fortress, columns of infantry were collected in the neighbourhood of Marialva, which, with five

regiments of cavalry and some artillery, early
on the morning of the 4th of July, crossed the
Azava, by the ford in front of Crawfurd's position; when the cavalry, coming on with great
rapidity, drove in the British videttes, and
then continued its advance, in spite of some
horse-artillery which opened upon them a galling fire. The allied infantry were compelled
to retire in the direction of Almeida, some
German and British horse covering their rear;
when, passing the bridge over a small brook
near Almeida, the French met with a temporary check by the spirited charge of the
German hussars, who, led by a gallant officer
named Captain Kraüchenberg, dashed boldly
at the advancing squadron while they were
attempting at a furious pace to follow the
British troops. The charge of this small body
was successful, and the enemy was for a moment driven back. The column of French infantry soon, however, crossed the stream at
various fords; but when in front of Almeida, instead of pushing on, they were easily
repulsed by a few volleys from the Portuguese
Caçadores, and gave up the pursuit. Crawfurd
was, notwithstanding, under the necessity of

falling back and taking up a new position near Fort Conception.

On the morning of the 11th, an affair took place which caused a considerable sensation in the army. General Crawfurd had discovered that the enemy's patrols were in the constant habit of pillaging the villages and hamlets in his front, and he determined, if possible, to cut them off in their retreat. Accordingly he arranged his movements by setting out at midnight, so as to get between them and their main body, with about six hundred cavalry; but by some accident Crawfurd, in an attempt to discover a shorter path, lost his way, and while his squadron was in an extended line, and not at all prepared for an attack, they came upon a French patrol, consisting of about two hundred infantry, with thirty troopers, posted in a kind of steep defile, up which the British had to pass in order to get at them. A charge was instantly made by the hussars in front; but as the infantry were quickly formed into square, they only succeeded in driving off the small body of the enemy's cavalry. They, however, rode boldly on to attack the square; but were received with so steady and well-directed a fire, that they were compelled to wheel and make way for the next squadron. But this was equally unsuccessful; the square was uninjured. A third attempt was, however, made: the brave Colonel Talbot, with four squadrons of the Fourteenth Dragoons, led the charge : they dashed rapidly forward, nor drew rein until the enemy's bayonets were at their horses' breasts ; when the French, having reserved their fire, poured in a volley which brought down fourteen troopers and their brave leader. The remainder wheeled off; when General Crawfurd, despairing of success against infantry, and being deceived by some bodies of his own cavalry into a belief that the enemy were advancing upon him in force, ordered a retreat. The loss sustained in this contest was thirty men killed or wounded, besides Colonel Talbot, who was amongst the slain ; while the effect produced upon the army, and more especially the cavalry, by this unsuccessful rencontre, was at this moment particularly depressing.

This affair took place the day after the fall of Ciudad Rodrigo, which, after a brave and protracted resistance, being unable any longer to contend unsupported against the over-whelming force by which it was surrounded, was compelled to surrender. Massena accordingly, after having lost many men and much time, which was to him the more valuable, was, at the expiration of ten weeks, enabled to take possession of this stronghold. By this success a large portion of his army was released, and he was at liberty to make a further advance against the English position. Accordingly, on the 21st, the French cavalry were pushed forward in the direction of Almeida; when Crawfurd, having blown up Fort Conception, fell back under the protection of Almeida; and it was generally believed that he intended by this retrograde movement to pass the river Coa, and again resume his position in the British line.

But it should here be observed, that Lord Wellington had given him positive directions " not to fight beyond the Coa:" his orders being, according to the Marquis of Londonderry, " that he should by every possible means avoid an action; and that, as soon as he became aware of the approach of an enemy, he should retire, with ample space between, to the opposite bank of the river:" and that these orders might be clearly understood, they were repeated. Nevertheless, instead of making sure of his retreat, he made every preparation to repulse the enemy. But the degree of obedience which he paid to these orders from Lord Wellington cannot be better expressed than by the following copy of his report, dated

" Carvalhal, July 25th.

" MY LORD,

" I have the honour to report to your lordship, that yesterday morning the enemy advanced to attack the light division, with between three and four thousand cavalry, a considerable number of guns, and a large body of infantry. On the first appearance of the heads of the columns, the cavalry and brigade of artillery attached to the division advanced to support the picquets; and Captain Ross, with four guns, was for some time engaged with those attached to the enemy's cavalry, which were of much larger calibre. As the immense superiority of the enemy's force displayed itself, we fell back gradually towards the fortress (Almeida), upon the right of which the infantry of the division was posted, having its left in some enclosures near the windmill, about eight hundred yards from the place, and its right to the Coa, in a very broken and extensive position, which it was absolutely necessary to occupy, in order to cover the passage of the cavalry and artillery through the long defile leading to the bridge. After this was effected, the infantry retired by degrees, and in as good order as it was possible for them in ground so extremely intricate. A position close in front of the bridge was maintained as long as was necessary to give time for the troops which had passed to take up one behind the river; and the bridge was afterwards defended with the greatest gallantry, though, I am sorry to say, with considerable loss, by the Forty-third and part of the Ninety-fifth regiments. Towards the afternoon the firing ceased; and after it was dark, I withdrew the troops from the Coa and retired to this place.

" The troops behaved with the greatest gallantry.

(Signed) " R. CRAWFURD."

" To Lord Viscount Wellington,
&c. &c."

The reader has here General Crawfurd's own statement of this affair; Colonel Napier has, however, given another. It is necessary to quote a portion of that writer's account of this transaction. It is not intended to bring an accusation against Colonel Napier of indulging in any personal ill-will towards the memory of Sir Thomas Picton. There is no reason to believe that these two officers were ever in communication; if they had been, it is not probable that Colonel Napier would have accused him of forgetting his duty to indulge in private animosity.

After giving the details of General Crawfurd's retreat to the bridge of Coa, Colonel Napier thus continues: " As the regiments passed the bridge, they planted themselves in loose order on the side of the mountain. The artillery drew up on the summit, and the cavalry were disposed in parties on the roads to the right; because two miles higher up the stream there were fords, and beyond them the bridge of Castello Bom; and it was to be apprehended, that while the sixth corps was in front, the reserves and a division of the eighth corps, then on the Agueda, might pass at those

places, and get between the division and Celerico. The river was, however, rising fast
from the rains, and it was impossible to retreat further. The French skirmishers swarm-
ing on the right bank, opened a biting fire,
which was returned as bitterly; the artillery
on both sides played across the ravine; the
sounds were repeated by numberless echoes;
and the smoke rising, slowly resolved itself
into an immense arch, spanning the whole
chasm, and sparkling with the whirling fusees
of the flying shells. The enemy gathered fast
and thickly; his columns were discovered forming behind the high rocks, and a dragoon was
seen to try the depth of the stream above;
but two shots from the Fifty-second killed
horse and man, and the carcasses floating between the hostile bands showed the river was
impassable. The monotonous tones of a French
drum were then heard; the next instant, the
head of a noble column darkened the long narrow bridge; a drummer, and an officer in a
splendid uniform, leaped forward together, and
the whole rushed on with loud cries.

" The depth of the ravine at first deceived
the English soldiers' aim, and two-thirds of the

passage was won ere a shot had brought down
an enemy; yet, a few paces onwards, the line
of death was traced, and the whole of the
leading French section fell as one man. Still
the gallant column pressed forward, but no
foot could pass that terrible line; the killed
and wounded rolled together, until the heap
rose nearly even with the parapet, and the
living mass behind melted away rather than
gave back. The shouts of the British now
rose loudly; but they were confidently answered; and, in half an hour, a second column,
more numerous than the first, again crowded
the bridge. This time, however, the range
was better judged, and ere half the distance
was won, the multitude was again torn, shattered, dispersed, and slain: ten or twelve men
only succeeded in crossing, and took shelter
under the rocks at the brink of the river. The
skirmishing was again renewed, and a French
surgeon coming down to the very foot of the
bridge, merely waved his handkerchief, and
commenced dressing the wounded under the
hottest fire. Nor was this touching appeal
unheeded; every musket turned from him, al-

though his still undaunted countrymen were preparing for a third attempt.

" The impossibility of forcing the passage was, however, become too apparent; and this last effort, made with feebler numbers and less energy, failed almost as soon as it commenced. Nevertheless, the combat was unnecessarily continued, by the French, as a point of honour to cover the escape of those who had passed the bridge; by the English, from ignorance of their object. One of the enemy's guns was dismantled, a powder magazine blew up, and many continued to fall on both sides, until about four o'clock, when a heavy rain caused a momentary cessation of fire; the men among the rocks returned unmolested to their own party, the fight ceased, and Crawfurd retired behind the Pinhel river. Forty-four Portuguese, two hundred and seventy-two British, including twenty-eight officers, were killed, wounded, or taken; and it was at first supposed that Lieutenant Dawson and half a company of the Fifty-second, which had been posted in the unfinished tower, were also captured; but that officer kept close until the evening, and then with great intelligence passed all the enemy's posts, and crossing the Coa at a ford, rejoined his regiment.

" In this action the French lost above a thousand men: the slaughter at the bridge was fearful to behold. But Massena claimed to have taken two guns, and it was true, for the guns intended to arm the unfinished tower near Almeida were lying dismounted at the foot of the building. They, however, belonged to the garrison of Almeida, not to the light division. That they were not mounted, and the tower garrisoned, was certainly a great negligence; the enemy's cavalry could not otherwise have fallen so dangerously on the left of the position, and the after investment of Almeida have been retarded. In other respects, the governor, severely censured by Crawfurd at the time for not opening his fire sooner and more vigorously, was unblamable; the whole affair had been so mismanaged by the general himself, that friends and enemies were mingled together from the first, and the shots from the fortress would have killed both.

" During the fight General Picton came up *alone* from Pinhel. Crawfurd desired the support of the third division; it was *refused*; and, excited by some previous disputes, the generals separated after a sharp altercation. Picton was decidedly wrong, because Crawfurd's situation was one of extreme danger; he could not retire, and Massena might undoubtedly have thrown his reserves by the bridge of Castello Bom upon the right flank of the division, and destroyed it between the Coa and the Pinhel rivers.

" Picton and Crawfurd, were, however, not formed by nature to act cordially together. The stern countenance, robust frame, saturnine complexion, caustic speech, and austere demeanour of the first, promised little sympathy with the short thick figure, dark flashing eyes, quick movements, and fiery temper of the second; nor did they often meet without a quarrel. Nevertheless, they had many points of resemblance in their characters and fortunes. Both were inclined to harshness, and rigid in command; both prone to disobedience, yet exacting entire submission from inferiors; and they were alike ambitious and craving of glory. They both possessed decided military talents, were enterprising and intrepid; yet

neither were remarkable for skill in handling
troops under fire. This also they had in common,—that both, after distinguished services,
perished in arms fighting gallantly; and being
celebrated for generals of division while living, have since their death been injudiciously
spoken of as rivalling their great leader in war.
That they were officers of rank and pretension
is unquestionable, and Crawfurd more so than
Picton; because the latter never had a separate command, and his opportunities were necessarily more circumscribed: but to compare
either to the Duke of Wellington, displays
ignorance of the men, and of the art they
professed. If they had even comprehended
the profound military and political combinations he was then conducting, the one would
have carefully avoided fighting on the Coa,
and the other, far from refusing, would have
eagerly proffered his support."

That General Picton refused to co-operate
with or assist General Crawfurd from a feeling of
personal animosity, is the charge which Colonel
Napier has thrown upon his memory. Concerning this affair, there is no written document whence information can be obtained;

and Colonel Napier's account is, doubtless, drawn from the memory of those who were present at this battle. With every paper relating to General Picton before us, we can discover no allusion to this circumstance; nor does it live in the memory of his most intimate friends. A charge so seriously implicating a soldier's character should not be made without ample proof; and such proof Colonel Napier has not advanced. Circumstances which occur amid the tumult of a battle are seldom remembered with precision or reported with accuracy. We may be allowed to doubt whether the request was ever made, or the refusal given, in the decided manner in which they are stated to have been. But even granting the facts, there are many means of accounting satisfactorily for such a refusal, without having recourse to a supposition which is the last that one officer should entertain of another; namely, that he sacrificed his fellow-soldiers to a private pique. Can Colonel Napier confidently affirm what were the private instructions which General Picton had received from Lord Wellington at this time? We feel convinced that he cannot: and although we are unable to say that there

did exist private instructions which compelled
General Picton to act as he is stated to have
done, we believe that Colonel Napier is equally
unable to declare that there did not.   But the
colonel was not inclined even to suppose that
Picton was acting in obedience to his orders,
when he left General Crawfurd to finish what
he had begun; and, consequently, attributes
to the worst of motives what might have been
only a point of duty.   Neither does this historian do Picton more justice when describing his general character: his uncompromising
sense of honour, his undaunted courage, his
devoted patriotism, and his love of glory — all
these weigh as nothing to Colonel Napier, to
prevent his representing him as endangering
the safety of the whole army, together with
his own and his country's honour, for the selfish
gratification of one of the worst and most ignoble sentiments of the human heart.   If any
feelings so contemptible had existence in the
mind of Sir Thomas Picton, then indeed his
most intimate friends had little knowledge of
his character, and those who were most constantly with him were most effectually deceived.

A gentleman who has contributed much va-

luable information to this memoir, and who, to
use his own words, " knew Picton intimately
both in the field and out of it," speaking of
his patriotism, observed : " No hero of ancient
Rome or Greece ever loved his country dearer,
or was a more devoted soldier in her cause,
than my lamented friend Sir Thomas Picton."
And is this the man who would sacrifice her
interests from so unworthy a motive as private
animosity ?   Of this at least his countrymen
must acquit him, and not allow the memory
of one whose whole life was devoted to their
cause to be thus traduced.   But it is not thus
that Colonel Napier must be met ; the accusation is made, and Sir Thomas Picton is not here
to answer it : one word from him might have
been sufficient to convince even the .gallant
colonel, that if he refused to bring up his division to support General Crawfurd, he was not
wrong.

The first question which now naturally occurs is, upon what authority does Colonel Napier ground his statement?   Did he hear of
Crawfurd's request and Picton's refusal, together with their sharp altercation, from either
of the generals themselves ? or did he hear it

amidst the din of battle, whilst serving as
lieutenant in the Forty-third regiment, then
warmly engaged in defending the bridge? That
he never heard of this rencontre from either
Crawfurd or Picton, the writer has little hesitation in asserting. He must therefore have
received the report from some third person,
who ought to have heard it,—not from General Crawfurd, after the occurrence; for, by-
Colonel Napier's own showing, he would not
have spoken well of Picton. But whoever informed him should have been present at the
interview; and the gallant colonel was not justified in publishing so injurious a report to
the memory of so distinguished an officer upon
any other authority than that of an auricular
witness.

Colonel Napier cannot be ignorant of the
fact, that no other writer upon the Peninsular
war mentions this interview. The Marquis
of Londonderry would certainly have been as
likely to hear the report of Picton's refusal, as
any other officer from whom the gallant colonel could have gleaned his information; but
the marquis does not even hint at the subject.

A still stronger evidence that Colonel Napier's information may be incorrect, is, that General Crawfurd, in his report to Lord Wellington already quoted, makes no mention whatever of having applied to General Picton for his support, and that it was refused. Now any military man will admit, that had General Crawfurd made this request to Picton, and met with a refusal upon no better grounds than personal altercation and disagreement, General Crawfurd would have reported his conduct to the commander of the forces, which would beyond a doubt have led to a public investigation; and at the same time it is not unreasonable to suppose that Crawfurd would readily have alluded to General Picton's refusal to assist him, to divert in some measure the asperity of remark to which he had exposed himself by his own rashness.

We have said, we think, sufficient to induce any unprejudiced person to reject this imputation upon Picton's character. It is a serious charge, unsupported by evidence and contradicted by probability; and, until further proof is adduced, we are justified in assuming that this passage in Colonel Napier's work was occasioned by erroneous information.*

It would be unsatisfactory to the reader to peruse the various reasons which, in a military point of view, might have induced General Picton to refuse bringing up his division. We have been assured by many a distinguished officer, that if Sir Thomas Picton did refuse to support General Crawfurd at the bridge of Coa, that refusal was not produced by any feeling of personal animosity, but was either in

---

* Since the publication of this work, the following letter from Colonel Napier has been addressed to the author.

" SIR,   Freshford, near Bath, Oct. 29, 1835.

" I have this moment read the first volume of your Life of Sir Thomas Picton ; the second I have not yet seen, but I lose no time in correcting an error into which you have fallen. I have not accused General Picton of refusing to support General Crawfurd, at the Coa, from motives of per-sonal animosity ; you have entirely mistaken the drift of the passage in question. If you will take the trouble to refer to it again, you will see that I make the refusal to support come *before* the altercation ; and consequently that I could not mean to impute the refusal to animosity arising from the altercation. My words will not, I conceive, either in letter or spirit, bear such a construction, and they were never intended to do so."

Perhaps the more judicious course will be, to leave this explanation of the gallant colonel's meaning to the reader.

accordance with the private instructions which
he had received, or a strong impression, the
result of a profound military judgment, that
by bringing up his division he would either
interfere with Lord Wellington's more enlarged designs, or bring on what that general
was most anxious to avoid—a general engagement with the enemy.

The result of the conflict, even by Colonel
Napier's own showing, proved that Picton's
" refusal" was not ill judged. The fight was
over before, in all probability, the third division could have been brought up; for General
Crawfurd, in his report, says, " towards the
afternoon the firing ceased."

But enough has been said upon this subject;
the writer's only object has been to show that
Picton was too much a soldier to sacrifice the
interests of the army. The comments of Colonel Napier upon the character and abilities of
General Picton, together with his concluding
remarks upon the ignorance of those who compare him to the Duke of Wellington, will be
again brought before the reader, after he has
had an opportunity of forming a judgment
from the actions of Sir Thomas Picton : one

thing however is evident ; namely, that Colonel Napier is apparently reluctant to give
strength to the comparison by the slightest
breath of praise, or even by a too frequent
mention of the subject of this memoir.*

* Since writing these remarks upon Colonel Napier's account of the affair at the bridge of Coa, we have been favoured with an introduction to an officer who belonged to
the third division, and who was actually with General Picton at Pinhel when the battle was being fought at the
bridge. This officer holds a high and distinguished name
in the service : it was, as he himself observes, his "good
fortune to hold an appointment on the staff of Sir Thomas
Picton :" but he adds, "I also enjoyed his friendship, which
I shall ever esteem as the greatest honour and happiness
of my life." To this high-minded individual we are indebted for many interesting particulars of Sir Thomas Picton, and especially for the following facts connected with
the affair at Coa. "We were quartered in the neighbourhood of Pinhel," observed this officer ; "General Picton's
head-quarters being at that place on the 24th of July. We
heard firing in the direction of General Crawfurd's position ;
but as this was so common an occurrence, it was thought but
little of. General Picton was, during the whole of this time,
either in Pinhel, or occupied with some of his usual duties ;
and as to riding out alone, it was a thing which he scarcely
ever did, and certainly not on this day : he was generally
accompanied by myself and several others of his staff : but
of this I am quite certain, that he did not ride out on this
day in the direction of the bridge of Coa ; neither do I think
that he was half a mile from Pinhel during the whole time.
And farther, I can state that the first intimation which we

received at Pinhel of the serious affair which had occurred
at the bridge, was by the body of an officer who had been
killed at the bridge being brought back on the following
day ; this officer had left us early in the morning of the 24th,
and was brought back dead on the 25th, having fallen during
the fight. Any attempt to bring up the third division in
time to support the light division, (unless information had
been sent to General Picton when General Crawfurd commenced falling back,) would have been ridiculous, as the
country could not have been traversed by infantry in less
than three hours. With regard to any personal ill-feeling
existing between Generals Picton and Crawfurd, I can only
say, that I never knew the former to express himself in any
but the most friendly terms of General Crawfurd. I certainly upon one occasion heard him observe. ' That d—d
fighting fellow Crawfurd will some day get us into a scrape :'
but this was not uttered at all in an unfriendly tone ; on the
contrary, I think he had a great respect for the daring courage in General Crawfurd's character, at the same time
that he always regretted his want of prudence and consideration."—This is a valuable and indeed conclusive testimony in favour of the judgment we have already formed
upon this subject: the officer from whom it was obtained
is certainly as valuable an authority as any that Colonel
Napier could select; his means of information being peculiarly favourable, as he was upon the spot, and speaks from
personal knowledge. The conclusion which probability favoured is thus confirmed by unequivocal and irrefragable
authority; and this ambiguous passage in the life of Picton
is henceforward clear.

CHAPTER XVI.

Fall of Almeida.—Plans of Massena.—Letter from General
  Picton to Colonel Pleydel.—Battle of Busacos.—Picton's
  Letter descriptive of that affair.—Whimsical incident dur-
  ing the Battle.

AFTER the fall of Ciudad Rodrigo, the next
place for investment was Almeida; and the
enemy having secured the former important
fortress, began to push some troops over the
Coa; thus cutting off all hope which the garrison of Almeida might have entertained of
relief from the allied army. As no effort was
made by the English general to drive them
back to their original ground, they advanced
on the 27th to the river Pinhel, when Lord
Wellington, unwilling to hazard an engagement in his present situation, determined upon
falling back to a more concentrated position.
The cavalry was therefore ordered to Alverca
to cover the retreat: the light division march-

ed to Celerico, where the head-quarters were formed; the first division proceeded to Penhancos; and General Picton, with the third, was ordered to Carapichina; while the fourth was to continue to occupy Guarda, in order to keep open the communication with General Hill. In this line the British army remained for several days, anxiously waiting and watching the movements of the enemy.

On the 3rd of August, however, the French again retired beyond the Coa, and the road to Almeida was once more free. The following letter from General Picton, at this period, gives an accurate picture of the then state of the allied armies.

"Linheres, 8th August, 1810.

" MY DEAR SIR,

" In consequence of the surrender of Ciudad Rodrigo, and the advance of the enemy, with very superior forces, we have withdrawn from the line of the Coa, which was no longer defensible, and the army is now cantoned about thirty-five miles in the rear of that river, in the neighbourhood of Alenio. By this movement we have gained two objects: we have transferred the theatre of operations to a more enclosed country, where numbers will lose many of their advantages ; and we have secured the re-union of the different corps of the army whenever events may render such a measure desirable.

" The enemy, certainly, show little disposition to force us to a general action : by a rapid movement, immediately after the surrender of Ciûdad Rodrigo, they might have compelled us to fight upon ground much less advantageous to us than that which we now occupy. They advance with great caution, and leave as little as possible to fortune. This campaign will be spun out for some months yet, and there will probably be a good deal of hard fighting before the enemy will be able to reach the neighbourhood of Lisbon : but as their losses will be supplied by continual reinforcements, and we shall be daily diminishing in numbers, without any hopes of succour, it is clear that they must eventually succeed. With this view of the subject we are throwing away immense sums of money to no useful purpose ; and all we can expect are a few barren sprigs of laurel for our labours and treasures. I have not heard a word from Trinidad since I have been in this miserable country, and I am, in consequence, desirous of knowing how *my affairs* are going on there.

"The troops in general are now much exposed to slight fevers, and, I may assert, fully ten per cent. of them are now *hors de combat* in consequence. I hope Mrs. M. and all your family have had good health to enjoy the air and amusements of the country: pray offer them my best wishes.

"My dear Sir,

"Very respectfully yours,

"J. Marryat, Esq."   "T. Picton."

But Lord Wellington did not alter his plans until Massena had set himself down before Almeida, which was not until the 14th, when the allies again took up the same position from which they had retired at the end of July. The fortress of Almeida did not, however, make that resistance which, from its strength, the British general had been led to expect. The French were dilatory in their proceedings; and had it not been for a disastrous occurrence, either the effect of accident or treason, which decided at once the fate of the fortress, they might have been

delayed for a considerable period in its reduction; but on the first day's firing the magazine
exploded, shattering the defences to a heap of
ruins, and compelling the defenders to accept
the terms which the French general thought
proper to propose.

Immediately Lord Wellington became acquainted with the fall of Almeida, he ordered
the army to fall back upon its previous position. But still much of inertness pervaded
the operations of Massena; he hesitated to advance, and seemed anticipating the inconveniences and disabilities to which he would be
exposed by driving Wellington into the fastnesses he had prepared.

By their depredations and cruelties the
French had rendered the inhabitants of the
country in their rear implacable enemies. They
had no regular commissariat, and in fact depended solely upon the chance resources of the
country for their support: these were of course
soon exhausted, and their only hope was then
placed upon France. But to have sent supplies through Spain with any escort short of an
army would have been absurd, as the Guerrilla
parties were so numerous, and their local know-

ledge so perfect, that they could at any time annihilate a small force with but little danger to themselves. Massena was accused of ignorance with respect to the defences prepared by Wellington; but it appeared as if he had a just idea of the difficulties which he would have to encounter; for although he was well convinced that the army under his command was nearly threefold as numerous as that of the British, still he would not commence his invasion of Portugal until assured of the co-operation of Regnier. That general, on the 1st of September, was at Sabugal, threatening to advance on Guarda, and turn the right of the English position; while almost at the same time the French cavalry attacked the British picquets in front. The plans of Massena appeared now ripe for execution, and Lord Wellington made every preparation for falling back upon the lines of Torres Vedras, the only position of defence which he could hope to maintain against the overwhelming force by which he was opposed.

The plan of the French general appears to have been at this period to enter Portugal by three different routes : a corps, under Junot, was to advance by the line of Pinhel; another, under

Ney, by Alverca; and a third, under Regnier, by Guarda. These intentions are now well known; but the following letter from General Picton to Colonel Pleydel will convey an idea of the uncertainty which at that time existed in the British army with respect to the movements of the enemy.

"Laurosa, 10 September 1810.

"My dear Colonel,

"Your kind letter of the 20th of July arrived in proper time, and I have very many thanks to return you for the satisfactory accounts it contained. After a variety of movements, which it will be superfluous to detail, as you will have seen them in the public papers, we at length arrived here, nearly in the centre of Portugal, on the 3rd instant; and there is no hazarding a conjecture when we may move, or in what direction, as our operations will depend entirely on those of the enemy, which we are watching. The enemy's force threatens the whole of the frontier from the right bank of the Tagus as far as the Douro; but a ridge of lofty and in most parts impracticable mountains (the Estrella) intervenes, and will confine their principal offensive operations to two lines—the one to the north, and the other to the south, of this extensive chain. The army under Lord Wellington is so distributed as to attend to both these objects. There are about twenty-five or twenty-six thousand, including Portuguese, with Lord Wellington, on the north line, where they can easily unite to oppose an enemy attempting to penetrate on that side; and the country affords many good posts, where we can contend advantageously with greatly superior numbers, without any apprehension of having our flanks turned or being circumvented.

" Lieutenant-general Hill, with nearly an equal force, is stationed in the rear of Castello Branco, in front of the river Zizzara, with his right resting on the Tagus, to oppose any attempt to penetrate on that side; and we are so relatively situated as to be able to communicate and interchange support by four easy marches; and by this distribution of our force we completely cover our line of communication with Lisbon. I think our position, generally considered, is much more advantageous than it has been at any period since my arrival in this country; and there is no doubt but the enemy will experience much difficulty

and hard fighting before they get the better
of us.

" Lord Wellington's plan appears calculated
to draw the enemy on into the interior of the
country before he engages in a serious affair : a
decisive defeat in such a situation would be followed by the entire destruction of their army ;
for the whole peasantry of the country are furnished with arms and ammunition, and are most
inveterate in their hatred of them, from a recollection of the recent enormities and cruelties they have everywhere committed on the
frontiers : and the mountainous and extremely
difficult nature of the country will allow them
abundant opportunities of acting without much
risk.   Lord Wellington has the full confidence
as well of the army as of the Portuguese nation ; and, as far as I am capable of forming a
judgment, I really think it was not possible to
have made choice of a person possessing more
essential qualities for so important and difficult
a command.

" This place (Laurosa) is situated in one of
the most beautifully romantic countries I ever
saw. It is a succession of hills and valleys,
most magnificently wooded, bordering upon

a stupendous ridge of mountains, which rise in succession above each other, and the remotest of which lose their summits in the clouds; and it is so thickly interspersed with towns and villages, that we everywhere find abundant cantonments for the troops.

"Since we have been in constant movement, I have enjoyed perfect health, notwithstanding the extreme heat we have experienced during the last and this month. It has become sensibly cooler within these few last days, and, in consequence of some heavy rains, the troublesome flies are beginning to disappear. I have very lately written both to my uncle and to General Este; therefore I shall only beg my remembrances when you see them.

"With my best wishes,

"My dear colonel, very faithfully yours,

"THOMAS PICTON."

It was within a few days after General Picton had written this letter, that the French general totally altered all the plans which by his demonstrations he was supposed to have formed. He suddenly concentrated the whole of his army, and commenced a rapid march along the

right bank of the Mondego, in the hope of securing Coimbra before the junction of General
Hill's corps should enable Lord Wellington to
offer him any effectual resistance.

"The road selected by Massena for his advance was of the worst description, full of
natural impediments, and by all the officers
by whom it had been surveyed considered almost impracticable. The direct, and in every
respect preferable road, to Coimbra and Lisbon
runs along the left bank of the Mondego. By
this Lord Wellington retreated in a line parallel with that followed by his opponent. Had
Massena determined on advancing by the road
on the south side of the Mondego, he must
have previously encountered the British army
in the strong passes of the Estrella, a high
mountain-chain extending from the Tagus
to the Mondego. This, however, did not
agree with his project of the campaign; and,
notwithstanding its numerous disadvantages,
he directed his march along the road to the
northward of the river. After passing Viseu,
the road declines from a ridge into a lower
and more level country, and is subsequently
crossed by the Sierra de Busacos, which ter-

minates abruptly on the Mondego. On the southern bank of that river there is another range, called the Sierra de Murcella, which forms an obstacle of equal magnitude to the advance in that quarter."*

One of these ridges must be crossed in order to approach Lisbon from the north; and so soon as Massena gave demonstrations of selecting the heights of Busacos, Lord Wellington pushed the whole of his force over the river, and took up a position a little in the rear of that mountain. This was during the 20th and 21st of September. Sir Rowland Hill, with his division, had not yet joined the army; and General Leith's corps was not come up, but was engaged in passing the river; consequently it is probable that if the French had at once made their attack, they might have succeeded in forcing the pass. But Massena was not on the spot; and although Ney, anxious not to lose the favourable opportunity, would at once have commenced battle, he was unwilling to do so upon his own responsibility, and the moment was lost. This produced a delay of several days, both generals

* Annals of the Peninsular Campaigns.

being desirous not to lose any advantage in this trial of strength.

The whole of Wellington's force was assembled before the enemy made any serious movement. By the 26th the British were thus posted:—General Hill, with the second division, had to guard the passage of the river, and prevent an attack by the declivities on the right of the British position. Next in the line was General Leith's corps ; and on the left of this, General Picton, with his division, protecting the pass of St. Antonio de Cantara, where it was expected that the enemy would make the greatest efforts to effect a passage. About a mile on the left of General Picton was the first division, commanded by General Spencer ; the line being then continued by General Crawfurd's light division ; and last of all, defending the extreme left, the fourth, under General Cole, the flank of which was protected by an almost perpendicular declivity. Here, then, Lord Wellington determined to wait, and, if necessary, to give battle: the position was one which hardly any but a madman would have thought of attacking, being covered in front by deep gorges and pathless defiles.

· The Marquis of Londonderry, in reference
to the position selected, remarks: "The principal inconvenience attending this place as a
fighting ground for our army arose out of
its extent, for it was manifestly too capa-
cious to be occupied aright by sixty thousand men; whereas it is essential to the constitution of a military post, that it be easy of
egress as it is difficult of access, and that its
flanks as well as its centre be well secured.
But when ground is too extensive for the
troops destined to hold it, the latter object can
never be perfectly attained; and in the present
instance we could not but feel, that any serious
endeavour to turn our left by the Milheada
road must in the end be attended with success.
Strange to say, however, Marshal Massena, an
officer whose reputation came second to that
of no marshal in the French service, made no
effort of the kind; on the contrary, he led
his columns through the passes above described, and up the face of heights approximating
very nearly to the perpendicular, and thus devoted them to destruction, from the hands of
men posted, as has been already mentioned,
on their summits. Had he acted by the ad-

vice of Lord Wellington," continues the gallant marquis, "I think he could not have adopted a course better calculated to insure defeat, and that too with a loss to the conquerors trifling, out of all the proportion which usually attends even upon success."

It fell to the lot of General Picton and his division to take an active and conspicuous part in repulsing the enemy upon this occasion; and it may be considered as the first opportunity which he had of distinguishing himself under the command of Lord Wellington. The post occupied by the third division was the key to the pass of St. Antonio de Cantara, and was in consequence the principal object of Massena's attack, as it was evidently his intention to force, and not to turn, the British position. From this ridge the enemy could be seen bivouacked on a mountain plain: their encampment was animated during the day by the glistening of bayonets, the movements of squadrons of cavalry and detached parties of tirailleurs, who were occasionally sent up the mountain steeps to skirmish with the advanced picquets of the allies. At night the watch-fires discovered their position.

On the 26th Lord Wellington's army was drawn up in expectation of an attack, every movement in the enemy's camp indicating such an intention. Towards noon a mass of infantry was observed filing into the French quarters : this was the eighth corps, consisting of about fifteen thousand men — an addition to their force which was not a very agreeable contemplation to the British. Still the position of the allies presented an imposing aspect, as the sun shone upon the glittering points with which every eminence was covered. But there was something more inspiriting to the English general than his position, — he could see confidence in the countenances of his men; and the cheer which greeted him as he rode along his line conveyed a happy assurance that he might trust them. They had long been submitting to retreat, but they were not disheartened; and now that they had hopes of meeting the enemy, the young soldier and the veteran felt alike anxious for the conflict: yet the 26th was passed without a battle.*

* The night was cold, and the position occupied by the troops exposed them to the inclement blast which swept over the mountains; even the hardy veteran shrunk within his scanty covering. The young soldiers, however, and

On the 27th, long before the dawn, the French were in motion. But the events of this day are described by Picton himself in the following letters to his friends Mr. Marryat and Colonel Pleydel.

even the young officers, endured with much less patience their mountain couch. A party of these latter, tired of the coldness of their situation, resolved to try whether the enemy were equally inactive; accordingly Captain Urquhart, with Lieutenants Tyler, Macpherson, and Ouseley, of the Forty-fifth, walked down the steep slope towards the advanced posts occupied by the enemy, and arrived at the spot from whence the artillery had been withdrawn only a short time previously. Here they found some straw, which offered so strong a temptation to obtain a few minutes' repose, that each ensconced himself beneath a heap, and prepared to enjoy their good fortune. They were soon fast asleep; even the roll of the drums was unheeded; and the first sound that broke their rest was the clash of fixing bayonets. This ominous sound effectually aroused them, and they scampered back to their regiments with admirable expedition,—a retrograde movement which was considerably accelerated by a strong impression that they could hear the enemy coming up the hill. Upon reaching their line, they found the regiments formed, and silently waiting the attack. To fall-in without being observed by the colonel (Mead) was out of the question; they had been long missed, and he had sent orderlies in all directions after them; and he now pounced upon them as they approached, full of indignation at this infringement upon military discipline. He called loudly to them, " There you are! I'll report every one of you to the general; you shall all be tried for leaving your ranks while in front of the enemy!" Ob-

"Cadaceira; 31st October, 1810.

" MY DEAR SIR,

". . . . . . . I shall say nothing to you about the action of Busacos, as you will have seen it in the Gazette — though not very clearly de-serving at this moment that they were attempting to fall-in and avoid further castigation, he assailed them with renewed eloquence. " Stop, sirs, stop,—your names, for every one of you shall be punished,—it's desertion." And a great deal more he would have added, but the French were on the move; and each officer having given his name, without waiting for any further observations, occupied his post in the ready-formed ranks, much chagrined at the unfortunate event of their expedition and its probable result. But the fight soon began, and every other thought was absorbed in the heat of battle.

After the enemy had been repulsed, and the firing had ceas-ed, and the allies were falling back upon Coimbra, Colonel Mead, who was a severe disciplinarian, and possessed a most inveterately good memory, resolved to fulfil his promise, and report the offending officers to General Picton. Seeing Lieu-tenant Macpherson, he called to him, and in a tone of seve-rity said, " Well, sir, you remember last night, I suppose ?" Macpherson bowed with no very enviable recollections. " Ah, it's a breach of discipline not to be forgotten," continued the colonel, with a stern and uncompromising look.

" Where is Urquhart?"

" Killed," replied the lieutenant.

" Ah !" grunted out the disciplinarian, " it's well for him. But where's Ouseley, sir?"

" Killed, sir," again responded Macpherson.

" Bah !" exclaimed the colonel in a still louder tone, as if actually enraged at being thus deprived of the opportunity

tailed. The serious attack was upon my divi_
sion on the right, that on the left being a mere
feint. The attack was made with great im_
petuosity, and *en masse*, but nothing could
exceed the determined bravery of our troops,
who repulsed them with the bayonet. I had
only three British regiments and three Portuguese engaged with two divisions, and in the

to punish their breach of military discipline. As a last resource, however, he inquired—" Where is Tyler "

" Mortally wounded, sir," was the reply.

This was too much for the old colonel's patience ; so, with
a look of anger, not at all allied to either regret or repent-
ance, he rode off, leaving his only remaining victim in a state
of much uncertainty. Two days after this rencontre, Lieutenant Macpherson, having received a message from his friend
Tyler, who with the rest of the wounded had been carried
into Coimbra, requesting to see him, applied to Colonel
Mead for leave to visit the town, stating at the same time
that his object in doing so was " to attend (as he thought)
the dying moments of his friend." The colonel had not,
however, forgotten Macpherson's offence, and he took this
opportunity to punish him. " No, no," said he in a voice
which seemed to forbid all further solicitation, " you shan't
go ; you haven't deserved it, sir : go to your duty." Macpherson shortly after this met General Picton, and to him he
stated the request which his chum Tyler had made, and
Colonel Mead's refusal to grant him leave. Picton was indignant: " What! not let you go !" he exclaimed in his
usually forcible and energetic manner ; " d—me ! you shall
go—and tell Colonel Mead I say so ; d'ye hear, sir ?" The
young lieutenant both heard and obeyed. Thanking the ge-

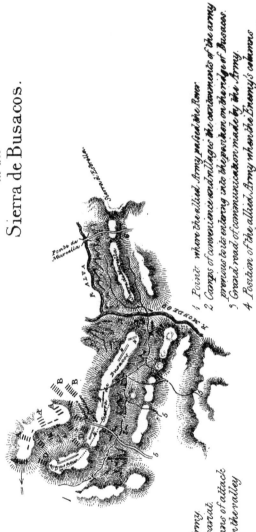

Plan of Operations
at the
Sierra de Busacos.

A Bivouac of the French Army.
B French Cavalry & Commissariat.
D Heads of the Enemy's columns of attack formed during the night in the valley below the ridge.
–– Direction in which the Enemy manoeuvred and the Road which he took to turn the left of Lord Wellington's Position.

Coimbra

1 Point where the allied Army passed the River.
2 Camps of convenience and villages the cantonments of the army previous to its entering into the position on the ridge of Busacos.
3 Grand road of communication made by the Army.
4 Position of the allied Army when the Enemy's columns attacked Gen.l Picton's Division, previous to Gen.l's Hill and Leith coming up to his support.
5 Roads by which the Army retired on the three Columns towards Coimbra.
6 General Pane's force marching the Bridge of Murcella.

four different attacks they made upon different points of my position, the enemy must have lost, in killed and wounded, nearly four thousand.

" Massena appears to have got into a scrape, and in all probability will be obliged to yield up his laurels to his more fortunate adversary. He is in a most critical situation, without provisions, in an exhausted country, with his communication cut off. Another such an affair as that of Busacos will completely do him up, &c.

" Your very faithful

" Humble servant,

" T. PICTON."

" Cadaceira, 3rd November 1810.

" MY DEAR COLONEL, .

" To give you some idea of the affair of Busacos, which took place on the 27th Septem-

neral, he set off first to deliver Picton's message to the infuriated colonel, who swore " that all discipline had ceased in the army ;" and then to Coïmbra, where he found his friend Tyler not dead or dying, but wonderfully recovered from the severe wound which he had received, and prepared with an excellent breakfast for Macpherson and some more of his companions, whom he had contrived to allure into a participation of the good cheer he had provided, by the invitation to " attend his dying moments."

great gallantry and perseverance, they never were able to gain an inch of ground, and were ultimately compelled to abandon the attempt in great confusion.

" During this time a very heavy column penetrated, on the left of my position, close to the hill of Busacos, occupied by the Eighty-eighth regiment, and four companies of the Forty-fifth regiment, which appeared to be engaged in an unequal contest with very superior numbers. These regiments, after the enemy had completely gained the summit of the hill, most gallantly attacked them with their bayonets, and drove them off with great slaughter. Convinced that the enemy would make no impression upon the pass of St. Antonio, from which they were completely repulsed, I galloped towards the left, to join the Forty-fifth and Eighty-eighth regiments, who still continued engaged, and, to my great surprise, found the enemy in possession of a strong rocky point in the centre of my line, and the light infantry companies of the Seventy-fourth and Eighty-eighth regiments (who had been stationed with the light corps in advance) driven in and retreating before them in disorder. With some difficulty I rallied them, drove the enemy from the rocky point with the bayonet, and with the assistance of a Portuguese battalion, which opportunely came up at that moment, I succeeded in forcing them to abandon the hill, and cross the ravine in great confusion.

" There was another feeble attempt made by the enemy to force the hill; but this was easily repulsed by Major-general Leith, who joined the army at that moment with the First, Ninth, and Thirty-eighth regiments: Lieutenant-general Hill also joined the army about an hour after, with ten British, and, I believe, eight Portuguese regiments. The evening of the 27th was employed by the enemy in a variety of movements and fresh combinations, and we fully expected a renewal of the attack on the following morning. Unfortunately we were disappointed: the enemy appeared in movement the whole of the 28th, as if concentrating for the purpose of attacking the left of the hill and convent of Busacos; but towards the evening very considerable columns were discovered filing off through the mountains on our left, towards the main road leading from Oporto to Coimbra and Lisbon, and it became apparent that they had given up all hopes of forcing our position, and were endeavouring, by a circuitous march, to turn our left, and occupy Coimbra before us. Lord Wellington in consequence marched in three columns, at two o'clock on the morning of the 29th, and took up a position to cover Coimbra on the same evening. Coimbra at this season, when the river Mondego is everywhere fordable, has no advantages of a defensive position; it became, therefore, necessary to retreat, and occupy the great line which covers Lisbon, at the distance of about thirty miles, with the right of the army resting upon the Tagus at Alhandra, and its left on the sea near Torres Vedras, where we have been since the 7th of October.

" Massena's army has its head-quarters at the village of Sobral, about two miles in front of the position occupied by the third division; and his army is cantoned in the villages in his rear, and extending towards the Tagus on his left. He is apparently waiting for reinforcements, very badly off for provisions, with his communication wholly cut off. His situation is every day becoming more and more critical, and his difficulty of procuring subsistence for his army must be daily increasing. If a considerable army is not despatched in time to his assistance, little less than a miracle can save him from ruin.

" Our army is healthy, well equipped in every respect, and regularly supplied with provisions. Our eating number, according to the commissary-general's returns, exceeds thirty-five thousand men; and we certainly have seven or eight and twenty thousand bayonets in the field, exclusive of cavalry. The Portuguese may bring nearly the same number; in addition to which we have about seven thousand Spaniards with the Marquis of Romana,—a miserable mob, on which we have no reliance. I do not much like our position; it is too extensive to be strong, and there is great difficulty in communicating between the different posts, on account of the extreme badness of the roads at this season of the year.

" I hope you have enjoyed your health. I learn from General Este that my uncle continues in good health and spirits. I wrote to him by the last packet. Will you have the goodness to offer him my best respects, and say that I am perfectly well? With my best wishes,

"My dear colonel,

"Very faithfully yours,

"THOMAS PICTON."

An incident occurred during this battle, which, although trifling in itself, at the moment caused much amusement to the soldiers. When General Picton had made every disposition for the reception of the enemy, and had visited the particular posts occupied by his division, after a sleepless night, he wrapped himself in his cloak a short time before the day broke, put on a coloured nightcap, (his usual custom,) and ·after giving orders to some of his staff that he might be called upon the least alarm, stretched himself upon the ground to snatch a short repose. Possessing that command over the senses peculiar to strong minds, he instantly fell asleep. Brief, however, were his slumbers: the sound of musketry on the left suddenly aroused him; when, throwing off his cloak and putting on his hat, he sprang into his saddle, and was the next moment at the head of his troops defending the pass of Saint

Antonio. Thence, when this point was secured, he galloped to the spot where the enemy
had obtained a partial success. Here his presence retrieved the lost ground; he rallied the
retreating troops, and urged them again to the
attack. Major Smith placed himself at their
head, and fell leading the attack. Picton, at
the same time, placed himself at the head of
a Portuguese battalion: the eyes of the men
were fixed upon him as he cried " Forward!"
and pointed towards the foe. When arrived
within a few yards, with some encouraging
words and a loud " hurra!" he gave the word
to charge, and at the same moment taking
off his hat, he waved it over his head, totally
unconscious that it was still covered by his
nightcap. His appearance at this moment was
sufficiently grotesque, and caused much merriment.

This incident for an instant diverted the
minds of the soldiers from the approaching
conflict: but it was only for a moment. Giving one loud cheer, they dashed boldly forward; the echo was a groan, as, borne back by
the impetuosity of this charge, the foe rolled
over the craggy steep.

While the attack was being made upon. General Picton's division, Ney advanced two columns; the one under Loison, and the other commanded by Marmont: these made an effort to force the heights occupied by the light division. They came on at a rapid pace with much intrepidity; the path was even more difficult and precipitous than in front of the third division; still they pressed on, and nearly gained the summit of one of the ridges, in the rear of which the Forty-third, Fifty-second, and Ninety-fifth were drawn up in line. These regiments allowed the foe to advance within a few yards without firing a shot; but as soon as they were near the edge, one volley was poured in with terrific effect. The advancing column staggered; but not so the English: Crawfurd, at the top of his voice, gave the word to charge, and in a moment the whole line was in motion; the enemy, tired and breathless with their exertions in ascending the steep, made but a feeble resistance to the destructive bayonets of our men. "The enemy, unable to retreat and afraid to resist, were rolled down the steep like a torrent of hailstones driven before a powerful wind; and not

nets only, but the very hands of some
rave fellows, became in an instant red
blood of the fugitives."*   The enemy
us foiled in all their attempts to force a
over this mountainous ridge ; and they
for the night with all the disappoint-
defeat, besides the loss of between four
thousand men in killed and wounded.

* Marquis of Londonderry.

·CHAPTER XVII.

Colonel Napier's account of the Battle of Busacos examined. — General Picton's letter to Lord Wellington. — Erroneous statements in the " History of the Peninsular War."

WE are compelled to advance a second complaint against Colonel Napier's " History of the Peninsular War." Any reader, in perusing the relation given of the battle of Busacos in that work, would be led to believe that General Picton was either not personally concerned, or was merely a spectator of the conflict. To General Leith and Colonel Cameron is attributed the merit of rescuing the third division from its " *critical situation.*" A few extracts from Colonel Napier's account of the battle of Busacos will assist the reader to form an opinion of the justice rendered to Picton by this historian. Referring to the attack upon General Picton's division, he observes :

" The allies resisted vigorously, and six guns

played along the ascent with grape ; but in less than half an hour the French were close upon the summit—so swiftly and with such astonishing power did they scale the mountain, overthrowing everything that opposed their progress. The right of the third division was forced back; the Eighth Portuguese regiment was broken to pieces ; and the hostile masses gained the highest part of the crest, just between the third and fifth divisions. The leading battalions immediately established themselves amongst the crowning rocks, and a confused mass wheeled to the right, intending to sweep the summit of the Sierra ; but at that moment Lord Wellington caused two guns to open with grape upon their flank ; a heavy musketry was still poured into their front ; and in a little time the Forty-fifth and the Eighty-eighth regiments charged so furiously, that even fresh men could not have withstood them."

*   *   *   *   *

" Meanwhile, the French who first gained the crest had re-formed their ranks, with the right resting upon a precipice overhanging the reverse side of the Sierra : thus the position was in fact gained, if any reserve had been at

hand ;. for the greater part of the third division,
British and Portuguese, were fully engaged,
and a misty cloud capped the summit, so that
the enemy, thus ensconced amongst the rocks,
could not be seen except by General Leith.
That officer had put his first brigade in motion
to his own left, as soon as he perceived the vigorous impression made on the third division,
and he was now coming on. rapidly ; but he
had two miles of rugged ground to pass in a
narrow column before he could mingle in the.
fight. Keeping the Royals in reserve, he directed the Thirty-eighth to turn the right of the
French ; and as the precipice prevented this,
Colonel Cameron, of the Ninth, who had been
informed by a staff-officer of the critical state
of affairs, formed his regiment in line under a.
heavy fire, and, without returning a single shot,
ran in upon and drove the grenadiers from the
rocks with irresistible bravery ; and yet, with.
excellent discipline, refraining from pursuit,
lest the crest of the position should be again
lost ; for the mountain was so rugged that it
was impossible to judge clearly of the general state of the action. The victory was, however, secure."

This, then,.is. Colonel Napier's. statement of the facts connected with the battle of Busacos: a statement so completely at variance with the private letter of General Picton, that if one be correct,.the other must be. erroneous. If Picton's account be false, it must be wilfully so: it is, therefore, of the utmost importance to his character that it should be investigated.

We have fortunately found, amongst the manuscripts of the general, a document of some value in deciding this point. It is a copy of a letter addressed to Lord Wellington, giving a minute and circumstantial detail of the disposition and conduct of Sir Thomas Picton's division, together with the support it received from any other corps belonging to the army.

"Cadaceira,'November 10th, 1810.
" My Lord,

"In consequence of an extraordinary report, which has been circulated with a good deal of assiduity, it becomes necessary that I should make a written detailed report to your lordship of the circumstances which preceded and attended the action which took place upon the height of Busacos on the morning of the 27th of September, inasmuch as they relate to my-

self and the troops I had the honour of commanding on that occasion.

" Major-general Lightburne, with the Fifth
and Eighty-third regiments, was detached to
the left, and did not act under my orders.

" On the evening of the 25th, by orders from
your lordship, I occupied that part of the Sierra de Busacos which is immediately connected
with the pass of St. Antonio de Cantara, with
Colonel Mackinnon's brigade, consisting of the
Forty-fifth, Seventy-fourth, and Eighty-eighth
regiments, amounting to about one thousand
three hundred rank and file; and with the
Ninth and Twenty-first Portuguese regiments
under Colonel de Champlemond: upon the
whole about three thousand men.

" All the movements of the enemy during
the 26th indicating a determination of attacking the position early in the following morning, I made what dispositions I judged necessary for the defence of the post that evening;
and there being an unoccupied space of considerably above a mile between my left and Sir
Brent Spencer's division, immediately after sunset (when it could not be observed by the enemy), I detached Lieutenant-Colonel Wallace,

with the Eighty-eighth regiment, to take up
an intermediate position, and communicate with
the hill of Busacos and the main body of my
division at the pass of Saint Antonio.

" The troops in the immediate neighbourhood of the pass were visited by me on their
respective posts by daybreak ; and, immediately after, Colonel Mackinnon returned from visiting the Eighty-eighth regiment, and reported
that the enemy was collecting in the ravine, opposite the position occupied by that regiment ;
in consequence of which I immediately detached Major Gwynne, of the Forty-fifth regiment,
with four companies, to reinforce that post.

" A few minutes after, when the day began
to clear up, a smart firing of musketry was
heard on the left, apparently proceeding from
the point where the Eighty-eighth regiment
had been stationed ; and after a short suspense,
a violent cannonade opened upon the pass of
Saint Antonio, and at the same time a heavy
column compelled the advanced picquet of the
division to fall back, and, pressing forward with
great impetuosity, endeavoured to push up the
road and force the pass. The light corps of the
division, unable to resist such a superiority of

numbers in front, was most judiciously thrown
in upon the flank of the advancing column by
Lieutenant-colonel Williams; and it was received with so steady and well-directed a fire
by the Twenty-first Portuguese regiment of
the line, and three companies of the Seventy-
fourth regiment, that moved up to their support on the left, that, after a long struggle, and
repeated desperate attempts to effect their object, (during which they suffered much from
the well-directed fire of the Portuguese artillery,
under Major Arentschild,) they were ultimately
under the necessity of desisting, though a severe
firing of cannon and musketry still continued.

"About this period the fire of musketry on
the left appearing to increase, and draw nearer,
I directed Colonel Mackinnon to take the immediate command of the troops at the pass of
Saint Antonio, and rode towards the left, with
the assistant adjutant-general, Major Packenham; leaving my aid-de-camp, Captain Cuthbert, and the assistant quartermaster-general,
Captain Anderdon, to bring up as fast as possible one battalion of the Eighth Portuguese
regiment, and the five remaining companies of
the Forty-fifth regiment.

" On reaching the high rocky point about half-way between the pass of Saint Antonio and the hill of Busacos, I found the light companies of the Seventy-fourth and Eighty-eighth regiments retiring in disorder, and the head of the enemy's column, already in possession of the strong rocky point, deliberately firing down upon us, and the remainder of a large column pushing up the hill with great rapidity. Whilst endeavouring to rally the light infantry companies with the assistance of Major Packenham, I was joined by Major Smith of the Forty-fifth regiment; and we succeeded in forming them under the immediate fire of the enemy, not more than sixty yards distant. Major Smith most gallantly led them to the charge, and gained possession of the rock, driving the enemy before him; but, I am concerned to say, fell in the moment of victory, for which we were chiefly indebted to his animating example.

" The assistant quartermaster-general having fortunately brought up a battalion of the Eighth Portuguese regiment, commanded by Major Birmingham, at this critical period, I personally led and directed their attack on the

flank of the enemy's column; and we completely succeeded in driving them in great confusion and disorder down the hill and across
the ravine.

" Not being able to discover any enemy upon
the ridge to my left, I immediately returned
to the pass of Saint Antonio, where the firing
of musketry and cannon still continued with
little apparent abatement. On my arrival I
learned from Colonel Mackinnon that the enemy had not been able to make any impression
during my absence.

" At this moment Major-general Leith's aid-
de-camp came to report the arrival of that general and his division; upon which I rode from
the post of Saint Antonio to the road of communication, and directed the leading regiment
of the brigade to proceed without loss of time
to the left, as I had no occasion for assistance.
General Leith's brigade in consequence marched
on, and arrived in time to join the five companies of the Forty-fifth regiment, under the
Honourable Lieutenant-colonel Mead, and the
Eighth Portuguese regiment, under Lieutenant-
colonel Douglass, in repulsing the last attempt
of the enemy.

" Your lordship was pleased to mention me
as directing the gallant charge of the Forty-
fifth and Eighty-eighth regiments; but I can
claim no merit whatever in the executive part
of that brilliant exploit, which your lordship
has so highly and so justly extolled. Lieutenant-colonel Wallace of the Eighty-eighth,
and Major Gwynne, who commanded the four
companies of the Forty-fifth engaged on that
occasion, are entitled to the whole of the merit,
and I am not disposed to deprive them of any
part. I was actively engaged at the time in
repelling the attack upon the post with which
I was principally charged, though I provided, as
far as the means I had at my disposal would
allow, for the safety of every part of the
position within my reach; and the moment
I could with propriety and safety to the service quit the principal point of my command,
I immediately proceeded to the post where
my services were most necessary, and was at
all times to be found where his Majesty's
service and my own honour required that I
should be.

" I shall not say anything of the conduct
of the troops under my command during the

whole of the trying service of the day : it was beyond eulogy, and can receive no additional splendour from my feeble praise.

" With many apologies for troubling your lordship with such long details, in which I am necessarily so much concerned,

" I have the honour to be,

" With high respect,

" Your lordship's very faithful,

" Humble servant,

(Signed) " THOMAS PICTON."*

" To Lieutenant-general Lord Viscount Wellington,
" Commander of the Forces, &c. &c."

---

* The extraordinary report alluded to in this letter had its origin in the following singular and unlooked-for circumstance :—It has been before remarked, that previous to leaving England to join the army, General Picton made a promise to the Duke of Queensberry that he would write to him an account of the different occurrences which took place in the progress of the campaign. In accordance with this promise, a short time after the battle of Busacos, the general wrote to his grace a brief statement of the affair, confining his details almost entirely to the proceedings of his own division, giving but a brief outline of the attack on the light division and the spirited manner in which General Crawfurd drove the enemy from the heights. The perusal of this letter gave the duke much satisfaction, and he read it over and over again to his friends ; some one of whom, thinking that it would be equally interesting to the public,

The clear and accurate description of the battle of Busacos contained in this letter, when

contrived by some means to obtain possession of it, and within a few days it was inserted in all the newspapers. Now it will readily be believed that the report contained in this letter was not intended for general perusal, but solely for those who felt an interest in General Picton, and wished for a detail of his own proceedings; and this was the whole which it was meant to convey. The effect produced upon the army, and especially upon General Picton, when the papers containing his letter were brought out, may easily be imagined.

General Crawfurd, with the officers and men of the light division, were annoyed at the trifling mention made of them; and the subject was discussed at some length in the army. Words cannot express the indignation of General Picton when he read his own letter in the public prints: he spoke of it as a most unjustifiable breach of confidence, but fully acquitted the duke of being a party to such a proceeding. The reader must remember, that, in writing this letter, he expressed that which was uppermost in his mind; while, being written only a few days subsequently to the battle, before he had an opportunity of being made fully acquainted with the proceedings on the left of the position, he was but ill able to give a detail of the engagement at that part of the line; and again, the army, and more especially his division, had ever since been in the field, checking the advance of the enemy, and covering the retreat. Still, coming from a general actively engaged in the field, this letter was looked upon almost in the same light as the despatch; whereas it was only intended to describe that part of the battle in which General Picton and his division had been personally concerned, and of which he had been an eye-witness. The pe-

assisted by the accompanying plan,* will convey an accurate idea of the conflict. The account given in the " History of the Peninsular
War" is strikingly at variance with that contained in General Picton's report to the commander of the forces. The necessary inference
to be drawn from these conflicting statements
is, either that Colonel Napier must have been
badly informed, and consequently published an
erroneous statement; or that General Picton
did not know the disposition of his men, in
what manner they behaved, or to whose assistance he was indebted for extricating his division
from its critical situation; or else, that knowing
these particulars, he ventured to make a false
representation of them to Lord Wellington.
Which of these conclusions is the most probable, it is for the reader to determine. But

rusal of this letter gave rise to a variety of reports respecting
General Picton, and the conduct of his division upon this
occasion; some of these reached his ears, and in consequence he was induced to draw up the above detailed report
for the satisfaction of the commander of the forces.

* This plan is engraved from the original sketch taken on
the spot by the quartermaster-general referred to, and enclosed in, General Picton's letter to Colonel Pleydel of the
3rd November 1810.

should a doubt arise in the minds of any, we
will point out more particularly a few of the
errors in the description of the battle of Busacos, as related in the "History of the Peninsular War."

In the first place, it may be desirable to refer
to an examination of the position of the British
army on the heights of Busacos previously to
the commencement of the attack.*   It will
there be seen that the corps of General Leith,
called the fifth division, was on the right of
Picton's third division ; while Sir Brent Spencer, with the first, was on his left.   Now General Picton in his report says, " There being an
unoccupied space of considerably above a mile
between my left and Sir Brent Spencer's division, I immediately after sunset (when it could
not be observed by the enemy) detached Lieutenant-colonel Wallace, with the Eighty-eighth
regiment, to take up an intermediate position,
and communicate with the hill of Busacos and
the main body of my division at the pass of
Saint Antonio."

This shows, that long before the commence-

* Vide Plan.

ment of the attack, the Eighty-eighth regiment
was more than half a mile on the left of the
third division; while, in the next paragraph of
the same document, he observes, " The troops
in the immediate neighbourhood of the pass
were visited by me on their respective posts
before daybreak; and, immediately after, Colonel Mackinnon returned from visiting the
Eighty-eighth regiment, and reported that the
enemy was collecting in the ravine, opposite
the position occupied by that regiment: in
consequence of which I immediately detached
Major Gwynne of the Forty-fifth regiment,
with four companies, to reinforce that post."

It is there proved that this part of the Forty-
fifth regiment was thus early sent to join the
Eighty-eighth on the left of Picton's position.
General Picton then commences an account of
the attack upon the pass of St. Antonio by
" a heavy column" of the enemy; who, according to Colonel Napier, scaled the mountain so
swiftly and with such astonishing power, that
they overthrew everything that opposed their
progress. The gallant colonel then goes on to
relate, that " the right of the third division was
forced back, the Eighth Portuguese regiment

was broken to pieces, and the hostile masses gained the highest part of the crest, just between the third and fifth divisions."

A statement more at variance from the above could hardly have been written than that contained in the following extract from General Picton's report, wherein he describes the reception and success of this column of the enemy, which, he says, "compelled the advanced picquet of the division to fall back, and, pressing forward with great impetuosity, endeavoured to push up the road and force the pass. The light corps of the division, unable to resist such a superiority of numbers in front, was most judiciously thrown in upon the flank of the advancing column by Lieutenant-colonel Williams; and it was received with so steady and well-directed a fire by the Twenty-first Portuguese regiment of the line, and three companies of the Seventy-fourth regiment that moved up to their support on the left, that, after a long struggle, and repeated desperate attempts to effect their object, (during which they suffered much from the well-directed fire of the Portuguese artillery, under Major Arentschild,) they were ultimately under the necessity of desisting, though a severe fire of cannon and musketry still continued."

The most astonishing part of Colonel Napier's statement, however, is contained in the concluding passage of the preceding extract from his work; where, after stating that "the hostile masses had gained the highest part of the crest, just between the third and fifth divisions," he continues, "the leading battalions immediately established themselves amongst the crowning rocks, and a confused mass wheeled to the right, intending to sweep the summit of the Sierra: but at that moment Lord Wellington caused two guns to open with grape upon their flank, a heavy musketry was still poured into their front, and in a little time the *Forty-fifth* and the *Eighty-eighth* regiments charged so furiously that even fresh men could not have withstood them."

The *Eighty-eighth* and four companies of the Forty-fifth regiments were at this moment defending themselves against an attack of the enemy, more than half a mile on *the left* of General Picton's division! the *remainder of the Forty-fifth being in reserve ;* how Colonel Napier could bring these regiments to charge on the *right* of the division is a mystery.

The colonel then observes, that " meanwhile the French, who first gained the crest, had re-formed their ranks, with the right resting upon a precipice overhanging the reverse side of the Sierra. Thus the position was in fact gained, if any reserve had been at hand ; for the greater part of the third division, British and Portuguese, were fully engaged, and a misty cloud capped the summit, so that the enemy, thus ensconced amongst the rocks, could not be seen except by General Leith. That officer had put his first brigade in motion to his own left as soon as he perceived the vigorous impression made on the third division, and he was now coming on rapidly ;· but he had two miles of rugged ground to pass in a narrow column before he could mingle in the fight. Keeping the Royals in reserve, he directed the Thirty-eighth to turn the right of the French ; and as the precipice prevented this, Colonel Cameron of the Ninth, who had been informed by a staff-officer of the critical state of affairs, formed his regiment in

line under a heavy fire, and, without returning a single shot, ran in upon and drove the
grenadiers from the rocks with irresistible
bravery," &c.

Now the ground of the whole of these proceedings is supposed to be on the *right* of the
third division, near the pass of Saint Antonio ;
but if any further proof should be wanting to
establish this fact, it is only necessary to re-
mind the reader, that General Leith's corps
was on the right of Picton's position ; and as
the Ninth regiment, which is stated to have
driven back the enemy after they had forced
the right of his position, belonged to that corps,
these operations must have taken place on
the right of the third division. The reader
has already perused General Picton's report
to the commander of the forces, wherein he
gives a most detailed account of the enemy's
attack and repulse on this part of his position ;
but so opposite is his statement to that given
in the " History of the Peninsular War," that
it will hardly be imagined to refer to the same
point of the action. In fact, so convinced was
General Picton that the enemy were effectually
repulsed in their attack upon the pass, and

that he had nothing to apprehend upon his right, that in his own words, which, although before inserted, are particularly applicable here, he actually quitted this part of his position, and proceeded to the left, where the attack was more warm. He says in the following paragraph to that last extracted—

"About this period the firing of musketry on the left appearing to increase and draw nearer, I directed Colonel Mackinnon to take the immediate command of the troops at the pass of Saint Antonio, and rode towards the left, with the assistant adjutant-general, Major Pakenham: leaving my aide-de-camp, Captain Cuthbert, and the assistant quartermaster-general, Captain Anderdon, to bring up as fast as possible one battalion of the Eighth Portuguese regiment."

"On reaching the high rocky point about half-way between the pass of Saint Antonio and the hill of Busacos, I found the light companies of the Seventy-fourth and Eighty-eighth regiments retiring in disorder, and the head of the enemy's column, already in possession of the strong rocky point, deliberately firing down upon us, and the remainder of a

large column pushing up the hill with great
rapidity."

It will be observed that the only point where
the enemy did succeed in gaining any advantage was nearly a mile on the extreme *left* of
the main body of the third division ; and, consequently, for General Leith to have seen the
enemy "ensconced among the rocks" from his
position, he must have looked through the
smoke arising from the firing at the pass ; while
for the Ninth regiment to have " driven them
from the rocks with irresistible bravery," it must
have passed with considerable expedition, either
in front or rear of the main body of the third
division : but this, even by Colonel Napier's
own statement, they did not do; while, by General Picton's report, the enemy were repulsed
by the troops of his own division. He continues, " Whilst endeavouring to rally the light
infantry companies with the assistance of Major
Pakenham, I was joined by Major Smith of
the Forty-fifth regiment, and we succeeded in
forming them, under the immediate fire of the
enemy, not more than sixty .yards distant.
Major Smith most gallantly led them to the
charge, and gained possession of the rock, driv-

ing the enemy before him ; but, I am concerned to say, fell in the moment of victory, for
which we were chiefly indebted to his animating example."

How different this to Colonel Napier's account ! In fact, there is no similarity between
the two, excepting that the position gained by
the enemy was "a rocky point:" but the local-
ity of that point is described as at least a mile
from its real situation, it being far to the left of
the third division, instead of immediately on its
right, and much nearer relief from Sir Brent
Spencer's division than the corps of General
Leith; while, so far from the enemy having
"no reserve" at hand, General Picton says,
"that the remainder of a large column was
pushing up the hill with great rapidity."

But a more important error in Colonel
Napier's account occurs where he so distinctly describes the formation under fire, together with the gallant and successful charge
made upon the enemy by the Ninth regiment,
under Colonel Cameron. Doubtless this officer
would have led, and his regiment would have
made, as brave and well-conducted an attack
upon the enemy as that described by Colonel

Napier—only it was not there: and as praise
is due only where it has been earned, some
degree of injustice is done to the memory of
Major Smith, in thus giving to another that
which is justly his. But another brief extract
from the report will further convince the
reader *who* it was that drove the enemy from
his rocky height, and forced him to abandon
his momentary success. Immediately after the
last extract General Picton observes:

" The assistant quartermaster-general having
fortunately brought up a battalion of the Eighth
Portuguese regiment, commanded by Major
Birmingham, at this critical period, I personally
led and directed their attack on the flank of the
enemy's column, and completely succeeded in
driving them in great confusion and disorder
down the hill and across the ravine."

Thus, then, it appears that it was Major
Smith, at the head of the light companies
of the Eighty-eighth and Seventy-fourth regiments, who drove the enemy from the rocky
point; and to his " animating example," General Picton says, " we were chiefly indebted
for success." But General Picton's biographer
may add more; praise is to him no longer

flattery. Picton himself, at the head of a battalion of Portuguese, by his example assisted greatly the intrepid charge of the major, and together they drove the French at the point of the bayonet, first from the "rocky, point," and then down the almost perpendicular steep. But the "History of the Peninsular War" is not only deficient in giving due credit to the leaders of this charge, but also to the officers and soldiers of the Forty-fifth, Seventy-fourth, and Eighty-eighth regiments. To them, and to them only, the merit of this contest is due. The light companies of the two latter, it is true, were compelled to retreat before the overwhelming numbers of the enemy ; but they gallantly retrieved what they had lost, unassisted by any other force than one battalion of the Eighth Portuguese ; the whole of which regiment, according to Colonel Napier's account, was "broken to pieces" at the attack upon the pass. General Picton then continues:

" Not being able to discover any enemy upon the ridge to my left, I immediately returned to the pass of Saint Antonio, where the firing of musketry and cannon still con-

tinued with little apparent abatement. On
my arrival I learned from Colonel Mackinnon, *that the enemy had not been able to make
any impression during my absence ;"* —proving at
once that the right of the third division *was
not* forced back at any time during the action ;
for the reader must be already convinced that
no . such reverse had taken place previously to
General Picton visiting the position on his left,
occupied by the Eighty-eighth and part of the
Forty-fifth regiments.

It was not until the return of General Picton from the left of his position, when in fact
the brunt of the action was over, that he had
any communication with General Leith, as is
evinced by the following remark contained in
the consecutive passage of the report to that
last quoted.

" At this moment Major-general Leith's aide-
de-camp came to report the arrival of that
general and his division ; upon which I rode
from the pass of Saint Antonio to the road
of communication,* and directed the leading regiment of the brigade to proceed without loss of time to the left, *as I had no*

* Vide Plan of Busacos.

occasion for assistance. General Leith's brigade in consequence *marched on,* and arrived in time to join the five companies of the Forty-fifth regiment, under the Honourable Lieutenant-colonel Mead, and the Eighth Portuguese regiment, under Lieutenant-colonel Douglass, in repulsing the *last attempt* of the enemy."

It thus appears, even by General Picton's report, that General Leith's division had a slight share in the conclusion of this battle ; and upon a reference to the letter to Colonel Pleydel, dated the 3rd of November, it will be seen that he there mentions the First, Ninth, and Thirty-eighth regiments, as being those which came up to his support. Still they were not engaged on the right, or in concert with the main body of the third division, but were directed to march by the rear to the left of the position. They did not, however, arrive at the point of attack until long after the enemy had been driven from the " rocky point" which they had succeeded in gaining, and were only engaged in repulsing the *last* feeble attempt made by the French before the close of the action.

It is evident, therefore, that the "History of the Peninsular War" has not done justice either to General Picton or to his soldiers for the share which they took in the battle of Busacos; and it is strange that a writer who takes so much pains to be correct, and who had so many sources of information, should thus have fallen into so palpable an error with respect to the details of this conflict. The authorities whence this memoir has been compiled are beyond question authentic; and it is submitted that if General Picton did not know the operations and disposition of his division, it may with safety be asserted that they were not known at all: and without any disrespect to the commander of the forces himself, it is not too much to say, that even *he* would forego his opinion with regard to the operations of the different corps of a division if opposed to the report of the general who at the time was in command.

But General Picton deserves unequivocal praise for his conduct in this affair. The foresight which he displayed in filling up the interval on his left, between the pass of Saint Antonio and the position occupied by Sir

Brent Spencer, which he describes as considerably above a mile in extent, is highly characteristic of military genius. With admirable judgment he despatched, unobserved by the enemy, one of his strongest regiments to occupy this ground, conscious that a small force could defend the pass. The event proved how necessary was this precaution : it was the first point of attack, and by far the most serious. The bravery of the troops and the presence of their general, alone obtained for them victory.

CHAPTER XVIII.

Operations of the allied army.—Massena's movements.—
Scene of horror and confusion.—Retrograde movement
of the allies.—Position within the Lines of Torres Vedras.
—Plan and defence of those lines.—Disposition of the
several allied corps.—Excesses of Massena's troops.—
Lord Wellington's masterly plans.—Massena's critical situ-
ation.—Pursuits and occupations of the allies.—General
Picton's rebuke of his men.

It is time now to follow the operations of the
army after they had thus successfully checked the progress of the enemy. The letter of
General Picton, dated the 3rd of November,
has already given a brief outline of the movements of the allies subsequently to the battle of
Busacos. It was fully expected that Massena
would make a further attempt on the following
morning to force a passage over this mountain
ridge, and every preparation was accordingly
made in the British line to give him as warm
a reception as he had experienced on the previous day. The French general had, however,

learned his lesson; the result of the conflict
on the heights had taught him to reflect that
there might be a better, if not a shorter route
to Coimbra, than over precipices defended by
a determined and well-disciplined enemy.

Acting upon this conclusion, Massena merely
occupied the attention of the British during
the day with some light infantry movements,
and at night put his army in motion to execute what he should have done at first, instead
of attacking the heights of Busacos. This was
to turn the left of the British position, by
marching his army through a mountain-pass in
the Sierra Caramula; a ridge which runs at an
obtuse angle with that of Busacos, and upon
which the right flank of the French had rested.
This pass led into the high road to Coimbra;
and, by a rapid movement, Massena hoped to
reach that place before the British could succeed in effecting their retreat. Lord Wellington, therefore, put his army in motion in
three columns at two o'clock in the morning
of the 29th of September, and in the evening took up a position with the apparent intention of defending Coimbra; but it does not
appear that this was any part of Lord Wel-

lington's actual plan : for General Picton observes, " Coimbra at this season, when the river
Mondego is everywhere fordable, has no advantages as a defensive position." The British commander, in fact, had no other object
in making this demonstration than to enable
the inhabitants of the city to effect their retreat in front of his army, while he retarded
the advance of the French through the narrow
paths by which they must necessarily pass.

On the 1st of October, the enemy attacked
the position occupied by the allies, driving in
the outposts : a retreat was immediately ordered ; and the army, with all expedition and some
skirmishing, crossed the Mondego at Coimbra.
This movement was full of danger, as the confined passes through which the army and retreating inhabitants had to defile admitted but
of a narrow front. The Junta had, at the instigation of Lord Wellington, issued a man-
date, calling upon all the inhabitants of the
provinces in the neighbourhood of Lisbon to
fall behind the lines of Torres Vedras, to drive
in their cattle, and bring with them their stores
of corn and provisions, and whatever else they
wished to preserve from the hands of the in-

vaders. This order was, however, but imperfectly obeyed; for, while the enemy was at a distance, and the British army between them, the inhabitants thought there was plenty of time; and not until they found the French in their cities, and plundering their houses, did they discover that they had neglected the opportunity of complying with the wise injunctions of their Government. So, at Coimbra, the rapid advance of the enemy and the sudden retreat of the allies left but little time for preparation; and a scene of horror and confusion ensued which can hardly be conceived.

Lord Londonderry says, " A crowd of men, women, and children, — of the sick, the aged, and the infirm, as well as the robust and the young, covered the roads and fields in every direction. Mothers might be seen, with infants at their breasts, hurrying towards the capital and weeping as they went; old men, scarcely able to totter along, made way chiefly by the aid of their sons and daughters; whilst the whole way-side soon became strewed with bedding, blankets, and other species of household furniture, which the weary fugitives were unable to carry farther."

When the British troops fell ~back. upon
Coimbra, all was confusion. As they passed through the city and over the bridge, the
whole population would have fled with them ;
they then, however, felt how ill-judged had
been their delay : the road was choked with
soldiers and guns, and the inhabitants were
compelled to give way, force even being employed for the purpose of securing a passage for the
army ; and the wretched inhabitants forgot in
their misery the folly which had occasioned it.
Little could be done to alleviate their sufferings or assist their flight ; they had neglected to
employ the means when in their power, and
they were now left by thousands to witness the
pillage of their homes and the destruction of
their city.   The French showed but little mercy : plunder was their object, and they returned
in full the rancorous hatred manifested by the
Portuguese towards themselves.

This retrograde movement of the allies was
one of choice, not of necessity ; and a pe-
culiarity characterized it, namely, that it was
the retreat of a victorious army. But Lord
Wellington did not wish to hazard another
engagement with the enemy : his plans were

more extensive, and, his efforts were all directed to reduce the result to a certainty. To effect this he took up a position within the first grand line of Torres Vedras: here it was that he staked his military reputation; this was the spot which he had chosen to convince the enemy that, although he had retreated, he was not vanquished. It was not only the French army that he had to check : that powerful opponent public opinion was now to be arrested; the current of defeat was to be turned; in short, by this measure, the result of mature judgment, he hoped not only to destroy the power of the French in the Peninsula, but at the same time to secure the confidence of his army and the British nation. Without this, he could not expect to obtain success; with it, he might obtain anything.

These celebrated military lines of defence, the formation of which entitle their distinguished projector to as much or more fame than any of the many victories which he gained, have already been fully described; and we are here only called upon to repeat General Picton's opinion of their capability, as expressed in his letter to Colonel Pleydel of the 3rd of November; wherein he remarks, that the position is "too extensive to be strong;" and then adds, " There is great difficulty in communicating between the different posts, on account of the extreme badness of the roads at this season of the year." These objections were doubtless reasonable; but it would be presumptuous at this period to hazard any observations in support of General Picton's remarks, as they could at once be met with the ready reply of success. A brief outline of the position of the contending armies and their resources shall therefore fill up the interval during which Lord Wellington locked up his army within the lines of Torres Vedras.

The Marquis of Londonderry gives an account of the plan and defence of these lines.

"Along the neck of the Peninsula," says his lordship, "at the extremity of which Lisbon is built, there extend several ranges of high and rugged hills, intersected here and there by narrow passes, and covered for the most part by deep ravines and defiles, in the usual acceptation of the term, impassable. Along these, at the distance of perhaps twenty-five English miles from the city, Lord Wellington had selected two lines, one considerably in advance of the other, but both of tremendous strength ; and he had bestowed upon their fortification so much of care, diligence, and science, as to place them almost equally beyond the reach of insult from any assailing force, however numerous and well supplied. The system pursued on this occasion was quite novel, and the works erected such as were not to be met with under similar circumstances in any part of the world."

In reference to the first line of this position, which was now occupied by the allied powers, he observes: " This line rested its right upon the acclivities of Alhandra, on the summit of which several formidable redoubts were erected, and was flanked by the fire of a dozen gun-boats at anchor in the Tagus. The faces of these hills were all carefully scarped, the road which led through them was destroyed, and it was with perfect justice concluded, that here, at least, our position might be pronounced impregnable ; — on the left of these heights, by a ravine or gully, called the Pass of Maltao, the gorge of which was effectually blocked up by two formidable redoubts; whilst it was completely commanded on one hand by the hills of

Alhandra, and on the other by those of Armeda.
The latter, like the former, were scarped, and
otherwise rendered inaccessible; and they communicated with the centre of the position, which
was a high mountain, crowned by a redoubt
more extensive than any other in the line. As
this mountain overhung the village of Sobral,
its castle kept completely at command the great
road which conducts from thence to Lisbon,
and rendered it utterly hopeless for any body of
men so much as to attempt a passage in that
direction. On the left of this redoubt, again,
some high and broken ground looked down
upon Zebreira, and stretched in formidable
shape towards Pantaneira. Just behind that
village there is a deep glen, succeeded by other
hills which cover the roads from Ribaldiera to
Exara de los Cavalleiros and Lisbon; whilst
on the left of the whole was a lofty mountain,
which crowded up all the space between these
roads and Torres Vedras.

"Such," continues the Marquis, "is a brief
detail of the leading features in this position;
than which it will be seen that, independently
of all that art had done for it, few can be imagined more formidable. But when it is fur-

ther understood, that the ascents were all steep, rugged, and rocky; that strong vineyards and deep ground everywhere covered the front, and that wherever natural obstacles chanced to be fewer in number or less insuperable in kind than could have been desired, labour had not failed to supply them ; and when these things are taken into consideration, an army once brought thither must either be false to itself, or it might defy all the force of the French empire seriously to molest it."

Such was the position of the army ; and it may now be desirable to show the disposition of the several corps. On the extreme right, with its right flank resting on the Tagus, were posted the forces of General Hill. The next on his left was Crawfurd, with his division, the particular duties of which were to guard the heights of Arruda. General Pack's Portuguese brigade followed, occupying the great redoubt before alluded to as overlooking the village and castle of Sobral.

The high ground above Zebreira was held by Sir Brent Spencer's first division, connected on its left with the right of Picton's division, which had to defend the ground from the village of Pantaneira, across a kind of ravine, until it joined the fourth division, under General Cole, by which the line of defence was continued across a succession of hills as far as the road leading to Exara de los Cavalleiros and Lisbon, where the corps of General Campbell occupied the extreme left of the British line at Torres Vedras.

The troops under Lord Wellington's command, and with which he had to defend this position, which extended about twenty-nine miles, amounted, according to General Picton's statement, to nearly seventy thousand men; but of these only thirty-five thousand were British; and this estimate was, as he observes, drawn from the "eating numbers," the amount of bayonets not exceeding eight-and-twenty thousand. The remainder of the seventy thousand was composed of Portuguese and Spaniards: the latter General Picton styles "a miserable mob;" while the former were hardly yet to be fully depended upon when unsupported by British troops. Still, as they were led, and in some instances officered, by English, it was hoped that they would not disgrace their allies.

The disposable force under the command of

Massena in front of the lines was about seventy thousand veteran soldiers; but the relative situations of the two armies was strikingly different. The French had Spain and the greater part of Portugal between them and France; their excesses had destroyed every favourable feeling which might have existed in the minds of the inhabitants of the Peninsula towards them; every means were therefore employed to destroy and harass them. The marauding and destructive spirit which prevailed, and which was in fact encouraged, in the French army, soon devastated the country occupied by their soldiers, and destroyed their resources. The decree of the Junta had been but imperfectly obeyed, and for a time their foraging parties contrived to collect together a miserable maintenance; but a thoughtless and wasteful expenditure soon exhausted the immediate neighbourhood, after which they were compelled to extend their depredations to a more enlarged circle. Then it was that the independent corps of both Spaniards and Portuguese, many of whom were instigated by bitter hatred, sought revenge for some desolated home or murdered relative. Those active but irregular forces,

taking advantage of the unsupported detachments, constantly surprised and attacked them
in their expeditions, and destroyed them with
as little mercy as they had shown to others.

These occurrences at length became so frequent, that the parties sent out by the French
more resembled small armies than detachments;
while it frequently happened that they could
only succeed in obtaining sufficient for their
own support, their unfortunate companions
being left without resources. An occasional
supply would sometimes arrive, sent from Madrid by King Joseph; but for ten that were
sent, not more than three reached their destination. No reliance, therefore, could be placed
upon their arrival. The numerous mountain-
passes through which they had to travel gave
the active and untiring guerilla bands every
advantage in their attacks upon the escort;
and although occasionally they were successful
in getting forward their charge, the contests in
every succeeding defile reduced their numbers;
until at length, the love of self-preservation su-
perseding every other consideration, they abandoned the waggons, and endeavoured by flight
to gain the army. But few even by this sacri-

fice contrived to escape the hostile Spaniards, and they were hunted and shot with the same savage pleasure as if they had been wild beasts.

Far different was the situation of the allies at that period, as, from their Alpine line, they looked down upon the host beneath. In conscious security, they could watch their movements and defy their attacks; while, with Lisbon in their rear, and the English fleet riding triumphantly in the Tagus, they were abundantly supplied with provisions. England, with her ample resources, was sending constantly her fleets of merchant-ships full of corn, ammunition, and in fact everything that could be desired for the maintenance and support of the army. In case of being driven from this their first position, they had another, and even a stronger, upon which they could fall back without confusion; while, supposing all should fail, this same fleet was prepared to receive them. The allies had nothing, therefore, to do but to await the retreat and probable destruction of their enemies; for it was certain that the French army could not remain long in its present position.

In confirmation of this, the following letters

from General Picton himself are here introduced :—

" MY DEAR SIR,

" I am much rejoiced at your victory over
the Secretary of State. *Entre nous,* the governor
is a weak man, wholly divested of anything like
firmness or independence of character. I find,
by my letters, that Dr. Sanderson is become one
of his most intimate friends !!

" Our relative situation, and those of the
enemy, is nearly what it was six weeks ago.
There has been a total suspension of all operations on both sides, and the two armies are
perfectly quiet in winter quarters. The accounts by deserters and prisoners state, with little disagreement, that the enemy suffer greatly
for want of provisions, forage, and supplies of
all kinds; and there is no doubt but the difficulty of procuring the primary indispensable
articles for the support of the army, is daily
increasing in an almost incalculable ratio. The
impression upon my mind at present is, that
the enemy will be under the necessity of falling
back upon their resources: for I have no idea
that it will be possible, during the winter

months and rainy season, to forward adequate
supplies from Salamanca, or any other depôts
in Spain, considering the length and imprac-
ticability of the roads. Lord Wellington has
certainly conducted the whole of this campaign
with great ability and prudence; and no one
can reasonably refuse him the character of a
great general.

"My dear Sir,

"Very faithfully yours,

"T. PICTON."

"Figarro, 26th Feb. 1811.

"MY DEAR SIR,

"We still remain quiet in winter quarters,
without any movement of consequence; the
enemy apparently suffering great hardships from
want of supplies, but continuing in the same
position, and carrying on their communications
with the frontiers of Spain with great difficulty,
and by means of numerous detachments.

"Nothing can exceed the misery of this part
of Portugal. Every article of human subsistence has long been consumed or destroyed.
The poor inhabitants are kept from perishing
by the contributions of the officers (British) of

the different divisions of the army. This division daily feeds above three hundred : but for
this resource, the greater part must have perished.   My dear Sir,

" Very faithfully yours,

" T. PICTON."

Lord Wellington had induced the French
general to attempt the conquest of Portugal in
order to destroy his army. Massena had not
discovered the plans of his opponent until too
late to retract from his fatal advance ; and he
found himself in one moment stopped, when
he was in full expectation of driving the English into the sea, and taking quiet possession of
Lisbon. He had now a choice of three ways
of attempting to extricate himself, but none of
these presented a very flattering prospect of
success ; one was, to force the lines of Torres
Vedras, and, by securing Lisbon, obtain for his
soldiers those supplies of which he stood so
greatly in need ; another, to fall back without
delay to the frontiers of Spain, until France
could send him some assistance by increasing
his force, and securing the passage of provisions for their maintenance ; the last was, to

make a flank movement, and, by passing the Tagus, form a junction with the army of Andalusia.

Posterity will doubtless give to Lord Wellington as much credit for his masterly plans, and the manner in which he made the French general unconsciously subservient to them, previously to taking up this position, as for any other acts of his life. Lord Wellington led on Massena with the constant shadow of victory; for it must be acknowledged that the British army was retreating. From Ciudad Rodrigo, from Almeida, from Busacos, it had successively retired, and " the Leopard was about to be driven into the sea." But at Torres Vedras the delusion was dispelled.

The plot was then ripe. Lord Wellington had lured his pursuer into the snare he had so long been preparing; at this spot his career of success was arrested; here he wasted his resources and his strength; here he discovered the error into which he had been betrayed, when, disappointed and discouraged by the formidable barrier before him, and ashamed to retreat, he remained in a state of mere inactivity. General Picton, even as early as the beginning of No-

vember, observed, " He is apparently waiting
for reinforcements, very badly off for provisions,
with his communication wholly cut off. His
situation is every day becoming more and more
critical, and his difficulty of procuring subsistence for his army must be daily increasing. If
a considerable army is not despatched in time
to his assistance, little less than a miracle can
save him from ruin." Thus, then, Lord Wellington, from as bad, or even a worse situation
than that of Sir John Moore, contrived to draw
success, to stop the tide of French conquests,
and, with an army which at first was laughed
at for its insignificance, to hold at defiance an
enemy flushed with conquest, and in numbers
almost double that of the allies. General Picton
gave a strong proof of his penetration, when,
in the early period of Lord Wellington's career,
before he had had an opportunity of evincing
the vast original resources of his mind, he observed,—" I think it was not possible to have
made choice of a person possessing more essential qualities for so important and difficult a
command."

A few movements in front kept our soldiers
on the alert. Massena made several demonstra-

tions to change the line of attack by uniting his
army to that of Regnier, and endeavouring to
force the right extremity of the British position
where it rested on the Tagus. The ground oc--
cupied by General Picton and his division was
of too important a nature to admit of its being
for a moment left unprotected, and therefore no
change took place in their position; but many
alterations were made in the situation of the
other corps; and Crawfurd with his light division
was more than once partially engaged with the
enemy, and upon one occasion, had it not been
for the opportune arrival of Lord Wellington,
it is more than probable that he would again
have involved the security of his division, if not
of the whole army.

The pursuits and occupations of the allies
cannot be better expressed than in the language
of the Marquis of Londonderry: "Neither the
time of our soldiers," observes the gallant Marquis, "nor that of their chief, was, however,
wasted in idleness. The former were busily
employed in the construction of new works
wherever their erection appeared at all desirable, and in giving additional solidity to those
already thrown up, till the lines became as per-

fect a specimen of a fortified position as it was
possible for nature and art to produce. The
latter was indefatigable in his exertions to bring
his army into a condition of general efficiency,
and his efforts were too judiciously applied not
to be crowned with success. The Portuguese being now thoroughly amalgamated with the British troops, learned from them all those lessons
which in after campaigns they turned to an
excellent account; and Beresford, to whom the
entire merit of their first training is due, was in
consequence removed from all farther responsibility in field operations. Every day brought
in its improvements among them; and the general was soon rewarded for all his trouble by
the conviction that he might rely upon them
almost as perfectly as upon his countrymen.
Nor was Lord Wellington inattentive to the
comforts and even luxuries of his followers.
Provisions were abundant; there was no want
of wine; and sports and amusements went on
as if we had been, not at the seat of war, but
in England. Officers of all ranks and every
department, from the commander-in-chief down
to the regimental subaltern, occasionally enjoyed the field sports of hunting, shooting, and

fishing: the men, too, had their pastimes when not employed on duty;—in a word, seldom had an army, occupying ground in the face of an enemy, enjoyed so many hours of relaxation, or contrived to unite so completely the pleasures of country life with the serious business of war. It is probably needless to add, that so great a show of security in their leader had the best possible effect upon the temper of the troops; or that the *morale* of the army was sustained, not more by a contemplation of things as they really were, than by a conviction that they must be going on prosperously, otherwise so much relaxation could not abound." -

Another writer, in relating the *amusements* of the officers and men at this period, after describing the pillage of a wine-store by some of Picton's division, and the consequent intoxication of the men, adds, " The first Sunday after the outrage already related, when the chaplain left his station, General Picton took his place, not to pray, but to give us a sermon. This was the first time he had addressed us. I felt anxious to examine the features of a man who had been so much the public talk on account of his reputed cruelty at Trinidad. I could

not deny that I felt a prejudice against him,
and his countenance did not do it away; for
it had a stern and gloomy expression, which,
added to a very dark complexion, made it no
way prepossessing: but when he opened his
mouth, and began to pour forth a torrent of
abuse on us for our conduct, and his dark eye
flashed with indignation, as he recapitulated
our errors,

' Hope withering fled, and Mercy sigh'd farewell."

*　　*　　*　　*　　*　　*

"But General Picton was not the character
which we by prejudice were led to think him.
Convinced of the baneful effects of allowing
his men to plunder, he set his face sternly
against it, but in other respects he was indul-
gent; and although no man could blame with
more severity when occasion required, he was
no niggard of his praise when it was deserved.
Nothing could surpass his calm intrepidity and
bravery in danger; and his presence in battle
had the effect of a talisman, so much had his
skill and valour gained upon the men under
his command."

CHAPTER XIX.

Retreat of the French Army.—General Picton's account of the advance of the Allied forces.—General Picton's accuracy proved by the statements of the Duke of Wellington, the Marquis of Londonderry, and Colonel Napier.—Indefatigable exertions of General Picton.—The " Fighting Division."—Depredations of the Enemy.—Discontent among Massena's Generals.

IT was not until the commencement of the year 1811 that the allied army was again called into active operations. Massena, despairing of sufficient reinforcements to enable him to advance, and having no certain means of communicating with Napoleon, by which he could represent to him the actual state of his army and the total exhaustion of all his resources, resolved upon that step which, had he taken some few months earlier, might have placed the allied army at this period in a strikingly different situation to that which it now held. He resolved to retreat; but it was now an act of necessity: his army was reduced, disheartened,

and disaffected, and he was obliged to fly before
the same enemy whom he had at the close of
the preceding year driven before him into the
lines of Torres Vedras. Disease had made sad
havoc amongst the French troops, and deser-
tions had been frequent; in short, every accumulated misery of a besieged city was endured
by this victorious and blockading army.

Massena was unwilling to betray his intention to the British general until he had got his
sick and baggage in advance of his march, and
he even showed some demonstrations of commencing active operations against the lines;
but it soon became apparent that the only preparations which the enemy had been making
were to deceive the allies, that they might
retreat as far as possible before their intentions
were made known. The correspondence of
General Picton, who was now again called
into action, and who had a fresh opportunity
of showing the activity of his disposition,
and that military genius which so strongly
marked his character, contains a description of
this retreat, and the part which his division
took in harassing the enemy. He wrote the
particulars contained in the following letter to

Colonel Pleydel; and the accuracy of his details cannot be more fully exemplified than by comparing them with the remarks of more modern and more elaborate writers.

> " Philadoze, fifty miles in advance of Coimbra,
> 24th March 1811 ; and Guarda, 29th.

" My dear Sir,

" It having been satisfactorily ascertained that the enemy was in general movement towards the rear on the 4th and 5th of March, the different divisions of this army were ordered to march on the 6th. The route of this division for five days was extremely laborious, running over excessively steep and rocky mountains, scarcely affording the trace of roads On the 11th, after a march of above twenty miles, we came up with the rear-guard of the enemy, strongly posted near the town of Pombal ; and the third division was ordered to make a movement to the left, to co-operate in a general attack upon the rear-guard : but the fourth division being delayed longer than was calculated, by the badness and narrowness of the roads, it was not carried into execution, and the enemy decamped during the night, leaving merely a few of their light troops to keep their fires up until morning.

"On the 12th the army moved in pursuit of the enemy at six o'clock, this division supporting the advance-guard. After a march of between five and six miles, we came up with them, strongly posted on a commanding ridge, with an extensive declivity in front, their right resting upon a woody mountain of difficult access, and their left secured by the village of Redinha and an impassable river. The third division was ordered to march to the right, through difficult woods, to attack the left of the enemy's position; whilst the fourth division, under the Honourable Major-general Cole, supported by the first, under Lieutenant-general Sir Brent Spencer, made the attack in front. After a well-supported though distant fire of about twenty minutes, the enemy gave way at all points, and retreated across the river by a bridge with which, unfortunately, we were not acquainted. I attempted to push the Honourable Major-general Colville's brigade over the river, to cut them off; but the attempt failed, as it proved too deep and rapid to be forded. The enemy retreated about three miles to a strong woody ridge, where they showed a disposition to make another stand ; but the third division being pushed along the mountains on their left, so as to threaten their rear and their communication with the main body of their army at Condeixa, they abandoned it the same evening, and took up a fresh position near the town of Condeixa, which is covered by an extremely difficult river.

"On the 13th the third division made a forced march over a tract of difficult rocky mountains, to make a demonstration in the rear of the enemy's left flank ; which had the desired effect, as they immediately abandoned the position with considerable precipitation, and fell back several miles. The division crossed the river at an extremely difficult pass the same evening, and took up a position within a mile of the enemy's rear-posts.

"On the following morning (the 14th) the light division was engaged with the enemy's rear-guard as early as half-past five, and it was a continual skirmish without any intermission until near four o'clock in the evening. The light troops of the third division harassed the

enemy's left during the whole of the day; and
the body of the division made such successive
demonstrations in their rear, as to deter them
from attempting anything like a serious stand
in any of the positions they took up during
the course of the day. The fog was so very
thick on the morning of the 15th, that we did
not commence our march until nine o'clock,
and it was nearly three o'clock in the evening
before we came in contact with their rear;
which was immediately attacked on the right
by the light division under Major-general Sir
William Erskine, supported by the sixth division, and on the centre and left by the third
division, supported by the first division under
Lieutenant-general Sir Brent Spencer. The
ground was particularly favourable to the enemy; being abrupt woody heights, connected by
narrow gorges, which were strongly occupied
by infantry and artillery. The division in consequence experienced an obstinate resistance;
but in the end we successively drove them from
all the points they occupied, but were prevented from taking advantage of their disorder by
the approach of night.

" The following day (the 16th) was employ-

ed in reconnoitring the position where the
enemy had concentrated the whole of his force,
about fifty thousand, upon a strong woody
ridge, covered by a rapid rocky river, nowhere
fordable, in his front. He decamped early on
the following night, and by a forced march
reached the river Alva, which he passed at
different practicable fords on the 17th and
18th in the morning. We were under the
necessity of relaxing in our pursuit through
a total deficiency of provisions, the convoys of
which could not keep pace with the rapidity
of our movements, and the country through
which we advanced affording no one article
of human subsistence, the enemy having destroyed everything with fire and sword. We,
however, followed the route of the enemy
by easy marches until the 29th, when, by a
combination of movements, we succeeded in
dislodging him from the position he had taken
up upon the heights of Guarda, the strongest
and most defensible ground I ever recollect to
have seen in any country. The most important
part of this day's business fell to the share of the
third division; and we fully succeeded in turning the left of the enemy's position, and taking

a strong position in his rear, within a quarter
of a milé of his head-quarters ; which so alarmed him, that he immediately withdrew the
corps which were opposed to the other divisions,
and commenced his retreat with great marks of
precipitation.

" Massena himself, with full twenty thousand men, was on the heights and in the city
of Guarda when I made my appearance at nine
o'clock in the morning, with three British and
two Portuguese regiments. This famous general certainly showed little determination or
talent on the occasion; with his great superiority
of force, he should immediately have attacked
me, notwithstanding the excellence of my position, which, independent of its strength, had
a most commanding appearance; but he allowed me to remain within four hundred yards of
his main body, threatening his rear, for above
two hours before the other columns made their
appearance; but of course their movements
alarming him, at the same time decided him
not to hazard an attack, the failure of which
would probably have brought on the total discomfiture of his army. This was wholly a
day of manœuvring, and did not cost us a sin-

gle man. If the light division and cavalry had been able to cross the country, it would probably have-been a decisive day; but the difficulty of the country and the badness of the roads rendered it impracticable. We have, however, driven them out of Portugal for the present; and their army is so perfectly disorganized in respect to every kind of military equipment, that it will require considerable time to reform it for active service. With about thirty-five thousand men we have been pursuing an army of sixty thousand, and of course Lord Wellington has been extremely cautious not to undertake anything which might eventually lead to a general action.

" The enemy's rear-guard, during the whole course of the retreat, was commanded by Marshal Ney in person; and all his movements afforded a perfect lesson in that kind of warfare. Moving at all times upon his flank, I had an opportunity of seeing everything he did; and I must be dull in the extreme if I have not derived some practically useful knowledge from such an example. Nothing can exceed the devastation and cruelties committed by the enemy during the whole course of his retreat;

setting fire to all the villages and murdering
all the peasantry for leagues on each flank of his
columns. Their atrocities have been such and
so numerous, that the name of a Frenchman
must be execrated here for ages.

"I shall write to the general by this occasion. My friend General Este writes to me,
that he continues to enjoy his usual health
and spirits, and had got so far over the winter, as far as February, without any indisposition. I hope you have escaped equally well ;
my health has been excellent. I fear you
will have great difficulty in deciphering my
miserable scrawl, which is rendered more so by
the badness of the paper.

"With my best wishes,

" My dear Sir,

" Very faithfully yours,

" THOMAS PICTON."

We are unwilling to forego this opportunity of showing the extraordinary precision
and accuracy with which General Picton remembered and described the dates, operations,
and successes of the allied armies ; a comparison with those writers who have had every

facility for obtaining correct information, and whose pages have had the advantage of criticism and correction, will be a gratifying proof that implicit reliance may be placed upon the statements of General Picton, notwithstanding the unfavourable circumstances under which they may have been written.

General Picton's account of the advance of the allied army is thus confirmed by the commander of the forces, who, in his despatch dated Villa Seca, March 14th, 1811, observes:—

"I could not collect a sufficient body of troops to commence any operations upon the enemy till the 11th. On that day, the first, third, fourth, fifth, and sixth, and the light divisions of infantry, and General Pack's brigade, and all the British cavalry, joined upon the ground immediately in front of the enemy, who had commenced their retreat from their position during the night. They were followed by the light division, the Hussars and Royals, and Brigadier-general Pack's brigade, under the command of Major-general Slade, and made an attempt to hold the ancient castle of Pombal, from which they were driven; but the sixth corps, and General Montbrun's

cavalry, which formed the rear-guard, support
ed by the eighth corps, held the ground on the
other side of the town; the troops not having
arrived in time to complete the dispositions to
attack them before it was dark.

*   *   , *   *   *   *

"The enemy retired in the night."

While the Marquis of Londonderry adds:
" On the 11th, dispositions were made for bringing the enemy to action, by the first, third, fourth,
fifth, sixth, and light divisions, assembled for
the purpose : but Massena, instead of waiting
to be assailed, broke up during the night."

Colonel Napier, in reference to this demonstration of attack, mentions it as having taken
place on the 10th; but as the three statements here given agree in representing it to
have happened on the 11th, it is only reasonable to suppose that he is in this instance
mistaken.

General Picton's statement relative to the
attack of the enemy's position near the village
of Redinha is borne out as follows :

Lord Wellington, in his despatch, says, in
allusion to this affair :—

"On the 12th, the sixth corps, with General

Montbrun's cavalry, took up a strong position
at the end of a defile between Redinha and
Pombal, with their right in a wood upon the
Soure river, and their left extending towards
the high ground above the river of Redinha:
this town was in their rear. I attacked them
in this position on the 12th, with the third
and fourth light divisions of infantry, and Brigadier-general Pack's brigade and the cavalry; the other troops being in reserve. The
post in the wood upon their right was first
forced by Sir William Erskine with the light
division; we were then able to form the troops
in the plain beyond the defile; and the third
division, under Major-general Picton, was formed in two lines in the skirts of the wood upon
the right; the fourth division, under Major-
general Cole, in two lines in the centre, having General Pack's brigade supporting their
right, and communicating with the third division and the light division in two lines on
their left. These troops were supported in
the rear by the British cavalry; and the first,
fifth, and sixth divisions were in reserve. The
troops were formed with great accuracy and
celerity.

*   *   *   *   *   *

"There was but one narrow bridge, and a ford close to it, over the Redinha river, over which our light troops passed with the enemy; but as the enemy commanded these passages with cannon, some time elapsed before we could pass over a sufficient body of troops to make a fresh disposition to attack the heights. on which they had again taken post. The third division crossed, however, and manœuvred again upon the enemy's left flank; while the light infantry and cavalry, supported by the light division, drove them upon their main body at Condeixa. The light infantry of Major-general Picton's division under Lieutenant-colonel Williams, and Fourth Caçadores under Colonel de Regoa, were principally concerned in this operation."

The movements connected with the enemy's retreat, as detailed by General Picton, are related in the same way by the Marquis of Londonderry. "On the 12th," observes his lordship, "a strong rear-guard was seen posted at the end of a defile in front of the village (Redinha). It was immediately attacked by three divisions of infantry, by General Pack's

Portuguese brigade and the cavalry, and, after an obstinate resistance, was driven through the defile to the plain beyond. It next retreated to some high and broken ground, where it again showed a front; but from this position it was also compelled to retire with some loss; and finally it withdrew to Condeixa, where the main body had established itself."

Colonel Napier's description is too detailed for entire extract: after alluding to the light division, then under Sir Wm. Erskine, "being formed in such a manner that it out-flanked the French right," he observes, " Picton seized the wooded heights protecting the French left; thus Ney's position was left bare."

In reference to the manœuvres of the 13th, the same uniformity of statement will be observed in the correspondence of General Picton; and from this confirmation of the accuracy of his details, which it is now our object to prove by comparison, we may in future claim for him, when relating facts peculiarly within his own knowledge, the praise of strict veracity, which cannot be shaken by any contemporary narrator.

Lord Wellington, in his despatch, observes:

" We found the whole army yesterday, with the exception of the second corps, which was still at Espinhel, in a very strong position at Con‑deixa.

*　　*　　*　　*　　*　　*

" I therefore marched the third division, under Major-general Picton, through the mountains upon the enemy's left, towards the only road open for their reception; which had the immediate effect of dislodging them from the strong position of Condeixa."

Colonel Napier, in allusion to the position held by the French at Condeixa, observes, in confirmation of General Picton's remark on that head :

. " For some time all appeared quiet in the French lines. Massena, in repairing to Fonte Coberta, had left Ney orders, it is said, to set fire to Condeixa, at a certain hour, when all the divisions were simultaneously to concentrate at Casal Nova, in a second position, perpendicular to the first, and covering the road to Puente Murcella. Towards three o'clock, however, Picton was descried winding round the bluff end of a mountain, about eight miles distant; and as he was already beyond the French left, instant confusion pervaded their camp; a thick smoke arose from Condeixa; the columns were seen hurrying towards Casal Nova, and the British immediately pushed forward."

The Marquis in his Narrative, referring to the same affair, says: " The third division, under General Picton, made a long and tedious *détour* to the right; but it succeeded in throwing itself upon the left of the enemy's line, which instantly broke into column of march and fell back."

Alluding to the attack by the light division, described in General Picton's letter, Colonel Napier remarks: " The enemy's ground was so extensive, and his skirmishers so thick and so easily supported, that in a little time the division was necessarily stretched out in one thin thread, and closely engaged in every part, without any reserve; nor could it even thus present an equal front, until Picton sent the riflemen of the Sixtieth to prolong the line. Nevertheless, the fight was vigorously maintained amidst the numerous stone enclosures on the mountain side; some advantages were even gained, and the right of the enemy was partially turned; yet the main position could not be shaken, until

Picton near, and Cole further off, had turned it by the left."

The accuracy of General Picton's description of the attack on the rear of the enemy on the 15th, is proved by Lord Wellington, in his despatch dated Louzao, March 16th, 1811, who observes: " We found the enemy's whole army yesterday in a very strong position on the Ceira, having one corps as an advanced guard in front of Foz de Aronce, on this side the river. I immediately made arrangements to drive in the advanced guard," &c.

*   *   *   *   *   *

" The light division, under Major-general Sir William Erskine, was ordered to possess some heights immediately above Foz de Aronce, while Major-general Picton's division was moved along the great road to attack the left of the enemy's position and of the village. The sixth division, under Major-general Campbell, and the Hussars and Sixteenth light dragoons, supported the light division ; and the first division and the Fourteenth and Royal Dragoons, the third."

In the " Annals of the Peninsular Campaigns," it is stated that—" On the following morning (the 15th) a thick fog retarded the march of the allies for several hours. About nine the day cleared up ; and the troops, renewing the pursuit, passed through the smoking ruins of Miranda de Corvo. The French army were found in a strong position on the Ceira, a tributary of the Mondego, with one corps at Foz de Aronce, on the left of the river. Lord Wellington immediately directed movements on the flanks of this corps, and attacked it briskly in front. By these measures it was driven rapidly back on the bridge in great confusion."

It is extraordinary how General Picton could obtain such accurate details of the proceedings of the other divisions, while he was himself, during nearly the whole of this retreat, on the extreme left of the allied army. Yet, allowing for the various modes of expression, General Picton's statements are corroborated by all those writers who have subsequently compiled their narratives of the war. It must be remembered that the letter from which these passages have been extracted was written actually during the advance of the allies in pursuit of the retreating French ; while, from

the position of Picton, he had not even the
advantage of communicating with the other
officers of division.

Those who had an opportunity of observing
the conduct of General Picton at this period,
speak of him in terms which, if inserted here,
would be considered merely the language of
panegyric. One who served with him in almost every field, declares that no pen could do
justice to the merits and indefatigable exertions of Sir Thomas Picton during this pursuit
of the French army. Long before the break
of day he was awake, and preparing his division for an advance so soon as there was
sufficient light to direct their footsteps. Constantly at their head, encouraging where they
faltered, and directing them where they were
at a loss, he might be seen by every man in his
division. The waverer was shamed into fresh
efforts, while the courageous but exhausted
soldier was cheered and encouraged by the example of his leader. The mountain steeps and
unknown and broken paths were traversed with
extraordinary rapidity, himself pointing the way
and leading on his men until he suddenly surprised the enemy by emerging from the mist at

those points where of all. others they least expected an attack.

. These unexpected and daring movements
prevented many a bloody struggle, by daunting
the enemy and compelling him to retreat in
order to save his flank from being turned. The
merit of planning these evolutions is doubtless
in many instances to be attributed to the distinguished chief of the British army, but the
merit of their execution is due alone to Picton.
After receiving his orders for the general line
of operations, the rest was left to his judgment
and his skill: all the active duty consequently
devolved upon him; and even at this period
Lord Wellington showed the estimation in
which he held him, by keeping his division
constantly in the advance, when, by traversing, the most dangerous and difficult paths, or
by outflanking the position of the enemy,
many an easy conquest was gained where it
might have been anticipated that the enemy
would make a determined stand.

This division had already obtained for
itself a name which it bore throughout the
war, and the "fighting division" soon became the most conspicuous in the whole army.

for its daring enterprise and indefatigable activity. It was not, however, its numbers that made it formidable to the enemy or distinguished in the allied army; it was the spirit of its soldiers and the heroic example of its leader. There were many older officers in the army at this period, both as to years and experience; for it must not be forgotten that General Picton had never seen a field of battle before he took the command of the third division of the army in the Peninsula: his early career had therefore been unmarked by any train of services likely to give him military knowledge or reputation. It has already been shown that many years of his life had been passed in all the inactivity of garrison duties in time of peace, many more in the retirement of private life, and a considerable period in the civil capacity of Governor of Trinidad: it will therefore be a natural inquiry how General Picton had been enabled to qualify himself for the important duties which he had now to perform. He had been in the field but one year at the period of this retreat; yet he distinguished himself above those whose whole lives had been passed in the camp, who had gone through every gradation in the school of war, but who now only lived and acted as well-drilled soldiers,—obedient and brave. Not so Picton: his whole soul was absorbed in the manœuvres of the two armies; he was born a soldier, and he took with him into the field a genius which enabled him soon to become a master of his profession. In one year he established for himself a name which was the admiration and envy of many a veteran. Lord Wellington was not slow in discovering his abilities, and he thus early placed that reliance on his judgment which Picton afterwards justified upon a more conspicuous occasion.

Pursuing a few steps further the comparative statements which have been already adduced in proof of the correctness of General Picton's account, the following extract from Lord Wellington's despatch, dated Oliveira de l'Hopital, March 21st, 1811, is here inserted.

"The enemy withdrew his rear-guard from that river (the Ceira) in the course of the 16th; and we crossed it on the 17th, and had our posts on the Sierra de Murcella, the enemy's army being in a strong position on the right of the Alva. They moved a part of their army on that night, but still maintained their position on the Alva, of which river they destroyed the bridges. We turned their left by the Sierra de Santa Quiteria with the third, first, and fifth divisions on the 18th, while the light division and the sixth manœuvred in their front from the Sierra de Murcella. These movements induced the enemy to bring to the Sierra de Morta the troops which had marched the preceding night, at the same time that they retired their corps from the Alva."

General Picton observes, " We were under the necessity of relaxing in our pursuit through a total deficiency of provisions, the convoys of which could not keep pace with the rapidity of our movements ;" a necessity which gave to the enemy an advantage which they could not otherwise have hoped for. They destroyed everything in their path, burning the villages, and apparently striving to revenge themselves upon the defenceless inhabitants for their own reverses.

Lord Londonderry remarks : " It seemed as if these men had resolved to make a desert of the country which they had failed to conquer; and that the war, which they professed at first to wage only with the English and their armed partisans, had been turned against its peaceable inhabitants."*

Whilst the allied army was halting for supplies, the enemy were continuing their retreat with the utmost expedition, being followed in their rear by the British cavalry and light infantry. Massena's object was evidently to endeavour to make an effectual stand against the advance of the allies, by concentrating his army upon the heights, and occupying the passes in front of Guarda. But much discontent existed at this time amongst Massena's generals: the impetuous Ney almost refused to co-operate

* The following additional particulars of the cruel and devastating principle upon which this retreat was conducted are derived from the letter of a gentleman who accompanied the British army in its pursuit of the French, and who was consequently a spectator of what he relates.

" It is impossible to describe the scenes of horror of which I have been an eye-witness, and which will for ever brand the name of Massena with execration. It is hard for anybody to believe that human nature could be guilty of such enormous and wanton wickedness. The city of Leyria had been eleven days on fire when I was there, and was burning still. Everything that could be taken away was removed, and the rest destroyed. The images in the churches were in pieces; the graves were actually opened for the sake of plunder. The nuns and friars, at all the towns where we came, had fled to the mountains; their convents were with him; while Junot, Drouet, and Regnier were equally opposed in opinion.

Retreat is ever a trying moment for a commander-in-chief; the movement is disliked by all, and opinions are hardly ever wanting to prove that it was produced by bad management, and that at any one stage it might have been stopped. Still, all the odium is made to fall upon the chief, and every subordinate without restraint boldly asserts that he would, and his superior might, have averted the evil; it is universally allowed that he alone is to be answerable for every casualty or mismanagement attending the movements. Thus Massena

destroyed, and we found none but a few Portuguese perishing with hunger and ill-treatment. At every place where we halted, if we saw anything like a house with a door standing, we made it our head-quarters, and took possession of any table or chair that might have escaped the general devastation, as the mansions had no tenants to dispute our invasion. All was dreadful silence and desolation. The floors of almost every house had been pulled up wherever we passed, particularly at Leyria, where there were about twelve miserable wretches who had been unable to move from wounds and famine, some of whom expired before us. This city, four years since, contained thirty thousand inhabitants. Libraries were burned and scattered; and it seemed to be the intention of the enemy to leave a dreadful memorial of their fury, which never should be effaced from the recollection of the country."

‚was accused by his whole staff of want of skill, while each in his turn accused the others of giving him bad advice; and, in consequence, the retreating army more resembled a number of independent bands, than the organized force of a great, and hitherto conquering, nation.

The master-hand of Napoleon was never more wanted than at this moment; and had he acted upon this occasion with any of that foresight and decision which had so long marked his character, by hastening with a few fresh troops to put himself at the head of this disorganized army, he would at once have smothered the flame of discord, silenced the voice of disobedience, and perhaps have prevented, or at least delayed, his ruin. But he was too much engaged in dreams of conquest in the North, to turn for a moment to the affairs of the Peninsula. Wrapped up in his gigantic project against Russia, what were the affairs of the Peninsula to him? what the success of Lord Wellington and his five-and-thirty thousand British? Let them advance; he could crush them in Spain, and there they would have no retreat! With such arguments as these he let the moment pass; and the progress of the allies towards the very heart of France was never arrested for any time, from the period when they commenced their advance from **the** lines of Torres Vedras.

END OF THE FIRST VOLUME.

LONDON :
PRINTED BY SAMUEL BENTLEY,
Dorset Street, Fleet Street.

MEMOIRS

OF

LIEUTENANT-GENERAL

SIR THOMAS PICTON,

G.C.B. &c.

INCLUDING HIS CORRESPONDENCE,

FROM ORIGINALS IN POSSESSION OF HIS FAMILY, &c.

BY H. B. ROBINSON.

SECOND EDITION REVISED, WITH ADDITIONS.

IN TWO VOLUMES

VOL. II.

LONDON:

RICHARD BENTLEY, NEW BURLINGTON STREET,

Publisher in Ordinary to His Majesty.

1836.

CONTENTS

THE SECOND VOLUME.

CHAPTER I.

CHAPTER II.

CHAPTER III.

CHAPTER IV.

CHAPTER V.

CHAPTER VI.

CHAPTER VII.

CHAPTER VIII.

CHAPTER IX.

CHAPTER X.

CHAPTER XI.

CHAPTER XII.

CHAPTER XIII.

CHAPTER XIV.

CHAPTER XV.

CONCLUSION.

APPENDIX.

APPENDIX.

THE LIFE

OF

LIEUTENANT-GENERAL

SIR THOMAS PICTON,

G.C.B.

CHAPTER I.

The route of the enemy followed.—Colonel Napier's History and General Picton's Letter.—Affair of Sabugal.—
Picton's projected attack.—Retreat of the French army.
—Battle of Fuentes de Onoro.—General Picton's letter
relative to this engagement.—Unsuccessful attempt to
relieve Almeida.—Battle of Albuera.—Siege of Badajoz.

THE allied army followed the route of the
enemy by easy marches until the 29th; General Picton having still to lead his troops over
almost inaccessible paths amidst the mountains.
The striking similarity of statements between
Colonel Napier's history and General Picton's
letter is here well worthy of remark. The

historian observes : — " Early on the 29th,
the third, sixth, and light divisions, and two
regiments of light cavalry, disposed in five
columns of attack on a half-circle round the
foot of the Guarda mountain, ascended by as
many paths, all leading upon the town of
Guarda, and outflanking both the right and
left of the enemy. They were supported on
one wing by the militia, on the other by the
fifth division, and in the centre by the first
and seventh divisions. A battle was expected, but the absence of Ney* was at once felt
by both armies : the appearance of the allied
columns for the first time threw the French
into the greatest confusion ; and, without firing a shot, this great and nearly impregnable
position was abandoned."

The colonel then adds, that " had the pursuit been as vigorous as the attack, it is not

---

* According to Colonel Napier's history, Massena had
deprived Ney of the command of the sixth corps, and given
it to Loison. Whether General Picton was aware of this
is uncertain ; but as he pays a high compliment to Ney
for the manner in which he conducted the retreat, it may
be necessary to remark that the change was only made
about one day previous to the date of General Picton's
letter ; consequently it is only reasonable to suppose that it
was yet unknown in the allied army.

easy to see how the second corps could have rejoined Massena. Regnier, however, quitted Belmonte in the night, and recovered his communication with a loss of only three hundred prisoners, although the horse artillery and cavalry had been launched against him at daylight on the 30th; and much more could have been done if General Slade had pressed his cavalry forward with the celerity and vigour the occasion required."

A reference to the passage in General Picton's letter relating to this movement will evince the correspondence of facts; but it should be particularly remarked, that the date of General Picton's letter is the very same as that upon which this operation took place, and it must actually have been written while the tramp of the retreating foe was almost sounding in his ears. Colonel Napier's observation that the pursuit of the enemy was not so vigorous as the attack, is certainly not borne out by General Picton's statement, wherein he says:

" Massena himself, with full twenty thousand men, was on the heights and in the city of Guarda when I made my appearance at nine

o'clock in the morning with three British and
two Portuguese regiments." This would imply
that the advance, at least, of the third division
was sufficiently bold and rapid to produce any
advantages which pursuit could obtain ; but
whether it was from any delay in bringing forward the other divisions, or that the enemy's
reserve was in too great force for the allies to
hazard any attack, a judgment may be formed
by the succeeding passage of General Picton's
letter :

" This famous general (Massena)," he continues, " certainly showed little determination
or talent on the occasion. With his great superiority of force, he should immediately have
attacked me, notwithstanding the excellence of
my position, which, independent of its strength,
had a most commanding appearance ; but he
allowed me to remain within four hundred
yards of his main body, threatening his rear,
for above two hours before the other columns
made their appearance. But, of course, their
movements alarming him, at the same time
decided him not to hazard an attack, the
failure of which would probably have brought
on the total discomfiture of his army."

From this it is quite evident, that whatever degree of censure may be attributed to the allies for not following up the pursuit with necessary vigour, still General Picton and his division are exempt; for it is shown that he had to wait two hours until the other columns made their appearance.* General Picton at the same time agrees with Colonel Napier, that much more might have been done had the cavalry been pressed on ; but Picton, it will be perceived, attributes the neglect of this important movement to the difficulties of the country and the badness of the roads, which, in his opinion, rendered it impracticable. Ap-

* As these columns came up, the different staff officers were making constant use of their glasses, in endeavours to discover the movements of the enemy. One of these, whilst looking at an unfinished fort on the left of the position, remarked to Sir Edward Pakenham, who was near, " We shall have some sharp work there; that place is full of men." The gallant Sir Edward immediately fixed his glass on the fort, and, after observing for a short time, said, " Full of men ! —yes, it is full of men ; but, by G—d, they 've all red jackets!". A further reconnoissance was quickly made, when it was soon discovered that this was Picton's division, which had thus early got possession of the fort, after driving the enemy out with such precipitation that they actually left their kettles on the fires, containing their meat, which thus became a most acceptable prize to Picton's soldiers.

parently unwilling to quit Portugal entirely,
Massena lost no opportunity of arresting the
progress of the allies ; and on the 3rd of April
he attempted to make another stand on the
Coa, which brought on the affair of Sabugal.
Colonel Beckwith's brigade of the light division,
four companies of the Ninety-fifth, with two
squadrons of cavalry, and three companies of
Colonel Elder's Caçadores, supported by the
Forty-third regiment, for a long time bore the
whole brunt of the fight. ; This was occasioned
by the attack being made somewhat prematurely. Colonel Napier, in speaking of this
affair, observes :

" The troops could not gain their respective
posts of attack with that simultaneous regularity which is so essential to success ; and in the
light division no measures were taken by Sir
William Erskine to put the columns in a right
direction ; the brigades were not even held
together : he carried off the cavalry without
even communicating with Colonel Beckwith ;
and this officer, who commanded the first brigade, being without instructions, halted at a ford
in expectation of further orders. While thus
waiting, a staff officer rode up, and somewhat

hastily asked, why he did not attack ? The
thing appeared rash, but, with an enemy in his
front, he could make no reply ; wherefore, passing the river, which was deep and rapid, he
mounted a very steep wooded hill on the
other side."

The rain and mist for a time concealed
their approach ; but, as they drew nearer, they
found that they were close to the left of the
enemy's main body, and opposed to a large
column in front. None of the other divisions
had yet reached their destination, and this
small force was consequently in a very perilous
situation. A most severe struggle ensued : attacked on all sides, and occasionally compelled
to give way to the overwhelming pressure of
the column to which they were opposed, still
they recovered their ground the next moment
at the point of the bayonet. Three successive
charges were made by the Forty-third regiment
with a resolution and courage which could not
be resisted ; thrice they beat back the solid
masses of the French, and repulsed the attacks
of their cavalry : but all would have been in
vain ; the whole force of the enemy had been
called up, and were about to close in upon this

heroic little band, when firing was heard on their left. This was from the leading brigade of the " fighting division," under Major-general Colville.

An individual who belonged to one of the regiments forming this brigade, alluding to its progress to the point of attack, observes, " As we advanced up the hill we formed line. General Picton rode up in front of us, with his stick over his shoulder,* exposed to the heavy fire of the enemy, as composed as if he had been in perfect safety. ' Steady ! my lads, steady !' said he ; ' don't throw away your fire until I give you the word of command.' " And not a shot was fired until within a few yards of the enemy's right ; but then a volley was poured in close and true. A cheer at the same moment was caught up by Beckwith's almost

* General Picton was in the constant habit of riding with a stick in his hand, and even in the heat of battle he sometimes retained it. When the firing commenced, he might be observed tapping the mane of his horse, at measured intervals, in proportion to its rapidity ; as it became quicker, and the fight grew warmer, this movement of the stick would be increased both in velocity and force, until at length the horse would become restive. But this seldom drew Picton's attention off, as his firm seat saved him from all apprehension of a fall.

exhausted soldiers, and the attack was renewed with fresh energy. The head of Major-general Dunlop's column was now seen crossing the bridge of the Coa, and ascending the heights on the enemy's right flank, while the cavalry appeared on the high ground in the rear of their left. These movements compelled Regnier to desist from his attack upon the apparently devoted band against which he was about to lead his reserves, and Colonel Beckwith and his brigade were rescued from the perilous situation in which they had been thus rashly placed.

It is, however, only justice to the memory of this brave officer and the soldiers under his command to conclude our account of this affair with the observations contained in Lord Wellington's despatch. " Although," says his lordship, " the operations of this day were, by unavoidable accidents, not performed in the manner in which I intended they should be, I consider the action that was fought by the light division, by Colonel Beckwith's brigade principally, with the whole of the second corps, to be one of the most glorious that British troops were ever engaged in."

The allies bivouacked on the field of battle, and consequently the victory, although dearly bought, was theirs.

General Picton was not, however, contented with merely driving the enemy, from the field; upon reconnoitring their position, he perceived what he considered to be a most favourable opportunity for attacking a hill in his front. A considerable force occupied this post with some artillery; but General Picton felt confident that he could drive back the French and seize their guns. The other divisions had already halted; but Picton was so convinced of the advantages to be gained by securing this post, that he was on the point of leading his men forward upon his own responsibility, observing to an aid-de-camp, "We must drive the enemy from that hill, or we shall have done no good." But at this moment an aid-de-camp came up from the commander of the forces, directing him to halt his division for the night. General Picton was always anxious to fulfil his instructions, although he sometimes ventured to give them a rather free interpretation; consequently, with much disappointment, he immediately halted his division. The advantages of his projected attack were, however, apparent. on the following morning ; for the enemy, upon the advance of the allies, hurried off, and with some difficulty were enabled to save nine guns, which were attached to this corps, and which, had the attack been briskly made on the previous evening, would in all probability have been captured.

The retreat was continued ; and on the 5th of April the whole of Portugal, excepting Almeida, was freed from French troops at the point of the bayonet. This invasion was calculated to have cost Massena above thirty thousand of his best soldiers.

The following letter from General Picton to Mr. Marryat, written about this period, will be read with interest :

"" Amedillia, Spain, 18th April.

"My DEAR SIR,

" I have had the pleasure of receiving your letter of the 12th of March, and one by Mr. ——, whom I took the earliest opportunity of recommending to the particular attention of Mr. Kennedy, the commissary-general, who, I am sure, will give him every opportunity of

becoming useful to the public, and eventually
to himself. This letter is written, as you will
not fail to observe, from Spain. We have effectually driven the French out of Portugal,
with the single exception of Almeida, (where
they have a small garrison,) which we have invested, but cannot besiege, for want of battering cannon; but as it is entirely cut off from
any possible communication with the French
army in Spain, it must submit in the course of
a few weeks.

" Whilst we have been employed in pursuing Massena, the rascally Spaniards took an
opportunity of treacherously giving the enemy
possession of Badajoz, which obliged Lord
Wellington, in the midst of his movements
after Massena, to detach Sir W. C. Beresford,
and a principal division of the army, consisting of sixteen British regiments, and nearly
as many Portuguese battalions, to oppose Marshal Mortier, who is now shut up in Badajoz
with about five thousand. If he succeeds in
compelling him to surrender, as we confidently
hope he will, the business of Portugal will be
completely settled for some time; but from
all I have seen of the Spaniards, I have little,

indeed no hopes of their ever being able to do anything.

" I find Maitland goes out to Sicily; he will be an honour to his country wherever he is employed.

" If anything can be done to prevent my being engaged with Mr. M'Donald's affairs, pray endeavour to effect it. I would willingly make great sacrifices to get rid of this last West Indian concern, which hangs so heavily about my neck.

" Nothing can be worse than the existing government of this country, and unless the Princess Regent of Portugal determines to get rid of all the rascally factions, by appointing Lord Wellington Vice-Regent, with full powers to administer the government, everything will shortly be as bad as ever here. The Portuguese army, for want of being properly recruited, is rapidly falling off every day. They scarcely bring twenty thousand bayonets into the field now, and in the course of another year they will not bring fifteen thousand, unless some more effectual mode of executing the existing laws be had recourse to. Two regiments attached to my division, the establishment of which is two thousand five hundred men, do not bring one thousand two hundred into the field, and this is pretty generally the proportion throughout the army. The men are well disposed, good subjects, and I have found them, on all occasions, show an excellent spirit, and no want of courage in the face of the enemy.

       " Your very faithful,

           " Humble servant,

              " T. Picton."

To reduce Almeida was the next important measure. The opportunity was favourable, and the army was in consequence placed in cantonment around this fortress, so as to effect its total investment. Having thus disposed of the allied army, Lord Wellington, leaving the command to General Sir. Brent Spencer, the senior officer, next proceeded to inspect the Army of the South, which still kept the field, with Marshal Beresford at its head. Massena had not, however, given up all hope of succouring Almeida: the allies were much pressed for provisions, but the fortress was quite destitute; and Massena knew, that unless he could succeed in throwing in some supplies, General Brennier (who was in

command) would be compelled to surrender.
Urging forward his reinforcements, the French
general resolved to attempt to raise the siege;
and on the 2nd of May he crossed the Agueda
near Ciudad Rodrigo, and marched upon Almeida, with the hope of supplying the garrison
with provisions. Lord Wellington returned to
the army on the 28th of April, just in time to
meet the plans of Massena, who, on the 3rd of
May, put his whole force in motion, with the
apparent intention of risking a battle for the
defence of the fortress.

The battle of Fuentes de Onoro ensued. The
third division upon this memorable occasion
occupied, in conjunction with the first, a position in the rear of the village of Fuentes de
Onoro, the light troops being in the houses and
defensible posts in front. Towards evening a
most furious attack was made upon this part
of the position by the whole of the sixth and
part of the ninth corps of the enemy. A heavy
cannonade was opened upon the village, which,
being partly situated in a ravine, was necessarily much exposed. The enemy's light troops
attacked the third and first divisions of the
allied army with great bravery and persever-

ance. The cannonade from the neighbouring heights, together with the numbers of the enemy, made them for a moment waver; but at this critical juncture a gallant charge made by the Seventy-first regiment, with Lieutenant-colonel Cadogan at their head, determined at once the question of occupation for the night; the Twenty-fourth and Seventy-ninth regiments being at the same time ordered to capture and maintain possession of the village.* The approach of evening put an end to the conflict; but with the morning it was expected that it would be renewed: Massena had, however, found greater difficulty than he had anticipated in forcing this post; and when the British line, with the first dawn of day, got under arms, no appearance of attack was perceptible. Still it was evident, as the day advanced, that preparations were being made for a more com-

* The spirited conduct of Lieutenant-colonel Williams of the Sixtieth, who commanded the light troops of Picton's division upon this occasion, and who in the most gallant manner defended the village against the repeated attacks of the enemy, called forth the warmest eulogiums from General Picton and the whole army. He was badly wounded during the action; but it was not until after this event that the light troops were arrested in their successful opposition.

bined and general movement: additional troops, especially cavalry, were seen coming in from all parts; staff-officers were galloping about in all directions reconnoitring the British position. The 4th, however, passed without a shot being fired. Lord Wellington and his whole army had not a doubt but that the attack would be made on the ensuing day; neither were they disappointed, as will be seen by the following letter from General Picton to his uncle, General W. Picton.

" Nava d'Aver, May 12th, 1811.

" MY DEAR UNCLE,

" I received the letter with which you favoured me when near Pombal, and take the first opportunity to acknowledge it. I know there is no subject so interesting to you as our movements; and while so near the enemy, I can think of no other to write upon. You of course know by this time that we have at length succeeded in driving Massena quite out of Portugal. Lord Wellington's plans throughout the pursuit appear to have been to avoid as much as possible a general engagement; for, although retreating, the enemy is still too strong for us to meet him on open ground. He is, in fact, more frightened than hurt, and more alarmed by what might have happened if he had stayed any longer in Portugal than by any real injury. In consequence, our movements have all been to keep up this alarm, by giving him no time for reflection, and, by constantly outflanking his position, compelling him either to continue his retreat, or give us battle at a disadvantage. Fortunately he has preferred the former; for the result of the latter would have depended a good deal upon the behaviour of our allies. Hitherto they have behaved very well, and will perhaps stand when it comes to a matter of importance; but they do not seem to handle the bayonet so well as our soldiers.

"Massena having crossed the frontier into Spain, we commenced the blockade of Almeida early in April; but, after lying in this state of inactivity for about three weeks, we were aroused by the sudden advance of Massena to succour the garrison. He crossed the Agueda on the 2nd of May with his whole army, and without much delay attempted to force a passage to Almeida; but we took up a strong position between him and that place, having rather an extensive line, the left resting on Fort Conception, and the right near Fuentes de Onoro. A good deal of skirmishing took place in this village on the evening of the 3rd May, during which the light troops of the division, under Lieutenant-colonel Williams of the Sixtieth, behaved in a very gallant manner, repulsing the French at every point, until Colonel Williams being badly wounded, the enemy's efforts were attended with some success; but he was repulsed by the Seventy-first regiment, which made a spirited charge and drove the enemy from the village for the night.

" We fully expected an attack upon the following day, but it was passed by the enemy in reconnoitring and making fresh dispositions, apparently for a more general attack: these dispositions were met by a corresponding change in our position. At daylight on the 5th we were again attacked by the French in great force, and we were soon engaged in rather a serious affair; when, as usual, the principal share of the fighting fell to the third division, which was supported on its right by the first, under Sir Brent Spencer; the light division under General Crawfurd, supported by the cavalry, occupying the ground on the extreme right of our position.

" The village of Fuentes de Onoro was still the principal object of attack; but it was defended in the most determined manner by the Seventy-first, Twenty-fourth, and Seventy-ninth regiments. The firing was kept up with great spirit by these troops, and they succeeded in keeping possession of the place for some hours against the repeated attacks of the French, supported by a tremendous cannonade. About two o'clock, however, these regiments began to give way, and fall back upon some more defensible ground in the rear of the village; when at this moment the Eighty-eighth regiment, under Colonel Wallace, and led by Major-general Mackinnon, was ordered to move up and support them. This was done in admirable order; and they made so overwhelming a charge through the streets, that they drove the enemy from the village with immense loss.*

* " General Picton had had occasion to check this regiment (the Eighty-eighth) for some plundering affair they had been guilty of; when he was so offended at their conduct, that, in addressing them, he told them they were ' the greatest blackguards in the army.' But as he was always as ready to bestow praise as censure where it was due,

Neither did he make any fresh efforts to re-gain it, but contented himself by keeping up a heavy but not very destructive cannonade upon the village.

" During these operations the light division, under General Crawfurd, was rather roughly handled by the enemy's cavalry; and had this arm of the French army been as daring and active upon this occasion as they were when following us to the lines of Torres Vedras, they would doubtless have cut off the light di-vision to a man, and probably have destroyed our cavalry; but they let the golden moment pass, and I hope they will never have another. Our loss has been very severe, more especially in the third division. We have got possession of the ruins of Almeida; for the commandant, General Brennier, after blowing up several of the fortifications, on the night of the 10th, con-trived to pass through our blockading regi-

when they were returning from this gallant and effective charge he exclaimed, ' Well done the brave Eighty-eighth !' Some of them, who had been stung by his former reproaches, cried out, ' Are we the greatest blackguards in the army now ?' Picton smiled, as he replied, ' No, no; you are brave and gallant soldiers: this day has redeemed your cha-racter.' "—*Eventful Life of a Soldier.*

ments without being observed until too late to do him any serious injury; and, in consequence, he was enabled to form a junction with Massena, having sustained but little loss.

"We have been inactive for a few days.; but affairs are assuming a threatening aspect in the south, and perhaps you will next hear from me near Badajoz.

*   *   *   *   *   *

"Always, my dear uncle, very sincerely and truly yours,

"Th. Picton."

The firing continued for some time after the French had been driven from the village of Fuentes de Onoro, but without doing any serious injury to those who held it; although much blood was spilt upon this occasion, with but little advantage to either party.

Lord Wellington still maintained his position between Almeida and the supplies which Massena was desirous of throwing into that garrison. The French general did not make a second attempt upon the following day, although a continuation of the battle was fully anticipated by the allies. It has been a subject of much discussion amongst military men, what could induce Massena so readily to abandon his object; as his loss was not sufficiently great, and his position remained the same; in fact, the French as well as the allies claimed the victory; although, as the British succeeded in their object of preventing supplies being thrown into Almeida, while the enemy failed in effecting that for which they fought the battle, the decision of this mere point of honour is obvious. Massena was so little satisfied with the result of the attack, that on the 8th and 9th his army was in motion to the rear; but whether to attempt to force the British line at another point, or recross the frontier, was at first doubtful. On the 10th, however, he drew his whole force over the Agueda, and thus left Almeida to its fate. The conduct of the governor of this fortress was both skilful and daring. As we have already seen from General Picton's letter, he contrived to elude the vigilance of the blockading regiments, and, after blowing up the fortifications, effected a junction with the second corps of the French army, under Regnier. This was a source of much disappointment to the British army; and the regiments whose duty it was to have prevented this manœuvre were for some time exposed to the jeers of their companions.

Upon the return of the French army to Spain after this unsuccessful attempt to relieve Almeida, the command was conferred on Marmont, who had been created Duke of Ragusa ; Massena being recalled to answer for the reverses which he had sustained, and to quiet the discontent of his subordinate generals.

A brief respite of a few days followed this second retreat, during which General Picton was ordered to rest his division at Nava d'Aver. But he was not long inactive, for some rather important events were now taking place in the south. Marshal Beresford had laid siege to Badajoz ; and about the period of Massena's defeat at Fuentes de Onoro and subsequent retreat it was fully invested, and the batteries of the besiegers had been erected. Soult, however, who was in command of the Army of the South, and was aware of the smallness of the force under Beresford and the inefficiency of his means, determined, if possible, to raise the siege before any assistance could arrive from Lord Wellington. But that general, as if anticipating the plans of his opponents, immediately he had made the necessary arrangements to guard against any further attack in front, and was convinced that no renewal of active hostilities was to be apprehended in that direction, placed the army in cantonments between Almeida and the Spanish frontier, and then set off with the utmost expedition to superintend the siege of Badajoz.

The third and seventh divisions were ordered to follow him without loss of time; and accordingly General Picton broke up the cantonments of his division, and with the seventh, under General Houston, commenced his march by the route of Castello Branco, Niza, Portalegre, and Campo Mayor. The very day, however, upon which these divisions were put in motion to reinforce Marshal Beresford, that general was compelled to give battle to Soult near the village of Albuera. Lord Wellington was proceeding at a rapid pace to the scene of threatened hostilities, while Soult was moving with equal rapidity to relieve the besieged garrison; and Beresford found himself under the necessity of either advancing to meet him, or of fighting under the walls of Badajoz. With much judgment he de-

termined on the former alternative; and having
carried off the whole of his stores, he put his
army in motion, consisting of the fourth division, commanded by General Cole, and the second division, under General Stewart; which
were the only British :troops under his command, with the exception of the Thirteenth
Dragoons and some artillery: the whole of
the remainder, amounting to about twenty-five
thousand men, being composed of Spaniards and
Portuguese, with one brigade of Germans, under
General Alten. The force under Soult was not
so numerous, but far superior in every other
respect, consisting entirely of French, and having above three thousand excellent cavalry and
between forty and fifty pieces of cannon. It
would be out of place here to give a detailed account of this sanguinary day, as General Picton
was not in the field; but we refer to the admirable description of this battle given by Colonel
Napier. It was one of the most desperately
fought general actions during this war; and, as
the Colonel well observes at the conclusion of
his relation, " the laurel is nobly won when the
exhausted victor reels as he places it on his
bleeding front."

Lord Wellington heard numerous and differ-
ing reports while on his road to Badajoz; some
that the French had been victorious, others that
the allies had retreated without a battle: but
as he got nearer to the scene, he was met at
Elvas by an officer sent by Marshal Beresford,
who brought him all the particulars of the conflict. The result, as may be imagined, gave him
great satisfaction; it was not however unmin-
gled with regret, for the loss sustained by the
English was immense.

On the 24th of May, General Picton arrived
at Campo Mayor with his division, where it
was halted for a few days until the military
stores and implements for the approaching siege
could come up. The apprehensions that Soult
would be enabled again to raise the siege were
not entirely removed by the partial success
which had attended the allies at Albuera. The
enemy had there yielded with a stubborn front,
which did not offer to the victors much security
against a renewal of the attack when he should
obtain a sufficient reinforcement; but as that
could not be immediately obtained, Lord Wellington determined, with his very slender means,
to secure Badajoz before Soult should be enabled

to make a second effort for its relief. While, therefore, Marshal Beresford was instructed slowly to follow and observe Soult, Generals Houston and Picton were ordered to bring up their divisions and immediately to invest the place.

On the 25th, the seventh took up a position on the right of the Guadiana. Two days afterwards General Picton crossed the river by a ford and established his division on the left bank, where the troops built themselves huts, and prepared to carry on the operations immediately. In modern warfare a hurried siege is, however, seldom a successful one if the defenders have a hope of relief.

On the 2nd of June, the batteries were completed, and opened upon the castle, and Fort Christoval. The poverty of the means at Lord Wellington's disposal for carrying on this siege was a subject of much merriment to the soldiers employed. General Picton remarked that " Lord Wellington sued Badajoz *in formâ pauperis ;*" and he was answered, that, " instead of *breaching*, the operations appeared more like *beseeching*, Badajoz." In fact, everything was wanting to bring this siege to a rapid termination. The means were deficient for the reduction of the place in *any* time; but to do so with expedition appeared, with such a force, to be impossible. On the 6th, the breach in Fort Christoval was reported practicable by Lieutenant Foster, who had minutely examined it, and in consequence an assault was ordered at midnight; but, after a brave, though totally unsuccessful effort, the assailants were compelled to retire with considerable loss. A second attempt was made on the night of the 9th, which, although better planned and conducted, was equally unsatisfactory in its result. The batteries again opened on the following morning, as the walls were supposed not to be sufficiently breached to render the assault successful; but towards noon orders were received at all the batteries to cease firing. Lord Wellington had received information of the enemy's movements, which at once determined him for a time to forego the reduction of Badajoz. Accordingly, after being engaged in unceasing efforts for nearly five weeks, the siege was raised, a blockading detachment being left to prevent the garrison from receiving any reinforcements or supplies.

The following letter from General Picton to Mr. Marryat gives a desponding view of the prospects of the British Army at this period.

"Campo Mayor, 2nd July 1811.

"My dear Sir,

"Smith, I see, has a large support in the House. The ministry support him to cover their own ignorance and folly in the appointment; and his former connexions, the Whigs and abolitionists, will not forsake an old friend in distress. You know I was always against *puppet-show* legislature in the country, and I have hitherto seen nothing to make me change my opinion. Generally speaking, and with few exceptions, it is a society composed of materials unfit to be trusted with the important power of legislation. It will be enough to give them good laws, and respectable, responsible people to execute them with impartiality.

"The approach of Soult and Marmont determined Lord Wellington to raise the siege, or rather, blockade of Badajoz, and we have now taken up a defensive line on the right bank of the Guadiana, behind the fortresses of Elvas and Campo Mayor.

"There is no probability of our undertaking offensive operations. Indeed, we are in no situation to attempt anything of the kind, considering the relative situations of the two armies: for, independent of the mixed materials we are composed of, in numerical force they exceed us at least by one-third. You appear everywhere to entertain sanguine expectations of our ulterior successes. I am concerned that I cannot say anything to keep up so pleasant a delusion; but believe me, it cannot last long.

" Ministry represent the Portuguese force as amounting to forty thousand regulars, and fifty thousand militia. *The regulars do not amount to twenty thousand,* and as for the militia, they are scarcely worth bringing into the account. If it is intended to carry on the war with a paper force of this kind, you will all very shortly be *undeceived.* There are independent bands of freebooters who harass the French considerably in several parts of Spain, but they are equally formidable to the Spanish inhabitants, who dread them to the full as much as they do the enemy. And you may depend upon it, the great mass of the inhabitants of the neighbouring provinces have submitted to the French yoke, and are not disposed to make any further struggle. We are playing, in my opinion, a very losing game in carrying on the war with

our own *money, at an immense expense,* whilst the
French army are wholly supported by the resources of Spain. This kind of contest cannot
last long. Portugal, whatever your wise heads
may say to the contrary, is a mere *caput mortuum,*
or a dead weight upon our hands in the contest,
and does not supply any force or co-operation
of consideration for the 2,000,000*l.* she receives.
Unless the whole resources of this country are
made subservient and applicable to her defence,
the contest cannot be carried on with any reasonable probability of ultimate success.

" You will think me a gloomy predictor, but
I fear, in the end, it will turn out that I have
drawn legitimate conclusions. I shall be most
happy to find them disproved by more favourable events than I look forward to at present;
but I must continue under similar impressions
until that period.

" Yours very faithfully,

" T. Picton."

In concluding his account of this siege, Lord
Wellington, in his despatch, observes,—" Major-
general Picton directed the operations on the
left of the Guadiana, and Major-general Houston on the right, and I am much indebted to
these officers."

CHAPTER II.

French forces on the frontier of Portugal.—Interval of
inactivity.—Position of the Allied army.—Lord Wellington's intention to blockade Ciudad Rodrigo.—Sudden
advance of the French.—Horsemen charged by Infantry.
—General Picton's critical situation.—Trying manœuvre.
—Retreat of the Allies.—Interval of repose.—Omen of
success.—Death of General Picton's uncle.

MARMONT, Drouet, and Soult were collecting
their forces on the frontiers of Portugal, to co-
operate against the allies in one more effort
to drive them from that kingdom. The main
body of the British army was still behind the
Agueda, under the orders of General Sir Brent
Spencer; and as the army of Portugal continued to move by its left to form a junction
with the corps under Drouet and Soult, the
British army was manœuvred so as to keep on
its front, and still protect Portugal, until it
effected a junction with the force around Bada-

joz. By the 26th of June, Lord Wellington
had concentrated the whole of his troops to
give battle to Marmont if he attempted the
invasion of Portugal.

The French in Badajoz were gratified by
the sight of their own army on the 19th, when
the united corps of Soult and Marmont came
to their relief. General Picton had been ordered to take up his old position at Campo
Mayor, and accordingly he marched his own
and the seventh division to that place, which
now formed the extreme left of the British
line, the right resting on Elvas; and in this
position the army remained for some weeks:
that of the French, amounting to about seventy
thousand men, under the united marshals, being
in cantonments along the course of the Guadiana, between Badajoz and Merida.

It was natural to expect that, while the two
armies were within so short a distance of each
other, something decisive would take place.
The enemy, at all events, came to fight;
and as their force was considerably greater
than that of the allies, they were expected to
commence the attack. This expectation prevailed for some time in the allied army; but

it soon became evident that the French marshals had learned to respect their opponents' and having succeeded in raising the siege of Badajoz, they appeared contented with their success. On the other hand, Lord Wellington was not anxious to risk a battle: he had lately received some reinforcements from England; the success of his plans had given confidence to the Government, and they were now making efforts to assist him. He determined, therefore, to fight if he could not defend Portugal without fighting; but, unless compelled to do so, to remain in his present inactive situation.

The position occupied by the allied army was one of considerable strength, and enabled Lord Wellington to concentrate his whole force with facility upon any one point which the enemy might think proper to select for attack. But the plans of the French generals seemed rather uncertain, and some weeks were passed in inactivity. A few cavalry skirmishes alone broke the monotony, in most of which the enemy were successful; and upon one of these occasions they succeeded in cutting off and making prisoners about one hundred and twenty men belonging to the Eleventh Light Dragoons. The "fighting division," while in these quarters, was quite out of its element; and General Picton, in a letter written at this period to his brother, observes, " We are here undergoing all the disagreeable and inactive routine of garrison duty, although with an enemy's force more than one-fourth larger than our own immediately in our front : but this cannot last long," &c.

For nearly a month the allied army remained in this position. About the end of July, however, Lord Wellington resolved to occupy a new line, and General Picton was ordered to march his division in the direction of Ciudad Rodrigo, which, Lord Wellington had been informed, was almost destitute of supplies. Picton accordingly recrossed the Tagus at Villa Velha; Sir Rowland Hill being again left with his corps to protect Alentejo. The position of the allies was therefore very similar to that which they had occupied the preceding year; but their prospects were widely different. At that period the English general was making every preparation to retreat with his small and inexperienced army, to seek protection behind the fortified lines which he had prepared for its reception, while the French were advancing full of confidence to drive Wellington and his soldiers into the sea. Now the state of affairs was much changed : Lord Wellington's army was augmented in numbers, and had driven the enemy before them out of Portugal; they had obtained confidence both in themselves and their leaders ; while the French, although better organized than they had been for some time, and greatly superior in numbers, were evidently afraid to hazard a battle. This was most satisfactorily demonstrated by an intercepted letter from General Tresion, chief of Marmont's staff, wherein he observed in most positive terms, that " the French troops were not able to cope with the English, and that their best chance of success lay in manœuvring;" an acknowledgment highly flattering to the courage and discipline of the British soldiers. On the 10th of August Lord Wellington established his head-quarters at Fuente Guinaldo ; it being his intention to blockade Ciudad Rodrigo, in consequence of his deficiency in all the necessary implements for a siege. It was known that a want of provisions was beginning to be felt in the fortress, and it was hoped that the garrison might be compelled to surrender before any movement could be made by Marmont for their relief. Lord Wellington immediately occupied the country between the rivers Coa and Agueda.

The following letter from General Picton to Mr. Marryat gives his view of the prospects of the allied army at this time :

"Alberguira, Spain, 12th Aug. 1811.

" MY DEAR SIR,

" We are again restored to our old theatre between the Coa and Agueda, and most probably shall move forward and cross the latter. The insuperable difficulty (from distance, and the nature of the roads) to the transporting forward the heavy ordnance and stores for a siege, will effectually prevent our attacking Ciudad Rodrigo, but we shall push on towards Salamanca, for the purpose of drawing the French armies from the rich countries where they are now cantoned. If this purpose should be effected by our manœuvre, we shall have gained a most important point. As soon as they find us moving, in force, upon Salamanca, they will be obliged to concentrate the whole of their force, now cantoned in the rich countries about Talavera de la Reyna, Placencia, and Coria, and march without loss of time upon Ciudad Rodrigo; when Lord Wellington, having effected his purpose, that of drawing them into a country where they cannot exist without separating, may either fight them to advantage, or take up a position behind the Agueda, in readiness to profit by any false movement they may make. If Buonaparte's attention should be taken up in the North, so as to prevent his amply reinforcing his armies in the Peninsula, I think we shall be able to afford him plenty of amusement here; but this war cannot be carried on without money, and if we cannot afford a liberal supply, we had better give it up at once. With money we can command abundant supplies on the frontiers of Spain, and can manœuvre to great advantage over an enemy who is under the necessity of separating continually to collect his means of subsistence; but without, we shall not be able to effect anything of consequence, as all our movements will depend upon the procuring supplies, which we draw from the sea-ports by a long, difficult land carriage. Our movements are not nearly as expeditious as they would be, were we not dependent on such considerations. As long as we have money in abundance, supplies of all kinds find us out; but as soon as the means fail us, we are obliged to go the Lord knows where in search of them. Dollars here are the only sinews of war.

"I had a letter from General Maitland, down from Gibraltar, on his way to Sicily. I find he was appointed to that command without any application or previous intimation of the intention. In a pecuniary view it is certainly by no means an advantageous change for him; as the revenue of a lieutenant-general will barely make the military pot boil, leaving the family entirely out of the question.

"I hope Mrs. M. and the young ladies continue in good health, and amuse themselves well with the rural scenes about Sydenham. Pray offer them my best respects. Has your elder son returned from his travels? I hope well stored with useful observations. My best respects to him and all the young ones.

"I am beginning to grow tired of this vagrant life. We have been since March in continual movement—sometimes in miserable abandoned cottages, and as frequently without any covering whatever. I have constantly, for a whole year, made use of a bundle of straw as a bed, and I do not see any probability of a change for some time longer.

"With my best wishes, my dear sir,

"Very faithfully yours,

"T. PICTON."

The third division was in a position of considerable extent, and even danger, on the heights of El Bodon. This was soon evinced upon a trying occasion. The intention of Lord Wellington in moving his army from the Guadiana was not apparently discovered by Marmont, and the allies had completed the investment of Ciudad Rodrigo long before that general put his columns in motion. At length, however, having formed a junction with the corps of Dorsenne, and collected a considerable quantity of provisions, he made preparations to raise the blockade, and, if possible, to drive the allies from the vicinity of the fortresses in the possession of the French on the Spanish frontier.

On the 22nd of September, Dorsenne and Marmont met at Tamames, a few leagues in front of Ciudad Rodrigo; their united forces amounting to about sixty thousand men, with six thousand cavalry, and nearly one hundred pieces of artillery. The force under Lord Wel-

lington at this moment did not exceed fifty
thousand men, some portion of which was necessarily occupied in the close investment of Ciudad Rodrigo. According to Colonel Napier,
"Lord Wellington's position was very extensive,
and therefore very weak." Certain it is, that
the third division, which formed the centre, had
to occupy ground which, to defend effectually,
should have been held by double the number
of men. At daybreak on the 25th the enemy
were in motion to attack the position occupied
by General Picton. Montbrun, with his cavalry,
shook the ground in their approach with a noise
as of thunder, and swept the height in the centre of his position: it was occupied by the Fifth
and Seventy-seventh, with the Eleventh Light
Dragoons, and some squadrons of German hussars. Fortunately the impetuosity of the French
cavalry led them so much in advance of their infantry, that they had for some time to contend
alone against the British.

The action was begun by the sudden advance
of the French, who, first traversing an open
plain, and then crossing a ravine, ascended a
steep rocky causeway, under a constant fire of
grape and canister from a brigade of Portuguese
artillery. Men and horses were struck down

in frightful numbers by this storm of shot; but still they persevered; and so determined and rapid was their charge, that the gunners were sabred and the guns seized before the smoke had cleared away sufficiently to show them that the enemy had gained the summit. At this critical moment the Fifth regiment, under Major Ridge, quickly deploying from square into line, poured in a volley of balls, and then dashed at the cavalry with the bayonet. Novel as was the expedient of charging cavalry with infantry, still it was in this instance successful: they drove the enemy before them, and being joined by the Seventy-seventh regiment, were enabled to re-capture and bring off the guns. Montbrun, however, came up with fresh troops, and putting himself at their head, attempted to ride through these two regiments; but they were rapidly formed into square, and received the attack in so cool and resolute a manner, that no impression could be made upon them.

General Picton, it should be observed, was during this part of the contest in the village of El Bodon, where it was supposed that the French would have made their attack. He had with him the Forty-fifth, Seventy-fourth, and Eighty-eighth regiments. An officer was instantly despatched from the scene of hostilities to El Bodon, when Picton prepared to concentrate his division by moving on his left to the support of the centre. The ground occupied by the three regiments with Picton, in the neighbourhood of El Bodon, consisted principally of vineyard enclosures and rocky ravines, difficult to be traversed; consequently it took some time to extricate the troops and push them forward to the point of attack. Before this could be accomplished, the French cavalry, having been totally repulsed in their repeated attempts to break the square of the Seventy-seventh and Fifth regiments, desisted for a while, and awaited the coming up of their infantry. During this interval these two regiments were enabled to manœuvre into line, and form a junction with the Eighty-third British, and the Ninth and Twenty-first Portuguese regiments, being the left brigade, under Major-general Colville; and almost at the same time Picton came up with his three regiments, and put himself at the head of his division. The following extract from the pen of a writer* who was engaged in this combat, will be read with interest. It is, we believe, a faithful account of this affair.

* Reminiscences of a Subaltern.

· " Montbrun, at the head of fifteen squadrons of light horse, pressed closely on our right flank, and made every demonstration of attacking us, with the view of engaging our attention until the arrival of his infantry and artillery, of which latter only one battery was in the field; but General Picton saw the critical situation in which he was placed, and that nothing but the most rapid and at the same time most regular movement upon Guinaldo could save his division from being cut off to a man. For six miles across a perfect flat, without the slightest protection from any incidental variation of ground, without artillery, and I might say without cavalry, (for what were four or five squadrons to twenty or thirty?) did the third division continue its march; during the whole of which the enemy's cavalry never quitted them. A park of six guns advanced with the cavalry, and taking the third division in flank and rear, poured in a frightful fire of round-shot, grape, and canister. Many men fell in this way; and those whose wounds rendered them unable to march, were obliged to be abandoned to the enemy.

*   *   *   *   *   *

" General Picton conducted himself with his accustomed coolness: he remained on the left

flank of the column, and repeatedly cautioned
the different battalions to mind the quarter
distance and the ' telling off.' ' Your safety,'
added he, ' my credit, and the honour of the
army are at stake ; all rests with you at this
moment.' We had reached to within a mile
of our entrenched camp, when Montbrun, impatient lest we should escape from his grasp,
ordered his troopers to bring up their right
shoulders, and incline towards our column.
The movement was not exactly bringing his
squadrons into line, but it was the next thing
to it, and at this time they were within half
pistol-shot of us. Picton took off his hat, and
holding it over his eyes as a shade from the sun,
looked sternly but anxiously at the French.
The clatter of the horses and the clanking of
the scabbards were so great when the right half
squadron moved up, that many thought it the
forerunner of a general charge. Some mounted
officer called out, ' Had we not better form
square ?' ' No,' replied Picton ; ' it is but a
ruse to frighten us ; but it *won't do*.' "

This was a most critical and trying manœuvre,
and its success was not more honourable to
General Picton than to the men under his com-

mand. The greatest order and coolness could alone save them from being annihilated by the furious charges of the enemy's cavalry; each battalion had in its turn to form the rearguard to repulse their advance, and then, having given a volley to stop their approach, to fall back at double time behind that which had formed in its rear. There is hardly any situation so difficult or so trying to the troops as performing this movement without cavalry. The least unsteadiness in forming or irregularity in retreat may lead to the instant destruction of the whole force: the only security, therefore, is the discipline of the troops, and the ability and firmness of their officers. General Picton in this instance saved his division, and, under such circumstances, that was more than could have been anticipated.

The day following this affair it was expected that the French would make an attack in force upon Lord Wellington's position, and every preparation was made to receive them; but again the allies were disappointed, and the day passed without a shot being fired. The demonstrations made by Marmont were, however, formidable; and Lord Wellington had not sufficient confidence in his present ground to wish to fight him. Accordingly, during the night of the 26th, the British army was ordered to fall back upon a new position, between the Coa and Agueda; the fourth division, under General Cole, being left at Aldea de Ponte. To this place Marmont pressed his advance on the following day, when a short but desperate conflict took place for the possession of the village, which, after much hard fighting, was left in the hands of the British.

On the same night the allies again retreated, and the following morning took up a strong and very defensible line behind Soita, where both flanks were protected by the river Coa. A singular circumstance attended this retreat; it was discovered in the course of the next day that the enemy also were actually retreating at the same time. Instead of pursuing the allies, Marmont had suddenly resolved to retrace his march, contenting himself with having relieved Ciudad Rodrigo and driven the British from beneath its walls. He now, therefore, returned to Spain, occupying cantonments in the valley of the Tagus, while Dorsenne resumed possession of Salamanca. A strong garrison and plenty of provisions were thrown into Ciudad Rodrigo ; but what further advantage was gained by this forward movement it is difficult to determine.

Lord Wellington was once more left to his own plans; the enemy had relinquished all intention of interrupting his operations, and he could now direct his arms against Ciudad Rodrigo with almost the same prospect of success as before. If Marmont came to its relief, he would have again to retreat until the French general was tired of the pursuit. But it was quite evident that the report of Massena respecting the lines of Torres Vedras was operating strongly upon Marmont: Portugal was still more exhausted than formerly, and he found that every step he took towards Lisbon increased the difficulty of obtaining sustenance for his troops.

With the example of Massena before him, there was little chance that Marmont would follow Lord Wellington in order to risk starvation and defeat before these impregnable lines ; but, to avoid all probability of being led into this error, he made a timely retreat, and at once put an end to the campaign of 1811.

The allied army went into cantonments, and it was anticipated that the winter would be passed in comparative inactivity. General Picton's division was ordered to occupy Aldea de Ponte, the remainder of the army being placed in quarters on the Coa ; the right resting on Penamacor, and the left on Celerico. During this interval of repose the losses in the army were extremely severe from a malignant fever, which spread with so much rapidity and violence, that at one period there were twelve thousand British in hospital, besides a considerable number of Portuguese. This frightful return of invalids was in some degree attributable to the want of occupation and excitement ; in addition to which, provisions were scarce and bad, while the weather, being cold and wet, made the huts occupied by the troops both comfortless and unhealthy. Lord Wellington took this opportunity to collect such *matériel* for the siege of Ciudad Rodrigo as would enable him to carry the place by a more rapid method than that of blockade. He had resolved, that while Sir Rowland Hill was diverting and even threatening the enemy in the south, he would make another attempt upon that fortress; but he determined to try to obtain possession by a *coup de main.* This was, in fact, the only course open at the present moment; for the garrison was now so well supplied, and the place in so complete a state of defence, that a blockade, unless supported by a much greater force than the English general could bring into the field, would certainly be disturbed before it could be successful. Marmont was aware of this; and Lord Wellington knew that Marmont depended upon it. It was, in fact, one of the calculations which the French marshal ventured to make with certainty: he knew the want of means possessed by the English for carrying on an active siege, and he ventured consequently to think this fortress perfectly secure.

A singular and rather fortunate event took place in the month of October, which was considered by the allies as an omen of success. On the 15th, Don Julian de Sanchos, one of the guerilla chiefs, celebrated alike for his activity and daring enterprise, whilst lying in ambuscade near the walls of Ciudad Rodrigo, fell in with the cattle belonging to the garrison. He and his band immediately dashed forward to secure them; when, having despatched or put to flight the drovers, they commenced driving off their prey. At this critical moment General Regnaud, the governor of the fortress, happening to be in the neighbourhood with a small escort of dragoons, came up, and seeing the position of affairs, put himself at the head of his troopers, and charged the guerillas. They, however, bravely defended what they had won, and, after rather a severe conflict, were enabled not only to keep their prize, but to defeat the escort and succeed in making the governor a prisoner. He was immediately conveyed to the British head-quarters, where he was treated by Lord Wellington with every respect: while the cattle, being driven into the English quarters, were hailed as a valuable reinforcement by the soldiers.

During the interval preceding the assault on Ciudad Rodrigo, General Picton received a letter from his brother, written on the 16th of October, informing him that his uncle, the veteran soldier under whose almost parental command he had commenced his career, had two days previously, breathed his last. This venerable officer had attained the advanced age of eighty-four years, with the rank of general in the army and colonel of the Twelfth Foot, in which regiment he had been for nearly thirty-six years. He left General Picton his sole executor and residuary legatee.

In his youth Picton had learned to esteem him as a parent, and these feelings only gained strength as he grew older: but when persecution assailed, and had nearly overwhelmed him, then it was that the sincerity of his uncle's regard was manifested : when almost every one had deserted him, he came forward, and was willing to spend his whole fortune in the defence of his nephew's honour.

An officer who had an opportunity of observing Sir Thomas Picton, and was constantly with him in all his campaigns, says, in a letter to the writer of this memoir :

"The effect produced upon General Picton by the letter announcing his uncle's decease was such as would hardly have been expected from a man who was accused of having set all the finer feelings of humanity at defiance. It is true, there were no external appearances of grief; his countenance was unchanged ; but even I, who esteem his memory for every vir-

tue, cannot say that his eyes were even mois-
tened by a tear : a slight exclamation of ' Good
God !' burst from him when he came to the
announcement of his uncle's death ; and as he
closed the letter which had brought him the
sad tidings, he in a low and melancholy tone
murmured, ' My poor uncle !' I saw little of
him for the remainder of that day, but a great
alteration was perceptible in his manner for
a long time afterwards ; every feature kept
rigidly its place, while the fire of his eyes was
unchanged ; but I, who knew him well, took
this opportunity to try and discover if he really
was as cold and hard as he had been represented : the conclusion at which I arrived was, that
never man felt more the loss of a friend or
relative than General Picton the death of his
uncle. I say he felt it more than other men,
because there was no outlet, no confidence ; but,
locked up within the very centre of his heart,
it preyed there with a strength which in any
other person would have burst forth with un-
controllable, unutterable grief: to him it produced want of repose, and even ill health, but
nothing would have offended him more than
even hinting that it was caused by regret. He

hardly ever mentioned his uncle's name; but when he did, it was with a slight falter in the voice, which could not deceive one who observed him so closely as myself."

In a letter dated Zamarra, January 25th, 1812, and which we shall again have to notice, General Picton observes: "The circumstance which you mention respecting my worthy uncle so shortly before his death is of that considerate nature, and so characteristic of him, that it convinces me he was as capable as at any former period of his life to dispose of his whole property; and I trust you will believe that I am more disposed to enlarge than diminish his benevolence."

This passage relates to an annuity which was left by General William Picton to an old and deserving officer, who had been obliged to sell his commission, and was living in humble and almost indigent circumstances. The general and this officer had in early life been for some years in the same regiment; and when the latter became reduced in circumstances, the general, with that kindly feeling which so distinguished him, assisted him, and at his death made that provision for his old companion in arms which

he thought would render the remaining years of.
his life free from care.

His nephew, as executor, of course paid this
annuity; but as Picton thought it likely that
his uncle had not indulged in the full extent
of his inclination towards the object of his solicitude, under the apprehension of reducing too
much the amount to be inherited by himself,
he immediately made an addition of fifty pounds.
a year to this annuity.

CHAPTER III.

Operations to reduce the Garrison of Ciudad Rodrigo.—
Commencement of the Siege.—Preparations for carrying
the place by assault.—General Picton's Addresses to his
soldiers.—His Letter descriptive of the Assault of Ciudad
Rodrigo.—The town taken.—Sanguinary excesses.—Con-
flagrations.—Characteristic anecdote of General Picton.—
Marmont and Lord Wellington.—Daring design.—Badajoz
invested.—Siege commenced.—Death of Captain Cuthbert.—Fort of Picurina taken.

OPERATIONS had for some time been carried
on, both by the guerillas and allies, to reduce as
much as possible the garrison of Ciudad Rodrigo. This was effected by means of detached
parties, who constantly intercepted the supplies
which the enemy attempted to throw in; but
although many were captured, still a sufficient
quantity reached their destination to prevent
any alarm on the part of the garrison lest they
should be straitened for provisions.

On the 4th of January 1812, the third division was in motion towards Ciudad Rodrigo. Snow, rain, cold, and wind combined to render this wintry march harassing in the extreme; but the example of their leader inspired the troops with fortitude and resolution to overcome every difficulty. Several, however, fell on the way; when, unless fortunately discovered in time, their destruction was inevitable,— a drowsy stupor soon crept over their senses, from which they never awoke. The carts, of which there were many, were entirely engaged in the transport of gabions and fascines, which the troops had been employed in constructing during the time they had passed in cantonments; consequently even an opportunity of placing an expiring soldier on one of these conveyances but seldom occurred. The best security against the inclemency of the weather was the exertion of the march; for those who had fallen from fatigue and cold were as likely to die upon an exposed cart as upon the ground. A long march brought the division into Robleda about eight o'clock in the evening. The following morning it was again in motion; and by the 8th the fortress was completely invested.

So rapid had been this movement on the

part of Lord Wellington, and so suddenly did the enemy find himself closely shut in, that he had not time to make any extraordinary preparations for defence. The battering train attached to the allied army was now in a respectable condition both in point of numbers and efficiency; Lord Wellington having by his strong representations induced the British Government to send out a considerable augmentation to this part of his force.

About forty thousand troops, including those engaged in the attack, were now in the immediate vicinity of Ciudad Rodrigo, and it was Lord Wellington's intention to lose no time in carrying the place by assault. It was ordered that the duties of the siege should be performed by four divisions,—the light, first, third, and fourth, which were to relieve each other every twenty-four hours. The trenches were immediately dug; the garrison the whole time keeping up a terrific fire of shot and shells, which did considerable execution amongst the workmen; still the works were carried on with alacrity and spirit.

" On the third day the garrison distinguished the batteries from the other parts of the work, and attained their range so precisely, that two-thirds of their shells fell into them, and their round-shot caused many casualties."[*]　The first battery was completed and opened on the 14th, being the sixth day of the siege, from which period until the 19th the firing was kept up without intermission.

Lord Wellington then made a close reconnoissance of the two breaches; this, together with the report of Major Sturgeon of the Royal Engineers that they were both practicable, induced him to direct the assault to take place the same evening.　Accordingly General Picton received orders to hold his division in readiness to make the attack, in conjunction with the light division and General Pack's Portuguese brigade.　The arrangements made by Lord Wellington were, that General Picton with his division should attack the great or right breach, while General Crawfurd, with the light division, should make a simultaneous assault on the left and smaller breach : General Pack with his Portuguese being ordered to make a feint on the opposite side of the town ; but with further instructions, that if he did not find the resist-

* Colonel Jones, in his "Journal of Sieges."

ance too great, and could succeed in forcing an entrance, he was immediately to lead his troops to the assistance of those at the breaches.

General Picton marched the left brigade of his division to the convent of Santa Cruz, situated on the right of the batteries, where the officers and men were made acquainted with the duties which they had to perform; the remainder of the division being formed in the first parallel. The night was calm, and the heavens studded with stars; and a young moon. shed a faint light upon the earth, which seemed to mock by its tranquillity the wild and sanguinary scene which was about to ensue.

The assault was ordered for seven o'clock; but Colonel O'Toole, with the light company of the Eighty-third regiment and the Second Caçadores, was directed to cross the Agueda by the bridge, and make an attack upon the outwork in front of the castle ten minutes before the time appointed for the general assault; his instructions being to destroy two guns planted in this outwork which might be the means of annoying the assailants by flanking the entrance to the ditch. At half-past six the division was ready, when General Picton and his staff rode

up to the ground : silence immediately prevailed amongst the troops. Major-general Mackinnon's right brigade, consisting of the Forty-
fifth, Seventy-fourth, and Eighty-eighth regiments, and five companies of the Sixtieth regiment, was to take the lead, and to be supported
by Lieutenant-colonel Campbell, (who upon this
occasion commanded the left brigade of the
division, during the absence of the Honourable
Major-general Colville,) with the Fifth, Seventy-
seventh, Ninety-fourth, and Eighty-third; the
whole of this force being directed against the
principal breach.

The animated detail given by a writer before
quoted,* when speaking of General Picton's
address to his soldiers previous to their advance
to the breach, is worthy of perusal:

" Long harangues are not necessary to British
soldiers, and on this occasion but few were
made use of. General Picton said something
animating to the different regiments as he
passed them; and those of my readers who
recollect his deliberate and strong utterance will
say with me, that his mode of speaking was
indeed very impressive. The address to each

---

* Reminiscences of a Subaltern.

was nearly the same; but that delivered by him to the Eighty-eighth (the Connaught Rangers) was so characteristic of the general, and so applicable to the men he spoke to, that I shall give it word for word. It was this: 'Rangers of Connaught! it is not my intention to expend any *powder* this evening; we'll do the business with the *could iron!*'

" I before said the soldiers were silent, so they were; but the man who *could* be silent after such an address, made in such a way, and in such a place, had better have stayed at home. It may be asked, what did they do? Why, what *would* they do, or would any one do, but give the loudest hurrah he was able?"

A few similar pithy remarks were made to all the regiments, in a tone which went home to the heart and feelings of every man in the line. An officer in the Seventy-seventh regiment upon this occasion, observes, that while talking to some officers just previously to the attack, " suddenly a horseman galloped heavily but hastily towards us — it was Picton. He made a brief and inspiriting appeal to us; said he knew the Fifth were men whom a severe fire would not daunt, and that he reposed equal confidence in the Seventy-seventh; a few kind words to our commander (Lieutenant-colonel Dunkin), and he bade us 'God speed!' pounding the sides of his hog-maned cob as he trotted off in a contrary direction."*—No man knew the nature of soldiers better than Sir Thomas Picton: it was not by words alone that he urged them on; his example was never wanting where they failed, and with such a leader none would have dared to pause.

After having thus raised the spirits of his men, General Picton and his staff dismounted, and the advance commenced. The following letter from the general to his friend, written six days after the assault, contains an accurate and animated account of its progress.

"Zamarra, 25th January 1812.

" My dear Colonel,

" I had the pleasure of receiving your letter by the last mail, and am most truly concerned to learn that your general health, as well as your complaint in the eyes, has been so troublesome: these afflictions, which we cannot hope wholly to get the better of, are only to be softened by patience. The circumstance which you mention respecting my worthy uncle, so

* The United Service Journal.

shortly before his death, is of that considerate nature, and so characteristic of him, that it convinces me he was as capable as at any former period of his life to dispose of his whole property; and I trust you will believe that I am more disposed to enlarge than diminish his benevolence.

" Since I had last the pleasure of writing to you, we have had a winter siege. The third division moved forward from its old cantonments of Alvazavia on the 4th instant, for the purpose of approaching Ciudad Rodrigo. It was the most miserable day I ever witnessed: a continued snow-storm, the severity of which was so intense that several men of the division perished of cold and fatigue. In consequence of this weather, we were not able to invest the place completely until the morning of the 8th; and the advanced work, which covered the point of attack, was very gallantly carried by storm (by Lieutenant-colonel Colbourne and the Fifty-second regiment) early on the same evening; an event which allowed us to open our first parallel within five hundred and thirty yards of the bastion intended to be breached.

" The siege was carried on by four divisions
alternately twenty-four hours each, and we had
to march about twelve miles every morning to
the trenches. The enemy kept up a tremendous fire of shot and shells during the whole
of the operations; we however paid no attention to this, but proceeded rapidly to erect our
breaching batteries, and thereby curtail our
operations; there being a probability that Marmont might be able to interrupt our progress
had we prosecuted our attack in a regular
manner.

" To make short of the business; on the
eleventh day, when the third division had the
trenches, two breaches were declared practicable, and the light division was brought up to
co-operate in the assault, which was determined
to take place immediately after dark, and to
commence at seven o'clock. The town is surrounded by an old wall, flanked with square
bastions, generally about twenty-five feet high,
covered by a modern *fausse-braye* and deep
ditch; and the point to be attacked by the
third division was elevated and commanding.

" The third division made five separate attacks
at the same moment; four in different parts

of the *fausse-braye*, and the fifth on the main breach. The enemy kept up a tremendous fire of shot, shells, and musketry, and made a show of an obstinate resistance; but on the forlorn-hope of the division reaching the foot of the breach, they prematurely sprung their mine, set fire to a great number of shells which they had arranged for the purpose, and retired to the entrenchments which they had thrown up on each side, and in front of the breach. The troops immediately took advantage of the explosion, rushed forward, and possessed themselves of the breach, where they were for some minutes exposed to a most destructive fire of grape and musketry, until, by scrambling over the parapets, they turned the entrenchments on both sides, and overcame all further resistance. About this time the light division, which was rather late in the attack, also succeeded in getting possession of the breach they were ordered to attack, and a miserable scene took place, which, notwithstanding every exertion, continued during the greatest part of the night. Our loss has been very severe, particularly in officers, having forty-one killed and wounded on the occasion.

" My poor friend Major-general Mackinnon, a most gallant, intelligent officer and estimable man, was killed by an explosion on the breach.

" Nothing could exceed the gallantry of the division, and it has most deservedly obtained the highest reputation of any division in this army.

" Accept, my dear colonel, my best wishes, and believe me to be very sincerely and faithfully yours,

" TH. PICTON."

So studiously does General Picton abstain from making any allusion to his own actions in his letters, that we are compelled to seek from those who fought by his side such details as are necessary to illustrate his personal heroism, and that character for cool and undaunted courage for which he was so justly famed.

General Mackinnon, whose fall he so warmly and feelingly laments, led the regiments which headed the attack. Whilst his soldiers were marching to the breach, Picton moved with them; at this moment, immediately after the leading columns had cleared the trenches,

the moon showed the advancing troops to the
defenders of the fortress. A tremendous fire
of every description of shot was instantly opened from the walls; but no check, no wavering
was apparent, for with a steady and determined
step they obeyed their general's command of
" Forward!" When near the *fausse-braye*, Picton stopped, and cheering on the storming parties, they rushed forward to the attack.

Lieutenant-colonel Campbell, with the Ninety-
fourth, Fifth, and Seventy-eighth regiments,
had been formed near the convent of Santa Cruz,
and ordered to enter the ditch on the right of
the breach, and then turning to the left, join the
attacking column. This force had commenced
its advance ten minutes before seven; and when
the soldiers of Mackinnon's brigade reached
the ditch, they found Colonel Campbell and his
men already there. Together, therefore, they
rushed up the great breach, where all were
striving to be first. The race was short; the
" fighting division" had now another opportunity of demonstrating that they deserved that
name, and the shout of defiance which burst
from them at this moment gave assurance to
Picton, who was anxiously watching their pro-

gress, that all was well. ͻ But in another moment every other sound was lost in one terrific explosion, which shook the earth, causing even those who were struggling on the breach to pause.

A magazine at the foot of the rampart had, as General Picton observes, "prematurely" exploded. The bastion was shaken to its base, while death was spread alike amongst friend and foe. Many a brave soldier fell upon this occasion, and amongst them Picton's lamented friend, Major-general Mackinnon,* who, after a long life of distinguished services, was thus shattered to death whilst leading his men in the assault. A fearful pause followed this explosion, but it was brief; the breach was much widened by the accident, and rendered more easy of access. Again the men rushed forward over dead and dying: the summit was soon won, but the entrenchments, behind which the enemy had, ensconced themselves with a deep ditch in their front, were yet to be gained; in addition

---

* This officer was uncle to the present Colonel Mackinnon of the Coldstream Guards, whose History of that disguished Regiment forms so interesting an addition to our military literature.

to which, two guns on each side of the breach, and cut off from the assailants by a wide gap in the wall, commenced pouring in a most destructive fire of grape and canister on each flank. These were difficult to get at, being entirely isolated from the breach, while the entrenchments stopped the advance in front. But the defenders, being thus compelled to bring a great force to repel this attack of Picton's divison, had weakened their other points of defence; and the small breach, after the first struggle, was quickly won:—but that struggle was wild and deadly.

Crawfurd led the van, and was almost the first up the breach cheering his men; but he fell, just as the shout of victory burst upon his ear. A ball had passed through his arm and penetrated his body, producing a hopeless wound in the lungs: he lived to hear the place was won; but that was the last sound which fell upon his ears. His soldiers were not, however, long without a leader; another instantly stepped forth. But they knew their work, and it was soon done. They drove the enemy before them in every direction, and moving by their right, joined the troops of Picton's division, which had

by this time also been successful. They had
with daring almost unparalleled seized the two
guns before alluded to, which the enemy considered unassailable, and then contrived to turn
the entrenchments by scaling the ditch which
the defenders had formed in front. Almost at
the same moment the brigade under General
Pack was in the town, having met with but
little resistance in its attack upon the castle.

The French were therefore taken in rear
and surrounded on all sides. Still, however,
they fought: they could not conquer, but they
could kill, and for some time the fighting was
continued in the streets. A conviction that
little mercy would be shown by troops thus
heated and excited protracted the sanguinary
conflict: all was now blood; and men who at
other times would have wept at the relation of
their own acts, now buried their steel in the
breasts of those who sued for mercy. The
flash and roar of musketry, the glare of the
reeking steel, the wild shouts of triumph, the
sullen cry for quarter, and then the moan of
anguish, which told the reply,—these were
amongst the terrors of that night.

General Picton was soon in the town, and,

according to the statement of one who was by his side, the efforts which he made to put a stop to this fearful tragedy were unremitting. He flew in all directions, calling in a voice of thunder on the frantic soldiers to remember that they were " men, and Englishmen — not savages!" and by exhortations and threats he contrived to bring back some to their senses; but the majority soon became intoxicated, and then every passion was let loose. Wherever the voice of distress was heard, thither Picton hastened, when his commanding and resolute tone was sure to make the offenders desist and fly.

In addition to the accumulated horrors to which the wretched inhabitants were subjected, frequent fires burst forth in various parts of the town, throwing a red glare over every object, and making the havoc of the night more frightfully conspicuous. Here again Picton was to be found, surrounded by his officers, directing and even assisting to subdue the flames, and giving protection to the affrighted sufferers.— But the mind willingly turns from the contemplation of scenes like these, and we would rather try to forget that our soldiers could ever have been guilty of such wild and inhuman excesses.[*]

The following account of the fall of Ciudad Rodrigo is given by General Picton in a letter to Mr. Marryat :—

"Zamarra, 27th Jan. 1812.

" MY DEAR SIR,

" Since I last had the pleasure of writing to you, we have been engaged in a most arduous undertaking; a winter's siege in a climate to the full as severe as that of England. Marmont, calculating that we were safely lodged in winter quarters, and would not, on various accounts, undertake anything of consequence at such a season, moved the whole of his army southward, for the purpose of co-operating with Soult and

---

[*] Lieutenant-colonel Macpherson, who has contributed many interesting particulars to these Memoirs, had upon this occasion been exerting himself to restrain some of the least disorderly of the soldiers, but without much success; for so soon as they were ordered to "*fall in,*" others fell out, until *he* was left almost alone. Picton seeing him in the square thus occupied, encouraged him in his laudable efforts; but Macpherson, tired of the endless task, observed to the general, " If you will keep them together, sir, I will collect them." The duty of each, however, was equally unsatisfactory; for, impelled by the hope of plunder and intoxication, even Picton was soon deserted.

Suchet, in overwhelming Blake and the Cata-
lonians before the opening of another campaign,
when their whole united force would become
disposable on this side. As soon as Lord
Wellington saw him so far advanced, as to
afford him a probable opportunity of being able
to capture Ciudad Rodrigo before he could
return to its relief, he suddenly assembled four
divisions of the army, and completely invested
the place on the 8th instant; and carried the
approaches and works on with such astonishing
rapidity, that there were two practicable breaches
in the body of the place on the evening of the
19th, when it was determined to assault at all
points. The business was divided between the
third and the light divisions. The assault took
place at seven o'clock in the evening. The
third division had by far the most difficult
attack on the main breach, where the enemy
were most prepared. The troops were, in consequence, exposed to a severe fire of hot shells
and musketry, as well as several explosions, from
which they suffered severely; but nothing could
damp their ardour for a single moment. They
rushed impetuously forward, drove the enemy
from the breach as well as the entrenchments

they had thrown up to defend it. The light
division shortly after seconded in the attack
allotted to them, and in a few minutes we drove
them from all their points of defence, and became undisputed masters of the city. Our loss
on the occasion was very considerable, particularly in officers, of whom forty-one (in the
third division) were killed or wounded. It
was necessary to accelerate the attack, as Marmont was returning rapidly, with a large army,
to its relief. Upon the whole, it has been a
most important as well as brilliant achievement,
and does *much honour* to the talents of our commander. By this enterprise he has gained two
great points. He has effected an important
diversion in drawing Marshal Marmont's army
back to this frontier, and he has, at the same
time, gained a position of the greatest importance to our ulterior operations. —I don't know
whether you will be able to decipher this scrawl.
My eyes are growing so bad, that I can with
difficulty make out any writing—particularly
my own. Be so good as to offer my best remembrances to Mrs. M. and all the family.

　　" My dear sir,

　　　　" Very faithfully yours,

　　　　　　" T. Picton."

Captain Kincaid, who upon this occasion led one of the storming parties against the small breach, remarks :*—" Finding the current of soldiers setting towards the centre of the town, I followed the stream, which conducted me into the great square ; on one side of which the late garrison were drawn up as prisoners, and the rest of it was filled with British and Portuguese intermixed, without any order or regularity. I had been there but a very short time, when they all commenced firing, without any ostensible cause ; some fired at the doors and windows, some at the roofs of houses, and others at the clouds; and, at last, some heads began to be blown from their shoulders in the general hurricane, when the voice of Sir Thomas Picton with the power of twenty trumpets began to threaten with his usual energy ; while Colonel Bernard, Colonel Cameron, and some other active officers, were carrying his orders into effect with a strong hand ; for, seizing the broken barrels of muskets which were lying about in great abundance, they belaboured every fellow most unmercifully about the head who attempted either to load or fire, and finally succeeded in reducing them to order."

* In his " Adventures of the Rifle Brigade."

Lord Wellington, in concluding his despatch containing the report of this important success, observes :—

" The conduct of all parts of the third division, in the operations which they performed with so much gallantry and exactness on the evening of the 19th, in the dark, affords the strongest proof of the abilities of Lieutenant-general Picton and Major-general Mackinnon, by whom they were directed and led."*

The morning following this night of blood the troops were again reduced to order, and it was remarkable to witness how quickly the

* Major-general Mackinnon had been an intimate and esteemed friend of General Picton, and his death caused him much concern. After the tumult was over and discipline again restored, his remains were found ; when Picton, after having taken a last look at them, calling to some pioneers, bade them prepare a grave in the breach. This breach had been won by the gallant-deceased, and a better or a nobler tomb could not have been selected ; and Picton appeared to take a melancholy pleasure in thus paying a last tribute to the remains of his friend. It was a soldier's fitting resting-place; and many a brave heart was buried there ; but the body was afterwards removed to Espija, where it was again interred with military honours. By Lord Wellington's orders, General Crawfurd was also buried in the breach which he had won, and no false notions or mistaken regard of friends disturbed the remains of that intrepid soldier.

wildest passions of men were subdued by discipline. The same man who but a few hours previously had broken through every bond of moral and physical restraint, was now the orderly and obedient soldier. An officer who served in the third division, relates, in his agreeable Reminiscences, a characteristic anecdote of General Picton, in allusion to the Eighty-eighth regiment getting under arms on the morning after the capture of this fortress.

"We were about to resume our arms," he observes, "when General Picton approached us. Some of the soldiers, who were more than usually elevated in spirits, on his passing them, called out, "Well, general, we gave *you* a cheer last night; it is *your* turn *now*." The general, smiling, took off his hat and said, "Here, then, you drunken set of brave rascals, *Hurrah; we'll soon be at Badajoz!*" A shout of confidence followed; we slung our firelocks, the bands played, and we commenced our march for the village of Atalaya in the highest spirits."

So soon as undisturbed possession of the town was obtained, the fortress was ordered to be repaired, and every addition made to the defences which skill could dictate. Marmont was at this very period advancing toward Ciudad Rodrigo; and it has since appeared that the French general was not acquainted with the investment of that fortress by the allies until the 15th of January, when immediate and hasty preparations were made a second time to relieve it. But the same want of correct intelligence still embarrassed him; all communication with the garrison was of course cut off, and not until eight days after the English had carried the place did Marmont know that fact. How much may be done in a short time by an active body of engineers, is demonstrated by the circumstance that, by the time Marmont was apprised of the fall of Ciudad Rodrigo, it was placed in almost as formidable a state of defence as before the breaches had been made.

The French general did not therefore think it prudent to make any immediate attempt for its recovery, but, as the weather was inclement and wet, he allowed the allies to retain, unmolested, this valuable fortress; probably in the expectation that Lord Wellington would be satisfied with his success, and continue no further operations until the severity of winter had passed.

If these were his views, however, he little knew the active mind of his opponent, and did not reflect upon the difference of their relative situations. Marmont was at the head of an army which belonged to a victorious nation; his force was already large, and his hopes of being reinforced almost amounted to a certainty. Spain was at this moment vir- tually a French province: Joseph Bonaparte was still king, although he had more than once rebelled against the imperious power which had made him so.

Marmont thought, therefore, that he had little to dread; he fancied he was not in an enemy's country, and consequently remained for a short but fatal period inactive.

The views and expectations of Lord Wel- lington were widely different: his army was composed of half foreigners, while the British troops were principally raw recruits, wanting confidence in themselves, and receiving little encouragement from the inhabitants, who, now tired and exhausted by war, made little distinc- tion between friend and foe ; as each of them consumed the produce of their soil, and made their dwellings the scene of their contest. Lord

Wellington had learned not to expect too much from the promises of the British government, and the levies now sent out were so few that they were little more than sufficient to fill up the heavy losses which the army sustained. The supplies of provision were equally scanty, and plunder was frequently resorted to by the soldiers in order to supply the mere wants of nature, although this was in defiance of the general orders issued by the commander of the forces. The physical disabilities under which Lord Wellington laboured compelled him to keep his army in the field in the depth of winter, and to subject his troops to every hardship and privation, in order to take advantage of the inactivity of his opponent, who did not give him or his soldiers credit for such daring and unexpected measures.

Apparently satisfied with the brilliant termination of his attack on the fortress of Ciudad Rodrigo, Lord Wellington kept the army perfectly quiet in its neighbourhood; but it was a deceptive calm, for he was at this moment preparing to accomplish an undertaking of a singularly bold and decisive character. This movement, together with its preliminaries, was

precisely one of those sudden but masked manœuvres which so greatly distinguished the plans
of Napoleon. A whisper spread through the
army that Badajoz was to be the next object
of attack ; but by the following extract from
a letter of General Picton's to a friend in London, it would appear that *he* at least was fully
aware of the intentions of the commander of
the forces. He observes in this letter, " I think
your reply will meet me at Badajoz ; for we
are making active although silent preparations
to invest that place," &c.

This letter is dated February the 9th.

The army remained in cantonments on the
Coa until March, when Lord Wellington established his head-quarters at Elvas ; in the
neighbourhood of which place the troops destined for the siege were collected. On the 15th,
pontoon bridges were thrown over the Guadiana ; and the following day the third, fourth,
and light divisions crossed the river; and with
little opposition invested the fortress of Badajoz
on the south and east sides, the north being
protected by the river ; and as the only bridge
was in the possession of the allies, but a small
force was requisite to confine the garrison in

that direction. The troops were under the
command of Marshal Beresford and General
Picton, the latter being appointed by Lord
Wellington to conduct the siege; and arduous
were the duties which he had to perform, —
even the weather seemed to conspire against
the besiegers, as it rained for several days together with so much violence that the river was
swollen so as greatly to endanger the safety
of the bridge : still no obstacle could overcome
the energy of the troops, or the perseverance
of their officers.

The first point of attack was an outwork
called Fort Picurina, of which it was absolutely
necessary to obtain possession before the batteries could be erected ; and accordingly, on the
night of the 17th, the first parallel was drawn
out, and the approaches were then continued
without intermission, although a tremendous
fire was kept up both from the fort and town.
On the 19th, the garrison (taking advantage
of a thick vapour produced by the continued
rains) made a sortie upon the trenches, both
with cavalry and infantry. The attack on the
workmen was sudden and unexpected ; they

were for a moment driven from the trenches in disorder; but some fresh troops being brought up, they quickly formed, and became in their turn the assailants, when they succeeded in driving the enemy back, although not before considerable damage had been done, and some loss sustained.

. General Picton, with one of his aides-de-camp, Captain Cuthbert of the Fusileers, was soon upon the spot, and assisted in rallying the flying workmen, who at his well-known voice regained confidence. The general was on foot, but Captain Cuthbert was mounted: Picton had just entrusted him with some orders, and he had scarcely left his side, when a shot from the fort struck him on the hip, killed his horse, and mangled the lower part of his body in a most frightful and fatal manner.

General Picton had a sincere regard for this aid-de-camp, and felt his loss doubly, not only for his services as a valuable officer, but also as an estimable young man. His death appears to have been much regretted throughout the division, as his manners whilst in the fulfilment of his duty were devoid of that arrogance which was assumed by many of those holding similar confidential situations.

The trenches during the greater part of this siege were half full of water, and the progress of the working parties was in consequence much retarded by the earth giving way, and filling up in a few minutes the labour of as many hours. In spite, however, of the weather, the fire of the enemy, and the circumstance of having to devote as much time to the repair of their work as in its execution, the besiegers were enabled to open six batteries, mounting in all twenty-eight guns, on the ninth day after the investment. The scene now became one of awful grandeur; every element of destruction and noise seemed concentrated upon this spot: but the result of a modern siege is always certain, unless some diversion is made from without; and the only calculation to be made before its commencement is, the manner in which it can be effected with the greatest expedition and the smallest sacrifice of life. The Fort of Picurina, against which the principal fire had been hitherto directed, presented on the 25th a most dilapidated appearance, nearly all the guns be-

ing dismounted and the walls in ruins; still,
however, it was strong as a place of defence.
But as the more important operations against
the town could not be pursued until this fort
was in possession of the besiegers, it was resolved that on the night of the 25th it should
be carried at the point of the bayonet.

For this important and hazardous undertaking five hundred men of the "fighting
division" were selected, and placed under the
command of Major-general Kempt. About ten
o'clock, every arrangement having been made
for the attack, the little band commenced its
march in three different detachments, advancing at the same moment; the right under
Major Shaw, the centre under Captain Powis,
and the left under Major Rudd. The fire which
met the assailants was most destructive; but
nothing could subdue their courage and perseverance. Three rows of strong palisades, protected by showers of musketry, offered a vain
resistance to their intrepidity; for when they
failed at one point they directed their efforts
to another. The garrison showed a degree of
resolution in their defence honourable to the
French arms; but with resistance the assailants

seemed only to gain determination : until, after as brave a contest as ever distinguished the troops of both nations, the British succeeded in driving the enemy from the walls, and compelling them to abandon the fort.

CHAPTER IV.

Siege of Badajoz.—Skill of the French governor in the art of defence.—Memorandum issued by Lord Wellington.—The attack made.—General Kempt badly wounded.—Desperate efforts of the besieged.—Anecdote of Lieutenant Macpherson.—General Picton wounded.—Anecdotes of Picton.—Dreadful havoc among the British.

THE siege of Badajoz is an event as honourable to our army as it was individually glorious to Sir Thomas Picton; for, regardless of the illiberal attempts which were made to take from him the glory which he there won, the veteran never relates the taking of Badajoz without a just eulogium upon him who, when every prospect of success seemed to have fled, sent his aid-de-camp to the commander of the forces with the gratifying announcement that *the place was captured!* It is necessary to give a brief outline of this siege in order

properly to appreciate the services of General
Picton, and to understand the critical moment
in which those services were rendered.

Picurina being taken, the guns of that fortress were immediately turned against the
town, while the batteries were all concentrated upon the ramparts, with the intention of
effecting two breaches; the one in the south-
east angle of the fort called La Trinidad, and
the other in the flank of the bastion called
Santa Maria.　Soult was now in motion, using
strenuous arguments to persuade Marmont to
effect a junction with him for the relief of
Badajoz; but that general preferred making
a diversion against Ciudad Rodrigo, in the
expectation of inducing Lord Wellington to
abandon the siege of Badajoz and hasten to its
relief.　The English general knew, however, too
well the local obstacles against which Marmont
would have to contend : he had received information that the rivers in the north were swollen,
so as to render the passage of an army a long
and tedious operation; and the only cause
of apprehension which Lord Wellington experienced at this period was, that the waters
might subside, or that Marmont, tired of wait-

ing, would by forced marches endeavour to
unite with Soult in sufficient time to prevent
his obtaining possession of Badajoz.

Soult made a movement towards the besieged
fortress, but did not dare to risk a battle with
the force under his command... Preparations
were, however, made by the English general to
fight him without stopping the progress of the
siege; for unless Marmont used extraordinary
exertions, he would be too late to save Badajoz,
as, without him, it was not supposed that Soult
would make any further efforts for its relief.
It was, therefore, a subject of much moment
that the proceedings against the town should
be carried on with the utmost activity.

Phillipon, the French general who commanded in Badajoz with a garrison of about
five thousand men, possessed great skill in
the art of defence, and every obstacle which
modern warfare could devise was thrown in
the way of the assailants; no opportunity was
lost; and when the outworks were destroyed
by the fire of the batteries, the besiegers
found others of nearly corresponding strength
prepared behind them; while the following
morning frequently showed the vigilance of

the defenders in the repair of the injury effected on the defences during the preceding day.
But the plan of Lord Wellington was simply to
make a practicable breach, and then trust to the
known and often-tried courage of his soldiers
to find their way through it into the town.

The operations of the besieged were, however, so daring, and their efforts to protract the
siege so constant and judicious, that the firing
in the breaches was ordered to be kept up during the night, in order to check in some degree the hardihood of their proceedings. But
by some neglect this order was not obeyed to
the extent desired, and on the morning of the
1st of April the garrison had succeeded in
raising several additional defences behind the
breaches; in consequence of which General
Picton issued the following order on the morning of that day :—

        " RESERVE ORDERS.

        "Camp before Badajoz, 1st April.

" It having been reported to the commanding officer by the commanding engineer, that
the batteries, with the exception of that commanded by Lieutenant De Goeben, did not
fire at the breach last night according to orders

given, he is determined to report every officer
to Lord Wellington who shall neglect this
duty."

On the 5th of April expectation was at its
height; the general impression amongst the
soldiers was that the attack would be made
that night. Lord Wellington made a close
reconnoissance of the breaches, attended by
several of his generals, when he came to a
determination that no longer time should be
lost, and directions were accordingly given to
the different officers to make the necessary preparations. The principal engineer was in the
mean while desired to make his own observations upon the state of the breaches, and the
defences which the enemy had erected on the
inside. Having with some difficulty been enabled to effect this to his satisfaction, he reported to the commander of the forces, that
although the great breach appeared sufficiently
easy of access, the works which the besieged
had thrown up in its rear would assist them in
making a formidable resistance, which could
not be overcome without a considerable sacrifice of men. Under these circumstances, it
was resolved to delay the attack until the fol-

lowing day, while in the mean time the whole
of the batteries should direct their fire against
the curtain of La Trinidad, " in hopes that by
effecting a third breach, the troops would be
enabled to turn the enemy's works for the defence of the other two." *   The morning of the
6th opened with the same heavy 'cannonade
which had for twelve successive days been continued almost without cessation, and by four
o'clock in the afternoon a third breach was reported practicable. Once more Lord Wellington made a reconnoissance; and upon this occasion being satisfied with the appearance of
the breaches, he gave directions for the assault
to be made at ten o'clock that night. But in
order that a correct idea may be formed of the
intended operations, the memorandum issued
by the commander of the forces is here inserted.

" MEMORANDUM.

" 1. The fort of Badajoz is to be attacked at
ten o'clock this night.

" 2. The attack must be made on three points;
the castle, the face of the bastion of La Trinidad,
and the flank of the bastion of Santa Maria.

* Despatch.

" 3. The attack of the castle to be by escalade; that of the two bastions by the storm of the breaches.

" 4. The troops for the storm of the castle, consisting of the third division of infantry, should move out from the right of the first parallel at a little before ten o'clock, but not to attack till ten o'clock.

" 5. They should cross the river Rivillas, below the broken bridge over that river, and attack that part of the castle which is on the right, looking from the trenches, and in the rear of the great battery constructed by the enemy to fire on the bastion of La Trinidad.

" 6. Having arrived within the castle, and being secured the possession of it, parties must be sent to the left along the rampart, to fall on the rear of those defending the great breach in the bastion of La Trinidad, and to communicate with the right of the attack on that bastion.

" 7. The troops for this attack must have all the long ladders in the engineers' park, and six of the lengths of the engineers' ladders. They must be attended by twelve carpenters with axes, and by six miners with crow-bars, &c.

"8. The fourth division, with the exception of the covering party in the trenches, must make the attack on the face of the bastion of La Trinidad, and the light division on the flank of the bastion of Santa Maria.

"9. These two divisions must parade in close columns of divisions at nine o'clock. The light division with the left in front; the fourth division, with its advanced guard, with the left in front; the remainder with the right in front. The fourth division must be on the right of the little stream, near the picquet of the fourth division; and the light division must have the river on their right.

"10. The light division must throw one hundred men into the quarries, close to the covered way of the bastion of Santa Maria; who, as soon as the garrison are disturbed, must keep down by their fire the fire from the face of the bastion of Santa Maria, and that from the covered way.

"11. The advance of both divisions must consist of five hundred men from each, attended by twelve ladders; and the men of the storming party should carry sacks filled with light materials, to be thrown into the ditch, to enable the troops to descend into it. Care must be taken that these bags are not thrown into the covered way.

" 12. The advance of the light division must precede that of the fourth division, and both must keep as near the inundation as they possibly can.

" 13. The advance of both divisions must be formed into firing parties and storming parties. The firing parties must be spread along the crest of the glacis, to keep down the fire of the enemy; while the men of the storming party, who carry bags, will enter the covered way at the place d'armes, under the breached face of the bastion of La Trinidad; those attached to the fourth division on its right, those to the light division on its left, looking from the trenches or the camp.

"14. The storming party of the advance of the light division will then descend into the ditch, and, turning to its left, storm the breach in the flank of the bastion of Santa Maria; while the storming party of the fourth division will likewise descend into the ditch and storm the breach in the face of the bastion of La Trinidad. The firing parties are to follow immediately in the rear of their respective storming parties.

"15. The heads of the two divisions will follow their advanced guards, keeping nearly together; but they will not advance beyond the shelter afforded by the quarries on the left of the road till they will have seen the heads of the advanced guards ascend the breaches :- they will then move forward to the storm in double-quick time.

"16. If the light division should find the bastion of Santa Maria entrenched, they will turn the right of the entrenchment, by moving along the parapet of the bastion. The fourth division will do the same by an entrenchment which appears on the left face looking from the trenches of the bastion of La Trinidad.

"17. The light division, as soon as they are in possession of the rampart of Santa Maria, are to turn to their left, and to proceed along the rampart to their left, keeping always a reserve at the breach.

"18. The advanced guard of the fourth division are to turn to their left, and to keep up the communication with the light division : the fourth division are to turn to their right, and to communicate with the third division by the bastion of San Pedro and the demi-bastion of San Antonio, taking care to keep a reserve at the bastion of La Trinidad.

"19. Each (the fourth and light) division must leave one thousand men in reserve in the quarries.

"20. The fourth division must endeavour to get open the gate of La Trinidad: the light division must do the same by the gate called Puerto del Pillar.

"21. The soldiers must leave their knapsacks in camp.

"22. In order to aid these operations, the howitzers, in number twelve, are to open a fire upon the batteries constructed by the enemy to fire upon the breach, as soon as the officers will observe that the enemy are aware of the attack, which they must continue till they see that the third division are in possession of the castle.

"23. The commanding officer in the trenches is to attack the ravelin of Saint Roque with two hundred of the covering party, moving from the right of the second parallel, and round the right of the ravelin looking from

H 2

the trenches, and attacking the barriers and gates of communication between the ravelin and bridge; while two hundred men, likewise of the covering party, will rush from the right of the sap into the salient angle of the covered way of the ravelin, and keep up a fire on its faces. These last should not advance from the sap till the party to attack the gorge of the ravelin will have turned it. That which will move into the covered way on the right of the ravelin looking from the trenches ought not to proceed further down than the angle formed by the face and the flank.

"24. The remainder of the covering party to be a reserve in the trenches. The working parties in the trenches are to join their regiments at half-past seven o'clock. Twelve carpenters with axes, and ten miners with crowbars, must be with each (fourth and light) division. A party of one officer and twenty artillery-men must be with each division.

"25. The fifth division must be formed, one brigade on the ground occupied by the Forty-eighth regiment, one brigade on the Sierra del Viento, and one brigade on the low grounds extending to the Guadiana, now occupied by the picquets of the light division.

" 26· The picquets of the brigades on the Sierra del Viento, and that in the low grounds towards the Guadiana, should endeavour to alarm the enemy during the attack by firing at the Pardaleras, and at the men in the covered way of the works towards the Guadiana.

" 27. The commander of the forces particularly requests the general officers commanding divisions and brigades, and the commanding officers of regiments, and the officers commanding companies, to impress upon their men the necessity of keeping together and formed as a military body, after the storm and during the night. Not only the success of the operation and the honour of the army, but their own individual safety, depend upon their being in a situation to repel any attack by the enemy, and to overcome all resistance which they may be inclined to make, till the garrison have been completely subdued."

We have been informed from many sources, that, according to the original plan of attack, the third division was only to have made a feint against the castle. As Lord Wellington doubted the practicability of a successful escalade, he had abandoned the idea of any serious attempt in that quarter: but upon the representation and arguments of General Picton, it was afterwards determined that *his* division should make the attempt. This determination decided the fate of Badajoz.

The original time appointed for making the assault was seven; but so many arrangements were necessary, that it was afterwards postponed until ten o'clock: a delay that enabled the enemy to construct defences which, it will be shown, offered such unexpected obstacles to the progress of the assailants, that even the undaunted resolution of our soldiers must have been shaken, had not an unexpected event paralyzed the efforts of the defenders. It will be seen by the arrangements, that the attack was to be made simultaneously at all points. Picton and his division were to move from the trenches a short while before the others; but they were to appear beneath the walls of the castle at the moment when the assault was to commence on the breaches,

and the diversion was to be made by the fifth
division on the opposite side of the town, near
San.-Vincente.

The number of troops directed to storm
Badajoz amounted to about nineteen thousand
men ; and never were soldiers in better heart or
condition : one spirit seemed to pervade them.
Some had already tried the strength of the
defences against which they were now about
to be led, in the unsuccessful attempt upon
Fort Christoval during the former siege ; but
any one who had seen the bearing of the men
when drawn up in preparation for the attack
could scarcely have doubted the result. It was
not alone the hope of conquest that now led
them on ; another, but not a better feeling,
was stirring in their breasts : they burned to
remove the stigma of former failures, and also
to satisfy their hatred of the inhabitants, who
had ever been unfriendly to the British troops.
These motives had raised a combination of
feelings which rendered this service a more
than ordinary cause of excitement. The
French in their turn were anxiously awaiting
the contest, relying on the activity and skill of
their distinguished commandant ; and, assured

by the success of their previous efforts, they'
anticipated the attack with confidence.   Prepared moreover on all hands and in every way
to destroy, they hoped to drive the assailants
back to their trenches, and compel them to
raise the siege.   As the hour approached, each
man made his preparation in silence ; for on-
such occasions it would be ill-timed and un-
kind to oppose the wishes of the brave and
devoted men upon whose exertions all must
depend.

The night was dark and damp; a cold vapour
hung around the town, partly composed of the
dense smoke which had been left by the day's
firing hanging heavily in the still air.   But
this stillness was not to last long.   Near the
appointed time, while the men were waiting
with increased anxiety, Picton with his staff
came up.   The troops fell in ;   all were in a
moment silent, until the general, in his calm
and impressive manner, addressed a few words
to each regiment.

The signal was not yet given; but the enemy,
by means of lighted carcases, discovered the
position of Picton's soldiers : to delay longer
would only have been to expose his men

unnecessarily; he therefore gave the word to
" advance." The regiments composing the
third division upon this occasion deserve. particular mention. The Forty-fifth took the
lead; and the Seventy-fourth, Eighty-eighth,
Fifth, Seventy-seventh, Eighty-third, and
Ninety-fourth, closely followed. But it would
be injustice to . pass over the two regiments
of Portuguese, the Ninth and Twenty-first,
under Colonel de Champlemond, who nobly
bore their part in the struggle of the night.
Advancing at a steady pace, they crossed a
small mill-stream called the Rivillas, but not.
unobserved : some fire-balls sent forth by the
garrison burning brilliantly in the air over
their heads, showed the silent march of the
column. The enemy's fire immediately opened,. and every available gun was brought to
bear upon their ranks. Still there was. no
pause; not a shot was returned; but quickly
filling up the intervals caused by this destructive fire, they moved on. The illuminated air
now showed them their path ; but the storm of
shot grew closer and hotter at every step as the
enemy saw more clearly their assailants, until,
having crossed the stream, Picton's soldiers set

up a loud shout, and rushed forward up the
steep, to the ditch at the foot of the castle
walls.

General Kempt, who had thus far been with
Picton at the head of the division, was here
badly wounded and carried to the rear. Picton
was therefore left alone to conduct the assault:
and the desperate nature of the service called
for all his energies.

Arrived in the ditch, the leading engineer,
Lieutenant Mac Carthy, of the Fiftieth regiment, who had volunteered for this service,
found that the ladders had been laid upon the
paling of the ditch. This brave officer, finding
that these palings had not yet been removed,
and that they formed a considerable barrier to
the advance of the men, cried out, " Down
with the paling !" and immediately applying
his own hands to effect this, with the assistance
of a few others, he succeeded in forcing them
down. Through this gap rushed Picton, followed by his men; but so thick was the fire
upon this point, that death seemed inevitable.
For a moment the soldiers were paralyzed, and
wavered; but the voice of their general was
heard above the din, and they again moved over

their fallen comrades, bearing the ponderous ladders on their shoulders, crowding to raise them against the walls; but the fire was so tremendous, that this forlorn-hope was all but exterminated.

It is said that each soldier on the walls had six muskets, which he fired in turn as they were loaded by others; at the same time vast fragments of stone like rocks, which had been kept poised upon the walls, were pitched down upon the assailants, crushing them in a frightful manner; whilst hand-grenades, shells, and guns loaded to the muzzle with grape and case-shot, all burst forth at once. The incessant flashes threw a terrible glare over the scene; and the men could be discerned running to and fro in the ditch, some pressing forward with the ladders, others endeavouring to raise them, and many falling in the act: quickly, however, was their place again filled up. They then strove to rest the ladders against the ramparts; but the defenders, prepared for every attempt, had long poles shod with iron, with which they forced them back, while those on the wall, pointing their muskets down on each side, swept off all who endeavoured to mount.

At length, however, the assailants succeeded in erecting three ladders;* but the rush of men and the fire of the enemy caused the ladders to break, when those who had succeeded in mounting them were thrown upon the bayonets of

---

* One of the first to make the daring ascent was Lieutenant Macpherson of the Forty-fifth, (whose name has been before mentioned,) closely followed by Sir Edward Pakenham. He arrived unharmed to within a few rounds of the top, when he discovered that the ladder was about three feet too short. Still undaunted, he called loudly to those below to raise it more perpendicularly; and while he with great exertion pushed it from the wall at the top, the men with a loud cheer brought it nearer at the base: but this was done so suddenly, that Macpherson was on a level with the rampart before he could prepare for defence, and he saw a French soldier deliberately point his musket against his body; and, without having the least power to strike it aside, the man fired. The ball struck one of the Spanish silver buttons on his waistcoat, which it broke in half: this changed its deadly direction, and caused it to glance off; not, however, before it had broken two ribs, the fractured part of one being pressed in upon his lungs so as almost to stop respiration. Still he did not fall, but contrived to hold on by the upper round of the ladder, conscious that he was wounded, but ignorant to what extent. He could not, however, advance. Pakenham strove to pass him, but in the effort was also severely wounded. Almost at the same moment the ladder broke: destruction seemed inevitable, for a *chevaux de frise* of bayonets was beneath. Still, even at such a moment as this, their presence of mind was unshaken: Pakenham, taking the hand of the wounded Macpherson,

their comrades below, where they met with a
horrid and lingering death. Hundreds had
fallen, and every moment added to the carnage.
Still there was no pause, not a soldier thought
of retreat; for a wild feeling of revenge now

said, " God bless you, my dear fellow ! we shall meet again !"
And they did meet again, but not where Pakenham meant,
for they both recovered from their wounds.

Macpherson contrived, by getting to the back of the ladder, to descend to the ditch in safety, where he lay for a
short time insensible. When reason returned, he found himself attended by two of his men, one supporting his head upon his knees, and the other holding a cup of chocolate to his
lips : the shots were ploughing up the ground in every direction around them ; but, unmoved and unhurt, they continued
their friendly occupation. Macpherson made a violent effort
to rise, during which the bone which had been pressing on
his lungs was forced from its place, and he obtained instant
relief. He arose and again mounted a ladder ; but the walls
were now gained : he therefore directed his steps towards the
tower, on which he had in the morning seen the French flag
waving in proud defiance ; his object was to gain it. But all
was now confusion and slaughter ; the enemy continued to
defend every tenable post, and the infuriated soldiers were
bayonetting them without mercy. " I at length," (to use his
own words,) " found my way to the tower, where I perceived
the sentry still at his post. With my sword drawn, I seized
him, and desired him in French to show me the way to the
colours. He replied, ' *Je ne sais pas.*' I upon this gave him
a slight cut across the face, saying at the same time, ' *Vous
le savez à présent;*' on which he dashed his arms upon the
ground, and, striking his breast, said, as he raised his head

led them on with sanguinary fury; every shot that struck a comrade to the earth filled the survivors with deadlier rage.

A ball had struck Picton on the groin a little above his watch, whilst leading his soldiers to the foot of the ramparts. A distinguished officer who was by his side at the time, and to whom we are indebted for much interesting information respecting the events of this night, thinks the ball had first struck the earth; still the blow was severe. He did not fall or bleed, but being assisted to the glacis, in a short time became extremely faint and almost insensible. He remained in this state for nearly twenty minutes; when the pain having in some degree

and pointed to his heart, '*Frappez, je suis Français!*' his manner at the same time indicating that the colour was there. I could not wait to provide for the safety of this brave fellow; so I called out loudly for a non-commissioned officer to take charge of him, so that he should not be hurt. One stepped forward; when, giving him instructions to protect the gallant soldier, I ascended the tower; but my precaution was vain, for I afterwards discovered that this noble fellow was amongst the dead."

Macpherson was rewarded upon reaching the top of the tower by finding the French colour still flying. He instantly tore it down; when, for lack of anything else, he took off his red jacket, and hoisted it on the staff as an honourable substitute for the British flag.

subsided, refusing medical aid, he again proceeded to direct the attack. He now saw his
men moving amidst the dying and dead, while
the incessant fire was still mowing them down;
he could also perceive that they had not yet
struck a blow in return, for during this period
the defenders had scarcely lost a man. Picton's
soldiers were amazed at the overwhelming fire
that was poured upon them; but they heard
their general calling upon them in a calm
energetic tone, not to desert him, but to make
one effort more. " If we cannot win the castle,"
he cried, " let us die upon the walls !"* This
was sufficient; fresh ladders were raised against
another part of the battlements, and hundreds
rushed forward to scale them, when the struggle
again commenced: this part of the wall was
not quite so high.

---

* " Picton, seeing the frightful situation in which he was
placed, became uneasy; but the good-will with which his
brave companions exposed and laid down their lives, reassured
him: he called out to his men, told them they had never been
defeated, and that now was the moment to conquer or die.
Picton, although not loved by his soldiers, was respected by
them; and his appeal, as well as his unshaken front, did
wonders in changing the desperate state of the division."—
Reminiscences of a Subaltern.

Colonel Ridge of the Forty-fifth, who had so
greatly distinguished himself at Ciudad Rodrigo,
was again foremost: a ladder was dashed against
the battlement, when, springing forward, he
rushed up, followed on every round by his fear-
less and devoted soldiers.   He had ascended so
quickly, that, before those on the top could
force the ladder back, the weight was too great,
and it pressed firmly against the wall.   But
who could hope to gain the summit and live?
The enemy were now concentrated round the
top to pour their fire on each man as he advanced; pikes, bayonets, and the unceasing
stream of musketry were to be passed before the
wall could be reached.   Ridge still, however,
pressed on, his sword guarding his head, and
the bayonets of those on the next rounds thrust
upwards to protect him.   Other ladders were
erected, and with better success; the enemy in
their turn were paralyzed at the unconquerable
resolution of the assailants.   Despair of being
able to repulse them seemed now to have seized
the defenders; it might even be supposed that
they were tired of killing: certain, however, it
is, that their efforts were becoming more feeble,
for Ridge, Canch, and several more, gained a

footing on the battlements. Then (for the first time during the night) did the tide turn in favour of the assailants. A continued rush of troops now followed up the ladders; as the enemy made but a slight resistance when the wall was gained. This conquest had cost the victors much, but the defenders paid a dear and bloody price for the injury which they had inflicted. From men so infuriated with the disappointment of repeated failure little mercy could be expected; few, very few of those who had assisted in raising the pile of dead that now nearly filled the ditch, were left to boast of their deeds.

The wound which Picton had received prevented his ascending the ladders to enter the castle, and he was in consequence compelled to remain in the ditch, but he was not inactive; for, calling up the whole of the straggling parties, he ordered them all to ascend the walls, and thus poured in a powerful assistance to co-operate with those already in possession in resisting any efforts on the part of the enemy for recovering the castle.

But we must now take a slight retrospect of the assault on the breaches, and the operations

of the fifth division against the Pardaleras and
San Vincente, in order to form an opinion of
the importance of Picton's success. It is not,
however, necessary to dwell upon the details of
these attacks.

The fourth and light divisions were ordered
on this fearful duty. They advanced a short
time after Picton's division had moved against
the castle. Their united numbers amounted to
about ten thousand men, commanded by Major-
general Colville and Lieutenant-colonel Barnard.
The attack made by these troops is perhaps one
of the most extraordinary instances of daring in
history: as an appalling proof of the wildness
and even madness of men when stimulated to
desperation by resistance and impelled by revenge, it stands unparalleled. But these were
not the only feelings which pervaded this gallant band; it would be injustice to them to
deny that in the breasts of many there lived a
nobler and better motive.

They moved from the trenches and reached
the glacis in silence: there the enemy discovered them, and the work of death commenced. The ditch was to be crossed: some
few availed themselves of the ladders; but, im-

patient of this slow mode of descent, the men rushed to the brink, and the column poured down like a falling cataract. The enemy had waited for this moment to set at work all their instruments of destruction.

" Never, probably, since the discovery of gunpowder," says Colonel Jones, " were men more exposed to its action than those assembled in the ditch to assault the breaches. Many thousand shells and hand-grenades, numerous bags filled with powder, every kind of burning composition and destructive missile, had been prepared and placed along the parapet of the whole front: these, under an incessant roll of musketry, were hurled into the ditch without intermission for upwards of two hours, giving to its surface an appearance of vomiting fire, and producing sudden flashes of light more vivid than the day. Description, however, conveys but a faint idea of the imposing nature of such a mode of defence. The doors of success were certainly thrown open; but they were so vigilantly guarded, the approach to them was so strewn with difficulties, and the scene altogether so appalling, that instead of its being a disparagement to the troops to have failed in forcing through them, is it not rather a subject for pride and exultation that they had firmness to persevere in the attempt until recalled ?"

Yet they did persevere in defiance of all these horrors, and the pile of dead and dying which was soon accumulated : the living still rushed on to gain the breach, or fill it with their bodies. Closely packed in the narrow ditch, every explosion and every shot found a victim, until it more resembled a grave where the living were interred with the dead. It would have been a hopeless effort to escape or even to avoid the destruction ; and the shell was frequently seen about to explode, without the beholder having power to move from its vicinity. But the hope of gaining the breach made them submit without a murmur to the havoc made in their ranks. Much confusion existed for a short time by the circumstance of an unfinished ravelin being mistaken for the breach : it was, however, too easily gained ; no enemy was on the summit. But it was not a position to be maintained : a murderous fire from the ramparts in the rear, on each side, and from the breach, swept the crown of this elevation, and many fell rolling back upon their advancing friends. Still, others pressed forward and jumped into the ditch which separated it from the ramparts; while some, moving to the right of the ravelin, joined them; when, forming in one close but irregular mass, they rushed up the crumbling ruins of the breach.

It would be vain to attempt an adequate description of this wild and sanguinary scene; to trace all its features is impossible. When the troops had arrived on the crown of the breach, an unexpected obstacle was found to exist; one that seemed at once to defy every effort of desperation to overcome. This was a *chevaux de frise* of sword-blades, fixed in beams of wood, the ends of which were buried deeply in the ruins, and chained to each other both inside and out; between these were rows of muskets, which poured forth a deadly and incessant fire upon the almost frantic assailants, as, goaded to desperation by this unlooked-for check, they dashed the butts of their muskets with wild fury against the firmly-rooted blades. While thus vainly endeavouring to overcome this barrier, the enemy, who lined the ramparts on each side, continued to send forth every missile of destruction, and at the same time kept up an incessant fire of musketry; so that the troops, unable to advance and unwilling to return, stood with reckless daring to be massacred by the enemy, who mowed them down with impunity. The sloping ruins were quickly covered with their bodies, some only disabled, others sadly mutilated; but all were soon alike, as their crushed and mangled remains were trampled into shapeless masses by their intrepid comrades. Unappalled by the havoc which strewed their path, fresh men still pressed up the breach: beneath that fire no man could live, but they could die; and hopeless but desperate, they crowded forward, unshrinking, unsubdued. The loud shouts of triumph sent forth by the defenders were answered by wild cries of defiance from the devoted English; and that was again echoed by the hollow moans and piercing cries of the trampled fallen. Many feats of daring gallantry were performed upon this memorable night by individuals, which, could they be recorded, would hand to posterity a list of names worthy of fame.

CHAPTER V.

Capture of the Castle of Badajoz.—Lord Wellington directs
it to be retained at all hazards.—Successful attack on the
breaches at the bastion of San Vincente.—The Governor
retires to Fort Christoval.—Attempt to retake the Castle.
—Death of Colonel Ridge.—Surrender of the Garrison.—
Anecdotes of Picton and his Division.—Picton's Letters
on the Siege destroyed; inference to be drawn therefrom.
—Lord Liverpool's eulogium on Picton.—Character of the
Third Division.

It would have been difficult to determine
whether the soldiers or the officers were most
conspicuous in this struggle for death; leaders
were never for one moment wanting, nor
hundreds to follow them: but it was still the
same hopeless strife—no single step was gained,
the same impenetrable barrier stood uninjured;
while the garrison, exulting in the success of
their stratagem, plied their muskets with increasing and frightful rapidity. To continue
this unavailing sacrifice of life would have been
inhuman. Lord Wellington received repeated

communications from the officers commanding the attack ; but no one brought him any change, or held out any prospect of success. The red glare upon the dark clouds, and the incessant din of arms, told him clearly that the contest was still raging with unabated fury. He knew well the slaughter attendant upon the assault of a breach ; a *brief* struggle is there surely a bloody one, but the long continuance of this promised a frightful return. He knew that his soldiers would not desist while an entire company remained to die ; but justice to these brave men demanded that he should put a stop to the work of destruction — and he ordered the retreat to be sounded.

At this moment, directed by the burning flambeaux to the post occupied by the com-mander of the forces and his staff, an officer rode up at speed — it was Picton's confidential aid-de-camp. " Who's that ?" said the chief, in his usual sharp but firm tone. " Lieutenant Tyler," was the reply. " Ah, Tyler, — well ?" observed his lordship. " General Picton has taken the castle, my lord," said Tyler. " Then the place is ours," exclaimed Wellington ; and Tyler was immediately ordered to return to

Picton, with directions to keep possession of the castle át all hazards. Tyler hastened back; but Picton, never for one moment forgetting or misunderstanding the spirit of his instructions, had already ordered parties to proceed along the ramparts to the breaches. The enemy, upon his retreat from the castle, had closed and strongly barricaded the gates communicating with the ramparts. To force these ponderous iron-bound barriers was a work of difficulty, with the means at their disposal.

Again, the enemy having received some reinforcements from San Vincente, were making demonstrations to retake the castle; when Picton sent in some fresh troops to repel the threatened attack, while others were employed in battering the gates. The success of Picton's escalade had, however, destroyed the security and confidence of the garrison. The castle commanded the whole town; and unless it could be retaken, the further efforts of the French in defending the breaches must be ultimately defeated. Other operations were, moreover, in progress against the fort of Pardaleras and the bastion of San Vincente. General Walker's brigade of the fifth division

had made a successful assault on the latter;
for the enemy's troops destined to defend this
post had been called upon to aid in the attempt
to recapture the castle, and in consequence
those that were left made at first but a feeble
resistance, and the British troops quickly succeeded in establishing themselves upon the
walls.   As soon, however, as the French had
recovered from their first panic, they were rallied
by their officers, and a desperate conflict ensued,
when the English were again partially driven
back ; but fresh troops were rushing up the
ladders, and these being formed by Colonel
Nugent as they reached the rampart, received
the French with so steady and close a volley,
that they were almost annihilated: the bayonet
finished the work, and the British troops advanced into the town, hurrying through the
main street to attack the breaches and retrench-
ments of the enemy in the rear.   Every exertion had been made during this period by
Picton's soldiers to force the communications
from the castle to the ramparts ; but some of
the gateways were filled up with solid masonry,
while others were of such massy workmanship

and so firmly secured, that all their efforts were vain.

General Picton, upon being made acquainted with this, sent the same aid-de-camp to inform the commander of the forces of the difficulty which his soldiers found in effecting a passage to the breach. Upon receiving this information, Lord Wellington, having ordered the light and fourth divisions to cease the attack, sent word to Picton to blow down the gates, but remain in the castle until daylight, when, with about two thousand soldiers, he was to sally out upon the ramparts, while the attack in front of the breaches was to be resumed by the two divisions which had already suffered so much and fought so well.

Picton accordingly prepared to obey the instructions of his chief; but the British bugles were now sounding in the rear of the enemy's entrenchments, and the English soldiers were rushing forward to clear the breaches. The light and fourth divisions were again ordered to advance against the breach of La Trinidad. But there was now no enemy: for, alarmed by the surrounding attack, and convinced that longer

resistance would be unavailing, Phillipon contrived to cross the bridge, and throw himself
and part of his garrison into Fort Christoval,
leaving to the allies the prize for which they
had so nobly fought. The two divisions mounted the breach, passed over the hill of dead, and
reached the *chevaux de frise;* but the resistance had ceased; instead of the showers of balls
which had before assailed them at that fatal
spot, they now stood uninjured. Still with
difficulty they forced the unguarded barrier;
but so soon as an entrance was effected, they
rushed like a torrent into the devoted city.

The last effort of the enemy to recover
Badajoz was an attack upon the castle; but
Picton's invincible and victorious soldiers beat
back the French with frightful slaughter,—
not, however, until as brave an officer as ever
fought had fallen by almost the last shot. This
was Ridge, who was the first upon the walls,
and whose daring example, both at Ciudad
Rodrigo and Badajoz, had rendered him an
object of emulation throughout the army.

A writer to whom we have before alluded, in
concluding his account of the siege of Badajoz,*

* In " The United Service Journal."

observes: " An attempt to retake the castle was made in vain. But the brave Colonel Ridge of the Fifth, who had so distinguished himself, lost his life by almost one of the last shots that were fired in this fruitless effort to recover a place which had cost the army the heart's-blood of the third division: and the army saw like a speck in the horizon the scattered remnant of Picton's invincible soldiers, as they stood in a lone group upon the ramparts of a spot that, by its isolated situation, towering height, and vast strength, seemed not to appertain to the rest of the fortifications, and which the enemy, with their entirely disposable force, were unable to retake from the few brave men that now stood triumphant upon its lofty battlements. Nevertheless, triumphant and stern as was their attitude, it was not without its alloy, for more than five-sixths of their officers and comrades either lay dead at their feet, or badly wounded in the ditch below them. All their generals, Picton amongst the number, and almost all their colonels, were either killed or wounded; and as they stood to receive the praises of their commander, and the cheers of their equally brave but unfor-

tunaté companions in arms, their diminished
front and haggard appearance told with terrible truth the nature of the conflict in which
they had been engaged."

Thus terminated this important siege, dearly
purchased, it is true, but never did soldiers
cover themselves with so much glory as those
who conquered Badajoz. France heard of it
with wonder and ill-concealed dismay; for the
details which were given to the French nation,
by exaggerating the amount of resistance in
the defenders, only added to the degree of skill
and courage demanded for its subjection. This
was the first perfect lesson which the enemy
had learned of the invincible nature of British
soldiers, and it produced its effect. Napoleon
is said to have observed in the memorable field
of Waterloo, " These English never know when
they are beaten."

As may be imagined from the details here
given, the loss sustained by the allies was very
great; nearly five thousand men had .fallen
from the commencement of the siege until
the moment when the flag of England was
seen floating over the city.

Colonel Napier remarks, that when the extent of the night's havoc was made known to Lord Wellington, the firmness of his nature gave way for a moment, and the pride of conquest yielded to a passionate burst of grief for the loss of his gallant soldiers.*

Phillipon and the remainder of the garrison

* We have met with several anecdotes relating to this siege in the accounts of those who witnessed the events of this night, and who shared in its dangers, but whose better fortune spared them to relate the deeds of those who fell. From that excellent periodical the United Service Journal the following anecdotes are extracted, which refer in particular to General Picton and his division.

A medical officer, whose more humane duties debarred him from entering into the sanguinary struggle at Badajoz, and who was necessarily better enabled to observe and note the passing events, after having remarked upon the repeated arrivals of aides-de-camp from the breaches, announcing the total failure of the attack, and that unless some reinforcements were sent the troops would be compelled to retreat, adds:

" Another staff-officer soon arrived, bringing information that General Picton had obtained possession of the castle.

" ' Who brings that intelligence?' exclaimed Lord Wellington.

" The officer gave his name.†

" ' Are you certain, sir?'

" ' I entered the castle with the troops—have just left it, and General Picton in possession.'

† Lieutenant Tyler, the officer before alluded to as sent by General Picton with this information.

surrendered early on the following morning.
Would that the pen could stop here, and close
the account of this brilliant achievement! But
it cannot be — the degrading tale is already
told, and those who have thus far admired
the brave and enduring soldiers for the devotion with which they fought, must look with
disgust upon the lawless plunderer and the

"'' With how many men?'

" ' His division.'

" It is impossible to imagine the change this produced in
the feelings of all around.

"'' Return, sir, and desire General Picton to maintain his
position at all hazards.'

" Having despatched this messenger, Lord Wellington
directed a second officer to proceed to the castle to repeat
his orders to General Picton."

Alluding to the failure of the soldiers to force the gates
and attack the breaches in rear, the enemy at the same
time threatening the recapture of the castle, and to defeat
which the troops were kept in order on the ramparts,
another writer observes: " Having continued formed as
above until morning, we received orders to advance into the
town, and were cheered by the generous admission of our
brave comrades, ' that Picton and the third division had
taken Badajoz.'"   And the Editor in a note to this remark,
adds: " We have now before us a letter from an officer,
written the day after the storm, eulogizing the magnanimity
of Lord Wellington on this occasion; his lordship having,
it was asserted, told Sir Thomas Picton that the ' third
division had saved his honour and gained him Badajoz.'"

violater of every human tie. When further apprehensions of resistance had subsided, the troops were allowed to leave their ranks, military discipline ceased, and the doomed city was made the sport of wantonness and crime. Colonel Napier says,

" Now commenced that wild and desperate wickedness which tarnished the lustre of the soldier's heroism. All, indeed, were not alike ; for hundreds risked and many lost their lives in striving to stop the violence : but the madness generally prevailed ; and as the worst men were the leaders here, all the dreadful passions of human nature were displayed. Shameless rapacity, brutal intemperance, savage lust, cruelty and murder, shrieks and piteous lamentations, groans, shouts, imprecations, the hissing of fires bursting from the houses, the crashing of doors and windows, and the reports of muskets used in violence, resounded for two days and nights in the streets of Badajoz ! On the third, when the city was sacked, when the soldiers were exhausted by their own excesses, the tumult rather subsided than was quelled."*

* Lieutenant Macpherson, the officer whose gallant efforts to ascend the ladder have already been mentioned, waited

We regret that we are unable to give original letters or documents from the pen of Sir Thomas Picton relative to the capture of Badajoz: those who had in their possession letters

upon General Picton the day after the assault, and presented to him *the flag* which he had taken in the castle the previous night. Macpherson's distinguished behaviour had been already reported to the general, and he received him in the most kind and friendly manner; even the words which he made use of to the young lieutenant are deeply impressed upon his memory. "Sir," he observed in a tone of deep interest, " I congratulate you on your gallantry, and thank you: this night you have allied your fate to mine," putting out his hand and warmly shaking that of Macpherson. He then continued: "There is a hand will never forsake you; from henceforth your promotion shall be my look-out." In how far he fulfilled this promise the reader will have a future opportunity of observing. General Picton would not accept the flag from the young officer, from a hope that it might do him more service in a higher quarter. " No," he said, " take it to Lord Wellington, and show him what the third division can do."

Macpherson was suffering much pain from his wound, and felt little inclination to intrude himself at head-quarters ; but Picton with friendly warmth insisted upon his going. Macpherson accordingly presented the flag to the commander of the forces. He was thanked, and invited to dinner; his wound, however, prevented him from accepting this invitation.

General Picton applied almost immediately to Lord Wellington to give him a company; but two years after the taking of Badajoz—he was still a lieutenant.

written by Sir Thomas Picton within a short
period after this siege have, from a friendly
but mistaken zeal, consigned them to the flames.
In no less than three instances has this been
the case, and amongst a consecutive packet of
letters from which this memoir has been in
a great measure composed, those that referred
in particular to the taking of Badajoz have been
in like manner withdrawn or destroyed.

This is the more to be regretted, as the parties
to whom these communications were addressed
are no longer living, so that even their memories cannot be appealed to. Unfortunately;
the inference to be drawn from this act on the
part of Sir Thomas Picton's friends is not of
a favourable nature; for it will necessarily be
presumed that he had in these letters expressed
opinions and passed comments upon the conduct of this siege and assault, which were not
calculated to advance his professional prospects,
and that for this reason they were destroyed.
The candid and unflinching statements of such
a mind as that of Sir Thomas Picton would
have been highly valuable; and although they
might have embraced some unpleasant or rather
severe truths, still they would have been es-

teemed as the sentiments of a man who never disguised his opinions, or shrunk from giving them utterance from any feeling of policy or fear of reproof.

The reader's attention should be directed to the following fact, and then he will be convinced, that when General Picton ventured to express anything like censure upon the manner in which the assault was conducted, he only did that which modern writers have not hesitated to do.

Immediately after the capture of Badajoz, admiration and respect for the commander of the forces, together with the exultation produced by success, made comment mute; and even those whose dearest friends and relatives had fallen on that fatal breach joined in the universal cry of praise to the great mind that had achieved this conquest. But a man of Sir Thomas Picton's stern cast was not to be carried away by the stream of public opinion; and it is only reasonable to suppose that these letters which his friends so zealously destroyed contained nothing more than those very remarks which are now brought forward without hesitation. He then saw circumstances to con-

demn in the conduct of this siege, which none
but himself dared. to allude to at the time,
but which are now freely commented upon.
Colonel Jones makes the following observations : " The hour originally named was half-
past seven, being immediately after dusk ; but
it was subsequently changed to ten, in consequence of the arrangements being found to require that delay. The garrison took advantage
of the interval between the breaching batteries
ceasing to batter and the commencement of the
assault, to cover the front of the breaches with
harrows and crows'-feet, and to fix *chevaux de
frise* of sword-blades on the summits."*

A gentleman who knew General Picton intimately, and to whom he more than once
spoke of the siege of Badajoz, still further con-
firms the supposition that the letters of which
we so much regret the loss, only referred to
the very point alluded to in the foregoing
extract ; for to this gentleman Sir Thomas Picton on one occasion expressed in rather strong
terms his opinion with regard to delaying the
attack, and the consequent sacrifice of life ; and
this is the only source from which the writer

* See his admirable work upon Sieges.

has been enabled to draw respecting the probable contents of these letters.   After this statement, it will naturally be asked by what means
any account has been obtained of General Picton's proceedings during the siege of Badajoz.
This has not been a difficult task; for many are
now living who were by his side nearly the
whole time of the assault; and they have given
every assistance which their memories could
furnish.   The only document amongst the gallant general's own papers which refers in any
way to the capture of Badajoz is the letter
from Lieutenant Mac Carthy to Sir Thomas
Picton, which has been before alluded to,
and from which an extract has already been
given;* but this affords no account of General
Picton's individual conduct.

The wound which General Picton had received rendered him for a time unable to
follow the same active routine which had so
long been his habit.   The soldiers of his divi-

---

* This letter is inserted at length in the Appendix, as an
interesting detail of the progress of an individual during the
escalade, and in order to assist in refuting the charge brought
against Sir Thomas Picton, of neglecting the interests of the
officers who served under his command.

sion had now learned to look up to him as their rallying point—as the chief who was ever ready to share with them every privation, and who had obtained for them the most distinguished name amongst the army. It was not his undaunted courage that alone made his soldiers value him; his collected and resolute demeanour, together with the calm firmness of his voice in the most trying moments of danger, gave them a confidence in his judgment second only to that which they reposed in the commander of the forces, and which made them follow wherever or whenever he led, depending on his skill and generalship to extricate them from any situation of peril in which they might be unexpectedly placed.

Lord Liverpool, during a debate in the House of Lords on the 27th of April 1812, after having eulogized collectively the services and abilities of the officers under the command of Lord Wellington, observed: " The conduct of General Picton has inspired a confidence in the army, and exhibited an example of science and bravery which has been surpassed by no other officer. His exertions in the attack on the 6th (Badajoz) cannot fail to excite the most lively feelings of admiration."

The third division was not so conspicuous for the regularity of its appointments or its parade-movements as for the more important duties of the field. One regiment in particular, the Eighty-eighth, or Connaught Rangers, as brave and steady a fighting set of fellows as ever handled a musket, were perhaps as determined a band of marauders as ever sacked a city or robbed a poultry-yard : their appearance was at the same time equally irregular, and Picton used familiarly to call them his *" brave ragged rascals."* But this irregularity in the regiments of the " fighting division" was not confined to the " Eighty-eighth," although the palm certainly rested with the *" Rangers of Connaught ;"* and Picton used to remark, that all the light division left in the way of plunder, was sure to be found by his *" ragged rascals."* Another observation of Sir Thomas Picton, when speaking of his soldiers, was, " I don't care how they dress, so long as they *mind their fighting."* And this was the only thing his division did mind—one unconquerable feeling seemed to pervade the whole. Picton had taught them to be daring, never to pause, never to retreat ; and so well had they learned their lesson, that it is a singular truth, that the third division was never repulsed when they attacked !

Success operates strongly on the minds of soldiers in making them respect their leaders ; it gives them confidence in themselves and in their officers ; they fight with a firmer front and think less of a reverse, and the victorious veteran becomes at length equal to a host of untried soldiers. The war waged by the "fighting division" was of that stern and unyielding description which defied opposition : their battle-front was terrible ; warmed by their chief, they rushed on, and never stopped until the enemy was overcome.

Picton often spoke in terms of the warmest admiration of the noble bearing of his soldiers when exposed upon several occasions to the most severe fire without returning a shot ; every gap in the line would be in an instant filled up ; when, close or unbroken, they would move on until bidden to pour in their deadly

answer, or charge with the bayonet. After
the escalade of the castle of Badajoz, he spoke
of them with an expression of gratitude for the
devoted manner in which they obeyed his orders, regardless of the fearful nature of the
attack, and undaunted by the fate of each succeeding comrade who had gained the summit
of the ladders. " Still," he observed to an officer who was with him for some time after he
was wounded,—" still they rushed to the foot
of the ladders, even striving who should be first
to mount; but they fell so fast, and the ladders
were so insecure, that even the bravest began
to waver. I called upon them, however, to
make another effort, when they poured on and
bore one another up until at length the wall
was gained;—nothing could resist them. Yet
I could hardly make myself believe that we
had taken the castle."

It was not, however, by words only, but
by a liberal gift, that Picton evinced the sense
he entertained of his gallant soldiers.*

* A few days after the capture of Badajoz, he desired
one of his aides-de-camp to pay to the remainder of the men
who composed the storming party of his division, one guinea
each, as a testimonial of their general's gratitude.

The following letter from General Picton to Mr. Marryat may be here inserted with little interruption to our narrative.

"Peno Dona, 8th May 1812.

" MY DEAR SIR,

" I had the pleasure of your letter by Mr. Henwell, who arrived in the camp before Badajoz on the morning previous to the assault of that place, and fortunately participated in that event. He was, in consequence, recommended for an ensigncy in the Forty-third regiment, to which there is little doubt of his succeeding. After the capture of Badajoz, we were under the necessity of moving rather expeditiously northward, as Marshal Marmont had made an incursion during our absence, with the view of drawing us from our main object, the siege of Badajoz; but in this expectation he was disappointed by the celerity of our operations, which he did not calculate upon. He, however, did very considerable injury in the province, and carried off cattle and other booty of no inconsiderable value; and, what is of very great importance, he has taught us what value to place upon a militia force, which the ministerial papers, with you, have so frequently and so loudly cried up as nowhere yielding to regulars. The militia of the northern provinces, under their generals, two English and one Portuguese, of established reputation, and whose names and exploits have frequently figured in the gazettes, were driven from the strong post of Guarda, and perfectly dispersed and dissipated, by about five hundred French horse. If we rely upon our vast establishment of the kind, we shall, some day or other, be woefully disappointed. These people, like ours, had sufficient mechanical discipline, and were equal in appearance and equipment to any regulars: but war is a practical science, and is only to be learned in collision with the enemy. I seriously apprehend that our military system will eventually lead to a great national misfortune, unless it be more practically organized in time.

" We are now approaching the river Douro, in order to be near our depôts of provisions, whilst our means of transport are employed in supplying Almeida and Ciudad Rodrigo with provisions; and I shall profit of this movement to visit Oporto, and, on my return, if Major-general Colville should be sufficiently recovered from his wounds to take charge of the division, I shall take my passage for England, where my affairs require my presence. The public despatches will let you know what we have been about, and I trust you will not think we have been idle or uselessly employed. The general idea is that we shall again move southward, to carry on offensive operations on that side; but we are not in sufficient force to act, at the same time, on the offensive there and the defensive here. We want at least fifteen thousand English troops more to do any thing decisive. I shall probably see you in August.

"My dear Sir,

"Very faithfully yours,

"T. Picton."

CHAPTER VI.

Advance of Soult to relieve Badajoz.—His retreat on hearing
of its fall. — Marmont threatens Ciudad Rodrigo. — He
marches upon Almeida.—Colonel Trant's stratagem.—
British move towards Castile.—French retreat upon Salamanca.—Skirmish at the Douro.—Friendly intercourse
between the hostile armies.—Marmont, reinforced, assumes the offensive.- Picton's dangerous illness.—General
Pakenham assumes his command.—Battle of Salamanca.
—Gallant conduct of the Third Division.—Temporary
success of the French.—Their complete rout.

UPON the fall of Badajoz, Marshal Soult resolved, after too long a delay, to advance from
Seville to the relief of the besieged fortress.
He arrived at Villa Franca, on the 8th of April,
only to hear from the flying garrison that the
place had been captured two days previously.
He halted upon receiving this information, for
his force was not sufficiently large to meet the
allies without the assistance of the garrison, and
immediately afterwards he commenced his retreat to Seville.

As soon as Lord Wellington was made acquainted with the advance of Soult, he made
preparations to give him battle. When it was
known, however, that he was in full retreat, the
cavalry, under Sir Stapleton Cotton, was ordered to follow on his rear; and several skirmishes
took place highly honourable to the skill and
courage of the pursuers. During this period,
Marmont had threatened Ciudad Rodrigo, with
about twenty thousand men; but finding the
garrison determined to defend the place stoutly,
although ill supplied with provisions, he left
one division to establish a blockade, while with
the remainder of his army he marched towards
Almeida.

Colonel Trant,* whose active and enterprising
operations at the head of a few militia had
drawn forth the warm praises of Lord Wellington, arrived at this moment in the neighbourhood, and contrived, with great daring and at
much personal risk, to establish a short communication with the governor of that fortress, Colonel Le Mesurier, when they agreed upon the
plans which they should pursue in co-operation
in order to deceive the enemy. By the simple

* Now Sir Nicholas Trant.

stratagem of making a great show of fires
during the night, they led the French to believe that a large force had advanced to the relief of Almeida; and they consequently abandoned their design of attacking this place, and
moved forward to take possession of Castello
Branco, which was occupied by their advanced
guard on the evening of the 12th of April.

After the trenches of Badajoz had been filled
up, the breaches repaired, and the walls height-
ened, Lord Wellington put his army in motion
towards Castile.   On the 15th the third division
was again on its march.   As this division passed
beneath the castle of Badajoz, which only a
few days before it had so daringly assailed, the
recollection of those who had fallen came sadly
on the minds of all; and there was not a man
among them who did not recognise, in the spots
around, the burial-place of many friends.

When the allied army was put in motion
towards the field of Marmont's operations, that
general at once betrayed a distrust either in
himself or the force under his command.   Even
the report of Wellington's success at Badajoz,
and his intention to advance to the North,
stopped the excesses which he had been com-

mitting on the frontiers of Beira; and as soon as he received information that the English general was upon his march, he commenced a retreat upon Salamanca. The allies again took up a position between the rivers Coa and Agueda, the head-quarters being established at Fuente Guinaldo; and for a while the army remained in cantonments to refresh after the severe services in which it had been engaged through all the inclemency of winter. It was during this period that Napoleon invaded Russia.

How the strength of France was wasted in this vast attempt, her fields left nearly untilled, and her cities deprived of their defenders, need not be repeated here. The affairs of the Peninsula became now a secondary consideration in comparison with this greater enterprise, to the result of which all Europe was looking with painful suspense.

On the 9th of May 1812, Napoleon left Paris to join the immense army with which he undertook this expedition: had he thrown himself into Spain with one-fourth of this army, the English general might probably have been driven to his ships. It is true that the number of French troops in the Peninsula was already great. According to Colonel Jones, " The French force within the Pyrenees, in May 1812, exceeded one hundred and seventy thousand, chiefly veteran troops, under distinguished officers. Soult commanded fifty-eight thousand in Andalusia; Marmont, fifty-five thousand in Leon; Souham, ten thousand (the Army of the North) in Old Castile; Suchet, forty thousand in Arragon and the eastern provinces; and Jourdan could dispose of fifteen thousand men, called the Army of the Centre, for the security of the intrusive king and the quiet of the capital."

But, large as this force was, it was not during any period of the subsequent war effective: a want of cordiality and co-operation existed amongst the different generals, which, fortunately for the liberties of Europe, enabled Lord Wellington to act against each army separately, and defeat them in detail; while reinforcements could not be expected from a country already exhausted of its population.

But the presence of the Emperor would have produced a great alteration in affairs; he would have been able to concentrate each corps, and silence at once all dissension among his officers; while his great military genius would have secured every advantage which the preponderance of his force might have entitled him to expect.

The force under Lord Wellington's command, with which he had to oppose that of Marmont, amounted to about forty-five thousand men. General Hill had at the same time about ten thousand infantry and one thousand two hundred cavalry, principally Portuguese; but this corps, after having carried the castle of Miravete by assault, and secured the bridge of Almaraz, was occupied in observing the operations of Soult, and preventing a junction between his army and that of Marmont.

On the 13th of June the allied forces once more commenced operations, and on the 16th they came up with the French in front of the town of Salamanca; but the enemy showed no intention of fighting, and the next morning they had passed the river Tormes, upon the right bank of which the city is built. Lord Wellington crossed in pursuit on the following day by two fords, one above and the other below the town. A good stone bridge is thrown over this river; but the French had erected some formidable works to prevent the passage, which were at the same time so constructed as to command the city. The inhabitants were not well-disposed towards their invaders; but received the English with every demonstration of friendliness and gratitude.

The following letter from General Picton to Mr. Marryat details the operations of the British army at this period.

"Before Salamanca, 24th June 1812.

" MY DEAR SIR,

" We passed the Tormes by difficult fords on the 17th, and I had a continued skirmish with Marshal Marmont during the whole of that day. We entered the city on the same evening, but the French occupied a strongly-fortified point, which they have ever since maintained with obstinacy; and we have lost many valuable officers and men in attempting to dislodge them. On the 19th, Marshal Marmont, being joined by the reinforcements he expected, advanced within three miles of our position in front of Salamanca, and he made every apparent disposition for attacking us, and extended his army along our front so as to almost bring the two armies in contact in various points. In this extraordinary situation we remained, with various skirmishes and trifling affairs of posts, during the whole of the 22nd. On the morning of the 23rd, we discovered that he had silently decamped during the night, with all the appearance of a retreat upon Valladolid. However, we shortly after discovered that he had made that nocturnal movement for the purpose of approaching his left to the Tormes, and he now appears to be meditating the passage of that river, for the purpose of getting into our rear and acting upon our line of communication. We have also passed the river with three divisions of the army, and are endeavouring to counteract this manœuvre. The armies are, I believe, nearly equal at present; but the enemy has the means of reinforcing himself at hand, and we have no hopes of any addition to our force. My hopes are far from sanguine. We may operate as an admirable diversion, and distract the enemy considerably by obliging him to concentrate his forces, which will lay him open to the enterprises of the Guerillas; but I have no

hopes of being able to effect anything substantial. I am perfectly tired with the continual movements and fatigue of this unceasing kind of warfare, in a country where we are
exposed to every kind of privation, and, I may
almost say, want. I mean to make my interest,
as soon as I find a favourable opportunity, for
some one to succeed me in the command of the
third division.

" Very faithfully yours,
" T. PICTON."

A battering train had already been ordered
from Elvas for the reduction of the forts erected to prevent the passage of the river. This
duty was given to the sixth division, under
Major-general Clinton; while the remainder of
the allied army was posted on the heights of
St. Christoval, three miles in advance of the
town: a position which cut off Marmont's communication with the troops defending the besieged works. It is unnecessary to dwell upon
the reduction of these forts. On the tenth day
after the batteries had opened, two breaches
were reported practicable in St. Vincente, the
principal, and one in Gaetano, the smaller fort.

" The troops," according to Colonel Jones, " were formed for the assault of the latter, when a white flag announced the intended submission of the garrison ; at the same moment the flames in the other work increased rapidly, and the commandant likewise demanded to capitulate. Each, however, required three hours' preliminary delay. Their offers were treated as statagems to gain time and get the flames under, and Lord Wellington limited them to five minutes to march out, promising them their baggage and effects. This message not being complied with, the batteries resumed their fire, under cover of which the storming parties advanced and carried the lesser fort at the gorge, the enemy offering little resistance : the Portuguese light troops even penetrated into the principal fort, making the number of prisoners above seven hundred."

The reduction of these works destroyed the last hold which Marmont possessed on Salamanca, and it was now quite evident that he must either fight or retreat. He was not long in forming his determination, the army being at once withdrawn towards the Douro, closely followed by the allies. The British

cavalry came up with their rear on the 2nd
of July, when a sharp skirmish ensued, which
terminated in favour of the English, who compelled the enemy to cross the Douro in much
confusion. Both armies took up a position
for the night on different sides of the river;
and here they remained until the 16th, the
third division being posted at the ford near
Pollos. The writer of the " Reminiscences of
a Subaltern" observes, that much intercourse
existed between the soldiers of the two armies,
more especially between the third British and
seventh French divisions—and he adds; " The
French officers said to us on parting, ' We have
met and have been for some time friends; we
are about to separate, and may meet as enemies. As friends we received each other warmly; as enemies we shall do the same.' In ten
days afterwards, the British third and the
French seventh divisions were opposed to each
other at the battle of Salamanca; and the seventh French were destroyed by the British
third."

During this interval of repose, neither general was desirous of becoming the assailant;
Lord Wellington on account of the strength

of the French position, and Marmont rendered cautious by his late reverses. He was
now however joined by General Bonnet, with
the Army of the Asturias, amounting to nearly
ten thousand men: thus augmenting the troops
under his command to forty-seven thousand
veterans. With this addition to his strength,
he again prepared to commence offensive operations. To cross the river with the army of
Wellington in his front, was an undertaking
which must necessarily be attended with considerable sacrifice; he therefore, after a variety
of brilliant and rapid movements, contrived
to throw his army over the Douro at a place
about twenty miles above Toro. By this skilful manœuvre he re-established his communications with the Army of the Centre, at the
same time that he threatened to cut off the
light and fourth divisions, together with Major-
general Anson's brigade of cavalry; but these
troops managed to rejoin the main body of
the allies, which now occupied a position on
the river Guarena. Several days were then
passed by both generals in a variety of movements and counter-movements; now marching
" in parallel lines, within half-cannon shot dis-

tance of each other ;" then the allies, falling
back, followed by the French, would suddenly
halt, as if to fight; upon which the enemy in
his turn would decline the proffered contest.
Still it was evident to every individual in the
army that a battle must ensue.

Picton's division alone seemed disheartened ;
for their leader, whose appearance at their head
they had now learned to consider as an assurance of success, was not with them. He
had for some time been inconvenienced by
the wound he had received at Badajoz; but,
still mounted on his cob, he had been frequently seen among his soldiers. He was now, however, dangerously ill with the fever which is
so common in these countries, and from which
our troops suffered greatly; although these
returns, being confined to the medical department, did not swell the list of loss which appeared in the Gazettes.

General Picton was confined in Salamanca
with this malady, which had attacked him in
its most virulent form. His life was for a
time despaired of; but the same iron constitution which had supported him through the
fever at Walcheren enabled him to withstand

this disease. His illness and consequent absence were much regretted by his soldiers. Going into battle without " Old Picton" at their head seemed, in the language of his men, quite unnatural. At the same time the illness of the general was greatly increased by constant anxiety respecting his soldiers; in fact, when made acquainted with the near approach of the two armies, and the various movements which had been made, he observed that they must lead to a battle; and it was with some difficulty that he was restrained from going to place himself at the head of his division, although so enfeebled that he could not stand without assistance. Lieutenant Tyler, his aide-de-camp, succeeded, however, in dissuading him from this rash design ; and when he heard that the honour of the " fighting division" was entrusted to General Pakenham, he observed, " I am glad he has to lead my brave fellows; they will have plenty of their favourite amusement with him at their head."

But although Picton was not present at this battle, the noble spirit which he had infused into his men was conspicuous.

On the 20th of July, the allies were again in

the same position on the heights of St. Christoval which they had occupied during the
attack on the forts. Marmont was still manœuvring; but both generals had the same
object, each trying to draw the other to commence hostilities while his army was in the
strongest position. In every particular these
movements resembled a game of chess where
the players are nearly equal: both were prepared to advance, but hesitated for some favourable moment; while the slightest oversight
being immediately observed on each side, the
greatest possible advantage which could be obtained from it was instantly seized upon.

On the evening of the 21st, the allied army
crossed from the right to the left bank of the
Tormes by the bridge of Salamanca; Picton's
division, with Brigadier-general D'Urban's cavalry, being however left to watch a large
corps which the enemy still kept on the
heights above Babilafuente. The French had
crossed in the morning of this day, when,
marching by their left, they threatened to
cut off the road between Ciudad Rodrigo and
the allies; and it was to counteract this, that
Lord Wellington also moved his army over

the river, and thus for a time re-established and secured his communication. Still Marmont had evidently determined to effect this object, while Lord Wellington resolved to prevent it; and it was this point which led to the battle of Salamanca. The night of the 21st was. tempestuous; and as the soldiers were kept under arms, the incessant rain and thunder, which kept them wet and sleepless, but ill fitted them for the exertions of the coming day.

Early in the morning, the third division, with D'Urban's cavalry, was ordered to cross the bridge with the utmost speed, and take up the ground allotted to them on the extreme right of the British position, just behind Aldea Tejada. Next to Picton's division was the fifth, under General Leith; General Bradford, with a brigade of Portuguese, occupying an elevated post between these two. On the left of the fifth, and immediately in the rear of the village of Aripiles, was the fourth division, under General Cole, supported in reserve by the sixth and seventh divisions, the former commanded by Major-general Clinton, and the latter by Major-general Hope: the first and light divisions, which occupied the ground on the left of the position, being also stationed in reserve.

The morning was passed in anxious suspense. The allied army expected a battle, and were prepared for a decisive conflict; but for a time the enemy gave no demonstrations of commencing the attack: some few alterations were made by Marmont in the disposition of his troops, but none which produced any effect upon the general arrangements; in fact, it appeared as if each party expected the other to begin. Lord Wellington's military skill was strikingly evident in this war of manoeuvre. He had left Marmont but little choice: the post occupied by the allies was strong, and each point easily supported. If the French general did attack, the chances would be much against him; at the same time that any movement which Marmont should attempt in order to pursue his plan would necessarily weaken his line, and Lord Wellington might then become the assailant with every probability of success. His military judgment and foresight were soon conspicuous. Towards noon much confusion was observed in the ranks of the enemy; but Lord Wellington saw nothing which induced him to make, any alteration in his position; when, about two o'clock, after having observed the movements of the French, " he gave his glass to one of his aides-de-camp, while he himself retired for a few moments to take some refreshment. He had scarcely commenced, when his aid-de-camp said, ' The enemy are in motion, my lord.' ' Very well : observe what they are doing,' was the reply. A minute or two elapsed, when the aid-de-camp said, ' I think they are extending to the left.' ' The devil they are!' said his lordship, springing upon his feet: ' give me the glass quickly.' He took it, and for a short time continued observing the motions of the enemy with earnest attention."

Marmont, by extending his left, was in hopes of being enabled to turn the right of the allies; but as this was done without a corresponding movement of the remainder of the French army, but by the extension of the line, it was a necessary consequence that the whole was comparatively weakened. It would appear by this manœuvre on the part of the French general that he was ignorant of the actual extent of the allied position ; as, when he had

thrown out his left as far as was consistent
with the security of his centre, he was still
outflanked by the third division. But this was
only one of those false moves which, whether
in chess or in war, are and ever will be made
by the best players, being in fact more frequently produced by impatience or loss of
temper, than by the want of judgment or foresight. Wellington instantly discovered the advantage which his adversary had given him,
and he resolved at once to begin the attack. In
his despatch he observes that he had long
been anxious to do so; and accordingly he ordered Pakenham to move on with the third
division, take the heights in his front, and drive
everything before him. "I will, my lord, by
G—d!" was the laconic reply.

The duty given to the third division upon
this memorable occasion was one of the most
conspicuous in the field. While the attack
was being made in front, they had to ascend the height upon which the enemy had
rested his left, and take the French line in
flank. It is a singular fact, and one which
redounds but little to the military skill of
Marmont, that while the allied forces were

advancing to give him battle, he was making his dispositions to receive them. The French army was, in fact, wavering between two positions, when they ought to have been prepared for the reception of their opponents.

The seventh French division had been ordered to march some distance on its left, to alarm the English general with the fear of being outflanked; but it was this very movement which induced Lord Wellington to become the assailant; and long, therefore, before this division had reached its intended ground, the British line was advancing in order of battle. An aid-de-camp was immediately sent after General Foy, who commanded the seventh division, with orders to return with all despatch and again occupy his former ground. This betrayed great want of foresight in Marmont: it was playing a bad game, resting the success of his plans upon the ignorance of his opponent; but he paid dearly for his presumption.

The confidence which Lord Wellington placed in the third division was strikingly justified upon this occasion; — moving in two lines, the first consisting of the Forty-fifth,

Seventy-fourth, and Eighty-eighth, led by Colonel Alexander Wallace of the latter regiment; and the second composed of the Ninth
and Twenty-first Portuguese, under Colonel
de Champlemond; the Fifth, Seventy-seventh,
Eighty-third, and Ninety-fourth. British regiments being kept in reserve. General D'Urban's cavalry, and Le Marchant's three regiments of heavy dragoons, were ordered to follow in the rear of the division, to protect it
from any flank attacks by the enemy's horse.
The heights which these regiments had to
carry were well provided with cannon, while
the bayonets of the French riflemen could be
seen moving hastily down the ridge : and a
plain of some extent was to be traversed
beneath the fire of these guns before the British could return a shot.

The word was given, and "forward" they
moved in open column of companies. The
crown of the hill was in a moment enveloped
in smoke as the artillery commenced their
play. The shot fell amongst the advancing
columns; but the height from which they were
directed, and the rain which had fallen during
the night, rendered them less fatal than might

have been expected, as they were soon buried
in the earth. Some British artillery, under
Captain Douglas, replied to this from some
high ground in the rear of the third division.
The English were thus between two fires;
the shot from their own guns flying over their
heads, while those of the enemy fell amongst
them. They moved on with unshaken resolution, the ranks being silently filled up as
their comrades fell: but this was only a slight
preface to the work about to ensue. A column,
consisting of above five thousand men, was
posted at the top of the hill, commanded by
General Foy, who had just reached this position with the seventh division. This mass
of men covered the summit, waiting until the
British should in their ascent of the hill come
sufficiently near to be annihilated by their fire.
They beheld them move steadily onward; they
saw the line occasionally close up as the shot
ploughed through their leading files; when,
within a short distance from the brow of the
hill, by Sir Edward Pakenham's orders, the
companies formed into line without halting.
By this well-judged manœuvre, which was performed with much regularity and expedition,

the enemy's light troops were at once driven in
to their main body ; for, expecting to do some
execution while the English were deploying
into line, they were surprised to see this effected without a pause. Now the British line presented a more formidable array, as, formed only
two deep, they pressed up. the remaining acclivity.

The French artillery continued a rapid discharge of grape and canister ; but Foy's division stood motionless, waiting until the English
should have gained the top of the ridge. In
consequence of the grand efforts of the enemy's
artillery being directed against the centre of
the British brigade, the two wings, which were
less exposed, advanced more rapidly ; and by
this means a kind of crescent was formed, the
horns of which were about to close upon the
enemy. Panting with their exertions, and
having left many dead and dying on their
path, the gallant line paused a moment on
the summit of the hill. Then came the attack
from General Foy. His column immediately
poured in a close volley, which almost crushed
the English. In a moment the earth was
strewed with the leading line of Wallace's bri-

gade ; but quickly recovering from this shock, and stepping over their fallen companions, the others rushed on before the smoke had cleared from the field, or the French could reload. Wallace, looking back upon his men, pointed to the enemy : it was enough—they knew well their work. The French, confident that this volley would paralyze their adversaries, were about to charge the remainder and drive them from the hill at the point of the bayonet ; but at that moment they saw through the smoke the faces of their opponents, who were advancing upon them with rapid but steady steps. This was a thrilling scene : for a moment there was almost a breathless silence, but it was the next instant broken by the French, who opened a quick but ill-directed fire. The assailants pressed forward.

The French fire had almost ceased, when a loud cheer was given by the British line. Pakenham, seeing the excited state at which his men had arrived, gave the word to " charge." A well-directed volley was poured in to the opposing column, the muskets were brought down to the " rest," and, emerging from the smoke of their fire, they rushed forward with the bayonet. The close phalanx for an' instant bent from the shock : then, for several minutes, the living mass was swayed backward and forward ; but at length it yielded ;—another effort, it was broken, and they fled ; when, in the words of a writer from whom many of these details are drawn, " the seventh French was destroyed by the British third."

The battle was not, however, only here ; in the centre it was raging with equal fury: the constant roll of musketry along the whole line made it evident that the same success had not yet crowned the efforts of the other divisions. But Pakenham remembered his instructions " to drive everything before him ;" and accordingly, having driven the French from the height, he next proceeded to turn the remainder of the enemy's positions. But cavalry were now wanting to complete the destruction of Foy's retreating column ; the infantry could only force them down the slope; while their very numbers and closeness made their retreat less decided than it would have been, could they have fled without interruption. Le Marchant's heavy dragoons were too far in the rear, and it was late before an officer was sent to order them forward.

When Pakenham had followed the French to a plain at the foot of the hill, Foy, instantly observing the absence of cavalry, brought up a fresh brigade, and by great exertions contrived to re-establish something like discipline, and persuade the men once more to face their pursuers. This part of the battle was now partially restored — the result was even uncertain ; but at this moment the hoofs of horses were heard in the rear of the British. Their line opened, and at a sharp canter three regiments of heavy cavalry rode through the intervals, quickly formed in front, and prepared for their charge. The suddenness of this evolution caused renewed confusion in the enemy's ranks ; they were instantly ordered into square, but they moved with uncertainty, and before they were half formed the cavalry were amongst them. Still they fought. The first close volley stopped the career of many a horseman ; amongst others, Le Marchant their leader was shot as his horse was at speed, and his body was precipitated upon the enemy's bayonets. Such a contest could not last long.   The broken French bravely but vainly resisted : it was a confused slaughter; the troopers hewed down the exhausted and almost helpless foe with unsparing fury, until at length they even fled to the British line for protection ; and there it was given so long as it was demanded : and, as the writer before referred to observes, " not a man was bayoneted, not one even molested or plundered ; and the invincible old 'third' on this day surpassed themselves; for they not only defeated their terrible enemies in a fair stand-up fight, but actually covered their retreat, and protected them at a moment when, without such aid, their total annihilation was certain."

And now the battle appeared to turn in favour of the allied army, as Foy's flying column spread confusion along the French line, and the British troops were seen advancing on their right.   On the left of the third division, Leith, with the fourth, had, during the fighting on his right, been warmly engaged for some time in firing volleys at the column to which it was opposed ; but when he saw that the charge of the third had proved successful, he gave the word to advance, and placed himself at the head of his division. The crash was terrible: Leith soon fell badly wounded, but his men still pressed on. Here also the allies were victorious; the French were driven up the hill in their rear, and the English were left in possession of the disputed ground. In the centre, however, affairs bore a different aspect, and for a while the result seemed doubtful.

Cole's division made a gallant attack upon Bonnet's corps, and after a severe struggle the French were thrown into confusion. Brigadier-general Pack, with nearly two thousand Portuguese, was to have carried a height called the Dos Arapiles, on the left of the fourth division. This was occupied by not more than five hundred of the enemy, with a few pieces of cannon. The security of Cole's advance depended upon the French being driven from this post, and the superior numbers of Pack's brigade rendered his success, by calculation, almost certain; but just as Cole had succeeded in throwing Bonnet's corps into confusion, the guns from this height opened with great effect upon the rear and flank of the fourth division: the Portuguese had failed in their attack; and the

French, who had beaten them back, now turned their fire against Cole's successful troops.
This unexpected event produced an immediate
panic amongst the British soldiers, as the storm
of grape, round-shot, and musketry did severe
execution in their ranks. Bonnet had been
carried from the field wounded, and the command had now devolved upon General Clausel, who saw at one glance that the advance of
the English had been checked, and as quickly
conceived the cause. He hastily re-formed his
troops, brought up a small reserve, and became
in his turn the assailant : the fourth division
gave way, and the Frenchmen, animated by
their success, renewed the attack with fresh
vigour. Cole fell wounded, while endeavouring to rally his men ; but all his efforts were
vain, for his troops were now retreating from
the position which they had gained. Clausel
was joined in his well-timed onset by the remains of the two broken columns, and he now
moved forward in great force, confident of
overthrowing all before him. Marshal Beresford, who happened to come up at this critical
moment, without delay ordered up a brigade
of General Leith's division, to try and stop the

current of defeat; but these regiments, composed principally of Portuguese; only added to the disorder, as the whole were borne back in one confused mass by the advancing line.

Beresford was himself wounded and carried from the field. An aid-de-camp had, however, been sent to apprize Lord Wellington of the state of affairs. Wellington galloped to the spot, and perceived at once the extent of the danger. The sixth division, under General Clinton, consisting of six thousand men, which had been in reserve, and had not yet fired a shot, was ordered to advance. Night was now closing in, but there was yet sufficient twilight to continue the battle. Clinton's soldiers, who had been looking on with ill-suppressed impatience, now pressed forward with ardour to the charge.

As the enemy saw this division coming on with unbroken ranks, they paused to receive them, and commenced a heavy fire. The contest was not, however, long one of musketry: the two lines soon closed, their bayonets crossed, and then a severe struggle ensued, and continued until there was scarcely light sufficient to distinguish friend from foe. The French, elated by their temporary success, fought with great obstinacy: but English troops have always displayed a decided superiority in the use of the bayonet; they destroyed rank after rank; and at length the enemy, disheartened at their loss, shrunk from the contest. The rout was complete; but their flight was protected by the darkness, which forbade any lengthened pursuit. Lord Wellington himself, with some cavalry, supported by the first and light divisions, followed them a short distance; while the remainder of the army slept upon the field. Both Marmont and Bonnet were wounded early in this battle, and General Clausel now conducted the retreat of the army.

It may perhaps be here inquired, why the third division did not continue its flank movement after the defeat of Foy's column, and thus extricate the fourth division from its perilous situation?

The progress of a battle may be seen at once by the commanders of the two contending armies; but it cannot be thus delineated: many of the movements which we are obliged to describe consecutively took place at the same moment. It was thus with the contests between

Pakenham and Foy, and Cole and Clausel: these successes and reverses were taking place at the same time. While the third division was driving Foy's column from the field, Clausel's were pursuing Cole's broken corps. The third upon this occasion took nearly five thousand prisoners, nine pieces of artillery, and two eagles: and Salamanca was justly added to the many glorious names already inscribed upon the colours of the regiments forming this division.

CHAPTER VII.

Anecdote of Picton during his illness.—Marmont retreats
to Burgos.—The Allies enter Valladolid.—Lord Wellington moves upon Madrid.—King Joseph evacuates the
capital.—Enthusiastic reception of the British.—Picton
returns to England.—Recovers his health at Cheltenham,
and revisits his native place.—The Allies invest the castle
of Burgos.—They raise the siege, and retreat to Ciudad
Rodrigo.—Picton created a Knight of the Bath.—He re-
joins the army.—His reception by his men.—Advance of
the Allies.

WHILST this glorious and decisive victory
was being achieved, Picton was, as we have
already mentioned, confined to his bed by a
severe and even dangerous fever. The intense
interest that he took in the proceedings of the
armies, and with which he listened to the accounts of the progress of the battle, and afterwards of its event and subsequent details, may
be readily conceived ; the excitement produced
by anxiety, and still more by regret that he was
not in the field, considerably increased the violence of the disease and retarded his recovery.

He heard with unmixed pleasure the account
of the part which his own division had borne
during the day, frequently interrupting the
narration with exclamations of delight as particular acts of bravery were described. At the
same time he spoke highly of Pakenham; calling him a " fit leader for his fellows," and passing high encomiums upon his conduct and
courage.

It was when recovering from this illness that
the following little incident occurred. Lieutenant Tyler, his aid-de-camp, accompanied by
a subaltern officer in the Ninety-fifth Foot,
one morning rather hastily entered his apartment. Both these officers were very young
men, full of spirits, and easily excited.

Tyler, who was in constant attendance upon
the general, familiar with his habits, and accustomed to his singularities, immediately accosted him with, " Well, general, how do you
do to-day ?" but the other was struck with the
singular appearance of the emaciated invalid,
as, raising himself on his arm, he displayed his
pale and haggard features beneath a nightcap
of more than ordinary dimensions. Picton was
about to make some reply to Tyler's inquiry,

when just at that moment the risible propen-
sities of Mr. C—— overcoming every control,
made him burst out into a loud and rather
boisterous fit of laughter.   The general, whose
natural irritability was augmented by his bodily
suffering and mental inquietude, instantly fixed his fiery glance upon the unfortunate C——;
he did not ask the cause of his ill-timed mirth;
but, in spite of his debility, made an effort to
leave the bed, in all probability to wreak his
fury upon the culprit; but he was too weak,
and he sank back.   His rage was, however, so
great that, finding it impossible to take personal
vengeance, he insisted upon the now repentant
ensign quitting the room, in terms too strong
to hazard a moment's delay.   After his retreat,
Tyler attempted to pacify the irritated general;
but it was no easy task, and he therefore left
him.

Shortly after this event, Ensign C—— returned to England, when he entered the Foot
Guards, and Picton did not see him again until
the battle of Waterloo; when, on the 16th,
riding over a part of the field occupied by his
division, be saw the enemy in possession of a
hill, which rather affected the security of his

position. He was near some battalions under
arms at the moment, and resolved to employ
them in driving the enemy from this post.

" Who commands these battalions ?" he cried
out in his usual loud, but sharp tone. " I do,"
said now Lieutenant-colonel C———. Picton
recognised him in an instant. " How do you
do, General Picton ?" continued the colonel;
" I am glad to see you looking so well."—" No
time for compliments now, sir," sharply responded Picton; " lead your men against that
hill, and take it." This was not easily to be
effected ; the enemy's numbers were about four
to one of the English ; but the colonel had his
orders, and away he went, fully determined to
execute them to the letter. Picton's attention
was almost immediately directed to other points
of the field, and he had probably forgotten
all about C——— and the hill, when that officer
rode up, and, as he waved a salute, said, " I
have taken the hill, general." Picton fixed
his eyes upon him for a moment, and then
without a word rode off with his staff. They
never met again.

Panic-struck by the signal defeat which they
had experienced, Marmont's retreating army

continued its flight until it arrived at Burgos;
and Lord Wellington, having no reason to apprehend that that general would again assume
an offensive position for some time, resolved
upon a bold and masterly manœuvre, strictly
in accordance with the most approved rules
of war. To beat the French armies in detail
was the system which his circumstances rendered it necessary for him to adopt. It must be
admitted that the French generals had made
but feeble efforts to guard against this; the
attempt to relieve Badajoz was little more
than a threat; while, not until Lord Wellington was on the point of attacking Marmont,
did King Joseph put his soldiers in motion,
or the Army of the North move up to his
support. Both were, however, too late; and
Marmont's retreating troops themselves announced their defeat. To the want of unanimity and co-operation amongst the leaders of
these corps may, in a great measure, be attributed their destruction; for had they by
retrograde movements, or falling back without
fighting upon some common centre, contrived
to concentrate their corps against the single
army of the allies, they would have been en-

abled to oppose Lord Wellington with one
hundred and fifty thousand men, instead of
allowing him to fight forty or fifty thousand at
different times, and in different places.

Having followed the French as far as
Valladolid, and driven them from thence, the
allied army entered that city amidst the acclamations of the inhabitants. The character
of our soldiers was here flatteringly appreciated; and the admirable discipline which the
commander of the forces had established, proved as beneficial to the comfort and security
of the men when amongst the inhabitants, as
it was destructive to the enemy in the field.
At Valladolid, Lord Wellington made that
sudden change in his movements, which, from
its rapidity, was so eminently successful.

Joseph Bonaparte, with the Army of the
Centre, consisting of about twenty thousand
men, was making demonstrations on the right
flank and rear of the allies; which rendered it
dangerous to continue the pursuit of Marmont.
Lord Wellington now, therefore, determined
by one bold effort, either to compel the intrusive king to fight him with his inferior forces,
or evacuate Madrid. And accordingly, having

impressed Clausel, who now commanded. for.
Marmont, with the idea that he intended to follow up the pursuit to Burgos, he on the 6th of.
August changed his route, and moved towards
Madrid with the whole of his army, except a
force under General Paget, which was left on
the Douro to watch the movements of the enemy. The advance of the allies caused much
consternation to the king, and he allowed them
to march unopposed through the mountain-
passes which they were obliged to traverse.
At first he ventured to hope that his subjects
would assist him in opposing the English ; but
the demonstrations of enmity to his government, and satisfaction at their approach, were
too evident to be misunderstood. Instead,
therefore, of awaiting their arrival, so soon as
they were seen on the mountains in the neighbourhood of the capital, Joseph with his army
and partisans evacuated Madrid, and retired by
the roads of Toledo and Aranjuez.

On the morning of the 12th of August the
British army marched into the city, when it
was received with the utmost enthusiasm. Banners, music, and acclamations greeted them at
every step ; and as our troops paraded through

the streets, flowers were strewed upon their path, and laurels thrown upon their heads from every window. The French had left some troops in occupation of a spacious entrenched post on the side of the Retiro; but when the governor perceived that the allies held quiet possession of the city, and that they were preparing to besiege this post, he offered to surrender upon honourable terms of capitulation. These were granted, and the garrison were made prisoners of war.

General Picton was not yet able to take the command of his division, the complaint under which he had been suffering having greatly reduced his physical powers, and rendering his recovery slow and tedious. His constitution was naturally hardy, but the variety of climates in which he had served, and his illness at Walcheren, had given it a severe shock; from the last in particular he had never totally recovered. Some of the internal organs had been greatly impaired either by the disease or the remedies, and he was ever afterwards subject to most distressing bilious attacks: these, after several long and tedious fits of illness, terminated in what is generally called a bilious

fever, every return of which was more violent.
The long confinements to which he had been
subjected, and which had kept him entirely
inactive, now that the original disease had been
overcome, produced a return of this equally
distressing complaint. The only effectual cure
for these illnesses, to which he was always
obliged ultimately to have recourse, was the
Cheltenham waters. On the present occasion,
the skill of medical men proved as unavailing as formerly to restore his strength; and
at length they informed him that the only
means of re-establishing his constitution was
to return home for a short period. Picton was
compelled, from former experience, to admit
the justice of this opinion, and he prepared to
act upon it. He was accompanied upon his
return by his aid-de-camp, Captain Tyler.

'By easy stages General Picton reached Lisbon, where he embarked for England. Upon
his arrival the sea air had in some degree restored his strength, but the germ of the disease
was not eradicated: He repaired directly to
Cheltenham; and the air and waters of that
place produced a rapid and favourable change.
After remaining at this place until his con-

stitution was restored, he revisited his native land. Here, as elsewhere, his military reputation had preceded him : the people of Wales had become justly proud of his renown ; many soldiers who had served in his division came from the same neighbourhood as himself; and in their correspondence they had mentioned with pleasure the high estimation in which their fellow-countryman was held by the whole army. For a short time he enjoyed the pleasures of retirement among his friends and relatives ; but it would have been wholly inconsistent with the character of Sir Thomas Picton to have remained long inactive from any other cause than absolute necessity.

The approaching spring gave promise of some great events : Napoleon, weakened by the destruction of his grand army, could with difficulty keep down the discontent of the various powers he had subjugated ; and he at length became sensible of the danger that threatened him from Spain. The perseverance and skill of Lord Wellington, together with the series of defeats he had inflicted upon the French marshals, determined Napoleon to make a more powerful effort to drive

the English from the Peninsula. It appears
that he would have placed himself at the
head of the army of Spain, but the Northern
powers were now threatening his dominions
with a more formidable invasion. Prussia,
Austria, and Russia, were forming a close
alliance; and France, exhausted by the efforts
which she had been called upon to make, was
now left almost destitute of the means of defence.

After the capture of Madrid, the allied
army, as we have already mentioned, remained
for a short time within that city to refresh.
On the 4th of September, the troops were collected at Arevola, except the third and fourth
divisions, which were left to garrison Madrid:
from Arevola they marched towards Burgos,
and, as they advanced, the French army evacuated all their fortified posts.

On the 11th the allies entered Placentia, and
on the 16th Lord Wellington was joined by
the army of Galicia, consisting of about five
thousand Spaniards. This corps was however
greatly deficient in discipline and organization.
To compensate for these disadvantages, the
Spaniards cherished an inveterate hatred to-

wards the French, and possessed a certain sparkling bravery, which, with judicious management, might be rendered highly effective.

On the 18th, the allies marched into the city of Burgos, and on the following day the castle was invested by the first, fifth, sixth, and seventh divisions. The proceedings for the reduction of this fortress were protracted and tedious ; the garrison made a brave and skilful defence ; and the allies were occupied for more than a month in unsuccessful attempts to compel them to capitulate. It was known that the French were using every exertion during this period to collect a sufficient force to make Lord Wellington raise the siege ; while he, aware of their intention, pressed it forward as much as possible.

About the middle of October, however, he received information that Souham was advancing towards Burgos with a considerable army on the north; while Marshal Soult was moving on Madrid with a large force from the south. Upon the confirmation of these reports, orders were immediately sent to Sir Rowland Hill, who commanded the troops left in Madrid and its vicinity, to fall back upon the Adejo.

On the 22nd of October, Burgos was evacuated, and the main army of the allies commenced falling back upon the frontiers of Portugal, at the same time that General Hill made
a retrograde movement to form a junction with
Lord Wellington. The enemy followed close
upon their rear, and constant skirmishes took
place between the retreating and pursuing
armies.

Early in November, the three corps of Soult,
Souham, and Joseph Bonaparte, united on the
Tormes, when their combined forces consisted
of eighty thousand infantry, and about twelve
thousand cavalry. They, however, relinquished the pursuit after they had reached the river; and Lord Wellington, having established
his head-quarters at Ciudad Rodrigo, directed
the army to prepare winter cantonments in its
vicinity: the third division occupying Fonte
Arcada and the neighbouring villages.

Thus, then, the campaign of 1812 was brought
to a close. The British army had gained many
battles and much glory: they had destroyed
the notion of the invincibility of French troops,
and had inflicted such severe losses upon Napoleon, that those of his friends and followers

who have traced the causes of his downfal,
have assigned to these reverses no trifling share
in the destruction of his power. They all agree
that the " Spanish ulcer" was only second to
the Russian winter. Still, Lord Wellington's
winter quarters at the close of the last campaign were within a few miles of those which
the allies now occupied; they had, it is true,
obtained possession of the two strong-holds of
Badajoz and Ciudad Rodrigo; and had *seen*
Madrid and Salamanca, but both these cities
were again in the hands of the French.

Lord Wellington was sharply animadverted
upon in England for his retreat from Burgos.
The popular outcry against him was very great,
and all that he had done was forgotten in
condemnation of this last act. The Government were fortunately not influenced by the
same sentiments; they were satisfied with the
explanation he gave of his motives for retreating, and resolved to send him every assistance which they could afford, in order to put
him in a position to open the ensuing campaign with a force which would enable him
to act upon more decisive and extended plans.
The British general himself was constantly

engaged during the winter months in making
exertions to render his army as effective as
circumstances and time would admit, and in
this he succeeded beyond expectation; for
early in the spring of 1813, the allied army
amounted to nearly one hundred thousand men,
of which forty-eight thousand were British,
thirty thousand Portuguese, and the remainder
Spaniards: the two former composing a highly effective army of seventy-eight thousand
men.

Lord Wellington had never before been
placed in so commanding a position: hitherto
he had been obliged to depend upon the errors
and over-confidence of his opponents; now he
was about to have the opportunity of forming his own plans and contending upon equal
terms. The power of Napoleon was now in its
decline. Russia had destroyed his grand army: the whole of the Northern powers were
combined against him, and Austria was already threatening his frontier. Still France,
with a blind but noble devotion, poured forth
her sons to fight his battles. Another army
was required; his old soldiers, those whom
he had so often led to victory, were almost an-

nihilated. The conscription with difficulty filled up his ranks. But the conscripts were young
and undisciplined : these, therefore, he sent to
gain experience in the Peninsula, in the place
of Soult and his veterans, whom he ordered
to join his Army of the North. The abilities
of this great general were therefore withdrawn,
and the conduct of the army of Spain was left
to King Joseph and his major-general, Marshal Jourdan. The former had long since
shown his incapacity, while the latter had yet
to prove it : for some time after the re-open-
ing of the campaign it was not even known
amongst the allies who actually held command
of the enemy, Joseph being always spoken of
as the ostensible chief.

Early in the spring Sir Thomas Picton again
returned to the Peninsula, his health having
been reinstated by his native air ; although, according to his own opinion, he was never so
well as when employed upon active service ;
for while away from the army he experienced
a constant feeling of anxiety and apprehension
lest some important action might take place
during his absence. He returned, therefore, to
his old soldiers with all the pleasure of a pa-

rent to his family; and he was received with
the same feeling. Before he left England to
resume his command in the allied army, his
Royal Highness the Prince Regent in the most
flattering manner created him a Knight of the
Bath; and he was nominated and invested at
Carlton House on the 1st of February, 1813.

A distinguished officer, who was a witness
of Picton's reception by his old soldiers, has
communicated to us the following account of
this interesting event : — "I was," he says,
"much surprised one afternoon by hearing
a kind of low whisper amongst the men of
my regiment, who were at the time variously
amusing themselves. This whisper was quickly
increased to a more general commotion, as they
all set off in the direction to which their attention
had been drawn, at first walking, and then running a kind of race, as each tried to distance the
others in first reaching the point of their destination. For awhile I was quite at a loss to account for this sudden movement; but at length
I discerned at some distance several mounted
officers riding slowly towards our quarters.
Curiosity led me to follow the men; but long
before I could reach the spot, the approaching

horsemen were surrounded by the soldiers, who had now collected from all directions, and were warmly greeting them with loud and continued cheers. As I came nearer, I soon recognised General Picton. Many of the men were hailing him with most gratifying epithets of esteem, one of which in particular struck me: this was, ' Here comes our brave old father !' The general seemed much gratified, and smiled upon them with a look of unaffected regard. I was not forgotten nor unnoticed. His eagle eye in one moment was fixed upon me, and holding out his hand, he observed, 'Ah ! my young friend; what ! you come to meet me too !' Nearly the whole division collected before he reached his quarters; and thus surrounded by his delighted soldiers, he returned again ,to lead them on to a still more splendid career of victory." This little incident is a sufficient reply to those writers who have so unhesitatingly asserted that " Sir Thomas Picton was not beloved by his soldiers."

Picton's division was now composed of the following regiments :

RIGHT BRIGADE. Major-General Brisbane.	45th Reg. 1st bat.; 74th Reg.; 88th Reg. 1st bat.; and three companies of the 60th Reg. 5th bat.

| Centre.
Lieutenant-General Picton. | { 5th Reg. 1st bat.; 83rd Reg.
2nd bat.; 87th Reg. 2nd bat.;
and the 94th Regiment. |
| Left.
Major-General Power. | { 9th Portuguese Reg. of the
line, 21st ditto ditto, and the
11th Caçadores. |

Picton, who had from the 6th of September 1811 held only the *local* rank of lieutenant-general, was on the 4th of June promoted to this rank in the army; and from that period dated his seniority. The custom of conferring upon officers a rank in the corps to which they were attached superior to that which they actually held in the British service, was an arrangement made for the purpose of preventing those officers who had seen much service, and obtained much experience at the seat of war, from being superseded in their commands by those sent from England, who in many instances were greatly inferior in abilities, although many years senior in rank.

That the army of Wellington was now about to commence operations under far more favourable auspices, has already been shown. King Joseph had, it is true, made every preparation to oppose the progress of the allies, but he wanted abilities for his task; and Marshal Jourdan was not an adequate substitute for Soult.

On the 16th of May 1813, the allied army was again in motion, in three separate columns ; — the right, under Sir Rowland Hill, marching by the route of Alba de Tormes to Salamanca; the centre, under Lord Wellington in person, taking the more direct road to that city ; while the left, being in fact the main body, under Sir Thomas Graham, now second in command, was ordered to cross the Douro at Lamego by boats, which had for some time been preparing for that purpose. General Picton and his division were attached to this corps, and the rapidity of their movements caused much consternation to the enemy.*

* In the " Recollections of a Soldier's Life," the writer, in speaking of this advance, after alluding to the passage of the division through some village on the march, observes :— " General Picton, who had joined from England a considerable time before, again commanded the division. To judge from appearances, no one would have suspected him of humour ; yet he often indulged in it. His wit was generally, however, of the satirical kind. On this advance, a man belonging to one of the regiments of the brigade, who was remarkable for his mean pilfering disposition, had lingered behind his regiment on some pretence when they marched out to the assembling ground, and was prowling about from one house to another in search of plunder. General Picton, who was passing through, happened to cast his eye upon him, and called out, " What are you doing there, sir ? why

The whole policy of the French commanders
appeared now to be changed. King Joseph
was unwilling to hazard an engagement wherein defeat would be attended with most disastrous consequences to his army and his throne.
Still, it appeared that it could not be long
avoided; for the allies were advancing rapidly
upon him, and he would soon be compelled
either to give them battle or evacuate Spain.

Joseph collected his whole force on the roads
to Burgos, with the apparent intention of arresting the progress of Lord Wellington; but
when that general, after having re-occupied Salamanca, concentrated his army at Valladolid
and moved on to the attack, the French again
abandoned their position without firing a gun,
and for some time appeared undetermined
where to make a stand. On the 7th of June,
the allied army crossed the Carrion in force,
still following the enemy. On the 11th, how-

are you behind your regiment?" The man, who did not expect to see the general in the village, had not an answer
very ready; but he stammered out an excuse, saying, " I
came back to the house where I was quartered to look for
my gallowses" (braces). " Ay, I see how it is," replied
the general: "get along, sir, to your regiment, and take my
advice—always keep the word *gallows* in your mind."

ever, Lord Wellington allowed his soldiers a short respite after the long-continued march which they had performed without a halt.

The following anecdote* of General Picton, in reference to the advance of the allied army, we have heard confirmed from various sources.

" General Picton had been for some time under a cloud; the principal cause of which is said to have been his rough and unpliant temper. The third division had always been called *par excellence* ' The Fighting Division,' being ever foremost where danger was the greatest. During the late advance, however, they had been saddled with the scaling-ladders, and other necessary lumber of the army; and this had greatly annoyed Picton, and contributed to produce still greater ebullitions of temper, which it would have been more prudent in him to have restrained.

" On the march, head-quarters' baggage has the privilege of continuing its route without turning aside to allow any troops to pass it.

* From the " Personal Narrative of Adventures in the Peninsula."

One day, Picton overtaking it with his division, ordered it off the road until he had marched by. A part complied; but Lord Wellington's butler refused to obey, pleading headquarters' privilege. Upon this, it is said that Picton struck him with the umbrella, which he usually carried to defend his eyes, which were weak, from the sun; and accompanied his castigation with a threat of having him tied up and flogged by the provost-marshal, if he did not immediately give way to the division."

CHAPTER VIII.

Joseph Bonaparte retreats to Burgos.—He blows up the castle, and continues his retreat.—Picton's account of the battle of Vittoria.—Picton's conduct in the battle.— Surprising efforts of the Third Division. —The French driven back upon Vittoria.—Total defeat of the French.— Narrow escape of King Joseph.—Southey's description of the booty.—The French fly to Pamplona.—They are refused admission.—Their flight continued to the Pyrenees. —Soult appointed " Lieutenant de l'Empereur."

JOSEPH was now falling back upon Burgos, the castle of which place had been strengthened. But the retreating monarch evidently had as little confidence in stone walls as in the issue of a battle. A slight show of opposition was made on the heights to the left of Hormaza; but this soon ended in flight, when, with much precipitation, the whole French army entered the town. This was towards night, and it was fully expected by the allies that they would have to fight the enemy in its neighbourhood. But Joseph had not yet gathered

sufficient resolution to stop his pursuers; and,
therefore, early on the following morning, the
castle of Burgos was blown up with a tremendous explosion, the report of which was stated
to have been heard at the distance of fifty
miles. By this unnecessary measure, between
three and four hundred French soldiers, who
were lingering in the town for plunder, were
destroyed.

Joseph now continued his retreat towards
Vittoria. It appears that his object at this
period was to prevent Lord Wellington from
crossing the Ebro: and to effect this he hastily
passed his army over that river, and took up a
strong position in its rear; strengthening at the
same time the castle of Pancorbo, to check
the advance of the allies along the great road
through Berbiesca to Miranda. But Lord
Wellington had anticipated this design of the
French general. Instead, therefore, of following the enemy with his whole army in the
direction which it was supposed was the only
practicable road, he suddenly changed the route
of his march, and moved the left wing higher
up the stream, over a country full of obstacles,
and which might have been defended by a

few hundred soldiers. This corps of the army was enabled to cross the Ebro on the 14th, by the bridges of St. Martin and Rocamunde. The rapidity of this movement entirely disconcerted Joseph's whole plan, and the passage of the Ebro was at once given up to the remainder of the allied army.

The French now hurried their retreat upon Vittoria, hotly pursued by the English; until both Joseph and Marshal Jourdan concurred in the opinion that they must now either fight or give up Spain. The result of a battle was uncertain, but even defeat would not be more disastrous than a retreat into France. Convinced at last of the necessity for decision, the French general now resolved to await the attack of Lord Wellington in front of the city of Vittoria. On the 19th, the rear-guard, which was strongly posted on some heights near Pobes, was driven back by the light and fourth divisions; when the enemy took up a position to await the advance of the allies.

Lord Wellington, having collected his scattered divisions during the day of the 20th, made every disposition for his intended attack. The soldiers were impatient for the contest; their continued pursuit of the enemy had made them almost despise them, and they looked forward with confidence to the result. The lines were formed at early dawn, and every preparation was made for the approaching battle. The centre of the British position was occupied by the third, fourth, seventh, and light divisions, in two lines; the right by the second, a Portuguese division, and a Spanish corps; and the left by Sir Thomas Graham, with the first and fifth divisions, Pack and Bradford's brigades of infantry, a Spanish division under Longa, and General Pack and Anson's brigades of horse. A small river, the Zadorra, separated the two armies; over this were several narrow bridges which would admit of a slow passage of troops, and it appears strange that the enemy should not have attempted to defend any of these against the allies. We give in General Picton's own words an account of this battle, as written by him to his friend Colonel Pleydel, only ten days after the event.

"Sanguessa, 1st July 1813.
" MY DEAR COLONEL,

"I had the pleasure of a letter from my friend General Darling, with an enclosure from

you; and I am most truly concerned to learn
that you have been so troubled with a recurrence and continuance of your obstinate old
complaints. I should have written to you
more frequently, but have been so affected,
with an inflammation and consequent weakness
of my eyes, that I have not even been able to
write the common report and official communications during the whole course of our operations. The rapidity of our movements will,
I conceive, have given you all no small degree
of astonishment in England.

" On the 16th of May, the division was put
in movement; on the 18th we crossed the
Douro, on the 15th of June the Ebro, and on
the 21st we fought the battle of Vittoria. The
third division, as usual, had a very distinguished share in this decisive action. The enemy's
left rested on an elevated chain of craggy
mountains, and their right on a rapid river,
with commanding heights in the centre, and
a succession of undulating grounds, which afforded excellent situations for artillery, and several good positions in front of the city of Vittoria, where King Joseph had his head-quarters.
The enemy's army amounted to about sixty-

five thousand men, with one hundred and fifty odd pieces of artillery,—four, eight, and twelve pounders. The battle began early in the morning, between our right and the enemy's left, on the high craggy heights, and continued with various success for several hours; and, whilst it still continued without any decisive advantage being gained on either side, (about twelve o'clock,) the third division was ordered to force the passage of the river, and carry the heights in the centre; which service was executed with so much rapidity, that we got possession of the commanding ground before the enemy were aware of our intention.

" We were scarcely, however, in possession before the enemy attempted to dislodge us with a great superiority of force, and between forty and fifty pieces of cannon; and. at that period the troops on our right had not made sufficient progress to cover our right flank; in consequence of which we suffered a momentary check, and were driven out of a village from whence we had dislodged the enemy: but it was quickly recovered; and. on the troops under Sir Rowland Hill (the second division, with a Portuguese and Spanish division,) forcing the enemy to abandon the heights, and advancing to protect our flank, we pushed the enemy rapidly from all his positions, forced him to abandon his cannon, and drove his cavalry and infantry in confusion beyond the city of Vittoria, when darkness intervened to protect his disorderly flight. We took one hundred and fifty-two pieces of cannon, the military chest, ammunition, and baggage; besides an immense treasure, the property of the different French generals, which they had amassed by their requisitions and extortions in Spain.

" The third division was the most severely and permanently engaged of any part of the army; and we in consequence sustained a loss of nearly eighteen hundred men in killed and wounded, which is more than a third of the total loss of the army on the occasion. The Portuguese brigade attached to the division was the admiration of the whole army : it advanced in line over difficult and broken ground in front of nearly fifty pieces of cannon and a continual volley of musketry, without ever hesitating, and drove the enemy from several commanding positions which they successively occupied. During this operation they lost above seven hundred men. We followed the enemy slowly to Pamplona, from whence they directed their retreat over the Pyrenees towards France. We have since been engaged in an unsuccessful pursuit of another French corps, which has effected its retreat upon Saragossa; and we are now returning to the siege of Pamplona, which has been closely invested by the corps under Sir Rowland Hill. During these operations we marched thirty-four days without a halt, and for several days through muddy roads up to our knees.

" The inhabitants of Navarre and Arragon we find active and intelligent people, and, in my opinion, much superior to those of the southern and eastern provinces. If the Northern powers should be able to continue the contest with Napoleon, I think we shall nearly clear Spain during the course of the campaign.

" I doubt much whether you will be able to decipher this miserable scrawl, which, for-

tunately for you, my eyes will not allow me
to continue.

"With my best wishes,

"My dear colonel,

"Yours very faithfully,

"TH. PICTON."

Another letter from General Picton, addressed to his brother, the Reverend Edward Picton,
and which, it will be perceived, was written
on the 27th of June, four days later than that
just given, and only six after the battle of
Vittoria, is also descriptive of this important
victory.

"Neighbourhood of Pamplona,
27th June 1813.

"MY DEAR BROTHER,

"I have been so affected with a weakness
and inflammation of the eyes, as to be wholly
unable to write; and we have been incessantly marching from the 16th of May, when we
commenced our operations. We had marched
nearly two hundred miles before we came up
with King Joseph's army, near the city of
Vittoria—a place celebrated in history as the

theatre of one of the Black Prince's victories, and which will be again rendered famous by the signal victory gained there on the 21st of June.

" The third division had again the principal part of this action, and, I may well say, covered itself with glory, having contended during the whole day against five times our numbers and fifty pieces of cannon. But, notwithstanding this great disparity of numbers, we bore down everything before us, during all which we were so situated as to have the eyes of all the army fixed upon us.

" Our loss was certainly great: out of five thousand six hundred men, we lost eighteen hundred in killed and wounded. There never was a more complete rout. About eight o'clock in the evening, the enemy ran off in the greatest confusion, abandoning one hundred and fifty pieces of cannon, with all their baggage, stores, and treasure; and they were indebted to the obscurity of the night and the lightness of their heels for safety. I was very fortunate, having escaped with only one shothole in my great-coat. I saw David Edwards' brigade several times during the action, and he appeared to be going on well.

" My eyes are still so weak that I cannot continue my letter.

" With best wishes to Mrs. Picton, my dear brother, very sincerely yours,

"TH. PICTON.

" Colonel Burgoyne is well, and just going to undertake the siege of Pamplona."

To give a just idea of Picton's conduct upon this important day, and of the part which he had in the victory, it will be necessary to enter into some detail, and to introduce the statement which we have received from several officers who were present with him at this engagement.

The battle, as has been already mentioned, commenced on the right of the allied army, and was continued there with much obstinacy; but the French were compelled at length to evacuate the heights for which they had been contending. Joseph was, however, tenacious of this point, and drew largely from his centre in order to make fresh efforts to regain

this part of his position ; but Lord Wellington
knew the value of this conquest, and sent immediate orders to Sir Rowland Hill, who commanded the right wing, to keep the post at all
hazards. That general sent fresh troops to reinforce those already engaged ; and they succeeded, after some hard fighting, in compelling the
enemy to abandon the attempt.

During this struggle on the right, the centre
was inactive. General Picton was impatient ;
he inquired of several aides-de-camp who came
near him from head-quarters, whether they
had any orders for him ? His soldiers were
anxiously waiting to advance : Picton knew the
spirit of his men, and had some difficulty in
restraining it. As the day wore on, and the fight
waxed warmer on the right, he became furious,
and observed to an officer who communicated
these particulars, " D—n it ! Lord Wellington
must have forgotten us." It was near noon,
and the men were getting discontented, for
the centre had not yet been engaged ; Picton's
blood was boiling, and his stick fell with rapid
strokes upon the mane of his horse ; he was
riding backwards and forwards, looking in
every direction for the arrival of an aid-de-

camp, until at length a staff officer galloped
up from Lord Wellington. He was looking
for the seventh division, under Lord Dalhousie, which had not yet arrived at its post,
having had to move over some difficult ground.
The aid-de-camp, riding up at speed, suddenly
checked his horse and demanded of the general whether he had seen Lord Dalhousie.
Picton was disappointed; he expected now at
least that he might move; and, in a voice
which did not gain softness from his feelings,
he answered in a sharp tone, " No, sir! I have
not seen his lordship: but have you any orders
for me, sir?"—" None," replied the aid-de-camp.
—" Then pray, sir," continued the irritated
general, " what are the orders you *do* bring ?"—
" Why," answered the officer, " that as soon as
Lord Dalhousie, with the seventh division, shall
commence an attack upon that bridge," (pointing to one on the left,) " the fourth and sixth
are to support him." Picton could not understand the idea of any other division fighting in
his front; and, drawing himself up to his full
height, he said to the astonished aid-de-camp
with some passion, " You may tell Lord Wellington from me, sir, that the third division

under my command shall in less than ten minutes attack the bridge and carry it, and the
fourth and sixth divisions may support if they
choose." Having thus expressed his intention,
he turned from the aid-de-camp, and put himself at the head of his soldiers, who were
quickly in motion towards the bridge; encouraging them with the bland appellation of
" Come on, ye rascals!— come on, ye fighting
villains!"

He well fulfilled his promise. A heavy fire
of artillery was opened upon the division, but it
moved steadily on, and the leading companies
rushed over the bridge, where they immediately
formed in open columns. They then moved
by their left so as to attack the entire centre of
the enemy. Still advancing in the same order,
they pressed up the heights, where they
quickly deployed into line. The enemy hardly
awaited the attack; for so ably and with so
much rapidity were these manœuvres executed,
that they were for the moment panic-struck.

Picton had gained the heights, but the divisions on his right had not yet made sufficient
progress to cover his flank; he in a moment
perceived this obstacle to his advance, and re-

strained his men from pressing too forward.
The seventh and part of the light divisions
crossed the bridge shortly after the third, while
the fourth, led by General Cole, passed over still
further on the right, at a place called Nanclares.
These divisions immediately closed up, and
came on at double-time to cover the right flank
of General Picton's attack. During their advance the enemy made several strenuous efforts
to dislodge General Picton from the commanding position which he had gained: between
forty and fifty pieces of cannon opened upon
him, at the same time that masses of infantry
were pushed forward on all parts of his line;
but the incessant fire which was kept up by his
troops made terrible havoc among the advancing columns.

Picton bade his soldiers charge: the bayonets crossed, and the result was certain. It was
from this period of the battle that " Picton's
division acted in a manner which excited at
once the surprise and admiration of the whole
army. For nearly four hours did it alone sus-
tain the unequal conflict, opposed to a vast
superiority of force. From the nature of the
ground, the rest of the army became witnesses

of this animating scene : they beheld with feelings more easily conceived than expressed the truly heroic efforts of this gallant band : they saw the general, calm, collected, and determined, leading them on in the face of danger, amidst a shower of cannon and musket balls. Nothing could appal, nothing could resist, men so resolute and so led ; they subdued every obstacle, bore down all opposition, and spread death, consternation, and dismay through the enemy's ranks." As the other two divisions ascended the heights, each took up its position in the line laid out by Picton, the third division still keeping the enemy's centre in its front ; and now the three divisions advanced in line.

The French had taken up fresh ground, a little in rear of the heights from whence they had been driven. The ardour of the third division made them again the first to come in contact with the enemy. The uneven and broken ground made their advance difficult and the line irregular ; but there was no confusion. After being exposed for some time to the fire of the enemy, they came within a short distance of their line: the word

was then given to "charge." So impetuous
was the onset, that the struggle could not
last. The enemy soon gave way; and so
hasty was their flight, that Picton's division
took from them twenty-eight pieces of artillery. The other parts of the line were pressing forward with equal bravery, but not with
equal success.

The seventh division met with a severe
check at a position which the enemy had taken
up in the village of Gomecha and the neighbouring wood; but a part of the light division
came up to its support, when Picton still
continuing to force their centre, the enemy
abandoned this ground, and again fell back
upon Vittoria with the rest of their columns.
When General Hill was made acquainted
with the success of the attack on the French
centre, he renewed his efforts against their left
wing, and, after some spirited fighting, succeeded in forcing their position, and driving
them back in some disorder.

The left wing, under Sir Thomas Graham,
had not, however, been so entirely successful.
Advancing early in the morning from Margina
along the Bilboa Road to Vittoria, they first

came up with the right wing of King Joseph's army on some commanding heights between Abechuco and Gomarra Major, which villages they also occupied. Sir Thomas Graham immediately ordered an attack ; and, after a determined resistance and much slaughter, they at length forced the enemy from the heights, and compelled them to evacuate the houses.

In the rear of these villages were two bridges over the Zadorra, and thence it was only a short distance to Vittoria. Had the left wing of the allies been successful in gaining a passage over the river at these places, it would in all probability have produced the surrender or destruction of the whole French army. The retreat to France by the way of Bayonne was already cut off by the occupation of Gomarra Minor, which was now possessed by Longa's Spanish division ; and in case of the Zadorra being passed at this point, Vittoria would no longer be left open. The consequence was then evident: Joseph would be driven to the necessity of either collecting his scattered troops and again giving the English general battle, or of surrendering to the allies. But the importance of this post was well known both to the king and his major-general: some of the choicest corps were therefore drawn from the centre to defend the bridges at Abechuco and Gomarra Major, when so strongly were the enemy posted, and so considerable were their numbers, that, after several attempts, Sir Thomas Graham was compelled to await the further successes of the right and centre.

The battle now presented a grand spectacle, as the three divisions moved forward in line. Here, again, that of Picton occupied a conspicuous position : surmounting every obstacle presented by the face of the country, they were ever the foremost in coming up with the retiring enemy ; and frequently the divisions on the right and left would see them charging into the very heart of the enemy's centre, and immediately afterwards the enemy retreating in confusion. Picton would then restrain his men, and form them in array to repel any fresh attempt until their flanks were again protected by the advance of the other two divisions. Thus was the fight continued for some miles; for Joseph, frightened by the prospect of hav-

ing his retreat intercepted by Sir Thomas Graham, slowly and in moderately good order fell
back upon Vittoria.

But this retrograde movement became more
rapid after every defeat, until within about a
mile of the city, where he made his last grand
stand. One hundred pieces of artillery played with great effect upon the pursuers, and it
might have been supposed that the victory had
still to be won. But the hearts and hopes
of the hostile soldiers were different. The
French were fighting on retreat, the allies
were flushed with conquest; the enemy had
no confidence in their leaders, while the English never thought of defeat when Wellington
was in the field. Night was approaching, and
it was desirable to drive the enemy from this
position before dark. The British divisions
paused but for a moment to close up their
ranks, and then once more advanced. Again
Picton and his soldiers were foremost: the ser-
ried line pressed up the steep against an incessant storm of shot; but the French soldiers
could not withstand the shock, — they wavered
and turned, and the day was irretrievably lost.

An officer of distinguished rank and ability,

who throughout the whole campaign enjoyed much of Picton's confidence, and who still bears him in affectionate remembrance, has assured us, that three times during this battle orders were sent by Lord Wellington for certain manœuvres to be performed by the third division, which in each instance General Picton had begun to execute upon his own judgment and responsibility.

A complete rout now ensued: from an organized army the enemy in a few moments became a wild and affrighted mob. The allies pressed hard upon their rear, and Joseph himself with difficulty escaped. The Tenth regiment of Hussars entered the town as he was leaving it in his carriage: Captain Windham, with a squadron, rode full gallop after him, and he only succeeded in escaping his pursuers by hastily quitting his carriage and mounting a horse. The Hussars were, however, rewarded by capturing his calash, in which were found all the portable valuables of his regalia,— a rich and well-earned booty. Such a victory could not but produce a powerful and animating effect upon the British nation: this was not an empty conquest—its effect was decisive.

Joseph had been forced into a battle and was beaten : but it was not only honour that the conquerors had earned,—they had gained possession of the whole *matériel* of the French army; and, in addition to this, all the spoils that had been plundered from Spain fell to the share of the allies.*

General Picton's letters to Mr. Marryat will be read with interest.

"St. Estevan, among the Pyrenees, 24th July 1813.

" MY DEAR SIR,

" The 'Gazette' account of the battle of Vittoria is a most incorrect relation of the circumstances of that memorable event ; most uncandidly attributing to arrangement and manœuvre alone, what was in a very considerable degree effected by blood and hard fighting. The arrangements and combinations preparatory to the action were certainly excellent : but the centre of the enemy's army did not immediately fall back upon Vittoria on seeing the arrangements for its attack, (as represented in the official despatch,) but, in fact, disputed

---

* The French had 152 pieces of artillery in the field; of these, 150 were taken by the allies, and one of the remainder was found in a ditch on the road to Pamplona.

every inch of the ground, and was driven from several strong positions by the third division alone, and with a loss, in killed and wounded, of eighty-nine officers, seventy-one sergeants, and one thousand four hundred and seventy-five rank and file, a number which exceeded one-third of the whole casualties of the army on that memorable day, and being in the same proportion to our own effective numbers, which were under five thousand. Upon the whole, the division has not had its proportion of credit; but its operations were in the view of the whole army, and murder will out in the end.

. " Soult is assembling the beaten army, and says that he will begin offensive operations in less than a fortnight. The whole of our army, except the cavalry, is either watching his movements or covering the siege of St. Sebastian; which is a fortress of importance, as well to cover the left of our line, as to facilitate our communication with England and, of course, our supplies. O'Donnel, with the Spanish army of reserve, is employed in the investment of Pampeluna, which may hold out for a couple of months longer. The surrender of this place, with that of St. Sebastian and Santona, will render us secure on this side, and then we must combine our operations with the unfortunate army of Alicant, and endeavour to eject Souchet from the south. Our numbers are naturally considerably diminished by the excessive fatigue of forced marches, as well as the casualties of war. It is of the greatest importance to replace them and augment our numbers, so as to enable us to do something decisive at so critical and favourable a conjuncture. *Now is the time, or never ;* fifteen or twenty thousand men would do more than fifty thousand under any other circumstances. I have been almost blind of an obstinate inflammation of the eyes, which, by a long continuance, is almost become cbronical. I must give over the business after this campaign, or it will give me up, which I must not run the risk of.

" I hope Mrs. M. and all the family continue in good health. We have already made great ravages in the jar of *mince-meat,* which is allowed to be unique ; and we have had the honour of celebrating her munificence in flaming bumpers of champagne. With my best wishes and compliments of the season to yourself and any part of your family, My dear sir,

" Very faithfully yours,

" T. Picton."

" MY DEAR SIR,

" I have just been favoured with your letters and enclosures, for which I return you many thanks. I am happy to find that you have at length succeeded in your privy council cause; for it would have been monstrous to have sent the judge back to Trinidad, under the whole circumstances of the case. I shall be very happy to have an opportunity of meeting the wishes of my old friend Mr. De Granville, and I will take an early opportunity of recom_ mending him for an ensigncy in my own regiment.

" I hope our operations here have not fallen short of your sanguine expectations. There certainly never was a more complete rout than that of the 21st ult.: a couple of hours more daylight, and we should have had nearly the whole of the army; but they dispersed, and saved themselves under protection of the night. The third division had more than its usual share, and swept everything before it, though opposed to about four times its number, and nearly fifty pieces of cannon. We had the satisfaction of exhibiting, from one o'clock until dark night, under the eyes of the whole army,

and I think I may say, to its admiration. Our
loss was of course great—more than one-third
of that of the whole army—seventeen hundred
and fifty men. The Portuguese brigade, if possible, surpassed the British in gallantry. The
whole of the cannon, military chest, ammunition, baggage, and equipment of the army—the
treasure of King Joseph, as well as that of all his
generals, and an immense booty in plate and
other valuable articles of plunder, fell into the
hands of the soldiers. The whole of the loss sustained by the fugitive monarch and his followers
must amount to between three and four millions
sterling. If ministers will send us ten or twelve
thousand to fill up our ranks, which have been
reduced by thirty-five days' forced marching,
we shall carry everything before us. Some of
our advanced troops are now in France.

" I hope Mrs. M. and all my young friends
enjoy good health. Pray offer them all my
respects and best wishes.

" My dear Sir,

" Very faithfully yours,

" T. Picton."

Southey's description of this mass of booty
is rather amusing. He says—

" The spoils resembled those of an Oriental, rather than those of an European army; for the intruder, who, in his miserable situation, had abandoned himself to every kind of sensuality, had with him all his luxuries. His plunder, his wardrobe, his sideboard, his larder, and his cellar, fell into the conquerors' hands. The French officers, who carried the pestilential manners of their nation wherever they went, followed his example as far as their means allowed; and thus the finest wines and the choicest delicacies were found in profusion. The wives and mistresses of the officers had gathered together in one house, where they were safe, and from whence they were sent in their own carriages with a flag of truce to Pamplona. Poodles, parrots, and monkeys were among the prisoners.

" Seldom has such a scene of confusion been witnessed as that which the roads leading from the field of battle presented; — broken-down waggons stocked with claret and champagne, others laden with eatables dressed and undressed, casks of brandy, apparel of every kind, barrels of money, books, papers, sheep, cattle, horses, and mules, abandoned in the flight. The baggage was presently rifled, and the followers of the camp attired themselves in the gala dresses of the flying enemy. Portuguese boys figured about in the dress-coats of French general officers; and they who happened to draw a woman's wardrobe in the lottery, converted silks, satins, and embroidered muslins, into scarfs and sashes for their masquerade triumph. Some of the more fortunate soldiers got possession of the army chest, and loaded themselves with money. 'Let them,' said Lord Wellington, when he was informed of it: 'they deserve all they can find, were it ten times more.'

"The camp of every division was like a fair; benches were laid from waggon to waggon, and there the soldiers held an auction through the night, and disposed of such plunder as had fallen to their share, to any one who would purchase it. Even dollars became an article of sale, for they were too heavy to be carried in any great numbers: eight were offered for a guinea."

Joseph hardly once looked back before he had reached the walls of Pamplona. The garrison would not open their gates to the retreating soldiers, who therefore attempted to force an entrance over the walls; but they were repulsed by a fire of musketry : upon which their flight was continued to the fastnesses of the Pyrenees, where Joseph collected the remains of his scattered troops. Provisions were, however, thrown into Pamplona, as the strength of that fortress promised, if well defended, to check for a while the advance of the allies into France.

General Clausel, with about fourteen thousand men, had commenced his march towards Vittoria, to support Joseph and General Jourdan ; but, hearing of the decisive nature of the battle which had taken place, he changed the direction of his march, and retired towards Logrono : and it is this corps to which General Picton alludes in his letter to Colonel Pleydel of the 1st of July 1813.

The third division, with the light, seventh, and fourth divisions, together with Major-general Ponsonby's brigade, the household troops, and General D'Urban's cavalry, were moved on the 24th of June towards Tudela, in the hope of intercepting this force, and of preventing a junction with the remains of Joseph's army. But Clausel, upon his arrival at Tudela on the 26th, was informed by the alcalde of the approach of the allies, and he therefore marched towards Saragossa, with the forces of General Mina and Don Julian Sanchez hanging on his rear, even up to the very gates of that city.

The blockade of Pamplona was, during this period, closely kept up by the Spaniards; at the same time that Sir Thomas Graham was directed to invest the fortress of St. Sebastian with the first and fifth divisions of the army. But another struggle was about to be made by Napoleon to retrieve his fallen fortunes. Soult, whom he now designated by the title of "*Lieutenant de l'Empereur*," was ordered immediately to assume the command of the Army of the South. It was now but a shadow; still this active and able general contrived by great exertions to concentrate the scattered forces and give them the appearance of strength. He had the confidence of the soldiers, and they freely rallied round his standard. His principal deficiency was in artillery; but this was forwarded to the frontiers with incredible despatch, and he was within a month from the signal defeat at Vittoria enabled to place himself at the head of an army amounting to above eighty thousand men. He issued a vaunting address to the soldiers, enumerating the number of victories achieved by the French army: he confessed they had been compelled to retreat, but denied any originality or military genius to the English general; while to the British soldiers he allowed only the merit of being apt scholars in learning the art of fighting; for he observed, "The dispositions and arrangements of their general have been prompt, skilful, and consecutive, while the valour and steadiness of his troops have been great. But do not forget that it is from you they have learned these lessons, and to you they are indebted for their present military experience."

"A change was now about to take place in the character of the contest," observes a writer, with much justice. "The allied army was to defend a series of mountain defiles, in a country where cavalry could not act, and in positions to which artillery could not be conveyed. They were about to enter into a struggle for which they were unprepared by any former experience; while the system of mountain warfare was one for which the lightness and activity of the French troops peculiarly fitted them, and in which they had hitherto been considered unrivalled. The high fame of the hostile commanders contributed also to invest this period of the war with extrinsic interest." *

* " Annals of the Peninsular Campaigns."

CHAPTER IX.

Advance of the French army under Soult.—Contest under General Picton between the allied forces and the French. —Battle of the Pyrenees.—Retreat of the French army. —General Picton's return to England.—Receives the thanks of the House of Commons.—His speech on that occasion.—Command of the Catalonian army offered to General Picton.

To meet the advance of Soult, the allied army was placed in a position occupying the whole of the passes of the Pyrenees between St. Sebastian and Pamplona. The left wing, under Sir Thomas Graham, composed of the first and fifth divisions, was employed in the siege of St. Sebastian; which operation was covered by a large corps of Spaniards, commanded by General Freyre, and Lord Aylmer's brigade, which were posted on the river Bidassoa. An intermediate space between this force and the left of the centre at Vera was held by General Longa's division.

The centre, under Sir Rowland Hill, consisted of the light, seventh, second, and the Portuguese division of the Conde de Amarante; while the sixth division, commanded by General Colville, was kept in reserve at St. Estevan, to support the troops at Maya or Echelar, as circumstances might require.

The army of the Conde de Bisbal, mustering about ten thousand Spaniards, was occupied in the blockade of Pamplona, which formed the extreme right of the allied position; the right wing of the army covering this operation. The pass of Roncesvalles, so famous in the border minstrelsy of Spain, was again occupied by Spanish soldiers; these were commanded by General Morillo, and supported by Major-general Byng's brigade of the second British division. Sir Lowry Cole, with the fourth division, occupied a second line in the rear of this advanced post; while General Picton, with his division, was in reserve at Olaque, ready to push forward and strengthen any part of this front which might be attacked by the enemy.

Thus posted, Wellington awaited the advance of Soult: the point of his attack was of course uncertain. The position of the two

armies was here strikingly picturesque, as, looking along the mountain summits, the eye rested
on some encampment perched on a cliff. These
unfrequented regions were now for a while animated with living masses; the world below was
left in peace, and the strife was now carried on
among the peaks of mountains and the alpine
streams, which bore down the blood of the
combatants to fertilize the valleys.

On the 24th of July, Soult concentrated the
right and left wing of his army. His design
was to relieve Pamplona; and, to effect this,
he resolved to attempt a passage through
some part of the British line. Roncesvalles and
Maya offered the greatest prospect of success,
as the force which could be opposed to him at
those passes would be weaker and less easily
supported than at any other part of the position. Early on the 25th he pushed on about
twelve thousand men, under General Drouet, to
force the pass of Maya, occupied by the second
division, under Sir Rowland Hill. A severe
contest here took place: the numerical strength
of the enemy was nearly double that of the
allies, but this consideration had long since
been laid aside; Drouet hoped by pressing for-

ward his large columns, to drive the allies from this pass. The English picquets were driven in, and the enemy then advanced with over-whelming numbers to attack the position : the confined nature of the ground did not, how-ever, give them that advantage from their nu-merical superiority which might have been ex-pected. A brave but sanguinary defence was made, the reserve being thrown forward by battalions to support the troops in front.

The force under Sir Rowland Hill was not sufficient to resist this corps; for the passes of Lareta, Ispegny, and Ariete were threatened at the same time that the attack was made at. Maya: a reserve was therefore necessary to defend and support these posts. General Hill was, however, unwilling to fall back; and re-inforcements were occasionally moved to the pass to relieve those troops which had been long engaged.

It was during this attack that Soult him-self, with thirty-five thousand men, advanced to force the position of the allies at Ronces-valles. General Byng's brigade was assailed by a superior force, at the same time that a large body of the enemy were manœuvred on his left along the ridge of Arola, which was occupied by the fourth division, under General Cole. The situation of the allies was at this moment one of critical interest; since, had one of these passes been gained, the security of their position would have been immediately destroyed, and Soult would have obtained a ready entrance into Spain.

The Marquis of Wellington was near St. Sebastian, not, it would appear, expecting so decided or sudden a movement on the part of the French. A despatch was instantly, however, sent to make him acquainted with the proceedings, at the same time that every preparation was made to check the progress of the enemy; while, in case of not succeeding in this object, a simultaneous retreat was resolved upon, so as to concentrate the whole of the divisions at one point, there to oppose their united strength to the further advance of Soult. But that general was aware of the importance of the moment, and of Wellington's absence; and he left no effort untried to force some of these passes by a *coup de main.* He pushed on his columns to attack Generals Cole and Byng, but for a long

time without success; for the soldiers under
their command repeatedly repulsed at the point
of the bayonet the heavy masses which were
sent against them: but General Cole, who knew
that his men would defend the post so long as
one entire company remained, felt it a duty to
fall back and assume a fresh and stronger position in the rear.

Soult then directed the whole of his force
against General Byng's brigade, extending his
line at the same time to the left, and compelling the Spanish corps under Morillo to
retire upon the fourth division. Byng, thus
exposed, also retreated; when the whole of this
force being concentrated under General Cole
near a place called Biscaret, about five miles
from the position which they had occupied in
the morning, it was thought advisable to continue the retreat to a strong ground still farther in the rear, near Lizoain.

The knowledge of these reverses on the right,
together with the information of General Cole's
retreat, induced Sir Rowland Hill to abandon
the defence of his position; and, accordingly,
after a severe and sanguinary conflict, he gradually fell back to some very defensible ground

in the neighbourhood of Trueta, by which the
security of the British line was still retained.
This was the situation of these two divisions on
the night of the 25th of July. General Picton
was at Olaque with his division, when information was brought to him of the success of
Soult's advance, and that Sir Lowry Cole was
in expectation of being again attacked by the
whole French force on the following morning.
Picton immediately put his division in motion,
and marched to the support of the fourth. He
here assumed the command as senior officer,
and proceeded forthwith to make every disposition to receive the enemy, and, if possible,
to stop his advance.

About two o'clock Soult commenced the
attack; when, as the superior numbers of the
French made resistance almost hopeless, Picton,
after consulting with General Cole, resolved to
fall back and occupy a more advantageous position in the rear, near Zubiri. Here, therefore,
the troops were withdrawn, skirmishing the
whole way; but the skill and judgment of Picton stopped every attempt of the enemy to press
his retreat and throw him into confusion. They
arrived in admirable order upon the ground

which they were to occupy, when they were once more thrown into line, and until night closed in, they succeeded in defeating every effort made upon the position.

Soult was thus checked for a while in his advance; still it was not possible to continue the struggle with such an inferiority of force. Picton knew that the position was not tenable without a considerable reinforcement, and that he must ultimately retire. He accordingly resolved to save the fruitless expenditure of life which must result from a continuance of the contest at this place, and determined to fall back upon the villages of Huerta and Villalba, where, by occupying a strong position between the rivers Arga and Lanz, he would be enabled to cover the blockade of Pamplona. In accordance with this plan, the two divisions were put in motion during the night of the 26th, the march being continued on the ensuing day, followed, but not very closely, by the enemy. Much chagrin was experienced by the officers and men upon this occasion, but the necessity for the measure was apparent to all.

Immediately Lord Wellington was informed that Soult was in motion, he set off to the scene of action ; but before his arrival General Picton had taken up a position about four miles from Pamplona : the right, which was composed of his third division, extending along a range of hills on the right of the village of Huerta ; and the left, consisting of the fourth division, with Major-general Byng's and Brigadier-general Campbell's Portuguese brigade, on the heights in front of Villalba, having their left at a chapel behind Sarausen, on the high road from Ostiz to Pamplona, and their right resting on a height which commanded the road from Zubiri and Roncesvalles ; General Morillo's division of Spanish infantry and a part of the Conde de Bisbal's corps being in reserve. The cavalry, under Sir Stapleton Cotton, was placed near Huerta on the right, being the only ground which would allow of the employment of this arm.

It was just as these dispositions had been made, and a short time before the enemy commenced the attack, that the Marquis of Wellington arrived. General Picton immediately acquainted him with the whole of his proceedings, and the arrangements which he had now made to meet the advance of Soult. The field-

marshal expressed his entire approbation of General Picton's conduct, and did not consider
it necessary to make the least alteration in his
present plans. Lord Wellington had, during
his journey from the left, issued orders for the
direction of the other corps of the army, so that
they should move by an organized arrangement to the point of conflict. The French
commenced the attack upon the allied position
by an attempt to obtain possession of a hill on
the right of the fourth division. This was held
by a battalion of the fourth Portuguese regiment and some Spaniards, who received the
enemy at this post with great firmness, and
drove them back in disorder.

But the importance of this post induced Lord
Wellington to reinforce it with the Fortieth
regiment. Early on the following morning,
(the 28th,) the sixth division, under Major-
general Pack, came up, when Lord Wellington
ordered it immediately to occupy some heights
and a valley on the left of the fourth division. This had hardly been effected, before
the enemy made a movement in considerable
force upon the troops in the valley, with the
intention of penetrating the line at this point,

and thus turning the left of the allies. But the
fire with which this column was received, both
in front and on each flank, was so destructive,
that the attempt was after a short time abandoned; while, to extricate their troops from
the dilemma in which this failure had placed
them, Soult directed an attack on the height
occupied by the left of the fourth division,
which was defended by a Portuguese regiment
of Caçadores. The French came on in great force
and with much impetuosity, and they succeeded
in obtaining a brief possession of the hill; but a
spirited charge which was on the instant made
by the brigade of Major-general Ross speedily
drove them back with great slaughter.

The firing was now opened along the whole
line. The French advanced with loud cries of
" *Vive l'Empereur!*" and an apparent determination to conquer : but they were young soldiers,
drawn by the conscription from the very last
resources of the country. They came on with
all their national enthusiasm, and exhibited
many daring feats of personal heroism; but
they were not equal to a conflict with Wellington's veterans. These had withstood the
old warriors who had fought under Napoleon,

and they now stood firm and confident until
the enemy was within a few yards of their
bayonets: then a volley was poured in upon
the advancing column which made it stagger.
The rear ranks were stopped by the bodies of
those who had already fallen, and the raw levies
saw, amidst the receding smoke, the whole line
moving forward at double-time. The first shock
tumbled the leading files back upon their rear,
and then drove the whole in confusion down
the precipitous heights. The slaughter was terrific; the ground was strewed with dead, while
the wounded implored, and received quarter.

Only in a single instance did the enemy
gain the slightest advantage during the attack.
This was against a Portuguese battalion on
the right of the position occupied by General
Ross. This battalion having given way, the
French succeeded for a short time in establishing themselves in this part of the line;
but two British regiments, the Twenty-seventh
and Forty-eighth, were immediately ordered to
drive them from this post: four times these
troops charged with the bayonet, and each
time did they succeed in driving the enemy
before them.

Soult now discovered the hopelessness of the attempt, and after having sustained a severe loss, desisted from any further efforts for that day. The result of this battle showed him that the troops which he now had under his command had no chance of success when opposed to the steady and well-disciplined soldiers of Wellington : he had come into the field with nearly double their numerical strength, but in no one instance had they withstood the charge of British bayonets. This was a disheartening conviction to a general who had so long been accustomed to lead veterans, and who had so often been victorious.

Sir Thomas Picton and his division had during this battle been watching a considerable corps of the enemy from some heights on the right bank of the Zubiri. The defence of this post was of the utmost importance to the security of the allied position, and Sir Thomas Picton was in momentary expectation of being attacked : but Marshal Soult confined his operations on this side of the river solely to demonstrations. Upon the least appearance of success in his grand efforts, he would nevertheless have moved this corps immediately forward, and en-

deavoured to force Picton's post, which would
have at once exposed the whole flank of the
allies. The result of his attack on the centre
did not, however, justify his making this movement; and, therefore, General Picton's division
was debarred from claiming their share of honour in this brilliant affair.

On the following day both armies were
inactive; but Lord Wellington was further
strengthened by the arrival of the seventh division, under Lord Dalhousie, near Marcalain,
by which the connexion with Sir Rowland
Hill's corps and the left of the allied army was
rendered secure.

To meet these movements, Drouet's army,
which had compelled Sir Rowland Hill to
fall back, marched by its left towards Ostiz;
at the same time that Soult, having given
up the hope of forcing the line of the allies,
moved the main body of his army by its
right, so as to form a junction with Drouet,
and concentrate his whole force. The troops
which had occupied the heights opposite Picton's division were likewise withdrawn. While
these movements were being effected on each
flank and in rear, he endeavoured to mask

his intentions by still keeping a strong force in front of Lord Wellington's centre.

Soult's plan was to open the communication between Tolosa and Pamplona, which would enable him to attack the left of the allied line; when, if successful, he might have it in his power to relieve Saint Sebastian, or compel the British general to fight upon ground of Soult's own selection. But Lord Wellington was not deceived by the show of force in his front. With the break of day on the 30th, the French were observed to be in motion towards the mountains on the right of the river Lanz.

Lord Wellington immediately penetrated Soult's plans, and conceived the means by which he could defeat them. He at once resolved to dislodge the French from the heights they still occupied; and, to effect this, Sir Thomas Picton was directed to cross the ridge which had been abandoned by the French troops, and, marching upon the Roncesvalles road, to turn their left flank; while Lord Dalhousie, with the seventh division, should scale a mountain opposite the left of the fourth division, and turn their right. Both these movements were performed with the most perfect success; when the centre of the allies moved forward, and, after a sharp but short conflict, drove the enemy from their position, which Lord Wellington in his despatch described as " one of the strongest and most difficult of access that he had ever seen occupied by troops."

After an unsuccessful attempt upon Sir Rowland Hill's corps by the right wing of the French army under Drouet, Soult abandoned all his plans and commenced a retreat, followed closely by the allies. The abilities of the general, however, were still apparent, and he conducted this retreat with his new and disheartened soldiers in a manner which well supported the character he had already established. Extricating his army by the pass of Donna Maria, he attempted to check the advance of the allies in that confined position: but Lord Dalhousie and Sir Rowland Hill ascending the mountains on each side, by a simultaneous attack, compelled him to abandon the post and hastily cross the Bidassoa; the allies still following up the pursuit until they had driven the French beyond the line which they had formerly occupied. On the 1st of August the British divisions were placed in the same relative positions which they had held previously to Soult's advance.

A short period of inactivity followed this second retreat of the French army. Lord Wellington did not consider it advisable to enter France, leaving the strong-holds of Saint Sebastian and Pamplona in the enemy's possession in his rear: active measures were therefore taken to reduce the former fortress, while the blockade of Pamplona was still more rigorously enforced. The almost impregnable strength of Saint Sebastian made its reduction a work of time and labour. An assault made on the 25th of July failed signally, and a renewal of the attack was not attempted until the 31st of August; when the admirable practice of the British artillerymen enabling them to fire close over the heads of their countrymen, and sweep the curtain of the enemy, rendered the attack successful.

The loss sustained by the British in this memorable siege was very great, and presented an unquestionable proof of the gallantry of the troops engaged. The blockade of Pamplona consumed a still longer period, as the garrison had received fresh supplies a few days pre-

viously to the battle of Vittoria: still, as Soult's
movement for their relief had been defeated,
and no further efforts were being made, it soon
became evident that these must soon be exhausted, and a bloodless victory achieved. Picton, with his division and the centre of the
allied army, was left to cover this blockade
against any operations which might be made
by Soult for its relief. To him who had now
so long been accustomed to a life of activity
and enterprise, this interval of repose was particularly irksome; and it is a striking fact connected with his history, that whenever Picton
was from necessity compelled to a life of inaction, his health was never so good as when
exposed to all the attendant toils and privations
of a campaign.

The prospect of a renewal of hostilities until
the ensuing spring was very uncertain, and,
tired of being locked up in these alpine regions
without any occupation, he resolved to take
the opportunity of visiting his native land for
a brief period. During the last election he
had been chosen by the inhabitants of Carmarthen to represent them in parliament, but he
had not yet taken his seat, and was now anxious

to do so. Having, therefore, communicated with the commander of the forces upon the probability of any active operations taking place during the short time which it was his intention to be absent, he left the camp in the month of October 1813, and repaired to England, accompanied by his aid-de-camp, Captain Tyler.

During this short residence in England, Picton received the thanks of the House of Commons. On the 11th of November, the Speaker, in accordance with the resolution of the House, addressed him in a strain of high encomium. After briefly adverting to the resolutions passed on the 7th of July and 8th of November, when the thanks of Parliament were voted collectively to the general officers serving under Lord Wellington, he continued:

" Lieutenant-general Sir Thomas Picton,— In this House your name has been long since enrolled amongst those who have obtained the gratitude of their country for distinguished military services; and we this day rejoice to see you amongst us, claiming again the tribute of our thanks for fresh exploits and achievements.

"Whenever the history of the Peninsular war shall be related, your name will be found amongst the foremost in that race of glory. By your sword the British troops were led on to the victorious assault of Ciudad Rodrigo; by your daring hand the British standard was planted upon the castle of Badajoz: when the usurper of the Spanish throne was driven to make his last stand at Vittoria, your battalions filled the centre of that formidable line before which the veteran troops of France fled in terror and dismay; and by your skill, prudence, and valour, exerted in a critical hour, the enemy was foiled in his desperate attempt to break through the barrier of the Pyrenees, and raise the blockade of Pamplona.

"For the deeds of Vittoria and the Pyrenees, this double harvest of glory in one year, the House of Commons has resolved again to give you the tribute of its thanks: and I do therefore now, in the name and by the command of the Commons of the United Kingdom of Great Britain and Ireland in Parliament assembled, deliver to you their unanimous thanks for your great exertions upon the 21st of June last near Vittoria, when the French army

was completely defeated by the allied forces
under the Marquis of Wellington's command;
and also for the valour, steadiness, and exertion so successfully displayed by you in repelling the repeated attacks made on the position of the allied army, by the whole French
forces under the command of Marshal Soult,
between the 25th of July and the 1st of
August last."

How grateful, how thrilling must the sensation of this moment have been to a man
like Picton! One who was near him informs
us that it was almost distressing to witness the
effect produced upon the general as he heard
this glowing eulogium of his conduct. "I will
not say," observed our informant, "that this
courageous soldier trembled; but certainly he
could with difficulty articulate the few words
which he attempted in reply : and it was really
painful to see a man who, the whole House
knew, had remained unshaken in the field of
battle, where death was flying in all directions,
thus unnerved and overcome by his feelings
upon an occasion like the present. The greatest respect was, however, paid to these feelings, and the whole House listened with the

most marked and silent attention to his observations."

The answer of Sir Thomas Picton was in the
following words:

" Sir,—Being entirely unaccustomed to speak
in public, I have great difficulty in expressing
the high sense of gratification which I feel at
the very flattering sentiments which this Honourable House has been pleased to entertain
of my services, and at the very handsome manner in which they have been communicated.

" I have always, sir, regarded the thanks of
this Honourable House as one of the highest
honours which could be conferred upon any
officer,—as the unquestionable evidence of past,
and the greatest incitement to future services.
But I can apply individually to myself a small
part only of the high commendations which
have been so liberally and handsomely bestowed. A great proportion is unquestionably due
to the generals and officers commanding brigades and corps in the division, for the judgment and gallantry with which the services
alluded to were invariably executed ; and to
the officers and troops in general, for the spirit
and intrepidity which bore down all resistance,

and secured complete success in all the important enterprises in which the division had the
good fortune to be employed during the whole
course of the war in the Peninsula.

" It will ever be the height of my pride
and ambition to share the fortunes of a corps
eminently conspicuous for every high military
qualification, and actuated by a spirit of heroism which renders it truly invincible. With
such instruments, sir, you will easily conceive
that it cannot be difficult to obtain success;
and it would be unfortunate indeed if we failed
entirely to reflect some of the rays of the great
luminary that directed us."

Sir Thomas Picton always spoke of this
distinguished honour as one of the most gratifying events of his life. He earned this
same reward, it is true, on a future occasion;
but his feelings were then soured by disappointment and injustice, and he stood in the
same distinguished situation with widely different sensations. It was a sigular coincidence,
that the very same day on which Sir Thomas
Picton was receiving the thanks of the House
of Commons for the gallant exploits of himself and soldiers, his division should be gain-

ing additional laurels on the precipitous banks of the Nivelle.

The remainder of Sir Thomas Picton's time while in England was passed in the society of his friends and relatives, by whom he was received in the most flattering manner. Wher-. ever he now went, he was looked up to with respect and admiration, as one of the foremost in the field of victory—as the leader of " the fighting division."

After the passage of the Nivelle had been gained by the allies, Sir Thomas Picton was impatient to return to the scene of hostilities; fearful that, as the winter in the South of France did not set in with so much severity, or for so long a continuance, it might not be passed without active operations. He therefore hastened over the various business which he had to transact relative to his private affairs, and then prepared forthwith to return to the army. Early in December he embarked at Portsmouth for the port of St. Jean de Luz; from which place, in a letter dated December the 26th, 1813, to a friend in London, he writes :

" I had a remarkably pleasant passage out, and arrived here in eleven days from Portsmouth. Previous to my leaving England, I declined entering into any engagement respecting the command of the Catalonian army until I should have an opportunity of consulting the marquis on the subject. Finding from my interview with his lordship that it was not intended to carry on any active operations with the force in that quarter, I have determined to resume the command of the third division, which I shall join as soon as my aid-de-camp and horses arrive. I had considerable apprehensions for their safety, as they left Portsmouth ten days before I sailed; but within these two days I have received a letter from Mr. Tyler, saying that they had been forced into St. Andro, and were there waiting for a vessel to convey them down to Passages. I was fortunate in only losing one of the worst of the horses during the severe gale to which they were exposed. The weather has been most miserable, and the rain has fallen in torrents ever since my arrival."

*　　　　*　　*　　*

The operations in Catalonia and the other eastern provinces of Spain had hitherto been anything but satisfactory: much feebleness of judgment and want of confidence in the Spanish troops had marked all the measures of the several generals who had been appointed to command the allied army in that quarter.*

* The author has been favoured, since the publication of the first edition, with the following statement by Sir Frederick Maitland, in answer to the animadversion contained in this passage. Although the name of that officer is not mentioned, still, as he for a time held the command in the eastern provinces of Spain, it becomes an act of justice to insert the communication.

" Near East Grinstead, Oct. 21, 1835.

" SIR,

" I have read with admiration your Memoirs of the life of Sir Thomas Picton; personally, however, I have suffered no small mortification from your allusion to the conduct of the generals who served on the eastern coast of Spain in 1812.—At page 236, Vol. II. you have said,—

' *Much feebleness of judgment* and want of confidence in the Spanish troops had marked all the measures of the several generals who had been appointed to command the allied army in that quarter.'

" I hope, sir, that should you publish a second edition, you will add to this comment a brief statement of the troops, and circumstances, with, or under which those officers acted: I give the latter condensed.—The division from Si-

General Picton's letter to Mr. Marryat will further illustrate the subject.

" St. Jean de Luz, 3rd July 1814.

" MY DEAR SIR,

" In consequence of an interview with Lord Wellington, when it clearly appeared that the

cily, which arrived on the shores of Catalonia on the last days of July 1812, consisted of 6000 men; *half* of these were *British*.

" Of the inefficiency of the Spanish troops you seem aware : upon this point I refer to Picton's words in his letter to Colonel Pleydel, p. 260,* Vol. II.—' Upon the Spaniards we have little reliance, as they are rather *an embarrassment than otherwise.'*

" Now turn to the enemy's force. You state from Colonel Jones's authority, p. 135,† Vol. II. that the French had 170,000 men within the Pyrenees; of these Suchet commanded 40,000 in Arragon, and the eastern provinces. You might have added, that the French possessed every fortified place, from the Pyrenees to Alicant, which were all prepared against attack. There was nothing but the open beach left for us, which at *that time of the year,* on the Catalonian shores, is exposed to, and suffers from very high surfs, which render it *impracticable* for landing or embarkation for many days together. Under these circumstances, I used the discretion entrusted to me, and decided *not* to land, but to proceed to Alicant, where a *point-d'appui* offered.

" The Spanish General Saarsfield wrote to me from Villa Franca, in Catalonia, 31st July 1812, these words:—' Ge-

---

* Page 283 of the present edition. † Page 146 ditto.

army in Catalonia was in no situation to undertake offensive or active operations of any kind, I have determined, with his lordship's approbation, to remain with this army, and resume my old command. We are perfectly in France,

neral Saarsfield is of opinion that 14,000 or 15,000 men, including the corps of Rooke and Whittingham, might overrun the province of Catalonia, *independent* of the fortified places; but to reduce them, a corps of 20,000 *British* troops (independent of the force now organized in Catalonia) will be required.'

" I purposely compress the subject, but I am satisfied to rest the merits of the case upon what I have here stated: yet I will add a request that you will read what Colonel Jones, Royal Engineers, has reported respecting these affairs; you will there see that I am borne out by him in what I have written to you.

" I hope, therefore, in justice, that should you have the opportunity, you will add to your Memoirs the representation which I have by this letter made to you.

" I have the honour to be,

" Sir,

" Your very humble servant,

" FRED. MAITLAND.

" H. B. Robinson, Esq."

In a subsequent letter, Sir Frederick says:—

" On my return to London I found the following return: I see that there were, a detachment of Royal Artillery, British, 250 men; a weak detachment of dragoons; three *British battalions;* three *foreign* battalions, and a detachment, 300 extending from the Nivelle across the Nive to the Adour; and if you will give us twenty thousand, we shall be able to make a most decisive, important, forward movement, which cannot fail to cause most serious apprehensions

men, of the *Calabrese* corps. Of the *foreign* battalions, two were of the King's German Legion—unexceptionable, with this reserve, that I cannot place them as equal to the British. The remaining foreign battalion was composed, one half from De Rolle's regiment and one half from Dillon's; and to show what I had to expect from this battalion, I inform you, that as soon as an opportunity offered, a party of *eight*, with their arms, ammunition, &c. deserted, intending to join the enemy; but the Spaniards intercepted them,—they were brought back, tried, convicted, and four of the eight were shot.

"This heterogeneous *corps d'armée*, which I had had no opportunity of seeing together (of which, remember, that raw Spanish levies composed a great part,) was expected to land and to take Tarragona; a large fortified place, with a garrison of about three thousand French *troupes de ligne*, and to oppose a relieving army of 20,000 men (veterans) commanded by Marshal Suchet.

"I confined my letter to one object, namely, the decision made *not* to land in Catalonia. I did so, because I believed it to be the only act or measure of mine which has been criticised, and because I was unwilling to write a very long letter, for which reason I conclude this.

"I am, Sir,

"Your most obedient servant,

"FRED. MAITLAND."

"To H. B. Robinson, Esq.'

at Paris: but without reinforcements to nearly that amount, we shall be able to perform no achievements worthy the Speaker's eloquence. The Spaniards, instead of being of any service to us in our operations, are a perfect dead weight, and do nothing but run away and plunder. We should do much better without these vapouring poltroon rascals, whose irregular conduct indisposes every one towards us. The inhabitants of the country appear remarkably well-disposed, and I believe wish us success from their hearts, as the only probable means of bringing about what they all most ardently sigh for—peace. As for Buonaparte, as far as I can observe, he is held in general detestation, and the better sort of people speak of their old master with affection and regret. If peace is not brought about during the winter, we ought to make a great dash from all points, and get rid of the rascal at once. This, I conceive, would be no difficult matter, and I have little doubt but we should meet with very considerable co-operation; or at all events, a perfect sympathy from the inhabitants everywhere. In this country, we all ride about as if we were in England, and go through all the towns and intricate bye-roads without even our swords, which is a strong evidence of the temper of the inhabitants towards us.

"My dear sir,

"Very faithfully yours,

"T. PICTON."

Sir John Murray had been leniently censured for his want of ability,—a charge which would have been more properly made against those who selected him for the situation: he acted to the best of his judgment and skill, but in both he was deficient. Lord William Bentinck superseded him in the command; but the improvement in the state of affairs was not very striking. A skirmish of outposts gave him a distaste for his soldiers, and led him to suspect their power to compete with the army under Suchet.

In October, Lord William Bentinck returned to Sicily, when Lieutenant-general Clinton succeeded to the command. The perfect knowledge possessed by Sir Thomas Picton of the character and language of the Spanish people, together with his high military reputation, induced the commander-in-chief at once to

select him as in every respect the most competent and desirable person to command this
army. The Duke of York made him the offer
in the most flattering terms; but General
Picton had always expressed his disinclination
to quit the grand army of the allies, and accept
a separate command of troops upon whom he
could place but little confidence, and with
whom little glory was to be won. He used,
in fact, to speak of these armies in no very
measured terms of contempt, considering the
command as entitling the individual to a rank
but little above that of a guerilla chief.

The army of Catalonia had a few British
and some German troops attached; but the
Spaniards, of whom the main body was composed, had on no occasion evinced either courage or discipline. This reflection induced Sir
Thomas Picton to pause before he placed himself at the head of an army with which he
could only hope to act on the defensive, or
incur defeat by becoming the assailant: for,
although he more than once had reason to
report favourably of the conduct of the Spanish regiments in his division, he always distrusted them when not fighting by the side

of British troops. A gallant and distinguished officer, alluding to the advantage which might have arisen to the public service by Sir Thomas Picton's acceptance of this command, remarked that, " co-operating as that small British force did with so many distinct Spanish authorities and armies, composed of a most heterogeneous variety of materials, he would have been precisely the man to have secured a uniformity of action amongst them, by the commanding energy which he would have assumed over all classes."

Picton felt a repugnance to parting from his old third division; still, as expressed in his letter of the 26th of December, he left the point open for his determination until he had an opportunity of consulting Lord Wellington upon the subject. A short time after his return, in an interview with his lordship, this opportunity presented itself, and he frankly asked him whether he considered his acceptance of this command as " likely to be conducive to his honour and reputation." — The commander of the forces gave him an equally candid opinion, by assuring him that he did not think it would, since it was not

intended to carry on any active operations in
Catalonia. This induced Picton, without any
further hesitation, to decline the proffered appointment, and to resume his old command.

CHAPTER X.

The British army crosses the Bidassoa. — Surrender of Pamplona.—Invasion of France by the British army.— Address of Wellington to his soldiers.—Defeat and re- treat of the French army. — Advance of the Allies to Bayonne.—The French again defeated.—Effective state of the Third Division when rejoined by Sir Thomas Picton. — His account of the prospects of the Allied army.—Lord Wellington's operations against Bayonne.— Advance of the Allies into the interior of France.

DURING Sir Thomas Picton's absence in England, his division had been gaining ad- ditional laurels under Major-general Colville. It was determined by Lord Wellington to force the passage of the Bidassoa early in Oc- tober; as, by securing this advanced position, the whole of his line could pour into France at the same moment, so soon as the reduction of Pamplona left him at liberty to enter the enemy's country. Before this fortress was in his possession, it was impossible to commence any grand scale of offensive operations : but during this interval every preparation was made for the projected invasion. The enemy occupied a remarkably strong post on the French side of the Bidassoa.

On the 7th of October, at three o'clock in the morning, the whole of the troops destined for this service were in motion, amidst a heavy thunder-storm. Every precaution had been taken to prevent the enemy from being made acquainted with this movement; and this was effected with so much success, that the allied force, which was formed into three columns, and crossed at three different fords, was not discovered until the heads of the leading regiments were half over the river. A brisk fire was then opened by the French upon the advancing columns: the water was soon stained with their blood, and all who fell there died. But they were quickly revenged: the light troops pushed rapidly forward, gained the opposite bank, and drove the enemy from their position. This done, as the British columns reached the bank, they quickly formed, and prepared to attack the French line, which was being drawn up on the nearest range of hills.

Notwithstanding the imposing nature of the

ground and its natural defensive strength, only a trifling resistance was made in comparison with what the British general had anticipated. The troops drove the enemy from each height in succession, until the French left the conquerors in undisputed possession of the field. Soult now concentrated his army behind a strongly fortified position on the Nivelle, which he had for some time been preparing; and here he resolved to make another stand against the march of his pursuers.

The point occupied by the right of the allied army, (to which the "fighting division" was at this time attached,) enabled it at once to pour down into the plains of France whenever the moment appeared favourable. The left of the army was now placed in an equally favourable situation, and nothing therefore remained to delay this movement but the reduction of Pamplona.

On the 1st of November, the Marquis of Wellington received a despatch from the commander of the Spanish forces employed in blockading that fortress, of which the following is a translation :—

" Most excellent Sir,—Glory be to God, and honour to the triumphs of your excellency in this ever-memorable campaign !

" I have the honour and great satisfaction of congratulating your excellency on the surrender of the important fortress of Pamplona; the capitulation of which having been signed by the superior officers entrusted with my powers, and by those delegated by the general commanding the place, I have, by virtue of the authority which you conferred upon me, just ratified.

" The garrison remain prisoners of war, as your excellency had determined from the beginning that they should, and will march out to-morrow at two in the afternoon, in order to be conducted to the port of Passages.

" Our troops occupy one of the gates of the citadel, and those of France the place.

" May God guard the precious life of your excellency !

   " Dated from the camp in front of Pamplona, 31st of October 1813.

(Signed)   " CARLOS ESPANA."

" His Excellency Field-marshal
 the Duke of Ciudad Rodrigo.'

Thus, then, the only impediment to the advance of the allies was removed, and the Marquis of Wellington made immediate preparations for invading France. To force the passage of the Nivelle, and the strong entrenched posts in its rear, upon which Soult had bestowed so much time and labour, was the first step. Napoleon was now encircled by toils. On the north and south-eastern frontiers, were the armies of the three great powers, Russia, Prussia, and Austria; England swept the sea; and Wellington, with his small but victorious force, was on the point of invading the south. Such was the position of affairs when the British troops with their allies were about to descend from the alpine heights which they had so long occupied, upon the fertile fields of the south of France; but, before effecting this grand movement, the commander of the forces issued a proclamation full of judicious and salutary instructions for the conduct of the troops whilst in the enemy's county. One passage of this proclamation deserves particular admiration.

" Officers and soldiers must recollect," he observes, " that their nations are at war with

France solely because the ruler of the French
nation will not allow them to be at peace, and
is desirous of forcing them to submit to his
yoke ; and they must not forget, that the
worst of the evils suffered by the enemy in
this profligate invasion of Spain and Portugal
have been occasioned by the irregularities of
his soldiers, and their cruelties, authorized
and encouraged by their chiefs, towards the
unfortunate and peaceful inhabitants of the
country. To avenge this conduct on the peaceable inhabitants of France would be unmanly,
and unworthy of the nations to which the
commander of the forces now addresses himself."

About three o'clock in the morning of the
10th of November the allied army was in
motion. A bright full moon lighted up the
mountain paths : the troops gathered in silence ;
and each division following its chief, moved
down the different passes with no other sound
than was unavoidable in the passage of a multitude of armed men. It was hoped that by
these precautions the enemy might be taken
unprepared ; but they were under arms at day-

light every morning, and the allies were received on their advance with a warm cannonade from some of the fortified redoubts in
front. The whole of the divisions moved
forward almost in line; Picton's third, which
was on this day entrusted to Major-general
Colville, being on the right of the centre.
After a sharp skirmish with the picquets, the
divisions each in their turn had to attack the
redoubts which lay in their respective paths.

In some instances the enemy deserted their
defences with much precipitation, not even
waiting the approach of the allies: others,
again, were defended with a good deal of resolution. But, on the part of the enemy, the
whole proceedings of the day appeared more
like a last effort made without hope of success,
than the enthusiastic onset of brave and excited
men. The third division had upon this occasion several opportunities of supporting its distinguished character: moving from the pass
of Echalar in almost a direct line upon St.
Pé; having, about a mile on its right, the
sixth division under Sir H. Clinton, Sir John
Hamilton's Portuguese division, with the se-

cond division commanded by Sir W. Stewart, and at the same distance on its left the seventh division under General Le Cor.

It happened that one of the strongest posts which the enemy occupied (the key, in fact, to their position) was in the route to be followed by the third division. This was a redoubt formed on the summit of a hill, with a deep entrenchment and stockade in front. Crossing several streams tributary to the Nivelle, in their path, they rushed on towards this formidable post, keeping a parallel movement with the corps on the right and left, by which the whole of the enemy's line of defences was threatened at the same time. The advantages of this simultaneous attack were strongly apparent; for the success of any one division of the allies, and their consequent advance, would threaten the rear of those fortified posts which still held out. Immediately behind, and on the left of the village of Sarre, the enemy had established his main body; but the attack of the third and seventh divisions drove them with considerable loss from the heights on the left of their centre. The light division at the same time attacked their right; while the fourth, with the reserve of Andalusia on its left, forced the enemy to abandon nearly the whole of these strongly fortified and commanding heights.

The defenders of one of these redoubts continued to resist until too late to retreat, and the centre divisions of the allies succeeded in occupying the ground in their rear: the whole of the garrison, therefore, consisting of six hundred men belonging to the Eighty-eighth French regiment of the line, were compelled to lay down their arms and surrender as prisoners of war. The enemy were now falling back in some confusion, and hastening to cross the river, in order to defend the three bridges over which the allies must pass. Lord Wellington having halted the divisions in the centre to give them a short respite from their continued exertions, about three o'clock in the afternoon ordered the third and seventh divisions to continue their route along the left bank of the river, and force a passage by the two bridges; one of which was in front of, and the other about half a mile below, St. Pé. This was, to all appearance, a service full of difficulty: a determined resistance was threatened to the passage of the third division; but, after a short though sharp affair, they drove the enemy before them, and the bridge was theirs. The day was by this time far advanced; and as the extent of the line of movement traversed by the different divisions of the allies rendered their exact positions rather uncertain, Lord Wellington directed the whole to halt for the night.

The rewards of this day of toil were fifty pieces of cannon, about fifteen hundred prisoners, and a considerable quantity of ammunition and military stores.* It was expected that the fight, or rather the pursuit, would be renewed on the following morning; but Soult took advantage of the night to fall back upon Bayonne. He was discouraged by the proceedings of the previous day: he had seen his soldiers beaten back with almost the first charge of their opponents; his few veteran troops had become dispirited by constant defeat, while his young recruits were unable alone

* During this series of conflicts, the Shrapnell-shell was employed to dislodge the enemy from the heights; and its novelty, and the destruction it caused, struck quite a panic into the enemy.

to withstand the habitual discipline of the veterans who composed the British army: even
the statements made by French officers confirm the assertion, that their soldiers " did not
fight on this day with their accustomed gallantry, as their spirits were lowered by repeated reverses."

This was the only affair of any importance
in which the third division was engaged
during Picton's absence. After the passage
of the Nivelle had been forced, the weather
became too bad for field operations, and the
army was placed in cantonments between that
river and the sea, the enemy occupying a position about two miles in front.

A line of defensive posts was now formed, in
order to prevent any unexpected hostile movement from the French. The third division
was quartered in and about Ustaritz until
the 9th of December, when, the weather being
much improved and the roads passable, the
army again took the field, Lord Wellington
having resolved upon crossing the Nive and
investing Bayonne. Upon this occasion the
left wing of the allied army advanced by the
road from St. Jean de Luz to Bayonne, and

Sir Rowland Hill crossed the Nive at Cambo; while Sir Henry Clinton, with the sixth division, effected a passage at Ustaritz. These movements were performed with trifling loss, and the enemy retreated within his entrenched camp around the city, which had been in preparation ever since the battle of Vittoria. Soult, however, made a determined effort to drive back the left wing of the allies. Of this attack, Captain Batty gives the following interesting particulars.*

"On the morning of the 11th, at dawn, the light troops of the fifth division drove in the enemy's picquets, and the most advanced sentries were again pushed forward to their old line. The rain had fallen during the greater part of the preceding day, and the troops began to experience the harassing effects of being constantly on the alert upon ground which was soon trampled into mud. Nothing material happened during the forenoon; the men received their rations, and parties were sent out unarmed to cut wood for cooking; the weather brightened, and all was tranquil in the out-

* In his admirable Account of the Proceedings of the left wing of the Allied Army.

posts. About two o'clock, however, some stir was visible in the enemy's line, and in some places the French were seen cutting gaps in the fences for the passage of their artillery. A few moments after, they commenced a furious attack along the Bayonne road, driving in the picquets upon their supports. The hill in front of Barrouillet again became the scene of a hard contest. There was a general shout of 'To arms!' the moment this attack commenced; and the soldiers, who had gone in front of Barrouillet to cut wood, ran back in all haste to get themselves armed and accoutred. The French, seeing a number of men running to the rear, imagined that the allies were seized with a panic, and set up loud cheers of '*En avant! en avant!*' In a few moments, however, the whole left wing was formed in perfect order."

The situation now occupied by Soult gave him every facility for masking his movements and concentrating the whole of his force upon any point of the allied position. His entrenchments around Bayonne formed the centre of a circle, within which he might effect any alteration in the disposition of his army without being observed by Lord Wellington: and of this the French general took advantage; for, finding that all his efforts to force the left wing of the allies were unavailing, on the night of the 12th he made an entire change in his plans, presuming, it would appear, upon his own opinion of Lord Wellington's military abilities.

The repeated attacks which Soult had made upon the left wing of the allies led him to believe that the whole of Lord Wellington's attention would be turned in that direction, and that, in expectation of a renewal of these attacks, the other divisions would be drawn towards that quarter, and thus, that the right and centre of the position would either be undefended or weakened. But Soult ought by this time to have learned to entertain a higher opinion of Lord Wellington than to venture any movement which could only be successful through his neglect or want of skill. Following the tactics of Napoleon, on the morning of the 15th he advanced with an overwhelming force against the right and centre of the allies. Lord Wellington, however, had divined his intentions, and made every preparation to defeat them. Sir Rowland Hill, who had under

his command about thirteen thousand men,
occupied that line of the position; and this
corps was further augmented by the fourth and
sixth divisions; while the third, which was still
on the left of the Nive, was held in readiness
to cross that river should any additional support be required. · .

Soult commenced the action early in the
morning with above thirty thousand men, his
force being principally directed against the
centre, or Sir Rowland Hill's position. The
numbers of the enemy made the movement
formidable, but the firmness of the British
troops was not shaken by this consideration;
they had in almost every contest fought against
nearly one-third more than themselves, yet
they had gained the plains of France, and
upon this occasion their conduct was worthy
of themselves. A severe contest was kept up
for some time: the enemy even succeeded in
gaining one of the heights occupied by the allies; but Sir Rowland Hill, perceiving at once
that nearly the whole of the French columns
were concentrated to attack his centre, immediately ordered the troops on each flank to
move up to its support; these at once drove

the enemy from their momentary conquest, and then the battle became general.

The French stood and fought for a time with much resolution; but towards evening Soult again retired within his entrenchments, after having sustained a severe loss both in officers and men, together with a still more certain conviction that his troops could not contend with their opponents; for "he had repeatedly attacked with an army and been repulsed by a division."* Still, the allies had suffered considerably during these five days of almost continued skirmishing; according to the returns, amounting to five thousand and twenty-nine in killed, wounded, and missing; three hundred and two of this number being officers.

The campaign of 1813 may be said to have terminated with this attack on the right wing of the allies. Soult, in his almost impregnable entrenchment, could defy Lord Wellington and his whole army; while that general, too circumspect to attempt to force this position at the sacrifice which must inevitably attend such a movement, placed his troops in can-

* " Annals of the Peninsular Campaigns."

tonments, (a measure which had now become indispensable on account of the inclemency of the season,) and awaited the result of events, which were advancing rapidly to a crisis.

Napoleon was now in Paris. Still confident of the affections of the French nation, he called upon them with the desperation of a gamester who sees his last stake upon the cast. He addressed his council of state in the following excited language: " Wellington," he exclaimed, "is in the south; the Russians threaten the northern frontier, Austria the south-eastern; yet, shame to speak it, the nation has not risen in mass to repel them! Every ally has abandoned me; the Bavarians have betrayed me! Peace! no peace, till Munich is in flames! I demand of you three hundred thousand men: I will form a camp at Bordeaux of one hundred thousand, another at Lyons, a third at Metz. With the remnants of my former levies, I shall have one million of men in arms. But it is *men* whom I demand of you—full-grown men; not these miserable striplings, who choke my hospitals with sick, and my highways with their carcasses. Give up Holland! rather let it be swallowed up by the sea. I am continually hearing the cry of *peace,* when all around should re-echo with the cry of *war!*"

· He asked for that which he might have known the country could not give. Such was the state of affairs when Sir Thomas Picton rejoined the army, and again placed himself at the head of his division; having, as has already been shown, declined the command of an army rather than leave his old soldiers. Some changes had been made in the division, and its numbers were considerably augmented; the following being the return of its effective force at the beginning of the year 1814.

" Statement of the Third Division of the army under Field-marshal the Marquis of Wellington, January 1st, 1814.

General in command, Lieutenant-general Sir Thomas Picton, K.B.

GENERAL OFFICERS COMMANDING BRIGADES.

Major-general Brisbane.
- 45th foot, 1st battalion.
- 74th ditto.
- 88th ditto, 1st battalion.
- 3 companies 60th regiment, 5th battalion.

Lieutenant-general Sir Thomas Picton.
- 5th foot, 1st battalion.
- 83rd ditto, 2nd battalion.
- 87th ditto, 2nd battalion.
- 94th regiment.

Major-general Power.
- 9th Portuguese regiment of the line.
- 21st ditto, ditto.
- 11th Caçadores."

This division was now placed in a position where it could observe the advanced posts of the enemy in the vicinity of Hasparren. For some time after Sir Thomas Picton's return, the army was comparatively inactive : on the 6th, however, a trifling affair took place, in which the third division bore a prominent part. This was produced by the attack of the enemy on the advanced picquets of the allied cavalry, posted between the Joyeuse and Bidouze rivers; Soult at the same time moving two divisions on the heights of La Costa, having forced Major-general Buchan's Portuguese brigade to abandon that post. These operations, together with some additional demonstrations in the rear of the enemy's line, induced Lord Wellington to resolve upon driving the advance of the French back upon their main body ; and, accordingly, Sir Thomas Picton was directed to attack the position which they had occupied. With this object the third and fourth divisions (the latter under Sir Lowry Cole, supported by General Buchan's brigade, and the cavalry under the command of Major-general Fane,) were ordered to make the attack on the morning of the 6th. But this was a bloodless day, as the enemy abandoned his conquests without firing a shot. The picquets and General Buchan's brigade were in consequence replaced in their former positions.

The remainder of the month of January was unmarked by any movement of importance, the weather still continuing too unfavourable for field operations. The position and prospects of the allies and their opponents cannot be better explained than in the following letter from Sir Thomas Picton to his old correspondent Colonel Pleydel.

"Hasparren, 10th February, 1814.

" MY DEAR COLONEL,

" We continue on the advance posts; always in sight of the enemy, and, of course, always upon the alert. There are three divisions immediately in our front, only separated by the small river Laran, which traverses the country from the Pyrenees to the Adour. The enemy have latterly detached two divisions of infantry, and nearly all their cavalry, to the interior,— they say towards Lyons; but the weather has been so very wet, and the roads consequently so bad, that it is not possible to take any advantage of their situation. In the mean time they are raising the levy *en masse*, and mean to oppose us with the whole population of the country: a most dangerous step, as it does not appear at all attached to the existing *régime*. We receive no reinforcements, notwithstanding the great losses we sustained in the many severe conflicts during November and December; and our army is in consequence reduced considerably below sixty thousand English and Portuguese. Upon the Spaniards we have little reliance, as they are rather an embarrassment than otherwise. Under these circumstances, it cannot be expected that we should make any considerable impression. They promised twenty thousand, and we have not yet received a man. If we do nothing, the fault will be with *them*.

" My health has been tolerably good, though I have yet some remains of my old complaint. I hope you will have escaped any attack of your old complaints, and will have got over the severe winter without any serious indisposition.

" My dear Colonel,

" Ever faithfully yours,

" TH. PICTON."

Lord Wellington's object was now, to divert Soult from the continued occupation of his very commanding position around Bayonne ;. but that general was unwilling to forego the advantages afforded him by the strength of his position. · A series of manœuvres was therefore performed by Lord Wellington to draw him. forth, at the same time that the intentions of the allies should be hidden.

On the fourth day after the date of Sir Thomas Picton's last letter, he was again in motion. Sir Rowland Hill, with the right wing of the allies, made a movement in advance on the left of the enemy's position, in order to cut off his communication with St. Jean Pied de Port. This enabled General Mina, with his Spanish forces, to invest the place without apprehension from the French corps of General Harispe, which was now compelled to fall back upon Garres ; at the same time that General Hill, advancing on the right of the centre, made a corresponding movement. The greatest difficulty which the army now had to surmount was the passage of the several rivers behind which the enemy successively ensconced themselves in comparative safety. The principal of these rivers was the Adour, which, even undefended, offered a considerable barrier to the march of an army, but, with a strong force posted on the opposite bank, presented obstacles of a most formidable nature. To obtain a passage over this river below Bayonne was, however, indispensably necessary in order to effect the perfect blockade of the city.

This important and arduous service was to be executed by the left wing of the army under Lieutenant-general Sir John Hope, Sir Thomas Graham having returned to England to command an expedition to assist in the liberation of Holland. An English fleet under Rear-admiral Penrose co-operated with this corps; and the hardihood of the seamen, combined with the abilities of the military artificers, under the direction of Major Todd, enabled the allies to form a bridge of boats over this rapid river, which, at the spot selected for the purpose, was two hundred and seventy yards wide.

Soult had relied upon the supposed impossibility of this movement: but before this great undertaking was completed, the allies had obtained possession of the right of the river; for, taking advantage of the enemy's confidence, Sir John Hope directed the first division to attempt a passage near the mouth of the Adour, by means of pontoons and the boats of the country. A picquet and battery could be observed by the allies opposite the situation which they had selected for crossing; but, strange as it may appear, although only six boats effected the passage in the first instance, each having only six soldiers, they met with no opposition : the picquet ran away without even giving an alarm.

The allies carried a hawser from one side of the river to the other ; and before the French had recovered from their surprise, about six hundred of the Guards, with some Congreve-rocket companies, had effected a landing on the opposite bank. Then, however, their further progress was stopped, as the flood-tide set in with so much violence, that a raft with from fifty to sixty soldiers, having got near the middle of the river, could not be moved either backwards or forwards ; and in this situation they were compelled to wait for the slackening of the tide, until which they were unable to continue their passage.

The French were not long in discovering the error of which they had been guilty in depending upon the river for their protection; and accordingly, towards evening, about fifteen hundred men were sent against the force which had already crossed the river, with the full expectation of surrounding them and making them prisoners. But Major-general Stopford, who commanded this small body, made such an admirable disposition of his men to receive the attack, while the rockets, which were at this time quite new to the French, produced so much terror and confusion in their ranks, that they made a precipitate retreat towards the citadel, leaving this little band unmolested for the rest of the night. The following day, the 24th, the remainder of the division was ferried over; when, moving up the river, it kept the right bank, and prevented the French from interrupting the formation of the bridge. The result of these operations was the perfect investment of Bayonne.*

* The following letter from a serjeant in the Coldstream Guards, written to his father, who resided in the neighbourhood of Swansea at the time, contains an accurate detail of these movements:—   " Camp

Soult, leaving a strong garrison, had now withdrawn his army from this place, and directed his march towards Orthes. He called upon the inhabitants of the country through

" Camp in front of Bayonne,
" March 18, 1814.

"MY DEAR FATHER,

" In my last I carried you on to the operations of the 9th, 10th, 11th, 12th, and 13th of December, and also to our movement from St. Jean de Luz in the early part of January, and subsequent return; since which nothing of any consequence occurred within the limits of my knowledge until the 14th of February, when the troops stationed in and about St. Jean de Luz (and, I suppose, the rest of the army) were put in motion; and the left column, under Sir John Hope, comprising the first and fifth divisions, with Lord Aylmer's brigade (British), and, I believe, two Portuguese brigades of infantry, were directed to invest Bayonne. Accordingly we encamped on the south-western side of that fortress until the 23rd, when a sufficient number of vessels, principally *chasse-marées*, with some gun-boats, having entered the mouth of the Adour, a bridge of boats was successfully attempted. During the necessary preparations for establishing the bridge; and in order to prevent any interruption from the enemy, the left wing of the first battalion (Third Guards), with the light companies, were detached to the right bank in boats; which the enemy observing, threw down a column of three battalions, at least eighteen hundred strong, to oppose about one-third of their number. Our small body certainly appeared in a critical situation at this moment, being separated from the brigade by the Adour on the right, at least six hundred yards wide, with their rear to the sea,—with no other alternative than a which he passed to rise and repel their invaders; but the wise policy of Lord Wellington gave them such perfect assurance of protection, that they remained quietly in their homes,

glorious resistance against such superior force, or a quiet submission to become prisoners of war. The enemy's troops were encouraged to their bold advance by their officers assuring them the force they were to attack were Spaniards. But they were soon convinced to the contrary; for a brigade of rockets having passed the river at this pressing moment, opened on them with such effect, that, consulting their safety, they sought it in flight, leaving some killed, wounded, and prisoners in our hands; and we proceeded without farther molestation in the completion of the bridge, which has since proved of the greatest importance to the ready communication of the army with the rear. Having completely established ourselves at this point, we remained quiet until the 27th, when a very brisk attack was made upon the enemy's outposts, and, after some sharp fighting, we succeeded in driving them within their entrenchments close to Bayonne; in which service considerable loss was sustained on both sides. We are now as close to that city as their batteries will allow us to approach, and our column, it would appear, are to carry on the siege.

" I am happy to inform you that Lord Wellington has gained a battle over Soult between this and Bordeaux:* he has taken immense stores at Mont Marsan. In fact, it is considered a victory of as much importance as that of Vittoria; and it gives me equal pleasure to inform you, that our countryman, Sir Thomas Picton, in command of the third division, behaved with his usual judgment and gallantry."

---

* Orthes.

and readily supplied the allies with the produce of the soil, for which they invariably received ample remuneration. Sir John Hope being left to continue the blockade of Bayonne, the remainder of the British army, consisting of the second, third, fourth, sixth, seventh, and light divisions, with a well-appointed park of artillery, and about eight thousand cavalry, were put in motion on the 24th of February, to penetrate into the interior of France.

Sir Thomas Picton marched simultaneously with the other divisions towards Orthes. The enemy's advanced posts uniformly fell back after a short skirmish as the British line moved forward : still the security afforded to the French by the difficulties of the country enabled them obstinately to dispute every advantageous post. Sir Thomas Picton kept the enemy in alarm by a threatened attack upon the bridge across the Gave d'Oleron at Sauveterre. This position was occupied by the French in great strength ; but General Picton determined upon attempting to gain the opposite side of the river, by means of a ford at some distance below the bridge. By effecting this, he would be enabled to take the enemy in flank, at the

same time that he made the attack in front. A
brigade was, consequently, ordered upon this
service ; when some light companies, covered
by a party of the Seventh Hussars, succeeded
in fording the river.

The rapidity of the stream and the nature of
its bed, which was composed of large round
stones, rendered this a difficult operation. The
enemy offered no opposition, and it was even
supposed that they had not anticipated such
a movement. Without waiting, therefore, for
any further support, the troops which had
crossed immediately moved forward up a hill,
through a narrow and steep lane.

Arrived at the top of this eminence, they
took up a position behind a high bank, when
the cavalry returned to the ford. They were,
however, surprised by seeing a considerable
corps of the enemy advancing at a rapid pace
to drive them from the post which they held.
So sudden was this attack, that before any
support could be thrown over the river, the
light companies, finding resistance against so
overwhelming a body quite hopeless, endeavoured by a hasty retreat to recross the river.
But the French pressed hard upon their rear ;

and, in the confusion of flight, they got jammed in between the two walls of the lane. In this situation they were exposed to a heavy fire from the enemy. The annihilation of the whole body seemed inevitable; some, however, succeeded in extricating themselves, when they rushed wildly to the ford, in the hope of re-joining their companions, who were watching them from the opposite side of the river. Still the French followed close upon them, firing at those who were struggling through the water. Many were now carried away by the current, and all who were wounded from the shore immediately sunk: it was doubtful whether a single man could escape; when the sound of artillery was heard on the British side of the river. A brigade of guns had been hastily ordered up to cover the retreat; these opened a heavy fire of grape upon the enemy, the rapidity and precision of which checked their advance, and enabled the few remaining English to regain the main body.

CHAPTER XI.

General Picton's account of the operations of the army before Bayonne.—Battle of Orthes.—Picton's important services in that battle.—Anecdote of Lieutenant Macpherson. — Advance of the British upon Bordeaux. — The French defeated at Tarbes.—The Allied army crosses the Garonne.—Observations of General Picton on Marshal Soult.

THIS affair, although so unfortunate in its results, had the effect of alarming the French, lest, by crossing the river at some other point, the allies should succeed in coming suddenly upon their position and compel them to fight. They were consequently induced to blow up the bridge during the night of the 24th, when, without offering any further resistance, they retreated. The day following, Sir Thomas Picton, having had a bridge of boats thrown across the river, led over his division and entered the town of Sauveterre. The Petite Gave was passed without difficulty, as Soult was now rapidly concentrating his forces behind the Gave de Pau near the town of Orthes. A similar movement was in consequence made by Lord Wellington, in order to unite the whole strength of his divisions at the same point; Sir Thomas Picton having, as the duke observes in his despatch, "passed his division over the river by means of a ford, which he fortunately discovered a short distance below the bridge of Bereux."

The following letter from Sir Thomas Picton to Colonel Pleydel describes the proceedings of the army upon this occasion.

" Cazeres, department of Landes,
4th March, 1814.

" My dear Colonel,

" You will have seen in the papers that we broke up our winter quarters about the middle of last month, and commenced our operations in the midst of a hard frost. Our first movements were not of any great interest, and were merely calculated to blind the enemy as to our real intentions. We had three considerable rivers to pass, and the enemy on our first movement prepared to blow up all the bridges. We succeeded, however, in effecting the passage of the Bedouse, the Petite Gave, and the Gave d'Oleron, at points where they did not expect us ; and, on the 26th instant, the third division forded the Gave de Pau about four P. M., drove in the enemy's advanced posts, and took up a position within four miles of the Duke of Dalmatia's army, which he had concentrated in a strong mountainous position in front of the town of Orthes, on the Gave de Pau.

" The light, fourth, sixth, and seventh divisions passed during the night or early on the following morning over a bridge of boats. His lordship having reconnoitred the position early on the morning of the 27th, immediately made his dispositions for the attack, which was to be made upon the centre and both flanks. The right flank, which rested upon a village of difficult access, was to be attacked by the fourth division, supported by the light and seventh ; the centre by seven battalions of the third division, and the left flank by the remaining three battalions of the third division, supported by the sixth division in reserve.

" The fourth division twice carried the village,

and was compelled to fall back with great loss :
but, upon the arrival of the light and seventh
divisions, the enemy was compelled to give it
up, with the loss of two pieces of artillery.
This afforded those divisions ground and opportunity to deploy and prosecute the advantages they had gained. In the mean time
the three battalions of the third division, supported by the sixth division, turned the enemy's
left flank, drove him from a very strong advanced position where he had a formidable
battery, and established themselves, notwithstanding a most obstinate resistance on the
flank of his centre. His position was a kind
of triangle, and the two extreme points of the
base line were hard pressed and unable to
maintain their ground, when the seven battalions advanced against the centre and forced
it also to fall back. At this moment he began
his retreat, which he protected with large solid
masses of infantry, successively taking up the
most advantageous ground that offered; and
this was for some time made in great order and
regularity; but, as the evening approached,
and we pressed rather hard upon their flanks,
the disorder gradually increased, and the dif-

ferent columns at length mixed and dispersed, running off in all directions, as at Vittoria.

" It soon became dark, and we were under the necessity of giving up the pursuit. We took, I believe, eight pieces of cannon, and about fifteen hundred prisoners. But the French army is greatly disorganized and much diminished by the desertion of the conscripts and national guards, so that I do not think they will volunteer meeting us again for some time.

" As usual, you will see by the Gazettes that we had a fair part in this memorable business; and our loss, which amounts to eight hundred and twenty-five, including fifty-three officers, exceeds that of any other of the divisions. My health has been remarkably good, and I think it will last to see the end of this memorable struggle.

" After we had gained the enemy's advanced position to the left flank, we were for nearly two hours exposed to the most continued and severe cannonade I ever witnessed ; one of our nine-pounders had every man killed by round-shot; and Captain Parker of the Engineers, who acted as my aid-de-camp on the occasion, was killed close to me by a cannon-shot, whilst carrying my orders. I hope this will find you free from indisposition.

" My dear Colonel,

" Believe me to be

" Most sincerely and faithfully yours,

" TH. PICTON."

The subjoined letter to his brother refers to the same events :

" Cazares, in the department of Landes,
South of France, 4th March 1814.

" MY DEAR BROTHER,

" You will have seen in the papers that we broke up our winter quarters and commenced the campaign in the middle of last month. There was, however, no circumstance of any great consequence which took place until the 27th; when we attacked the Duke of Dalmatia in a strong position which he had taken up on a chain of elevated mountains, in front of the town of Orthes, on the Gave de Pau.

" After a severe conflict of several hours, during which the enemy fought with a considerable degree of obstinacy, we succeeded in forcing the position on all sides, and he fell back, covering his retreat with large masses of infantry. It was made for some time with great regularity and order; but as he became pressed towards evening, he fell into confusion, dispersed and made off in all directions so fast that we were unable to follow him sufficiently close to make many prisoners; and dark night coming on very shortly after he became in this state, we were under the necessity of giving up the pursuit, and he continued his flight during the whole course of the night, so that we were not able to come up with his rear-guard until the following evening, too late to attack it. We have since followed him slowly, and we are now on the right bank of the Adour, on the road to Toulouse; but our means of subsistence will not allow us to follow much farther. We, as usual, had a principal share in this memorable battle, and our loss exceeded that of any of the other divisions. The enemy is reported to have had forty thousand men in position; we certainly did not bring more than twenty-three thousand into action. We have lost about two thousand five hundred in killed and wounded: there is no estimating

with any correctness that of the enemy, which
I conceive must have been more considerable.
But, what is of greater importance, the loss of
the battle has occasioned the desertion of more
of the conscripts and national guards, with
which the marshal's army had been reinforced
after his repeated defeats in November and
December last.

" My health has been remarkably good since
my resumption of an active life, which appears
to suit my body and mind. We are here in
the country of excellent wine; better, in my
opinion, than that of Bordeaux : but the French
army has so exhausted the country, that every
other necessary of life is extremely dear. The
country we have passed through is most beautifully picturesque; and appears like a continued village, it is so remarkably well settled.
The inhabitants are an exceedingly fine race,
and perfectly uncorrupted.

" Property is well divided in Navarre and
the departments of the Lower Pyrenees. I
have never seen a beggar, or anything like misery; the inhabitants are all well dressed, well
lodged, and well fed : I wish the population of
England were as well off, and generally as well-

disposed. There are none of the vices of great riches or poverty here. The state of agriculture is very favourable; they pay great attention to the collecting and working of manure, and irrigation is general throughout this part of France. I hope you have all passed the severe winter without accident or injury to your health. May it long continue! My best respects to Mrs. Picton.

"Very sincerely yours,

"Th. Picton."

"To the Reverend Edward Picton,
"Llynceaer, near Bridgend, Glamorganshire."

During the battle of Orthes, Sir Thomas Picton commanded the centre of the allied army, consisting of the third and sixth divisions, with Lord Edward Somerset's brigade of cavalry. The left wing, under Marshal Beresford, commenced the attack upon the right of the enemy at the village of St. Boes; and here the struggle was continued for a considerable time, with but little success on the part of the allies. When possession of the village was obtained, Marshal Beresford next proceeded to drive the enemy from two com-

manding heights which they occupied in the
rear; but the only approach to this point of
their position was along a narrow ridge of land,
with a deep ravine on each side, the whole space
being ranged by their artillery. The difficulty
of advancing over this exposed ground will
easily be conceived. The fourth division made
the attempt with a courage which merited
success; but the enemy's fire sweeping dia-
gonally across the exposed summit, caused a
terrible slaughter: the front and centre were
alike exposed, and the havoc which was made
in the ranks of the division proved the stern
materials of which it was composed. They
still, however, pressed on; for they had been so
long inured to victory, that they could not
conceive themselves, defeated: but the ground
strewed with their fallen comrades presented a
frightful picture of the hopelessness of the attempt. A Portuguese brigade, after standing
for some time exposed to the destructive fire
of the foe, at length gave way, and commenced
a disorderly retreat. The French pressed hard
upon their rear; and nothing but the timely
support of some fresh troops from the light
division could have rescued them, and pre-

vented their spreading confusion throughout
this wing of the army. The battle now assumed a threatening aspect: the French were
redoubling their fire upon the broken Portuguese; while the fourth division, paralyzed
and wavering, bent beneath the storm.

Again it was reserved for Sir Thomas Picton
to change the fate of the day. At this moment,
when the issue of the contest was yet doubtful, he received orders from Lord Wellington to advance against that part of the enemy's
position between the right of his centre, where
it rested upon the left of the right wing. This
attack was made with his wonted energy and
resolution; the British troops carried every
point which the enemy attempted to defend,
with a spirit and daring intrepidity which were
irresistible.

The whole eleven regiments of the third
division were desperately engaged, and drove
the enemy from every height on which they
ventured to make a stand. This unexpected
movement at once changed the front of battle:
the French columns opposing the advance of
Beresford's corps, alarmed for their flank and
rear, now in their turn gave way, while their

artillery was partially withdrawn. Then the fourth division rushed over the ground upon which so many had fallen, and the whole quickly deploying into line, charged the heights, driving the enemy before them with immense slaughter. The British artillery was now brought to some high ground near the right of the third division, from which they poured a destructive fire along the entire line of the enemy's centre. This may be said to have concluded the battle; for Soult, seeing his centre totally discomfited and preparing to retreat, became apprehensive for his wings, and, therefore, after another futile effort to retrieve the fortunes of the day, the field was abandoned.

General Picton has sufficiently detailed the retreat of the enemy, which, as he observes, was after a time changed into a complete rout; for Sir Rowland Hill, having succeeded in forcing the passage of the river above the town of Orthes, was moving quickly to the rear of their left, threatening to cut off their communication with Sault de Navailles, which, with the exception of Dax, was the only road calculated for the passage of artillery. Even

Vittoria was not a more decisive victory than the battle of Orthes. The enemy, it is true, were not now rich with the spoils of a plundered nation, and the acquisition of the allies was not great in anything save glory. Their brilliant success upon this occasion was, however, tinctured with a feeling of apprehension for the safety of their commander; the Marquis of Wellington was himself amongst the wounded; for, during the action, a grape-shot struck the pommel of his sword, driving it with much force against his side, and producing a severe contusion. This wound, although not dangerous, was sufficient to alarm his soldiers, and prevent his directing the pursuit of the enemy.*

* The following anecdote connected with this battle, relating to Lieutenant Macpherson, whose heroism at Badajoz we have already recorded, will not be uninteresting. He was still a lieutenant at the period of the battle of Orthes, attached to the light company of the Forty-fifth foot. Just before the attack commenced, the regiment was drawn up in line, partly hidden by a kind of hedge or bank. The bugles had sounded the recall, and the light troops were hastening back to form in the rear. As the files opened to let them through, some of the enemy's tirailleurs had followed them nearly up to the line, which made Macpherson anxious to see the whole of the men fall in before he himself retired. The skirmishing was still kept up as they fell back, and an occasional man fell on both sides, as these expert

The results of this battle were highly important, by striking another and powerful blow at the empire of Napoleon. At the same time, the conscripts who had been forced into the ranks of Soult's army took the op-

shots rapidly loaded as they moved, and then with deadly accuracy turned to stop the advance of their enemy. The gallant Macpherson, in his anxiety to do his duty, was left almost the last, when he was about to effect his own retreat; but just at this moment he perceived one of the enemy's sharpshooters, within about twenty yards, raising his piece to take a deliberate aim at him. This man had ventured thus far alone; for his comrades, having come within range of the fire from the line, had begun to retire.

Colonel Macpherson's own description of his reflections are at once amusing and painful. " I saw the man," he observes, " taking a deliberate aim at me. What to do I did not know. I could not get at him before he could fire, while to run would have been equally useless—I should then be shot in the back; for I knew that he was one of those picked men who never missed anything;—in fact, I could think of nothing else to do but stand fire. The fellow was a confounded long time taking his aim, as if determined to make sure of his mark: so I put myself in an attitude, by presenting my right side to him, putting my arm straight down to cover me, and screwing myself up as small as possible;—but I can assure you I felt smaller than I looked, as I thus stood like a target to be shot at by a fellow that could hit any one of my buttons that he pleased. At last, bang went his piece, and I felt in a moment he was all right. I did not fall, but staggered a few paces backwards, and then felt very much inclined to reach my soldiers, some of whom had seen the whole affair without being able to portunity of this retreat to quit a service in which they took no interest and for which they felt no inclination. In fact, the impolicy of raising the country *en masse,* which Sir Thomas Picton so justly condemned, was now strikingly

lend me any assistance. My right arm was rendered unserviceable, and I felt confident that the ball had entered my body; but I was uncertain whether or not it had found its way out. I staggered towards the line, but must have fallen, had not a brave fellow named Kelly, (an Irishman, and one of our crack shots,) seeing that I was hit, run forward to support me. As soon as I felt his friendly grip round my body, I mustered fresh strength, although bleeding profusely both inside and out. Kelly commenced a dialogue, observing, ' By my sowl, sir, you're badly wounded, sure !'

" I felt very faint, but replied, ' Yes, Kelly, I think so: feel if the ball is out.' Kelly watched its course; and then placing his hand upon my loins, where it should have made its exit, exclaimed,

" ' No, by my sowl, then it isn't, and you're spaking yet. But where's the man that did it ?"

" Without at the moment any feeling of revenge towards him whom I then thought my destroyer, I pointed in the direction from whence he had fired ; and there, on the very same spot, stood this daring fellow, deliberately re-loading to have another shot at my assistant or to finish me. But Kelly quitted hold of me for a moment, and I saw his unerring gun raised to his shoulder: the French soldier was unmoved—Kelly fired—and he fell dead."

The colonel, in relating this incident, spoke with much regret of the fate of his gallant enemy.

apparent; for these southern provinces were always known to be well affected towards the Bourbons, and they now gladly availed themselves of the success of their cause to forsake the service of the Emperor.

It is not necessary here to follow the course of events in the North; which, in conjunction with the invasion of France by the British army under the Marquis of Wellington, led to the overthrow of the power of Napoleon. It is sufficient to observe, that he gave brilliant instances of his masterly military skill, and, by his rapid movements, even for a while paralyzed the operations of his opponents.

But he either would not or could not see the extent of his difficulties; and he thought that he was now become so necessary to France, that the nation would make any sacrifice to support him. The French people were now, however, tired of a war which was no longer accompanied by conquest and glory: a reaction had taken place. The veteran guards were, it is true, still attached to him; but these alone could not withstand the vast invading force.

Still Napoleon thundered out his proclamations, calling upon the nation to rise and crush the invaders. But the cry was made to deserted hearths; the manhood of France had fallen to support his power, and the feeble efforts of age and youth would not avail his cause.

His ambition urged him, however, to delay his answer to the proposition of the allied powers until he had tried his strength. This trial gave confidence to his opponents, and he consequently lost all; for when they had gained Paris at the point of the bayonet, negotiation was at an end—Napoleon was then an usurper. This was the position of affairs in the North.

To return to the proceedings of Lord Wellington's army in the South, and the subject of our memoir. After the battle of Orthes, Marshal Soult fell back by the most direct road to St. Sever, closely followed by the allies. The enemy destroyed the whole of the bridges in his rear, and by this means contrived to effect a tolerably secure retreat. The ardour of Sir Thomas Picton and his division gave them a conspicuous position in this advance; and on the 1st of March, with the centre of the allied army, they crossed the Adour, and entered the town of St. Sever. The rain having

greatly swollen these rivers, Lord Wellington
was induced to delay for a few days his further progress, in order to give the soldiers a
short interval of rest, while he sent working
parties forward to repair the bridges which
the enemy had destroyed. But as the French
had considerable stores at Aire, on the Adour,
a few miles above St. Sever, Sir Rowland Hill
moved forward to dislodge them from that
position. This service was performed in the
most gallant style; the French, after a smart
action, being driven from some heights which
they had occupied with considerable loss:
when, being forced from this vantage ground,
and finding no other tenable position near the
town, they made a precipitate retreat, and abandoned to the allies the whole of the stores.

Soult now felt himself beaten both in tactics
and in force; even the Portuguese soldiers were
now equal to the French; for these troops
had so often fought by the side of the British
that they had learned to imitate their steadiness, and caught their daring. Soult evidently
thought that his soldiers were inferior to their
opponents, for he still continued his retreat.
Again he committed an error; and to err with

Wellington as an opponent, was to ensure defeat. He appeared to have assumed the fact that Lord Wellington would not venture to advance upon Bordeaux, leaving so strong a place as Bayonne unreduced in his rear. But the commander of the allied forces had received confident information of the disaffection which existed in Bordeaux towards Napoleon. He determined, therefore, to take advantage of this feeling; and as the Duc d'Angoulême had a short time previously repaired to St. Jean de Luz, it was resolved to put the sincerity of the Bordelais' professions to the test. Accordingly, as a deputy had arrived from Bordeaux, bearing assurances from the corporation of their warm attachment to the House of Bourbon, and that nothing but the presence of a small French garrison prevented the inhabitants from giving proof of their sentiments, the Duke repaired to head-quarters at St. Sever; when Lord Wellington, who had hitherto refrained from assisting him too warmly without the concurrence of the British Government, no longer hesitated, but sent Marshal Beresford with three divisions to drive out the garrison, and secure to the Duc d'Angoulême an uninterrupted entry. This measure was entirely successful; the French garrison evacuated the place without any resistance, and the hereditary Prince of France entered the city amidst cries of "*Vive le Roi!*"

"Crowds pressed round him," observes Southey, in his elaborate History of the War, "if they might but touch his clothes or his horse. Some cried, ' He is our blood; he was born a Frenchman, and feels like a Frenchman.' Numbers fell on their knees and blessed him, and blessed God that they had lived to see this day. Mothers pointed him out to their children, and said, ' Now we shall no longer lose all our sons in the war.' And thus one hold was taken in the enemy's country : a great and influential city had openly declared against the longer continuance of Napoleon's empire."

During these political movements, confidence was given to the inhabitants of the southern provinces of France, by Lord Wellington, to follow up the example which had thus been set. The mere fact of seeing the French army driven before the English was enough in itself to make the people discontented; and they are ever prone to favour the strongest side. Soult was now falling back upon Toulouse; the inhabitants were apprehensive that he would defend their city, and, had they dared, they would readily have shut their gates against him: for though he could not fight the English, he could beat the French; they were therefore obliged to wait patiently the course of events.

The direction which Soult had taken was dictated by sound military policy: he hoped to draw off the allies from Bordeaux. Thirteen thousand men were still there with Marshal Beresford; and the French general thought, and hoped, that Lord Wellington would not dare to withdraw them from watching that city. In this again he was mistaken: no doubts were entertained of the sincerity of the sentiments expressed by the Bordelais, and Lord Wellington did not hesitate to withdraw the whole force under Beresford, with the exception of the seventh division, under Lord Dalhousie, which was reserved to keep in check any reaction of French policy which might occur. Having, therefore, again united his force, Lord Wellington continued his advance against Soult with undiminished confidence. That

general, however, finding he could not cover
or save Bordeaux, and being alarmed lest the
reanimated loyalty should spread, made a show
of firmness by an attack on the right flank of
the allies at Canchez and Viella, occupied by
Sir Rowland Hill. This took place on the
17th March, when he drove in the British picquets, and threatened to turn the line with his
whole force. But Sir Rowland Hill immediately retired upon some strong ground behind the Gros Lyes; and Lord Wellington,
being now convinced that the French marshal
intended to carry the war to the eastward, ordered two divisions from the centre to move
to the right of the allied position, for the purpose of supporting Sir Rowland Hill, should
Soult attempt any more important operations.

On the 18th, the whole army advanced, occupying each side of the Adour, and marching
up the stream; the French slowly falling back
on their front towards Toulouse. The "fighting division" was on the right; and on the
morning of the 19th they drove a large body
of the enemy from some singularly defensible ground which encircles the town of
Vic Bigorre. This position was capable of

a very obstinate defence, and its acquisition would in that case be necessarily attended with great loss. About the middle of the day, the division entered a wood composed entirely of vineyards, thickly occupied by the enemy's light troops. To force these to retire was indispensable before the division could advance. Lord Wellington and Sir Thomas Picton, protected by a squadron of German dragoons, reconnoitred the position, and after a short time the division was ordered to close up for the attack. .

It was expected, from the nature of the ground, that the enemy would make considerable efforts to maintain this strong post; but the light companies of the division, supported by the Portuguese brigade, met with little opposition, as they drove the French before them. The main body of the division moved close in their rear, so that any attempt made in force by the enemy would have been immediately overcome; and the result was, that, before evening, Sir Thomas Picton and his division encamped about three miles beyond the town of Vic Bigorre. On the following morning, Sir Thomas Picton was joined by Sir

Rowland Hill, with the second division, that
general having moved round the vineyards on
the right of the third division; and they now
marched together towards Tarbes, which formed the left of Soult's position, his right extending in the direction of Rabastens.

The intentions of the French general were
still uncertain: he was continually threatening
to give battle to the allies, but as continually
retreated when they came up. He was drawing Lord Wellington back upon the Pyrenees;
but he was leaving the country which he had
to defend unprotected; and, in fact, it appeared as if he would abandon France to the
allies, provided he might have Spain. It was
said that Soult had expressed his determination
to defend the heights of Tarbes to the last man;
but whether his own resolution or the courage
of his soldiers failed, is uncertain.

A general movement was made by the allies
on the whole of the French line; the third
division, with Sir Rowland Hill's corps,
moving, as before observed, upon Tarbes,
while three other divisions crossed the Adour
and advanced to attack the right of the enemy
at Rabastens. The whole of these arrange-

ments were admirably planned and executed. The French marshal had again assumed a very strong and commanding position, so that the feebleness of his defence is quite unaccountable. Sir Henry Clinton commenced the attack upon the right of the French line, while the two divisions advanced upon Tarbes. This place was quickly occupied by the British light troops. These succeeded in forcing the enemy to abandon the town, who then crossed the river, and ascended the heights in its rear, which were occupied by their main body. The two divisions now marched through the town with colours flying and the bands playing, during which they were loudly cheered by the inhabitants, who greeted them with acclamations of " *Vivent les Anglais!* " " *Vive l'Angleterre!*" the sincerity of which expressions might readily be doubted, as they were not interspersed with any cries of loyalty to the Bourbons, or of attachment to the cause in which the allies were engaged. The troops did not, however, pause in the town; but, marching quickly through, proceeded to follow up their success. Great, however, was their surprise when they saw a large French army drawn up on the heights to receive them, and those soldiers whom they had driven from the town hastening up the acclivity to form in their ranks.

It was judged expedient both by Generals Hill and Picton to await the further advance of the corps under Sir Henry Clinton before an attack was made upon this strong position: Nothing was, however, done before evening closed ; the troops, therefore, bivouacked upon the ground which they had gained, in full expectation of a renewal of the contest on the following day ; but, as usual, Soult took advantage of the night to retreat, and fell back to the vicinity of Toulouse. The dawn showed the heights deserted by the enemy, and the allies continued their march in pursuit. . Soult made as little delay as possible upon the way, being anxious to get the defences. which he had been preparing in as perfect a state as possible before the arrival of the allies. The enemy were not again overtaken until they were formed in the neighbourhood of Toulouse.

The broad and rapid river Garonne was to be passed by Lord Wellington's army before

Soult or the city could be attacked; and, to
effect this, a pontoon train was indispensable.
The conveyance of this heavy appendage necessarily delayed the movements of the troops,
and they did not succeed in reaching the vicinity of Toulouse until three days after the
French. Soult appeared to have resolved to
make a determined stand against his pursuers
at this place, as he had fortified every approach
and outwork with the utmost care; no point
that presented the least facility for defence had
indeed been neglected. The army, therefore,
looked forward to some severe fighting;—and
they were not disappointed.

On the 29th of March, Sir Thomas Picton
halted his division at Plaisance, about five
miles from the city; the other divisions of the
army occupying positions along the banks of the
river Garonne, opposite Toulouse. General Picton was directed to have his division under
arms two hours before daylight on the morning of the 1st of April, and it was generally
supposed that on that day the battle would be
fought. The division was accordingly formed
at the appointed time, and remained in momentary expectation of being ordered to advance

until late in the afternoon, when the men were again sent back to their quarters. It was intended that the second and third divisions should attempt to force a passage over the bridge in front of the town; but, upon reconnoitring, it was discovered to be so strongly fortified, and blocked up with so many obstacles, that it was not deemed advisable by the commander of the forces to make the attempt. Again, Sir Rowland Hill had succeeded in establishing a pontoon bridge on a bend of the river a short distance below the city : over this he had passed with his corps; but the passage thence to Toulouse was found to be almost impassable in consequence of the great quantities of rain which had recently fallen, and upon this conviction he withdrew his troops.

Lord Wellington now resolved to attempt the passage of the river below the city, at Grenade; and the pontoon bridge was therefore thrown across at this place by the 4th. The third, with the fourth, sixth, and light divisions, were then ordered to cross : but this was a slow and tedious operation, as the cavalry were compelled to dismount and lead their horses in single files. During the day,

by great exertions, a large force was enabled to effect a passage in the following order:—
" Colonel Vivian's brigade of hussars, horse artillery ; sixth division, foot artillery ; fourth division, foot artillery ; Lord Edward Somerset's brigade of hussars, horse artillery ; third division, foot artillery.; six regiments of heavy cavalry."

By the time these troops had passed over, the day had closed; and during the night the wind and rain caused so great and unexpected a swell in the river, that, in order to save the pontoons from destruction, they were removed. At the same time, the enemy, who had at length discovered the bridge, were trying every device to destroy it, by floating down large pieces of timber and boats loaded with stones. But their designs were frustrated by the skill and activity of the British engineers. The position of the allied army was now, however, rather precarious; its strength being divided by a wide and impassable river. Sir Thomas Picton, when afterwards alluding to this position, observed, that he considered Soult betrayed more timidity and less generalship upon this occasion than from the preceding actions of his life and acknowledged abilities could ever have been expected. But he added, " I suppose the anticipated downfall of his master had produced a corresponding depression in his own confidence."

The Marquis of Wellington was on the opposite side of the river, and Sir Thomas Picton, as senior officer, assumed the command; and had Soult taken advantage of this accident which chance had thrown in his way, left his entrenchments, and come down in force to attack these divisions, he would have had the advantage of fighting about seventeen thousand men with his whole army; while the rest of the allied forces would have been compelled to remain inactive spectators of the struggle. Albuera had witnessed how much could be done by a still smaller band; and with that example before us, what would have been too much to expect from these men, had Soult acted on the opportunity thus presented to him, and come down to the attack ?

CHAPTER XII.

Decisive Battle of Toulouse. — Abdication of Napoleon.—
Evacuation of Toulouse by the French, and entry of the
Allied army.—Intelligence of the arrival in Paris of the
Allies.—Unnecessary effusion of blood.

On the 6th, Lord Wellington and Marshal
Beresford crossed the river in a small boat
and visited the troops. By the 8th, the water
of the river had run out sufficiently to enable
the pontoons again to be laid down at a fresh
place nearer to the city, when the Spanish army,
under General Freyre, was passed over. The
divisions which had already gained the opposite side advanced nearer to the town; the
third division taking up a position in some
meadows, with their picquets occupying some
closely-wooded ground, near a fortified bridge
over the Canal du Midi. On the left of the
third was posted the sixth division, under
Baron Alten; the object of this corps being
to observe and divert the enemy in the sub-

urbs, between the canal and the city, and
threaten an attack upon the whole of that
part of the town to the river.

Sir Rowland Hill's corps was on the opposite side, on the left bank, protecting the right
flank of the third division by a cannonade,
and threatening the *tête de pont*. It was not,
however, on this side of the city that the battle was to be fought: a ridge of bold and
commanding heights to the east of the town
offered to Soult a strong defensible position
for nearly his whole army ; these heights were
therefore fortified with some redoubts and entrenchments, by which the line of communication was kept up to the canal, and thence
to the walls : his right flank was protected
by the river Ers, and his left by a strongly
fortified redoubt and entrenchments; so that
the whole line from the Ers to the Garonne
was prepared to resist the advance of the allies.
Circumstances rendered it necessary for Lord
Wellington to force this position of the enemy,
or obtain possession of Toulouse. To effect
the former object appeared the most expeditious ; and having made every disposition for
attacking the heights, on the 9th of April the
British army slept on the field.

On Easter Sunday, 1814, the dawn was scarcely visible when the columns of the allies were moving to their different points of attack. The following extract from Lord Wellington's despatch, dated Toulouse, April 12th, will convey to the reader's mind a perfect idea of the plan of the intended assault, and of the duties which Sir Thomas Picton had to perform upon this occasion, — remarkable alike as the last grand struggle of this long-protracted war, and on account of the particular circumstances under which it took place.

" The plan according to which I intended to attack the enemy, was for Marshal Sir W. Beresford, who was on the right of the Ers with the fourth and sixth divisions, to cross that river at the bridge of Croix d'Orode, to gain possession of Mont Blanc, and to march up the left of the Ers to turn the enemy's right; while Lieutenant-general Don Manuel Freyre, with the Spanish corps under his command, supported by the British cavalry, should attack the front. Lieutenant-general Sir Stapleton Cotton was to follow the Marshal's movements, with Major-general Lord Edward Somerset's brigade of hussars; and Colonel Vivian's brigade, under the command of Co-

lonel Arentschild, was to observe the movement of the enemy's cavalry on both banks of
the Ers beyond our left.

" The third and light divisions, under the
command of Lieutenant-general Sir Thomas
Picton and Major-general Charles. Baron Alten,
and the brigade of German cavalry, were to
observe the enemy on the lower part of the
canal, and to draw their attention to that
quarter by threatening the *tête de pont;* while
Lieutenant-general Sir Rowland Hill was to
do the same on the suburb on the left of the
Garonne."

The third. division was formed in three separate corps by Sir Thomas Picton early in
the morning; the one being posted on ,the
left, its flank resting on the light division near
the road from Paris, the right being supported by the Portuguese; Major-general Brisbane's
brigade having to move along the banks of the
river and occupy in force the plantations which
were still held by the advance picquets.

" The- business of this dreadful day commenced about seven o'clock, when Sir Thomas
Picton drove in the French picquets in front
of Port Jameau, at the point where the Canal

de Brienne joins that of Languedoc. The action became warm here; and the enemy retiring, set fire to a fine large chateau, in the cypress avenues of which they had sought in vain to cover themselves."* Too much importance is here ascribed to this skirmish. The enemy had no intention of withstanding the attack of the third division in this quarter; and from the information we have been enabled to collect, it does not appear that any portion of the third division was engaged at this period, except some of the rifle companies, who occupied the enemy's attention by skirmishing across the canal. The battle commenced on the left and in the centre of the allied position, in front of the heights upon which the enemy were posted.

Marshal Beresford, with the fourth and sixth divisions, moved along the left bank of the Ers, carried the village of Mont Blanc, and then advanced steadily over the level ground at the foot of the heights, exposed the whole time to a tremendous cannonade, which was poured down upon them with great precision and rapidity. At the same time the Spaniards,

* Southey.

under General Freyre, were ordered to attack
the redoubts from which this fire was opened.
But in this they failed, although they continued to advance with much gallantry, until,
elated by a slight success, and then panic-
struck by the tremendous fire to which they
were exposed, they wavered; when, before
they had recovered from their alarm, the French
charged them with the bayonet. The steady
courage of our soldiers was then strikingly
contrasted with the exhausted impetuosity of
the Spaniards : they turned and hastily retreated down the hill, followed, but not hotly, by
the French.

This was a critical moment; for, had the
enemy succeeded in driving this corps over
the Ers, the force under Marshal Beresford
would have been cut off from the rest of the
army. But Lord Wellington, always prepared
for emergencies, immediately ordered the light
division to move by its left, to arrest the flight
of the Spaniards and check the progress of
the enemy. Marshal Beresford, during this
reverse in the centre, continued his advance.
Having marched each column of the fourth
and sixth divisions opposite to their respect-

ive points of attack, they were rapidly wheeled into line. Then came the struggle. The ground up which these troops had to move was rugged and broken, offering every protection to the enemy's tirailleurs, and being occasionally exposed to the fire of the main body, which was posted on the more elevated heights. So true and close was the fire of the artillery, that nearly every shot told, mowing down the files as they unhesitatingly pressed on. But no fire could appal these men : they at last gained the summit, and drove the French from a formidable redoubt on their right flank. The enemy had, however, by means of planks laid over the broken and irregular ground, contrived to carry off their guns, which were withdrawn to redoubts further to the rear, from whence they opened afresh upon Beresford's troops.

The allies were without artillery to reply to this destructive fire ; for the guns attached to these divisions had been placed in battery in front of the village of Mont Blanc, to cannonade the enemy's works on the heights. An officer was now, however, sent to hasten it forward, while Beresford's soldiers covered themselves as well as they could within and behind the redoubts which they had taken. At this period a singular, and apparently unaccountable, pause ensued: the firing had almost ceased on the left, and the battle seemed suspended. It was even suspected by the third division and Sir Rowland Hill's corps that the allies had been defeated. But Sir Thomas Picton, who had been observing with anxious interest the progress of the fight, now rode up at speed; and the whole division was in an instant on the alert. He had seen the retreat of the Spaniards, and justly concluded that the left wing would have a frightful struggle against an immense superiority of force. This at once decided him in making a diversion in their favour, which has since been canvassed with some degree of severity by military men.

The right brigade, under the command of Major-general Brisbane, was immediately ordered to leave the plantation in which they had been hid, and attempt to force a passage over the canal, by means of a bridge situated near its junction with the river Garonne. The bridge was covered by an extremely strong redoubt in front, and a formidable range of artillery on each flank. Sir Thomas Picton personally directed this attack, which was made by the Forty-fifth, Seventy-fourth, and Eighty-eighth regiments, with three companies of the fifth battalion of the Sixtieth, in the usual style of "the fighting division," moving to the assault with that impetuous courage which nothing could daunt. The artillery attached to Sir Rowland Hill's corps, perceiving the intention of Sir Thomas Picton, opened a heavy fire across the river; but unfortunately they struck down some houses which had served to protect the light troops of the division, and this left them exposed to the incessant shower of grape which was kept up by the enemy.

The works which Sir Thomas Picton was now about to attack had been prepared with the utmost skill and care; everything that art could devise to render them impregnable against assault had been done; but it was not until the counterscarp had been gained that General Picton discovered the formidable nature of the defences. Here such a blaze of musketry and artillery was opened, while the ditch itself presented such an insurmountable barrier to any further advance, that a retreat was

immediately sounded,—but not before many
had fallen. The body of the gallant Colonel
Forbes, of the Forty-fifth regiment, was left
upon this fatal spot; but his soldiers afterwards obtained leave to carry it off, and gave
it a soldier's grave. Major-general Brisbane
was wounded, and the command of the brigade
devolved upon Colonel Taylor of the Eighty-
eighth foot; who had, however, only to lead off
the remnant of the troops, and establish them
in their former position, where Picton and his
division were condemned to remain inactive,
listening with intense anxiety to the thunder
of battle, which had now broke forth with
renewed fury on their left. · The light division
had succeeded in arresting the Spaniards in
their flight, and in checking the pursuit of
the French. When Beresford, who had now
been joined by the artillery, was informed
of this effectual check to the enemy's success,
and that the Spaniards were again formed
and about to renew the contest, he resolved
to continue his advance along the ridge with
the fourth and sixth divisions.

As there was a considerable space between
the two advancing divisions, Soult, imitating

Napoleon's tactics, endeavoured to crush one before the other could arrive to its support. For this purpose he collected the whole of his disposable force, and prepared to surround the sixth division with cavalry and infantry. But Sir Henry Clinton did not wait to be attacked; he ordered his men to charge the assembling army. They did so, rushing upon them with a fury which could not be withstood. It was a burst of impetuous courage; but it was sustained by the stern valour of Englishmen. The French fought with much resolution: never, according to some writers, did they fight better. They even checked for a while the advance of the allies; but they could not make them desist. A terrible carnage ensued: it was a contention of numbers against invincible courage and determination.

At length the enemy, unable longer to withstand the fury of their assailants, fled: this may be said to have decided the fate of the day, although another grand effort was made by fresh troops, sent across the canal, to recover the lost ground and redoubts. The sixth division again conquered, and the heights were cleared by a simultaneous charge of the British and Spaniards. The enemy then retired across the canal, the bridges over which were all strongly fortified; and about four o'clock the battle terminated, nearly five thousand men being left upon the. field. The futility of this battle is well known: at the very time that this carnage was going on, the Northern allies were in Paris, and Napoleon was held a kind of regal prisoner by the commissioners of the confederation.

On the 31st of March the city of Paris capitulated, when the sovereigns forming the alliance made their entry. Napoleon fled to Fontainebleau; but his hopes and much of his energy had left him. He made an offer to abdicate in favour of his son, the King of Rome. This was of course rejected; and he then submitted to their will, and abdicated upon a treaty by which, as a kind of satire upon his ambition, he was allowed to retain his imperial name, with the miniature dominion of Elba. The news of this abdication and the consequent peace was actually received in London six days prior to its being made known at Toulouse. The probability, — nay, almost certainty, is that, as any communication to this.

effect must of necessity have come through the French lines, either Soult or some of his officers intercepted the despatch. It is difficult to find a reason for such an inhuman act : the only one that presents itself is, that the sting of defeat had rankled so deeply, that they would not listen to peace before they had sought revenge. There is much reason to suspect that this is the truth.

On the 11th of April, the day following the battle of Toulouse, the divisions were again under arms; when Lord Wellington sent in a flag of truce, calling upon the French army to surrender as prisoners of war, in order to save the city from destruction. The situation of Soult was precarious : he replied, that he would rather bury himself and soldiers in the ruins of the town. But he knew that he should have the whole of the inhabitants against him if he remained, and Lord Wellington would bombard the place; while, if he waited until the allies had effected a perfect investment, he would in all probability be compelled to surrender. He therefore formed his resolution, and evacuated the city during the night of the 12th, taking the road to Ville Franque.

On the following day Lord Wellington entered the city, with a grand procession of English and foreign officers, together with those of the corporation. Even here, and by the French themselves, Picton was greeted with acclamations as he rode early in the morning across the square.

The allied army was now halted for a while. The report had spread widely through the city that the Northern allies were in Paris. Still Lord Wellington received no official intimation until towards evening on the 12th of May, when Colonel Cooke arrived from Paris, bringing a confirmation of the report. A French officer, Colonel St. Simon, also arrived, who was charged by the provisional government to make this news known to Marshal Soult. After having spread the glad tidings at Toulouse, these two messengers repaired with a flag of truce to the French camp. But Soult did not receive the information with any appearance of satisfaction, and even refused to acknowledge the authority by which the notification was received. An armistice was, however, agreed upon; when Soult, hearing within a short time that the Emperor was about to embark for Elba, settled the conditions, and the French army in a short time dwindled into a few regiments.

A still further, although equally unnecessary, effusion of blood had, however, taken place before this event was brought about. The two messengers in their way from Paris had passed through Bordeaux, from whence they sent information of the peace to Sir John Hope, who was still blockading Bayonne. Sir John did not communicate this intelligence to General Thouvenot, who commanded the garrison, as he did not conceive he was justified in so doing until he had received the announcement direct from Lord Wellington; in consequence of which delay, the enemy made a sortie during the night of the 14th, which was attended with the most distressing results; nearly two thousand French, English, and their allies, having fallen within the trenches. This was, however, the last of these sanguinary struggles; after which the British army went into cantonments, previously to its return to England.

CHAPTER XIII.

Breaking up of the army.—Tribute of respect to Sir Thomas
Picton by his division.—His return to England.—His
services apparently undervalued by the Government.—
His remark on that subject.—Picton again receives the
thanks of the House of Commons.

DURING this protracted war the Spaniards
and Portuguese had learned to respect and ad-
mire their British allies, and they now looked
upon a separation from these companions with
a feeling of regret. But other and closer ties
were to be broken: those regiments belonging to the same divisions, which had so long
been formed into a kind of fraternal band,
were now about to be ordered into different
parts of the world. In the third division
especially this was much felt, as several regiments were ordered to embark for America.

As a proof of the error of the assertion that
Sir Thomas Picton was not popular amongst
the officers and soldiers of his division, we
may refer to the circumstances of his parting

from the division at the close of this war.
From the very best authorities, we are enabled
to state that, with but one exception, a strong
feeling of regret was evinced by every soldier
of the division when "old Picton" inspected
their ranks for the last time previously to his
embarkation for England. The heartfelt, animating cheer,—the reply to his brief address
as he thanked them for their gallant services
and bade them farewell,—was, as he himself
remarked, "a gratifying and convincing proof
that the regiments composing 'the fighting division' would never forget their old general."

The officers of the division exhibited, however, a more substantial, but not more convincing proof of the esteem in which they held
him : and it will hardly be believed by those
who have heard that Sir Thomas Picton never
reported the services of any officer under his
command, or attempted to procure for them
any reward, that those very officers whom he
is thus accused of having neglected, before the
division was broken up, subscribed amongst
themselves a sum amounting to nearly sixteen
hundred pounds, for the purpose of presenting
" *old Picton*" with a service of plate. One ex-

ception must, however, be made to this apparently universal sentiment of regard : this was on the part of the officers and men of the Eighty-eighth Foot. This regiment has already been alluded to upon more than one occasion as having called forth the anger of General Picton. We have since been informed by an officer of distinguished rank who saw much of this regiment, that they were altogether the most singular set of fellows that ever handled a musket. " For days together," observed this officer, " they would be the most orderly, well-behaved soldiers; then all at once they would break out into the wildest and most irregular courses it is possible to conceive, pillaging everything spiritual or temporal; for being almost without exception Irish and good Catholics, they were always the first to find their way to church, when their love and veneration for the holy utensils made them greedily appropriate them to their own share, doubtless that they might not fall into the hands of their heretical comrades. But this was not all," added our informant; " for frequently, just before going into battle, it would be found upon inspec-

tion that one half of the men of the Eighty-
eighth regiment were without ammunition,
having acquired a pernicious habit of exchang-
ing the cartridges for *aguardiente*, and substi-
tuting in their place pieces of wood cut and
coloured to resemble them." Picton never
found fault with their conduct in the field;
but, on the contrary, gave them most unqualified praise whenever it was deserved ; and
this was often. But the frequent reprimands
which he gave them for their behaviour upon
other occasions, and which the officers in a
great measure applied to themselves, produced
a kind of ill feeling which was never entirely
destroyed, and now broke forth in not a very
Irish-like manner; for, almost without a single
exception, the officers of this regiment declined subscribing towards this testimonial of respect and esteem from the 'fighting division'
to their gallant general. With this exception,
the feeling which dictated this offering was
universal throughout the division. The money
for the purchase of this plate was remitted
to the Honourable Colonel H. R. Pakenham,
who was then detained in England by a severe
wound, and he with some brother officers had

the ordering and management of this handsome
present.*.

The services of Sir Thomas Picton being
no longer required, he embarked at Bordeaux

---

* Major-general the Honourable Charles Colville (now Sir
Charles), Major-general Brisbane, Major-general Power, and
Lieutenant-colonel Stovin, were the chief officers in promot-
ing this testimony of the high esteem in which Sir Thomas
Picton was held by his division. For the following letters
relating to the presentation of this gift we are indebted to
Sir Charles Colville :—

" Valley of Bastan, in Spain, Aug. 27, 1813.
" DEAR SIR,
     " It has long been the wish of the officers of the three
brigades which we have had the honour to command under
you in the third division, as also of the divisional staff, to have
an opportunity of offering you an ostensible mark of that high
respect, gratitude, and esteem, which we so sincerely feel in
our hearts.   Every objection seems now removed in point of
time, and otherwise, when, on the recurrence of severe illness,
which has in four successive seasons assailed you, you at
present only await sufficient degree of convalescence to admit of your trying change of climate, with but too little prospect, we lament to think, of your returning to your command
in this country.   Services such as yours cannot but have
been acknowledged before this, by the offering of one or
more swords from your attached military brethren, or a grateful corps; we, therefore, for ourselves, and those who desire us to represent them, request you will do us the honour to accept of a piece of plate, with a short inscription
commemorative of the circumstance, and of the corps which
composed the third division under your command in the Pen-

upon his return home. But he was there doomed to suffer further disappointments, which, if they did not call forth any warmth of expression, caused him to feel deeply how

insula. With most sincere wishes for your early convalescence, followed by confirmed good health, on leaving a climate that has proved so unfriendly to you, we have the honour to subscribe ourselves,

"Dear sir,

"Your ever faithful servants,

(Signed) "C. COLVILLE,

"T. BRISBANE, Major-general.

"M. POWER, Major-general.

"For the Staff of the Division,

"H. STOVIN, A. A. General.

"To Lieut.-gen. SIR THOMAS PICTON, K.B.

"Commanding the Third Division of the British Army."

"London, 18th Sept. 1813.

"MY DEAR GENERAL,

"I lose no time, after my arrival in England, to return an answer to the letter which you were so good as to forward me from the general officers commanding brigades in the third division, and which you will have the goodness to communicate to them. I am very sensible of the kindness of their intention, and feel much flattered by so handsome an expression of their sentiments.

"I was fortunate in finding the President frigate ready on my arrival at Passages; and my friend Lieut.-colonel Hood of the Guards immediately called upon me, and introduced me to Captain Mason, his brother-in-law. We sailed on the 9th, and arrived at Portsmouth on the 16th. My health improved but very slowly during the voyage, and I have not little dependence could be placed on merit and long services to obtain their reward, when opposed to the more powerful claims of courtly favour and ministerial influence.

It will readily be believed, that those who had distinguished themselves in this glorious campaign were hailed upon their return to England with enthusiastic admiration. Amongst these Picton stood in a proud position. All

yet been able to shake off the remains of the disorder which continues to incommode me. My nights are still restless. I can give you no news, not having yet seen any one.

"My best wishes attend you.

"My dear general,

"Most faithfully,

(Signed)   "Thos. Picton.

"The Honourable Major-general Colville."

"London, 18th Sept. 1813.

"My dear Generals,

"In the extreme weak state to which I was reduced, previous to my leaving the Peninsula, my feelings were too powerful for my spirits, and it was not possible for me adequately to answer the kind letter of the general officers commanding brigades in the third division, which you did me the honour of forwarding to me from the Valley of Bastan on the 27th of August last.

"I cannot but highly value the testimony of gentlemen to whose talents, zealous co-operation, and gallantry, on every occasion of difficulty, I feel myself indebted for the honours that have been conferred upon me, and for the degree of re-was now rejoicing: and many who read these pages well remember the feelings of admiration with which the millions who attended the numerous spectacles in commemoration of the peace gazed upon those who had fought with Wellington throughout the Peninsula. The often-tried Picton, the gallant leader of the " fighting division," was deservedly amongst the most popular of these.

putation to which I have risen in the service; and I shall receive any memento of their esteem and regard with corresponding sentiments and feelings of the heart. ·

" The period of my life to which I shall always recur with the greatest satisfaction, is that which was passed at the head of the third division, where I always experienced such a spirit of unanimity and heroism as never once failed to secure success in any one of the difficult enterprises we were employed upon. Though I may never again have the honour of commanding so distinguished a corps, I shall ever feel myself identified with the third division in all its operations, and shall take as strong an interest in its success as I ever did whilst I had the honour of presiding at its head.

" Accept of my many acknowledgments for your kind attention, and of my sincere and constant wishes for your success and prosperity on all occasions.

" Your devoted and very faithful humble servant,

" Thos. Picton, Lieutenant-general.

" The Hon. Major-general Colville.

" Major-general Brisbane.

" Major-general Power.

" Lieutenant-colonel Stovin, &c."

Within a short period after Sir Thomas
Picton's arrival in England, a Gazette was
published, containing the names of the following distinguished officers who were elevated to
the peerage:—Sir William Beresford (Viscount
Beresford), Sir Thomas Graham (Lord Lyne-
doch), Sir Rowland Hill (Lord Hill), Sir John
Hope (Hopetoun and Niddry), Sir Stapleton
Cotton (Viscount Combermere).

The friends of Sir Thomas Picton were naturally disappointed, as they unhesitatingly asserted that the claims of General Picton were
equally strong with more than one of those
who had been thus rewarded. Can it then be
a matter of surprise that Sir Thomas Picton,
who was greedy of honour, and who was fond
of the remark, and often used it, that "he never
envied anybody excepting when they did something great," should now experience a feeling
of silent reproach and degradation, when he
saw his services thus passed over, and a decided
and publicly marked preference shown to those
officers with whom he thought he had at least
equal claims? The people of England were
more familiar with his name than with some
of those who were thus exalted; but Sir Tho-

mas Picton could not deign to ask, and there were none to speak for him. His own spirited remark, when a friend asked him why his name was omitted amongst the new creation of peers, is characteristic of the man: "If the coronet were lying on the crown of a breach, I should have as good a chance as any of them," was his reply; and the world will *now* admit that there was no vanity in the assertion.

It appears that his Majesty's Ministers found it necessary to give some reason for this unaccountable omission, and *that* a more satisfactory one than the comparative merits of the parties. The following letter, however, which appeared in one of the daily papers at the time, will demonstrate the nature and justice of this ministerial vindication.

" SIR,

" You will confer a great personal obligation upon myself, as well as be the medium, I hope, of satisfying the curiosity of thousands, by inserting in your paper the following quære, which will probably be answered by those who alone are competent to solve it:

" What is the reason that Lieutenant-general Sir Thomas Picton has not been created a peer of parliament, as well as those distinguished officers whose names have appeared in the Gazette?

"I have, sir, a very extensive acquaintance in London, and am continually stopped by one person or another with the inquiry, 'Pray, colonel, can you tell me the reason why General Picton has been left out of the batch of peers?' As I do not *pretend* to know that of which I am really ignorant, I reply to my friends universally in the negative; and I content myself with asking them, what is the current solution of the problem? I am told, and indeed it is the only attempt at an answer which I have heard, that the reason is,—because the honours were thought to be due to those officers only who had the good fortune to have had, at some time or another of the Peninsular war, what they call *distinct commands;* by which, I presume, they mean, *commanding corps* at a certain *distance* from the chief, although not *moving* without his orders.

"Give me leave here to assure you most sincerely, that in requesting you to offer this enigma to the public, and in presuming to give my reasons for not thinking the general reason so assigned a sufficient one, it is by no means my intention to throw any stigma upon the conduct of the Prince Regent's ministers for the advice which they have thought proper to give his Royal Highness on the occasion; still less is it my wish to sow the seeds of discontent amongst that class of officers who may, perhaps, conceive themselves equally entitled to this distinguished honour : quite the contrary. I do believe that the noble person who is supposed more particularly to direct those counsels is not only an honourable and disinterested man, but I have good reasons to think that he entertains a very high opinion of the abilities of Sir Thomas Picton.

"It is, therefore, with a view as much to relieve *them* from the imputations to which they are subject, that I solicit your publication of this letter. Now, sir, as to the particular reason before assigned for the exception of Sir Thomas Picton, I cannot bring myself to admit its validity ; for, to hold good, the reason must be general, as well as apply fully and completely to all the officers mentioned in the Gazette. This cannot be disputed. But is this the fact? Let us examine:— There are Sir William Beresford, Sir Thomas Graham, Sir Rowland Hill, Sir John Hope, and Sir Stapleton Cotton. We shall take it for granted that the first three may be brought within *my* exposition of the words 'having had distinct commands.' Then come Sir John Hope and Sir Stapleton Cotton. The first was, on Sir Thomas Graham's leaving the army in the Peninsula, considered nominally, or *titularly*, as some classes would call it, second in command. He has been but a few months with the army; was left a few weeks at Bayonne to superintend the siege, and taken prisoner there.

"Sir Stapleton Cotton has commanded the cavalry: this is the sum of his good fortune. Now, sir, I beg to know, even in the strictest military definition that can possibly be given of this latter situation, whether it can *fairly* be considered to come under that class behind which, as it is said, his Majesty's Ministers entrench themselves, in the strict limitation of the rule they appear to have prescribed to themselves. I contend not: I assert that it is no more than the mere command of a division of the army; that it is straining too hard for a distinction, to endeavour to support it by calling it a '*distinct command;*' and that, where the honour and feelings of an officer of such high rank, of such distinguished and acknowledged abilities, and of such a length of brilliant services, are intimately concerned, it is in my humble opinion an unlucky endeavour to find out *words* instead of reasons for the exception of Sir Thomas Picton.

" I shall say nothing as to the rank, fortune, or relative merits of those officers : they are all men of ancient families, good fortunes, and unquestionable characters. But, in the view which I take of the question, those points are quite immaterial. The question is, Is the reason assigned for Sir Thomas Picton's exception a good one? Does it admit of his feelings being at once reconciled to it? With a reason that does so, I shall be perfectly contented ; and so I believe will be the whole army. But if it does not, or that he has not *refused* the proffered honour, then I assert without fear of contradiction, that by thus excepting him, a positive injustice and insult have been offered to him.   I am, sir,

" An Old Subscriber."

As a solace for the disappointment which he had experienced in not meeting with that reward which his countrymen agreed he had earned, he was again called upon by the Commons of England to receive from them their thanks; this being the *seventh* time upon which he had been thus complimented by this honourable assembly. On the 24th of June, the Speaker rose, and addressed Sir Thomas Picton thus:

" Lieutenant-general Sir Thomas Picton, you stand amongst us this day to receive our thanks for great and signal victories won by British arms in the fields of France.

" Descending from the Pyrenees, surmounting in adverse seasons all the difficulties of a country deeply intersected, and passing with unparalleled skill and boldness the formidable torrents of Navarre, after a series of arduous and sanguinary conflicts you came up with the collected forces of the enemy, posted upon the heights of Orthes. Attacked on all sides by British valour, the troops of France at length gave way, and commenced their retreat. Pressed, however, upon each flank, that retreat was soon changed into a flight, and that flight to a total rout. Pursuing their broken legions across the Adour, and seizing upon their strongholds and accumulated resources, you then laid open your way on the one hand to the deliverance of Bordeaux, and on the other to the lamented but glorious day of Toulouse.

" It has been your fortune to reap the latest laurels in this long and memorable war ; and leading forward your victorious columns from the Tagus to the Garonne, you have witnessed, with arms in your hands, the downfall of that gigantic tyranny which your own prowess has so materially contributed to overthrow.

" Informed of these triumphant exploits, this House lost no time in recording its thanks to all who had bravely fought the battles of their country : but to those whom we glory to reckon amongst our own members, it is my duty and happiness to deliver those thanks personally,— and I do now accordingly, in the name and by the command of the Commons of this United Kingdom, deliver to you their unanimous thanks for your able and distinguished con- duct throughout all those operations, which concluded with the entire defeat of the enemy at Orthes, and the occupation of Bordeaux by the allied forces of Great Britain, Spain, and Portugal."

The gallant Picton was only able upon this as upon a former occasion to express, in brief and simple terms, how deep were his feelings, and how totally unable he was to give them utterance.

CHAPTER XIV.

Sir Thomas Picton retires into private life.—Elevated to the rank of Knight Grand Cross of the Bath. —His inde_pendence as a Member of Parliament. —Recalled from his retirement by the return of Napoleon. — His conse_quent correspondence with the Duke of Wellington.— His last letter from home. — Presentiment of his death. —Anecdotes relative thereto.—His arrival at Brussels, and reception by the Duke of Wellington and the Army.— March of the troops to the field. —Enumeration of the forces under the command of Picton. —His advance to Quatre Bras. — Defeat of the French. —Anecdotes of the battle and of Picton.—Morning of the decisive battle of Waterloo.

SIR THOMAS PICTON now resolved to retire to his seat in Wales, and pass the remainder of his days in the quietude of a country life. At this period, indeed, he expressed to several friends his determination to give up active service; in fact, to retire from the army: and with this intention he left London.

The circle of acquaintance of Sir Thomas Picton was now greatly extended; the whole principality of Wales was proud of him and loud in his praise. He was contented, however, with the intimacy of a few choice friends, and with them he looked forward to enjoy the decline of life. Foreign as this wish may appear to his nature, and contrary to his professed inclinations, he nevertheless had firmly resolved to serve no longer in a public capacity. He had perhaps discovered that his unbending disposition would not advance him in his professional interests ; and as he was by far too independent in spirit to endeavour to suit the manners of the age, he determined to leave for others that path which he could only follow with advantage by the sacrifice of his feelings.

Upon the extension of the Order of the Bath at the commencement of the year 1815, he was elevated to the rank of Knight Grand Cross, being the highest class of that distinguished order ; and this was the last and utmost honour which was conferred upon himself or his family.

His time was now principally occupied in attending to his estate, and devising plans for the improvement of the surrounding country ; for the activity of his mind would not allow of his remaining long at rest. His health had been greatly impaired during the constant and arduous services in which he had been engaged for so many years, and in such a variety of climates. This did not, however, prevent him from being regular in the performance of his parliamentary duties, his conduct in which gave the most perfect satisfaction to his constituents. He did not pledge himself to any party, but, regardless of the favour of either, gave his vote for or against any measure, as he considered it likely or not to benefit his country; and with this feeling he was justly considered as one of the few really constitutional members of that period. He was not long, however, to enjoy the repose of private life, or the honours of a representative for his country.

Napoleon was once more in the field. After breaking his parole, and every engagement into which he had entered when he abdicated the throne of France, he now again returned, breathing threats of vengeance against those who had deserted, and those who had subdued him. The excitement produced by this unexpected event is still well remembered. No time was lost by the allied powers in making efforts to secure the peace of Europe; and it was soon apparent that a decisive blow would ere long be struck; for Napoleon was quickly at the head of a formidable army, ready to march against the first power that should take the field. England offered her millions to set the machine in motion, while every regiment which she could send forth was ordered to repair without delay to the Netherlands; at the same time that those officers who had distinguished themselves during the recent war were summoned from their retreats, again to meet the common enemy.

The note of warlike preparation was now sounding in all directions. Instead of the peace which the people of England had been so long anticipating, hostilities were about to be commenced with renewed activity. Sir Thomas Picton expected that he should be again called upon to take the field, and he was not long kept in suspense. An application was forwarded from the War Office, requiring him to join the army in the Netherlands under the Duke of Wellington's command. But the general hesitated: he had not exhausted his patriotism or his love for a military life; but during his command of the third division he had, upon more than one occasion, been exposed to a variety of petty annoyances from officers having intermediate commands between the commander of the forces and himself, and he now wrote to the Duke of Wellington, declaring his readiness to serve under his grace's command, but not under any other general officer; when, upon an assurance that he would be exclusively employed under the duke, he expressed his intention immediately to join the assembling forces.

This in some degree accounts for the delay which took place before Sir Thomas Picton repaired to the Netherlands; for it is not likely that the commander-in-chief would have neglected to call upon Sir Thomas Picton, or that his assistance would have been thought lightly of at such a period, when the whole moral and physical strength of the country was demanded to re-establish the peace of Europe. It has, however, been implied, in no friendly terms, that Sir Thomas Picton did not join the army at an earlier period, in consequence of the Duke of Wellington not having called upon him for his services. His enemies did not hesitate to

give publicity to the insinuation that the Duke
of Wellington thought so lightly of his abilities, that he doubted whether he should call
upon him to join at all. It is only necessary
to remark, that this was not the fact.

Having come to the determination of again
entering upon active service, Sir Thomas sent
the following letter to his aid-de-camp, Captain
Tyler, which possesses a melancholy interest,
as being the last he wrote from home.

" Iscoed, 26th May 1815.

" My dear Tyler,

" You must get ready as soon as you can ;
and you will be so good as to communicate to
Captains Chambers and Price that I have received orders for Flanders.

" Look out for some active horses, not above
fifteen hands ; but do not purchase without
the opinion of Mr. Price, who I dare say will
give you all the assistance in his power.   I
shall bring up the old horse and the mare, and
there is one in London.   Three others will be
about my mark.   I shall be in town during the
course of the next week.

"Yours faithfully,

" Th. Picton."

" Carmarthen, 26th May 1815."

Sir Thomas Picton forthwith made every preparation for the approaching campaign. He had a presentiment that it would be his last; and he did not hesitate in expressing to his friends the force of this impression. The calmness of his manner when he alluded to the subject made them at first hope that this anticipation might be the result of impaired health; but when it was known that he expressed this conviction in the most serious manner to the different branches of his family, and that he was arranging his affairs with all the exactness and attention of a man who knows that he has but a short time to live, the fact then became apparent. He never, however, betrayed for one moment the slightest dread of the fate which he believed to await him; and the following incident will illustrate the composure with which he anticipated death. He was walking during a fine evening, a few days before his departure, with Sir John and Lady ——, when they came to a churchyard, in which a grave was dug for the reception of some humble individual. The party was induced to ascend the newly thrown-up earth and look down. Sir Thomas Picton, after commenting upon the neatness with which it had been dug, observed, " Why, I think this would do for me ;" at the same time jumping in and laying himself at full length along the bottom, he observed that it was an exact fit. On scrambling out, he was surprised to find Lady —— much affected, as she declared this incident was ominous of his fate. Picton only smiled, and tried to persuade her out of such melancholy reflections.

After having made every preparation, he left Wales and repaired to London, where he made a short stay among his numerous friends. Twice he expressed the conviction which had taken such strong hold of his mind that he should die. In the one instance he observed to an intimate friend, " When you hear of my death, you will hear of a bloody day :" prophetic words which were but too faithfully verified. The second instance was when bidding adieu to the Honourable Colonel Pakenham, who was at the time prevented from joining the army by a severe wound. " God bless you !" said the general as he shook him warmly by the hand ; " if we never meet again, you will at all events *hear* of me." He had, in fact, determined to win all the honours that the most daring courage could obtain, or to fall in the attempt; and this determination he frequently expressed: he resolved not to leave an excuse for any neglect either to his name or to his memory.

Mr. Wynne, during a debate in the House of Commons, when reverting to this period of Sir Thomas Picton's career, observed, " He had heard that nearly the last words which the gallant Picton uttered before he left this country, were to express a hope, in the presence of two members of that House, that if he should fall, which he seemed to anticipate, he might not be forgotten, but receive the same distinctions that had been conferred upon other officers who had died in the service of their country." It will be seen that he never for one moment shrunk from the resolution which he had formed; but that, wherever danger was greatest, there he was foremost, until he found that heroic death which he neither sought nor shunned. His was not the daring of rashness or despair; if he exposed himself, it was not from any weariness or discontent of life; the lingering impression that death was in his path could not turn his steps or make him seek to avoid it.

On the 11th of June he left London, with his aid-de-camp, Captain Tyler; and on that day dined at the Fountain Tavern, in Canterbury. This dinner was given to Sir Thomas Picton as a mark of respect and admiration by some of the inhabitants of the place; upon which occasion the general was as cheerful and his manner as unconcerned as in the happiest moments of his life. From Dover on the following day he embarked for Ostend, where he arrived early the next morning, the 13th. Here he held a levee to receive the numerous officers who were desirous of paying their respects to their own general.

At Ostend at this period all was activity and confusion; troops and horses were landing day and night, while the whole *matériel* of war was rolling on to one point—Brussels. Sir Thomas Picton lost no time in pursuing the same route; and so soon as his horses and baggage were landed, he hastened forward, and arrived in that city on the evening of the 15th. The Duke of Wellington greeted his old companion in arms with a friendly warmth; and there can be no doubt but that his grace gained additional confidence as he beheld himself surrounded by so many of those distinguished soldiers who had been with him in his former hard-fought fields. Picton had never known defeat ; and there was not a soldier in this hastily-collected army, many of whom were raw recruits, who was not anxious to serve under his command : for at such a moment as this, when all appears confusion, and the minds of men are excited beyond their usual tension, they turn to those who have been in many such scenes before, with a peculiar confidence. It will readily therefore be believed that Picton was greeted with shouts of congratulation as he appeared among the young and admiring soldiers : their veteran comrades, many of whom had seen him in the midst of death, as calm as now, took delight in repeating to them the events of past days, when Picton led and they conquered.

The Duke of Wellington had just received information from Marshal Blucher, that the French army was in motion, and had com-

menced an attack upon the Prussians.   This
unexpected announcement quickly changed
the scene of merriment which was going on
in Brussels.   Orders were issued for the troops
to make every preparation to advance at a
moment's notice; while the Duke of Wellington, surrounded by his generals, waited with
some anxiety for further information.   An
officer who was present upon this occasion
observes:

"It was past midnight, and profound repose
seemed to reign over Brussels, when suddenly
the drums beat to arms, and the trumpet's loud
call was heard from every part of the city.
It is impossible to describe the effect of these
sounds, heard in the silence of the night.   We
were not long left in doubt of the truth; a
second courier had arrived from Blucher.   The
attack had become serious; the enemy were
in considerable force; they had taken Charle-
roi, and had gained some advantage over the
Prussians, and our troops were ordered to
march immediately to their support.   Instantly
every place resounded with martial preparations.   There was not a house in which military were not quartered, and consequently

the whole town was one universal scene of bustle. The soldiers were seen assembling from all parts in the Place Royale, with their knapsacks on their backs; some taking leave of wives and children; others sitting down unconcernedly on the sharp pavement, waiting for their comrades; others sleeping upon packs of straw, surrounded by all the din of war; while bât-horses and baggage-waggons were loading, artillery and commissariat trains harnessing, officers riding in all directions, carts clattering, chargers neighing, bugles sounding, drums beating, and colours flying."

It is unnecessary to recapitulate all the details of the following days. Every incident connected with the battle of Waterloo is fresh in the memory of our countrymen: every village and tree upon this sanguinary field has obtained immortality.

Sir Thomas Picton, immediately on his arrival, was appointed to the command of the reserve, consisting of above ten thousand men. It is, however, to be understood that his particular command was the fifth division, consisting of the following force:—

BRIGADES.	REGIMENTS.	FORCE.
8th brigade, Major-general Sir James Kempt.	28th foot	530
	32nd ditto	649
	79th ditto, 1st battalion .	675
	95th ditto, ditto . . .	542
9th brigade, Major-general Sir D. Pack.	1st ditto, 3rd ditto . .	592
	42nd ditto, 1st ditto . .	557
	44th ditto, 2nd ditto . .	424
	92nd ditto	586
Hanoverian 5th brigade, Colonel Vincke.	M. B. Hameln . . .	585
	—— Hildesheim . . .	575
	—— Peina	550
	—— Giffhorn . . .	550
	Total . .	6,815

The remainder of the reserve being composed of the sixth division, consisting of the

10th brigade, Major-general Lambers . . .	2,401
Hanoverian 4th brigade, Colonel Best . . .	2,345
7th Brigade, Major-general Mackenzie . .	2,500
8th brigade	

The Duke of Wellington being now confident in the opinion which he had formed of Napoleon's intended point of attack, arranged his plans so as to co-operate with the movements of Blucher at Ligny. It may not be superfluous to state that the enemy's grand object at this period was, either to defeat the army of Wellington or that of Blucher before the one could receive any support from the other; or, failing in that object, to gain such a position between the two armies, that their communication should be cut off, and their junction rendered impossible. This was the basis of Napoleon's plans, and it was for the Duke of Wellington and Marshal Blucher to defeat them.

The Duke of Wellington was convinced that the French would renew their attack on Blucher's position on the following day, the 16th. It would appear that he fully expected that the Prussians would be enabled to keep their ground; but, to guard against the accidents of war, the army of the Netherlands, consisting of between five and six thousand men, was ordered to march to Quatre Bras, while several other corps of the army were to move in the same direction.

The fifth division was, however, to advance with the utmost expedition to support the army of the Netherlands, in case the French should attack the position at Quatre Bras. Upon receiving these orders, Sir Thomas Picton hastened forward his troops; and before morning they were all marching, full of confi-

dence and courage, towards the scene of expected hostilities. Sir Thomas himself left
Brussels just after daylight, accompanying the
Duke of Wellington and his numerous staff.
Picton was at this period in more than usually
good spirits; and, as he passed through the city,
seeing many of his old companions in arms, he
accosted them in the most familiar and encouraging manner.

As had been anticipated, the French made
an attack upon the troops of the Netherlands
at Quatre Bras, first by skirmishing, in which
the Belgians behaved with some degree of courage. This commenced as early as five o'clock
in the morning, and was continued without
any more important movement or any decided
success until the middle of the day: then the
enemy, having sent fresh troops to support their
advance, succeeded in forcing the Belgians to
give way. But at this moment the British
colours were seen waving in the distance, and
the scarlet jackets hastening through the standing corn.

Sir Thomas Picton, as he approached the
field with his division, had heard the continued
and increasing fire kept up by the skirmishers,

which made him push forward to the support
of the Belgians, and by this means he succeeded 'in reaching Quatre Bras before any other
British force. Nearly at the same time, however, the first division of Brunswickers, led
by the gallant duke, arrived to share with
Picton and his soldiers the honour of arresting the progress of the French in this first
stage to Waterloo.

The Prince of Orange was anxiously looking for the arrival of some of his allies, when
he was gladdened by the spectacle of this reinforcement pouring forward with steady but
quick steps to relieve his almost exhausted
troops. Before half-past two in the afternoon,
fourteen thousand men were in the field. These
consisted of Picton's division, six thousand
eight hundred and fifteen; first division of
Brunswick Oels, five thousand; one regiment
of Brunswick cavalry, containing about nine
hundred; and the Second Belgian Hussars,
amounting to one thousand two hundred men.

The force which the enemy had now concentrated to attack this position amounted to
forty thousand men, under the intrepid Ney:
the odds were therefore fearful; but the firm-

ness of the allies was not shaken by the reported strength of their opponents. As the different regiments arrived on the ground, they instantly took up the posts to which they were directed by their respective commanders.

Immediately the enemy perceived that this additional force had taken the field, Ney moved down with two columns of infantry and a cloud of cavalry to the attack. The English and Brunswickers had but just taken up their ground, when they were exposed to a furious and galling fire from the immense park of artillery attached to this wing of the French army. The receding smoke showed the advancing columns rushing on to break the line of the allies: the brunt of this movement fell upon Picton's soldiers, and " Sir Thomas Picton's ' superb division' was singly engaged with the enemy for nearly two hours. Every man fought with a desperation which no language can describe." Picton was himself amongst his soldiers, calling upon them to stand firm and receive the enemy with a steady front. A murderous conflict now commenced; a rolling discharge of musketry from Picton's line was answered with deadly rapidity and closeness by that of the

French: the havoc was terrible; but Picton was in the midst, watching the progress of the fight; wherever death was thickest, there could he be seen encouraging—exhorting the soldiers to be firm.

After the French infantry had been repulsed, and before the heavy smoke had cleared off, the cavalry came thundering on. The English were instantly formed into squares to receive them. Upon the steadiness and celerity with which this was executed the safety of the men depended: then it was that Picton's calmness and penetration were conspicuous in watching and directing each movement; before the French cavalry was upon them, the squares were closed up.

" Another furious onset was then made by the Lancers, which obliged General Kempt to take refuge in the square; but they again repulsed their assailants; and at that moment Sir Thomas Picton riding up, ordered them to advance, for the enemy were giving way. Picton led them to the charge himself, and they drove the French from their position with great loss." *

* Mudford.

In reference to this movement, and the enemy's cavalry having surrounded the British squares; Captain Kincaid also makes the following remarks:* " This was a crisis in which, according to Bonaparte's theory, the victory was theirs by all the rules of war, for they had superior numbers both before and behind us: but the gallant old Picton, who had been trained in a different school, did not choose to confine himself to rules in these matters. Despising the force in his rear, he advanced, charged, and routed those in his front; which created such a panic amongst the others, that they galloped back through the intervals in his division, with no other object in view than their own safety."

But the progress and result of this sanguinary preface to the battle of Waterloo are too well known to require repetition here. Towards evening fresh troops arrived at Quatre Bras; and the struggle was continued until dark with unabated fury. The many heroic feats that were performed upon this memorable day are all recorded; and never was the courage of our army more called for, and never was it more

* Adventures of the Rifle Brigade.

brilliantly displayed, than in resisting the overwhelming numbers of the enemy. The vital
importance of this point, by which the line of
communication with Blucher and his army was
maintained, rendered success of the utmost importance; and perhaps the Duke of Wellington could not have evinced more satisfactorily
the high esteem in which he held the military
judgment and skill of Sir Thomas Picton, than
by appointing him to command the British
forces at Quatre Bras; and all who saw him
upon that occasion concur in stating that his
confidence was well placed. For awhile he
was in chief command of the troops engaged
in this battle; for the Duke of Wellington,
after having ordered the dispositions to receive
the attack, rode across the country to Bry, to
arrange with Blucher the subsequent movements of the allied armies.

Marshal Ney, finding that he could not succeed in forcing this position, at night desisted
from the attack, and left the allies in quiet possession of the field which they had so nobly
but dearly won; and the living slept amidst
five thousand of their dead and dying comrades. The loss of the French was supposed

to have been much greater; but the policy of Napoleon would not allow of any returns being made,—in fact, he boasted that he had gained a victory,—that the vanquished English were flying before his victorious soldiers.

While this battle was being fought by Ney at Quatre Bras, Napoleon himself was with the remainder of his army attacking the Prussians in the neighbourhood of Ligny, Bry, and Sombrel. Blucher and his soldiers fought long and bravely; a mortal and personal enmity appeared to exist between the two armies, for they slaughtered each other without mercy, neither asking nor giving quarter. The fight was continued with this sanguinary feeling from three in the afternoon until the approach of night, when the French succeeded in forcing the Prussian army to abandon the field.

" The bulletins of the Emperor announced two victories of the most dazzling description as the work of the 16th. Blucher would be heard of no more, they said; and Wellington, confounded and amazed, was already within the jaws of ruin." *

If anything could have removed the fatal

* Life of Napoleon.

presentiment of his approaching death, which still existed in the mind of Sir Thomas Picton, it would have been his remarkable escape through the perils of the 16th. He observed to his aid-de-camp, Captain Tyler, that he never had had so hard a day's fighting; and added, " I shall begin to think that I cannot be killed after this."

The night of the 16th was cold and wet; but the exhausted troops slept soundly on the field of Quatre Bras. Towards daylight they were however aroused by some skirmishing between the outposts, and it was supposed that the enemy were about to renew the attack. The allies were soon under arms; but no enemy was visible, and they in consequence proceeded to pay those attentions to the wounded which the darkness had prevented them from doing during the night.

A great change was now made in the Duke of Wellington's plans. The defeat of the Prussians compelled him to fall back, in order to keep up his communication with Marshal Blucher; who had instantly, after the reverse which his troops had experienced, despatched a courier to make the duke acquainted with his future movements. The English general had brought up nearly the whole of his force to Quatre Bras; but, upon receiving intimation of the defeat which the Prussians had sustained, a retrograde movement was ordered, and at ten o'clock on the morning of the 17th the allied forces were falling back upon the field of Waterloo.

Sir Thomas Picton was much inconvenienced during this day for want of a horse: that which had carried him on the 16th was injured; and as his staff servants, who were fresh from England, could not be found during the night, he was under the necessity of taking a trooper's horse; and we are assured that the general was riding about on the 17th upon a horse without a saddle; while Captain Tyler, who was constantly with him during the whole of this day, was mounted on a pony with a halter. Towards night, however, the servants came back; when the account which they gave of themselves caused the general and his staff no little amusement. Picton commenced reprimanding them in rather severe terms for presuming to leave the field; but one of the men, who undertook to be spokesman on the

occasion, explained their absence by saying,
" About the middle of the battle of the day
previous, 'the shot had flown about them so
thick, although a good way in the rear, that
they all agreed it was better to go farther off,
for fear some of the *horses'* should be hurt."
This quite disarmed the general of his anger,
and he laughed heartily at the simplicity of
this careful guardian of his property.

Before night the whole of the allied army
was formed in position on the plains of Waterloo. The soldiers were ordered to sleep upon
their arms; for it was known that Napoleon
was now concentrating the whole of his force
against this point, and a great battle was fully
expected to take place on the morrow.

But, as before observed, it is not our object
to recapitulate the details of this eventful day;
although in order to follow the subject of this
memoir to the termination of his glorious career
it will be necessary to relate some few particulars immediately connected with that event.

The tempestuous night of the 17th was passed by both armies on the field, which were exposed to all its inclemency. Sir Thomas Picton sought a few hours' repose in a small cot-

tage in the village of Waterloo; and, for some time after the battle, his name was written in chalk upon the door :—there he slept last !

The morning was wet; but between nine and ten the weather became clear. Picton was on the field at daylight, watching the movements of the enemy, and making every preparation' for the approaching conflict. He was con- stantly being recognised by some of his old soldiers, and many a hearty cheer welcomed him upon this last morning of his earthly ca- reer. He fully anticipated the stern nature of the battle which was about to ensue; and doubt- less then felt that silent conviction on his mind which he had so often expressed, and which was so fatally realized within a few hours.

At half-past eleven the battle began on the right by an attack on the Chateau of Hougou- mont. The obstinate defence of this building, together with the surrounding wood, is well known : this was, in fact, the key of the Bri- tish position, and its loss would consequently have exposed the whole line of the allies.

Picton, with his " superb division," as it was justly called from being composed of some of the finest regiments in the army, was posted on the road to Wavre, behind a straggling hedge, which extended from the farm of La Haye Sainte to Ter la Haye. This hedge is called straggling, because it was broken, and in some parts nearly levelled with the ground; and the troops were in consequence exposed to the attacks of cavalry, and not even protected from the enemy's artillery.

But Napoleon, finding so much difficulty in making any impression on the left of the allied position, now sent some heavy masses of infantry against the left of the centre, on the right of the road to Brussels. This force advanced, supported by about eighty pieces of artillery, which opened upon the British line. A brigade of Dutch formed Picton's centre; Sir James Kempt, with the Seventy-ninth, Twenty-eighth, and Thirty-second, on their right; and Sir Dennis Pack, with the Scotch brigade, consisting of the Ninety-second, Forty-second, Forty-fourth, and First, on their left; and again, on the left of these regiments, the Hanoverian brigade, under Brigade-colonel Vincke. As the enemy's formidable mass of infantry advanced against Picton's position, they were received with a most destructive fire from the British artillery, which was ranged along the whole front of his line : this swept down hundreds, but the columns still advanced. Some Belgian infantry were posted a short distance in front of the fifth division : Picton rather distrusted the steadiness of these troops : and about this period Captain Tyler, who was by his side when the French were coming up, observed, " I am sure, general, the Belgians will run." " Never mind," said he; " they shall have a taste of it, at all events." The truth of Captain Tyler's remark was, however, immediately evident; as the French no sooner came within musket range, than these troops fled with precipitation. And now came that contest in which Picton fell.

CHAPTER XV.

Battle of Waterloo. — Death of Sir Thomas Picton. — His concealment of a previous wound.—Announcement of his death in the House of Commons.—His body conveyed to England. — The Funeral. — National monument to the memory of Picton in St. Paul's Cathedral.—Pillar erected at Carmarthen to commemorate his services.

THE French columns were marching close up to the hedge; the English advanced to meet them, and the muzzles of their muskets almost touched. Picton ordered Sir James Kempt's brigade forward; they bounded over the hedge, and were received with a murderous volley. A frightful struggle then ensued; the English rushed with fury upon their opponents, not stopping to load, but trusting solely to the bayonet to do their deadly work. The French fire had, however, fearfully thinned this first line, and they were fighting at least six to one. Picton, therefore, ordered General Pack's brigade to advance. With the exhilarat-

ing cry of "Charge! Hurra! hurra!" he placed
himself at their head, and led them forward.
They returned his cheer as they followed him
with a cool determination, which, in the words
of the Spanish chief Alava, "appalled the
enemy."

The general kept at the head of their line,
stimulating them by his own example. According to the Duke of Wellington's despatch,
"This was one of the most serious attacks
made by the enemy on our position." To defeat it was therefore of vital importance to the
success of the day. Picton knew this, and
doubtless felt, that his own presence would
tend greatly to inspire his men with confidence. He was looking along his gallant line,
waving them on with his sword, when a ball
struck him on the temple, and he fell back
upon his horse—dead. Captain Tyler, seeing
him fall, immediately dismounted and ran to
his assistance: with the aid of a soldier he
lifted him off his horse; but all assistance was
vain—his noble spirit had fled.

The rush of war had passed on, the contending hosts had met, and none could be idle
at such a moment. Tyler, therefore, placed

.the body of his lamented friend and general beneath a tree, by which he could
readily find it when the fight was done;
and he rode forward to report to Sir James
Kempt the loss which the army had sustained. That general, as senior officer, immediately assumed the command of the division:
but "Picton's intrepid example had done its
work. Animated by their gallant chief, the
men fought with a degree of fury which
nothing could appal or resist: at one moment
formed into squares, they received and repulsed the dreadful assaults of the lancers and cuirassiers; at another deploying into lines, their
vigorous arm and undaunted courage drove
back the enemy's masses at the point of the
bayonet."*

How the British fought, and how they
conquered upon this day, is already fully recorded upon the pages of many a history.
As long as the name of Waterloo shall be
repeated with national exultation, so long will
Picton's death be remembered as one of the
noblest of the sacrifices by which that victory
was purchased.

* Mudford.

When the sanguinary struggle had ceased, and the victorious English were called back to the field of battle, leaving the Prussians to pursue the enemy, Captain Tyler went in search of the body of his old general, with feelings which even the events of the day and its surrounding horrors could scarcely moderate. He found it easily. Upon examination, the ball was discovered to have entered near the left temple and passed through the brain, which must have produced instant dissolution: after this, meeting with some resistance, it glanced downwards, and was found just under the skin near the articulation of the lower jaw.

Upon looking at the dress of Sir Thomas Picton in the evening of the 18th, a few hours after his fall, it was observed that his coat was torn on one side. This led to a further examination, and then the truth became apparent:—on the 16th he had been wounded at Quatre Bras; a musket-ball had struck him and broken two of his ribs, besides producing, it was supposed, some internal injuries: but, expecting that a severe battle would be fought within a short time, he kept this wound secret, lest he should be solicited to absent himself upon the occasion. Regardless of every selfish consideration, he only divulged this secret to an old servant, with whose assistance he bound up the wound; and then, with a command over his feelings almost incredible, he continued to perform his arduous duties. The night of the 16th and the whole of the following day he was in constant activity. By the morning of the 18th the wound had assumed a serious aspect; but the assurance that the French were about to attack the British position roused every energy of his almost exhausted frame; he subdued his bodily anguish; and when the moment came which called for his great example, the hand of death, which it is supposed was even then upon him from the wound alluded to, could not, while sufficient life yet remained, check for a moment his lofty courage.

The following brief recapitulation of Sir Thomas Picton's death was made by General Gascoyne in the House of Commons on the night of the 29th of June :—

" In the battle of Quatre Bras, previous to the great victory of the 18th, he had been dangerously wounded. From the moment he had left this country until he joined the army, he had never entered any bed—he had scarcely given himself time to take any refreshment, so eager was he in the performance of his duty. After the severe wound which he had received, he would have been justified in not engaging in the action of the 18th. His body was not only blackened by it, but even swelled to a considerable degree: those who had seen it wondered that he should have been able to take part in the duties of the field. He had afterwards fallen gloriously at the head of his division, maintaining a position which, if it had not been kept, would have altered the fate of the day, and its issue might have been different from that which now occasioned such well-founded rejoicings."

In so bad a state was the wound which Picton had received on the 16th, that it was supposed that, from having been neglected, from the great personal exertions which he had gone through, and the excitement necessarily attendant upon so great a victory, the result would have been fatal, even had he escaped entirely on the 18th.

Of Picton's four aides-de-camp, not one remained unhurt after this sanguinary battle: Captain Barrington Price was rode over by a charge of cuirassiers, and died a few months afterwards; Captain Algernon Langton was wounded on the 16th, and on the 18th Captain C. Chambers was killed; Captain Tyler was also slightly wounded.*

Picton's remains were conveyed to Brussels, where they were placed under a guard of honour until Tyler received further orders respecting their destination. This was indeed a duty which called for all the fortitude of his nature;

* This officer experienced the following most singular and providential escape upon this occasion :—Early in the morning of the 18th, Sir Thomas Picton, surrounded by his staff, was observing the movements of the French from a slight eminence near the position occupied by his division. This cavalcade of officers being observed by the enemy, they despatched a couple of guns in order to compel them to retire. After firing several rounds without any effect, or meeting with much attention, they at length succeeded in getting a better range. This was evinced by a shot striking Captain Tyler's horse directly on the hind-quarters, shattering the unfortunate animal in the most distressing manner. Before, however, he had quite fallen, two musket-balls struck him, the one in the head, and the other in the shoulder. But, strange as it may appear, this was nearly all the injury which these shot did; for Captain Tyler escaped with a slight wound in the knee, and some severe bruises by the fall of his horse.

Sir Thomas Picton had been to him more than an officer. During the last years of the Peninsular campaigns he had been constantly with him, his companion and friend: he had left England with him a few days before, full of life and energy—he now lay before him a corpse.

When it was known to the Duke of Wellington that the body of his old general was in Brussels, his grace directed that Tyler should convey it to England, where he expressed a wish that it might be received and interred with every honour due to his distinguished merit. Having received these instructions, Captain Tyler made every preparation for his melancholy journey. By slow steps he proceeded to Ostend, where the cavalcade embarked for England.

When arrived in the Downs, so soon as it was known that the ship which carried her flag half-mast high bore the body of Sir Thomas Picton, every vessel there assumed the same funereal form; and when the coffin was lowered into the boat to be conveyed ashore at Deal, the men-of-war fired minute-guns in honour of the dead. Upon reaching the land, a procession, formed of all the naval and

military in the place, was waiting to receive
the body and accompany it on the road to Canterbury; where, by a strange coincidence, the
remains of Sir Thomas Picton were placed in
the very same room at the Fountain Hotel
in which he had that day fortnight been entertained by his friends. — The funereal pall,
surrounded by the war-worn veterans who had
been selected for the guard of honour, seen
in the faint glimmer which found its way
through the closed shutters, — this was the
change which had come over the scene.

On the whole line of road, wherever it was
known that this mournful group was attending the body of a Waterloo hero, and that
that hero was Sir Thomas Picton, every means
were employed to express the high sense entertained of his merits. When the body reached
London, it was immediately conveyed to a
house which he had long occupied, No. 21,
Edward-street, Portman-square; all the members of his family who could possibly attend
being in town to receive it.

It was moved by General Gascoyne in the
House of Commons, that the ashes of Sir
Thomas Picton should be deposited in St.

Paul's Cathedral; but the subject was allowed to drop.   It was at length determined
that the body should be interred in the family
vault, in the burial-ground of St. George's·
Hanover-square;* and so soon as this was
made public, a great number of noblemen, officers, and gentlemen, sent to announce their
intention to follow the body to the grave.

The funeral took place on the 3rd of July,
and the body was followed by a vast concourse
of people, the most profound silence reigning
among the assembled multitude as the remains
were lowered into the tomb.

It now merely remains to observe, that his
country, grateful for his services, resolved to
raise a tablet to his memory, which should
hand to posterity the estimation in which he
was held.

On the 29th of June 1815, Lord Castlereagh
moved in the House of Commons, " That an
humble address be presented to his Royal
Highness the Prince Regent, that he will be
graciously pleased to give directions that a
national monument be erected in honour of

---

* The burial-ground of this parish is situated in the Bays-
water-road, a short distance from the end of Oxford-street.

the splendid victory of Waterloo, and to commemorate the fame of the officers and men of
the British army who fell gloriously upon the
16th and 18th of the present month, and more
particularly of Lieutenant-general Sir Thomas
Picton and Major-general the Honourable Sir
William Ponsonby."

Mr. Wynne upon this remarked, that he
" was anxious that distinct monuments should
be erected to those two general officers who
were mentioned in the motion; especially when
it was recollected what their services were,
and in how many hard-fought battles they
had participated."

Lord Castlereagh warmly seconded the sug-
gestion of the honourable member, observing,
"that the House might readily accede to it,
as they had only one object in view, — that of
distinguishing the eminent services of those
lamented officers. He would, therefore, subjoin, as an amendment to the original motion,
'And that funeral monuments be also erected
in memory of each of those two officers in the
Cathedral Church of St. Paul, London.'"

A monument was, in consequence, erected
in the north-west transept of that cathedral,

having a bust of Picton on the summit of a
marble column, with an emblematic group,
consisting of Fame, Genius, and Courage ; the
base bearing the following inscription :

Erected at the public expense,
To LIEUTENANT-GENERAL SIR THOMAS PICTON, K.G.C.B.
Who, after distinguishing himself in the victories of
Busacos, Fuentes de Onoro, Ciudad Rodrigo, Badajoz,
Vittoria, the Pyrenees, Orthes, and Toulouse,
Terminated his long and glorious military services
In the ever-memorable battle of Waterloo,
To the splendid success of which
His GENIUS and VALOUR eminently contributed,
On the XVIII. of June M.DCCC.XV.

But a still more costly edifice was some years
afterwards erected at Carmarthen in commemoration of the brilliant services of this distinguished soldier.   A subscription for this purpose was set on foot, and in a short time
a sufficient sum was collected to construct a
monument worthy of the name of Picton ; and
amongst the earliest subscribers to this national
undertaking was his Majesty King George IV.
who directed the following gratifying communication to be forwarded to the treasurer :

" Whitehall, May 5th, 1825.
" DEAR SIR,

" Inclosed I have the pleasure of sending
you a draft for one hundred guineas, being the

sum which the King has been graciously pleased to contribute towards the erection of a
monument at Carmarthen to the memory of
Sir Thomas Picton.

" His Majesty is gratified by this opportunity
of marking the estimation in which he holds
the name and services of that gallant and distinguished officer.

"I am, dear Sir, very faithfully yours,

"ROBERT PEEL."

" J. Jones, Esq. &c."

On the 16th of August 1825, the first stone
of this edifice was laid by Lady Dynevor.*

This elegant structure was not completed
until August 1828, when it was opened to
public view ; the nobility and gentry of the surrounding country proceeding from the Guildhall
for that purpose. On this occasion sixty Waterloo veterans carried silk banners, bearing in
letters of gold the names of the different battles in which the gallant Picton had fought,
Upon the arrival of the procession at the column, the member for Carmarthen, J. Jones,
Esq. addressed a few words to the assembled
crowd, in allusion to the occasion.

* See Appendix.

Ireland's national bard, Moore, must have fitly appreciated the character of Picton, since he has in the following stanzas paid that tribute to his memory which, as in ancient times, was the poet's meed for heroic acts.

Oh ! give to the hero the death of the brave,
    On the field where the might
    Of his deeds shed a light
Through the gloom which o'ershadows the grave.

Let him not be laid on the feverish bed,
    There to waste through the day,
    Like a taper, away,
And live till the spirit be dead.

Oh no ! let him lie on Fame's deathbed of pride,
    On the hoof-beaten strand,
    With his sword in his hand,
And a fresh welling wound in his side.

No—not with the stealth of disease should he die ;
    He should bound o'er the flood
    Of his fame and his blood,
To the glory that waits him on high !

For the lifeblood whose stream to our country is given,
    In the pride of its worth
    Shall be hallowed on earth,
And the soul shall be honoured in heaven.

Such fate, gallant Picton ! was thine, when the few
    Who survived thee in fight
    Won the day by the light
That thy deeds shed around Waterloo !

CONCLUSION.

Character of Sir Thomas Picton. — Anecdotes of him. — Character of Picton in a letter from the Duke of Wellington

HAVING thus followed Sir Thomas Picton through his splendid career to his glorious death, it remains but to make a few remarks upon his character as a private man and as a soldier.

In private life he was kind and generous, warm in his friendships, but strong in his enmities. He had a strict sense of honour, which would not admit of the slightest misconstruction or prevarication; it was to him one straight line, from which he never swerved, even in thought. The artificial forms of society were in many instances too nearly allied to deception to meet with his approbation: and this made his manners too unstudied and natural to be polite in the modern acceptation of the term.

In him there was no sacrifice of opinion or tacit acquiescence for the sake of obtaining favour. He was generous almost to a fault, and his purse was open to all who came with a tale of distress. A gentleman who knew Sir Thomas Picton intimately, and who does not hesitate to acknowledge that he was himself an object of his munificence, observes : " He was the most generous of men ; the warmth ·of his heart or the extent of his liberality knew no bounds ; but this only appeared to those beneath him, together with the poor and miserable—to these he was ever kind and considerate ; while to rank or presumption he was unbending and uncompromising. But perhaps the extraordinary degree of feeling possessed by Sir Thomas Picton cannot be better illustrated than by the following anecdote which came under my own observation.

" I was one day riding with him on horseback a short distance out of town, when an Irish beggar-woman, with a child in her arms, came by the side of his horse, and commenced asking alms in the usual dolorous tone of this class of mendicants. Our horses were walking, and we were deeply engaged in conversation. I happened to know this woman's face, and had always strongly suspected that she was an impostor : so, seeing the general fix his eyes upon her with some degree of attention, I imagined that he was about to relieve her, and therefore expressed to him my suspicions; upon which he desired her in rather a severe tone to be gone, and turning his head we continued our conversation. The woman, however, with national perseverance, still trudged on by the general's side, looking piteously up in his face, and pouring forth a strain of natural eloquence, depicting in strong colours a long train of miseries. I suspected my companion's attention was gradually leaving the subject of our discourse, as his replies lost much of their usual force, and he seemed absent. The woman (doubtless a better judge of the effect produced upon the object of her solicitation) opened a fresh battery, held up her babe, said she had four more at home unable to crawl from disease and starvation; that her husband was dying on the floor, without a morsel of food or a soul to give him a drink of water, while she came out, half-mad, to rob or beg a few half-pence

to make his last moments comfortable. God
knows, this tale might have been true; it
made me relent, and forget my suspicions; but
General Picton did more : the woman added
something to what she had already said, — I
think, that her husband had been a soldier.
The general had not uttered a word for nearly
two minutes; and as she continued heighten-
ing the picture of her woes, I could perceive
the blood rushing to his face, until no longer
able to bear the contention of his feelings, and
unwilling to believe all he had heard, he cried
out in a most singular tone, as if almost stifled
by the fulness of his breast, ' *You lie!*' threw
her a piece of gold, and then, without any
notice to me, put spurs to his horse, and it
was some time before I could overtake him."

It is unnecessary to multiply the instances
which might be given in proof of the kindness
and benevolence of Sir Thomas Picton's heart.
In passion, the most humane man may inflict an
injury ;—his reason for the moment is estranged,
and when he returns to himself he generally
suffers more real pain than he has inflicted.
Sir Thomas Picton was accused of possessing
a cruel disposition, Those who knew him best

are most thoroughly convinced that such an
accusation is wholly unfounded.

A great and apparent change was however
produced upon the character of Picton by the
incidents of his life; he was naturally candid,
open, and confiding, thinking every man as
honourable as himself. But his disposition
underwent a change in consequence of the
persecution he had to endure; and its long
continuance caused in him a moroseness foreign
to his nature, which was rather increased by
the scanty reward bestowed upon his services.
Had there been the least disposition to cruelty
in the breast of Sir Thomas Picton, it is only
reasonable to suppose that it would have been
augmented by the severe mortifications and
injustice to which he had been subjected; but
this was not the case. Whenever a city or fortress was taken, his indefatigable exertions to
save the unfortunate inhabitants from the lawless soldiery are well known by all who served
under his command: upon all these occasions
he appeared to make their cause his own, and
he frequently risked his own life in order to
save that of others. To his men he was always
kind and considerate; and some old soldiers

who are still enjoying the comforts of Chelsea Hospital, and who served under him, yet remember and speak of him in the most gratifying terms for his general attention to their comforts.*

Perhaps the disposition was never more strongly portrayed in the expression of the countenance than in that of Sir Thomas Picton. Lavater would have pointed to him as an evidence of the truth of his system. Firmness, penetration, courage, honour, and decision, were

* One of them, who was a serjeant in the Forty-fifth, thus spoke of him.

"General Picton, or ' old Picton,' as we used to call him, was always very well liked by the division : he was very strict sometimes — in particular about any little bit of plunder that the men would sometimes pick up; and he used always to be talking about how wrong it was to take from the poor people because the countries happened to be at war. He used to have the men flogged when they were found out: but when he flogged, many others took life ; so our fellows always thought ' old Picton' a very kind general. Besides this, the men always thought he had their welfare at heart ; for every soldier in the division knew that if he had anything to complain of, ' old Picton' would listen to him, and, if he could, set him right. As to his fighting, I always thought that it was he who made the third division what it was. Somehow the men never used to trouble their heads about anything but fighting when they went into battle ; for they all depended so entirely upon the general. to know what the enemy was doing in our front and on our flanks, that they never bothered their heads about anything strongly marked when his features were in a quiescent state; while energy, candour, sympathy, and benevolence, were by turns expressed in the features as these qualities arose in the mind. But in moments of excitement, when the fiery temperament of his nature was called forth, his whole countenance betrayed the overwhelming influence of passion; and he then gave utterance to a storm of bitter reproofs,

but what he ordered them to do; and I really think, if the general had placed himself in the thickest fire we were ever in, that, so long as he remained, his division would have stayed with him to a man."

Another, who served during the whole time that Picton commanded the third division, takes particular delight in repeating the following incident. He had told it over and over again in the guard-room as *his* tale, and dwells upon it now as the only instance in which he was thrown in immediate communication with his general. It is here given in his own words. His name is Jonathan Reynolds. "I was a serjeant in the Fifth foot. One day, while we were in the Pyrenees, there was a general movement in the whole army. The captain of my company, Captain Culley, commanded the light companies of the Fifth, Eighty-third, and Eighty-seventh regiments. We were lying under some heights, when our general, Sir Thomas Picton, came up. After looking about him for a moment, he desired Captain Culley to send a serjeant and six file round a corner that hid us from the enemy. I was ordered upon this duty; and Sir Thomas Picton spoke to me before I went, and told me not upon any account to let my men fire, and to keep as much under cover as possible. He then told the captain, which, for a while, subdued the most disorderly to good behaviour.

With a disposition so frank and generous, great natural abilities, a strong desire for information, tenacious memory, and an eloquent flow of language, it will readily be believed that he must have been an ornament to social life: in fact, he has left a most enviable impression; and all who knew him, now speak

that as soon as the signal gun had fired, he was to advance with the three companies and carry a hill occupied by the French just round the corner where I was to be posted: and before he went away he said to Captain Culley, that he should be there himself in about half-an-hour. ' Oh, then,' said my captain, who was a droll old soldier, ' I suppose I must be there in a quarter of an hour to get things ready for you.' The general smiled and then rode off. When I and my men had got round the corner, we could see a number of French officers reconnoitring on the hill. But the signal gun soon fired, and the companies advanced, when we fell in, and soon drove the enemy from their position. There was very little to do; and we only lost one man, a corporal of the Eighty-seventh, besides a bugle-man wounded. We drove the enemy above a mile and a-half, and halted near three houses, the Caçadores having come up with us. When Sir Thomas Picton and his staff arrived, Captain Culley spoke to him just by me, and said, ' General, my three companies have done all the work: I hope you will give them comfortable quarters.'—' Well, Culley,' said the gallant old general, ' there are three houses, put a company into each— that 's the best I can do for you.' "

of his loss with strong feelings of regret. We cannot better conclude these remarks than by quoting the following corroboration of our opinion by a distinguished officer, to whom we are greatly indebted for many interesting particulars of his life.

" Sir Thomas Picton was uniformly so kind to me during frequent, and sometimes prolonged, occasions of intercourse in Spain, that I cannot fail bearing him in the most affectionate remembrance. I feel also on higher grounds than personal sentiments, the strongest reason to respect his character as that of a thorough good man and soldier. A very wrong impression was formed of him by the world in general. He had certainly but little of the courtier about him; but an abruptness of manner was added to, in effect, by a rigid countenance and appearance, which amounted to roughness and to a seeming hardness of disposition; yet there never was a man more thoroughly kind-hearted and benevolent."

The abilities of General Picton as a soldier are attested by actions which need no commentary; but it is justly observed that " any officer, however high his rank or great his abili-

ties, who served under the command of the
Duke of Wellington, must necessarily have
been obscured by the lustre of his grace's
fame;" and this reflection may justify a few
observations upon the military character of Sir
Thomas Picton.

As remarked in the course of this memoir,
General Picton had made the art of war his
principal study; but this alone would never
have made him what he was,—one of the most
distinguished officers under the Duke of Wellington's command; in fact, as he was sometimes styled, " *his right hand*." A strong power
of combination, great foresight, calm judgment,
unshaken nerve, and undaunted courage;*—
these were the qualities, which fitted him so admirably for the profession which he had chosen,
and which enabled him to reach that eminence

---

* The following anecdote of Sir Thomas Picton has recently appeared in a periodical publication.

" Sir Thomas Picton went to witness the exhibition of Ireland (the famous gymnast) throwing a somerset over a
dozen grenadiers, standing at ' present arms,' with fixed
bayonets: but when he saw the men placed, he trembled
like a leaf, and kept his head down whilst Ireland jumped;
nor did he look up until he had first asked, ' Has he done
it?' when assured he had, he said, ' A battle is nothing to
that.' "

which mere study and experience could never otherwise attain. " He had," observes one who knew him long, and had many opportunities of observing the bent of his disposition, " a firmness of mind, independent of animal courage, which was remarkably striking. The train of his ideas, for instance, was always turned, even in the hours of greatest difficulty, rather upon the enterprises which we could undertake against the enemy, than upon the injury which they could do to us ; and his actions, if in chief command, would have been more offensive than defensive."

The remarks made by Colonel Napier upon the military abilities of Sir Thomas Picton, are certainly not supported by the evidence of his actions. Colonel Napier desiring to draw a comparison between Picton and Crawfurd, first proves that they were composed of such conflicting elements that they did not often meet without a quarrel, and then he implies that they were each compared to the Duke of Wellington by some ignorant people. It must be obvious to every military reader, that in no one respect could any comparison obtain between Generals Picton and Crawfurd. The lat-

ter was impetuous and headstrong; the former
calm and reflective. The commander of the
forces had the most perfect reliance on Sir
Thomas Picton for fulfilling his orders; but
perhaps the words of a gallant and distinguished
officer, who was intimately acquainted with Sir
Thomas Picton, will more satisfactorily express
this confidence. Extracts have already been
given from this officer's correspondence; and it
may here be observed, that the situation in
which he was placed was one which gave him
a favourable opportunity for remarking the intercourse which subsisted amongst the respective generals. He says, " It was the common
opinion that the Duke of Wellington and Sir
Thomas Picton did not get on smoothly together when they happened to have personal
intercourse, which was seldom. I cannot vouch
for the fact, but can readily believe it, from
the habitual frankness with which Sir Thomas
would offer his opinion, without respect to persons. I know, however, the high sense he entertained of the talents and character of the
great commander, and I am satisfied that the
Duke had a most favourable opinion of the
merits of Sir Thomas Picton as a general and

soldier; indeed, nothing could exceed the zeal with which he carried the orders that he received into execution; this was not, however, done to the *letter,* but to the *spirit,* when he was *quite sure* what that spirit was."

No person who has read Colonel Napier's admirable history, can pretend that such observations could with the least shadow of justice be applied to the character of the intrepid Crawfurd. How little would they accord with the actions which are related of, and the disposition which is attributed to, that general by the author of that work! Sir Thomas Picton was remarkable for calm judgment and immovable resolution when in the field; and this it was which produced the remark from Lord Liverpool, that " the conduct of General Picton had inspired a confidence in the army, and exhibited an example of science and bravery which had been surpassed by no other officer." Without the slightest intention to depreciate the merits or abilities of General Crawfurd, it must be acknowledged that the army had not, and never could have had, a similar confidence in him. His impetuosity and fiery temperament, together with his thoughtless daring, would have rendered him a very unfit officer to command an army; for Colonel Napier well knows that a general-in-chief must possess some other qualifications besides mere courage, and that prudence and judgment are indispensably necessary to inspire confidence in the minds of his soldiers. By Colonel Napier's own showing, General Crawfurd did not discover either of these qualifications, as will readily be seen by a reference to those pages in the Colonel's own history which record General Crawfurd's proceedings on the Coa,* at Alemquer when falling back upon the lines,† and at El Bodon.‡ Colonel Napier has himself ventured to censure Crawfurd for his spirited though ill-judged proceedings upon these occasions; whereas, in candour and justice, he must acknowledge that he could not find in the course of Sir Thomas Picton's military career any one act which did not call for eulogium; and yet Colonel Napier says, " they were both officers of mark and pretension ;" and immediately afterwards remarks that " Crawfurd was more so than Picton, because the latter

* Chap. iv. vol. iii.   † Vol. iii. p. 349.
‡ Vol. iii. p. 241.

never had a separate command, and his opportunities were necessarily more circumscribed."
It is perfectly true that Picton had not equal
opportunities with Crawfurd; but it may be
safely asserted that, had he been placed at Coa
in the same situation, and with the same orders
as Crawfurd possessed, he would not have acted
in such a manner as to call forth the just reproof which Colonel Napier has thrown upon
the conduct of that officer.

This remark is not made without proof. It
has already been fully established by many instances of masterly judgment, foresight, and
determination, far removed from ill-judged impetuosity, or untimely daring. It may not be
superfluous to recapitulate these instances,—
his foresight at Busacos — his calmness and
masterly skill at El Bodon — his persevering
resolution and heroism at Badajoz—his intrepid
advance, now bearing the enemy back, and
then checking his impetuous troops until his
flanks were covered, at Vittoria—his able generalship on the Pyrenees, in checking the advance of Soult; nay, even his attack, and timely
retreat at Toulouse; and, last of all, when on the
"red field of Waterloo" he fell, in the Duke

of Wellington's own words, while " gloriously leading his division to a charge with bayonets, in which one of the most serious attacks made by the enemy on our position was defeated." These brilliant services will place the. character and military abilities of Sir Thomas Picton in a far more elevated position than they could possibly have attained by the comparison which Colonel Napier has instituted with General Crawfurd.

This is not the only instance of erroneous judgment which Colonel Napier manifests as regards the character of Sir Thomas Picton; he asserts that he was " inclined to harshness, and rigid in command." .

" Where others took life for offences against military discipline, our general only flogged," was the remark of several of the old soldiers of the " third division." Each of these veterans had served long under Picton's command, and it is certain that better evidence could not be obtained of the feelings and opinions of this class of the army.

Picton acquired a lasting place in the hearts of his soldiers: true, he was severe in enforcing a strict attention to the duties of. the field, at the same time that he punished any offenders who were found committing depredations upon the peaceful and unoffending inhabitants.*

* The following anecdote has been reported of Sir Thomas Picton :—

" During the Peninsular war, when provisions were rather difficult to be obtained, a young and dandified commissary had been instructed to supply the rations for the third division at a given place by a certain time; but by some mismanagement this officer forgot to fulfil his engagement, and the division was in consequence left to its own resources, which were bad enough. A report of this neglect was brought to General Picton, and he forthwith sent for the commissary. " Well, sir," commenced Picton, as he came in, " where are the rations for my division?" This being the very question that the commissary was not prepared to answer, he hesitated for a short time, and then stammered out some well-worn excuse. Picton was not, however to be cajoled by excuses while his men were kept with empty stomachs; so he led the alarmed commissary to the door, and pointing, said, " Do you see that tree ?"—" Yes, sir," was the reply. " Well now," continued Picton, "if you don't get the rations for my division at the place mentioned by twelve o'clock to-morrow, I will hang you up there at half-past." He was then released, when he proceeded forthwith to Lord Wellington, and told him, with an appearance of injured dignity, of General Picton's threat; but the commissary was dreadfully alarmed when his lordship coolly remarked, " Ah! he said he 'd hang you, did he ?"—" Yes, my lord." " Well, if General Picton said so, I dare say he will keep his word. You 'd better get the rations up in time." Further advice was unnecessary—the rations were there to the moment.

Colonel Napier also asserts that Picton was " prone to disobedience, yet exacted entire submission from inferiors." The character of Sir Thomas Picton appears to have been totally misunderstood by Colonel Napier. This is perhaps as severe a charge as can be brought against the character of a soldier. Severe, however, as it is, we would not attempt, solely upon our own judgment, to vindicate Sir Thomas Picton, or to deny the justice of Colonel Napier's assertion : there is indeed no necessity for this; for the opinions of many officers, who served with him, completely refute this accusation; and their testimony is confirmed by Picton's whole career. There can be little doubt but that this erroneous impression of his character had its foundation in the manner in which he carried his orders into execution,—" not to the *letter*, but to the *spirit*, when he was *quite sure* what that spirit was." If at any time he saw what he conceived to be a favourable opportunity for extending the letter of his instructions, he never hesitated to avail -himself of it, and by this means he frequently did *more* than he was expected to do, but never *less ;* but this surely cannot be designated " disobedience."

At the battle of Vittoria, it may be remembered, that he acted almost entirely upon his own responsibility; still he did not *disobey* the orders of the commander of the forces, simply because he had received none; and he there only anticipated the time of his movement, because he considered the moment favourable, and the result proved the soundness of his judgment. Had Lord Wellington ordered him *not* to advance, and he had afterwards done so, then indeed that would have been an act of disobedience; but whenever General Picton received any orders either to advance or retreat, he in every instance on record strictly obeyed them; if, having no positive instructions, he thought he could obtain any important advantages, he invariably availed himself of the opportunity.

That Sir Thomas Picton exacted entire submission from inferiors, as a trait in the character of an officer, would not call for any remark; but, when coupled with the former charge of " disobedience," it implies an unjust and tyrannical disposition.

An accusation has been brought against Sir Thomas Picton with much injustice and acri-

mony, of having neglected the interest of his officers, by not reporting their services to the commander of the forces. When considering this
accusation, the unbending disposition of Sir
Thomas Picton must be borne in mind, for
we know that the opinion entertained by nearly all the officers of the third division, who
served under General Picton, is decidedly in
opposition to this assertion. It was in fact
generally believed that Sir Thomas Picton had
every inclination to reward the services of his
officers, and to advance their interests. It was
also known that he made frequent representations to the commander of the forces in
favour of his officers; but these were seldom
successful: and this circumstance, it is said, produced so unfavourable an effect upon his proud
spirit, that at length he ceased any longer to apply in that quarter, and in future addressed his
application solely to the commander-in-chief.

We are enabled to offer one, and that a
striking proof, that General Picton did not
neglect nor forget the interests of those who
served under his command. Colonel Macpherson, whose name has been before mentioned in
these volumes, was at the close of the war in

1814 still a lieutenant! A noble independence prevented him from soliciting promotion, and he thought that his services ought to ensure for him some unasked reward. He was un-known to Sir Thomas Picton in any other way than as a deserving soldier: upon three separate occasions he had been thrown in the path of his general, fresh from some daring achievement, and Picton never allowed early merit to pass unnoticed, nor, if he could help it, unrewarded. He had made repeated applications for his promotion, but without success.

The last occasion upon which Macpherson had seen Sir Thomas Picton was at Bordeaux, when he was suffering severely from a wound received at the battle of Orthes. Picton invited him to dinner, when, although much debilitated, he accepted the general's invitation. He was taken ill whilst at table, and was compelled to retire; Picton would not, however, allow him to leave the house, but insisted upon his taking up his quarters in his own apartment, and sent at once for his baggage. In a few days after this, Sir Thomas Picton embarked for England, but before his departure he recommended Macpherson to the

care of Lord Dalhousie, who was then commanding the British troops in the town.

Macpherson neither saw nor heard anything
more of General Picton for some time. He
applied to the War Office for a company, supporting his application by a memorial, which
recorded a list of services that equalled those
of any officer of his years, and surpassed those
of many a veteran; and upon this he depended
for success; but a cold official reply was the
only notice taken of either his letter or memorial.

The young soldier felt acutely this neglect,
and in consequence actually contemplated retiring from the army. About this period, as
he was walking one day along Pall Mall, he
saw Sir Thomas Picton coming towards him,
with several other officers. This was some
months after his departure from Bordeaux.
Macpherson hesitated to address his general:
he thought, to use his own words, " that now
Sir Thomas Picton was in London, surrounded by so many men of equal rank, he would
wish to avoid a humble lieutenant." Accordingly, as the general approached, he made no
attempt to stop him. Picton had not, appa-

rently, seen him, for he was deeply engaged in conversation; and Macpherson was passing him, as he thought, unnoticed. But Picton seized his arm, and in his sharp though friendly manner exclaimed, " D——e, sir! are you going to cut me?" The lieutenant was startled; but immediately collecting himself, bowed and observed, " No, sir; any officer who served under Sir Thomas Picton's command would be proud in the honour of being recognised by him. But I thought," added the lieutenant, " you might have forgotten me."— " Forgotten you!" repeated Picton: " No! no! sir, I have not forgotten you. But come along, sir," and he took his arm; " come home with me, I have got something I want you to copy." Macpherson accordingly walked to the Grosvenor Coffee-house with the general, who, upon entering his room, bade him be seated, when he presently put in his hands a paper for his perusal. This was a memorial of Lieutenant Macpherson's services, drawn up with much care, and dictated by a tenacious memory. In fact, every incident of the intrepid career of the young soldier was there set forth in the most forcible language.

Macpherson was greatly surprised at this marked instance of friendly consideration, and expressed his acknowledgments in the most grateful terms. But Picton did not want thanks, neither would he have them; but, stopping him short, he desired that he would without delay transcribe that paper into a more legible text, that he might at once send it to the Horse Guards. A few days after this, Lieutenant Macpherson called upon Sir Thomas, at his desire, to know the result of his application. He found the general foaming with rage, with a letter crumpled violently in his hand. "There, sir, read that!" he said, at the same time giving Macpherson the mutilated letter to peruse; "there is an answer to my application." It did not take long to read. The lieutenant knew it by heart; it being, in fact, a secretary's circular. "No vacancy," but "shall be appointed to the first vacancy. Your obedient, humble servant," &c.

Picton thought, and justly, that he deserved something more than this; his proud spirit could not submit to repeat his applications to the commander of the forces sufficiently often to render them successful; for certain-it is, that very few of those for whom he applied received any reward through his intercession. His application was now, however, made where he had a right to expect something more than the formal reply which would be deigned to a subaltern. Dissatisfied and annoyed, he told Macpherson to accompany him to the Horse Guards, when, as it was levee-day, he was readily admitted into the Duke of York's presence: the substance of his remarks during this interview are not known, for Macpherson was not present. The result was, however, soon apparent; for within a week from that day the lieutenant was gazetted as a captain, and received instructions to repair to Chatham to raise a company, there being actually at the time no *vacancy*. The well-known sense of justice and consideration for merit which distinguished that zealous public servant the late Duke of York, doubtless upon this occasion operated powerfully in behalf of Macpherson, and rendered Sir Thomas Picton's application successful.*

* We gladly avail ourselves of the permission of the able writer, to insert the following sketch of the character of the gallant general, which appeared in the Metropolitan Magazine for December 1835.

Having discussed the military and private character of the subject of this work, we

" When Picton fell, England lost a soldier never surpassed in bravery, and seldom equalled in genius. He was a soldier every inch of him; his character as such was never mistaken — as that of a man, greatly. His country appeared to know him only when it lost him, and the revulsion in his favour became as great, as was formerly the prejudice against him. That he was a man of the kindliest disposition, the numerous instances narrated in these volumes, and the still more numerous ones with which we were ourselves acquainted, evidently prove. But early in his career, he had been misrepresented by many, and most foully slandered by a base few. The few obtained a temporary credence, and then Thomas Picton coated his heart with a mail, not impenetrable, as a thousand instances show, but which opposed a harsh and hard exterior to most, whilst all was generous and soft within.

" His galling early injuries had turned his manly firmness into sternness, and his features in some measure were a reflection of his character, at least to the stranger. What he was, even in his looks to his intimate friends, they alone know, and for them it would be bootless to tell. Many of the bosoms that he gladdened are now mouldering in their graves, and the few that remember him in the hours of domestic relaxation, are now content to view him only in the light of an unapproachable star of the first magnitude in the galaxy of British military glory.

" Many pages of these Memoirs are occupied in disproving invidious charges brought against him on many military subjects. We think that his elaborate justifications were needless, and we would have had them omitted, as they reflect so little honour upon the distinguished characters cannot close the memoir more happily than by inserting the following letter from the Duke of Wellington.

To H. B. ROBINSON, ESQ.

" London, August 28th, 1835.

" DEAR SIR,

" I have received your letter, and I have the greatest satisfaction in giving you the assurance, that not only I was not on bad terms that have brought them forward. Not only was he not indifferent to the interests of those who, under him, distinguished themselves by their merits, but extremely though not importunately zealous. Picton become importunate!— there seems an absurdity in the very idea, a palpable catachresis. A man who commanded so much awe by the strength of his character, could not possibly win a favour by the smile of sycophancy. Yes, he was the steel upon which men rely in the hour of peril ; not the jewelled bauble to be praised and fondled in the period of enervation and luxury. Unfortunately for the brave, appointments are no longer bestowed and honours granted in the battle-field still slippery with gore ; but in the essenced hall, and in the courtly chambers, among silken parasites and luxurious hangers-on. Had the former been the case, how many of Picton's gallant companions of his brilliant third division would have now, if living, stood high on the army list! Alas! the stern brave warrior could only show them how to gain glory—they gained that, and but little else.

with the late Sir Thomas Picton, but that in the whole course of the period during which I was in relation with him, I do not recollect even a difference of opinion, much less anything of the nature of a quarrel.

" My first acquaintance with Sir Thomas Picton was when he joined the army in the Peninsula as a general officer on the staff. I had solicited his appointment, because I entertained a high opinion of his talents and qualities, from the report which I had received of both from the late General Miranda, who had known him in the West Indies. I never had any reason to regret, on the contrary, I had numberless reasons to rejoice, that I had solicited his appointment. It was made at a moment at which an unmerited prejudice existed against Sir Thomas Picton, the recollection of which was effaced by his services.

" I afterwards solicited his appointment to the staff of the army in Flanders; than which I cannot give a stronger proof, not only of my sense of his merits and former services, but likewise that I never was otherwise than on the best terms with him. The country was deprived of his valuable services on a glorious field of battle, in a short time after he joined the army ; and there was no individual in that army or in England who lamented his loss more sincerely that I did.

" I have the honour to be,

Dear Sir,

" Your most obedient humble servant,

" WELLINGTON."

APPENDIX.

No. I.

Port of Spain, 25th May 1798.

SIR,

Previous to your excellency's departure for England, I feel myself called upon to furnish you with such details and information respecting this island and the neighbouring continent, as may enable his Majesty's ministers to judge of the means necessary to be employed for the attainment of the objects they may have in view.

This island, possessing the most extensive, and perhaps one of the best and finest harbours in all America, wholly free from hurricanes, (the effects of which are so dreadful in all the other West India ports,) is so situated as to command the commerce of an immense continent, extending from the banks of the Rio de los Amazones to those of La Madalina, including the rich provinces of Guiana, Barinas, Santa Fé, Venexuela, Caraccas, and Cumana, with which there are navigable communications by means of the different rivers, which, traversing those extensive countries, at length lose themselves in the great river Oronoque, which discharges itself into the Gulf of Paria, by a number of small canals, navigable by vessels drawing from ten to twelve feet water, and by one large channel (capable of receiving frigates) opposite the north-east point of Trinidad.

The island has also a communication with the interior of the province of Cumana, by the navigable river of Guarapiche, which also falls into the Gulf of Paria.

These provinces are inhabited by Spaniards from Europe, who generally hold all offices and employments under government; Creoles, or such as are descendants of Spanish settlers; Indians, who are collected in missions, and kept in the profoundest ignorance by their Capuchin governors; Negroes, and a mixed race, resulting from the communication of all the others: the latter class and the Indians are by far the most numerous.

Throughout these fine provinces the oppressions and exactions of the persons entrusted with the government have totally annihilated all enterprise and industry; and the inhabitants of all orders are reduced to the most pitiable state of misery. They are entirely without manufactures of any kind, and now wholly depend upon the stranger for everything they wear. The usual intercourse between the mother-country and the colonies being almost entirely cut off by the war, the inhabitants of these countries are literally in want of everything. I know a gentleman of the province of Cumana who has 30,000 head of horned cattle, and is in absolute want of a coat.

The government, possessing no public force to compel obedience, and having entirely lost the confidence of the people, keeps up its authority by arming every individual against his neighbour, ordering every subject to seize another carrying on a prohibited trade, and to kill him in case of resistance; and authorising him to apply whatever he may so seize to his own use, as a

reward. Corrupted by these means, every person is suspicious of his neighbour, and regards him as a spy and
informer; so that they appear more a set of insulated
individuals than a nation. They however agree, op-
pressors and oppressed, that nothing can be more vex-
atious and corrupt than the government they live
under, or more deplorable than their own situation;
and every individual, with the exception only of those
who, placed in the highest offices of administration,
have the means of oppressing and plundering the inferior ones, looks forward to a deliverance from some
foreign hand with a degree of confident hope.

They have not yet been able to recover from the
habitual dread of a sanguinary government, and are
of themselves incapable of an independent, unassisted
struggle to subvert it. Conscious of a want of union
and energy, weak and defenceless as they know their
government to be, they acknowledge themselves incapable of any enterprise against it, unless favoured by
the countenance of some foreign power.

What I have the honour to propose is not in the
nature of a conquest, difficult and expensive to be maintained. I have to submit to your excellency, for the
consideration of his Majesty's ministers, a plan which
has for its object the opening an immense commerce
to the industry of his Majesty's subjects, and securing
them advantages of an incalculable value, to be obtained
by no other means.

The town of Cumana is centrically situated, so as
easily to communicate with the province of Guiana on
the one hand, and that of Caraccas on the other, with
the intermediate towns of Barcelona and Cariacco. The
town itself is capable of no defence, being open on all

sides, and will probably be evacuated on the first appearance of a force; at least, such was the determination some months ago.

If about three thousand troops could be collected,
with a sixty-four gun ship, a frigate, and some forty-
four, or India transports, to make an appearance or
impression—for a squadron would be no otherwise useful—I would propose immediately taking possession of
Cumana. The public mind has long since been prepared, and the people in general look forward to it as
the most favourable event which can befall them. The
prejudices against the English nation, which the government had sedulously cultivated by every species of
misrepresentation and artifice, have happily been dissipated by the extensive communication and intercourse
they have had with this island since the conquest.
The governor has no regular force, and the militia
have repeatedly signified that they would not expose
their families and property by an unavailing resistance.
I have also had an opportunity latterly of learning the
spirit of the Capuchins, who are determined to keep
their Indians entirely out of the business, and capitulate for their missions. I have seen a letter from one
of the principals of that order, giving such advice to
the missioners governing the dependant missions. The
government has latterly betrayed considerable jealousy
of the authority which this order has acquired amongst
the Indians; and the Fathers, recollecting the fate of
the Jesuits in Paraguay, appear a little suspicious of
their intentions; and this has in a considerable degree
loosened their attachment. A declaration that the intentions of his Majesty are to give the inhabitants of
South America an opportunity of asserting their claim

to an independent government and free trade, will, I am convinced, decide them at once to forsake a go-vernment which has energy only to oppress them; and the situation of the neighbouring provinces, long in a state of revolt, affords reasonable grounds to think that it will become the centre of a general movement, which might there be left to itself, and would only require occasional supplies of arms and ammunition. The expense of the expedition I propose would, com-paratively, be very inconsiderable. It will not be ne-cessary to employ horses or pioneers, and the ordnance necessary would be a few light field-pieces only. The principal objects to be attended to will be arms for cavalry and infantry, for the purpose of arming the inhabitants, and a liberal supply of ammunition.

There is a native of Caraccas, I understand, now in London, (Miranda,) who might be useful on this occa-sion : not that he possesses a great local knowledge, or has any considerable connexions, being the son of a shop-keeper of Caraccas who left the country at a very early period ; but as a native of the country, who has made himself a good deal talked of, he might fix the atten-tion of those people, and thereby make himself service-able. For reasons very obvious, I would advise his not being consulted on the business, or acquainted with it, until the moment of execution. The beginning of November will be the best time for an expedition to that part of the Main: the dry weather sets in much sooner there than in the islands. The situation is re-markably dry and healthy.

The expedition should go down immediately to its object, without stopping at Trinidad, which would in a certain degree indicate the point menaced : but it will be necessary to apprise me early of the intention, as the success will in a great measure depend upon the previous steps I may take to secure it.

I have a person perfectly master of the Spanish language, who can prepare all the necessary declarations and papers.

A subordinate expedition might be undertaken from Trinidad, with five or six hundred men, up the river Guarapiche, which would essentially contribute to the complete success of the undertaking: and this might be performed without any additional expense, as I should be able to provide the vessels necessary for their transport on the spot.

Having now sufficiently enlarged on this subject, and furnished your excellency with materials to form your own opinion from, I shall take my leave, with an assurance that a doubt does not exist in my mind respecting the success of the expedition I have the honour of recommending; and which, if entrusted to the command of an officer of prudence and conduct, cannot fail to produce the most extensive and important advantages.

I have the honour to be, &c.

(Signed)   THOMAS PICTON.

To his Excellency
Lieutenant-general Cuyler,
Commander-in-chief, West Indies.

APPENDIX, No. II.

First—Upon motion made and seconded, Resolved,
That the first Commissioner, Colonel William Fullarton, in taking possession of the criminal records deposited in the office of Francisco de Castro, (a public
scrivener, and regidor of Cabildo, one of the public
archives of this colony,) without the knowledge and
consent of Brigadier-general Picton and Commodore
Hood, (as declared by them at this board,) both being
present in the government, and without giving a receipt
or specific acknowledgment for the same, *has acted
contrary to his duty to his Majesty*, who appointed him
joint governor, and not sole governor, of Trinidad.

Resolved, That the said Colonel William Fullarton
has, in the opinion of this board, for the above reason,
acted in breach of duty to his colleagues in the government of this colony.

Resolved, That the said Colonel William Fullarton
has, in the opinion of this board, for the above reasons,
also treated the council with contempt and insult, because, at its meeting of the 17th day of March, the
following motion was made and carried, Colonel William Fullarton presiding, and of which he could not
plead ignorance; to wit: "As the first commissioner's paper, No. 4, contains insinuations of a most in-

sidious nature, calculated to impress his Majesty's
ministers with opinions injurious to the government,
at the head of which the brigadier presided during
dangerous and perilous times; he thinks it his duty
to move, that the alcaldes in ordinary be called upon
to produce copies of all the criminal proceedings that
have been carried on in their respective offices since
the 1st day of March 1797; and that they be remitted by the clerk of the council to the office of his
Majesty's Secretary of State, the Right Hon. Lord
Hobart:" and these aggravations this board conceives
to be the greater, as Colonel William Fullarton put
himself in the situation of public informer and de-
nouncer against the whole military and civil authority of the late government of this colony ; *and it is the*
first time this board ever learnt that an accuser was to
wrest the strongest means of defence out of the hands
of the accused, (which these public records must be sup-
posed to do,) and to vest them exclusively in his own.

Resolved, That the first commissioner, Colonel William Fullarton, in his conduct at the house of the
Honourable John Black, alcalde of the first election,
in the evening of Monday last, in the manner just read
and stated before this board, was guilty, in their opinion,
of an insult to the board of council, who had recommended proceedings against the said Francisco de
Castro for breach of public duty, *and an outrage of the*
most violent kind against the laws ; as the persons and
houses of all magistrates are, or ought to be, deemed
sacred ; and prisoners once in legal custody, never at-
tempted to be rescued, but suffered to remain until dis-
charged by due course of law.

Resolved, That Colonel William Fullarton, by nominating Francisco de Castro (when a prisoner in legal custody for a breach of public duty on the evening of Monday last) to the honourable and confidential post of commissary of population, in the room of Major Williamson, as proved by the declaration of Mr. Black, *lost all respect for his colleagues, for this board, and for this colony.*

Resolved, That Brigadier-general Picton and Commodore Hood be requested to give out in public orders, that the military attend to the calls of the magistrates, commandants of quarters, and alcaldes, whose houses may be entered against their consent, their persons insulted, and their authorities attempted to be weakened or brought into contempt.

Resolved, That the first commissioner's application to the board, soon after his arrival, for the establishment of a schooner to serve in the surveyor-general's department, (although two brigs were sent out by government and offered by Commodore Hood for that service,) was, on the ground of the excessive expense it would incur, and little utility to accrue from it, rejected: That the same application having been afterwards made, for the same reasons was again rejected; and the schooner Start, in both instances proposed, being now hired, affords just reason to this board to suspect, *that the first commissioner's design, in making such applications, was to impose fictions on this board, to effect his present purpose of deserting his post in the said schooner Start, and concealing the public records.*

Resolved, That his Majesty's first commissioner, by connecting himself with the disaffected characters and classes of inhabitants inimical to the former govern-

ment, hath produced the effects such conduct was calculated to promote : for this board views with sorrow
and indignation, that a spirit of party and faction is
kindling among the white inhabitants of all nations and
languages ; that the legal authority of the master over
the slave is weakened ; that mutinous ideas are excited
in the minds of the numerous bands of free coloured
people, who, by steady government and vigilance, particularly immediately before his administration, were
tranquil, loyal, and happy ; that the authority of the
commandants of quarters is brought into contempt and
insult, and the whole civil and criminal administration
committed to their charge, with the wise system of
police established, and found efficacious for six years,
and even in time of war, to keep good government,
in the most imminent danger of being overset and
extirpated.

The board having taken into its serious consideration
*a retrospect of the whole conduct of the first commission-
er*, Colonel William Fullarton, since he has been in the
exercise of this government, and compared it with the
present desertion of his post, withdrawing from the
commission and the council, *enlevement of the public
records*, and the contempt with which official requests
to produce these records, or to inform where they are
deposited, have been treated ;

Resolved, *That he, the first commissioner, has lost
the confidence of this board ; and that these resolutions,
with all respect and humility, be laid before his Majesty,
together with all the minutes of council, instead of the
proposed address, and that his Majesty's ministers be
humbly prayed to advise his Majesty to remove him for
ever from the government of this colony.*

EXTRACT FROM THE ADDRESS OF HIS MAJESTY'S COUNCIL OF THE ISLAND OF TRINIDAD TO HIS EXCELLENCY THE LIEUTENANT-GOVERNOR, THOMAS HISLOP, ESQ.

We, his Majesty's council of the said Island of Trinidad, beg leave to assure your excellency, that we have seen with just concern an attempt made to interrupt the peace and tranquillity of the colony, by *assertions* advanced in a pamphlet written by Colonel Fullarton, and by him forwarded to your excellency. We have, in a committee of the whole board, *resolved them to be libels on your excellency,* and meant to throw reflections upon the present government and the members of his Majesty's council, and to *sow discord, disunion, and mistrust among them,* &c. &c.

(Signed)   Hon. J. RUTHERFORD.
                         Hon. JOHN SMITH.
                         Hon. J. RIGBY.
                         Hon. JOHN NIHELL.
                         Hon. ST. HILAIRE BEGORRAT.
                         Hon. ARCHIBALD GLOSTER.

EXTRACT FROM THE ANSWER OF HIS EXCELLENCY THE LIEUTENANT-GOVERNOR TO THE FOREGOING PART OF THE COUNCIL'S ADDRESS.

GENTLEMEN,

I beg leave to offer you my warmest and most grateful acknowledgments for the very flattering and kind address with which you have been pleased to honour me ; and you may be assured, that it is with no less concern that I have seen an attempt made to interrupt the peace and tranquillity of the colony, *by assertions*

advanced by Colonel Fullarton, one of which was trans-
mitted to me by his directions.

The resolutions which your board have thought proper unanimously to adopt on the occasion cannot fail
to stand recorded on a basis the most impartial, and
must be to the world convincing of the pure and
honourable motives that have actuated you in the steps
you have deemed necessary to adopt, *to refute unmerited calumnies, and most effectually to stop the possibility
of introducing the seeds of discord, disunion, and distrust in the colony;* which, through the never-ceasing
determination which you, individually as well as collectively, have manifested for the maintenance of union,
of action, and sentiment in the discharge of your public
duties, as well as in your private capacities, has hitherto maintained its rightful authority with requisite
energy, and is thereby capable of resisting *every species
of attempt which can in future be invented to shake it,*
&c. &c.

THOMAS HISLOP,
Lieutenant-Governor.

APPENDIX, No. III.

Inconstant, Spithead, 4th December 1804.

MY DEAR SIR,

I have received your letter, enclosing Colonel Fullarton's extract, and should have answered it immediately, but waited to see the letter you mentioned having sent by Captain Maxwell, who has not yet come this way.

With respect to the extract in question, it is notoriously false. I never went on any predatory enterprises whatever : those undertaken by your orders, and executed by me, were for the sole purpose of destroying French privateers and bodies of brigands who had taken post on the Spanish Main, and threatened the destruction of the Island of Trinidad ; and I trust my public letter to Admiral Harvey, of the 6th of December 1798, stating the account of the expeditions to Rio, Caribe, and Carussano, which you will see in the " Naval Chronicle" for that month, printed for J. Gold, Shoe Lane, London, will refute most fully his assertion. I have enclosed you a copy of the proclamation I sent to the commandants of Rio, Caribe, and Carussano, which is another strong proof that our mission was not to plunder or bring off cattle, either for ourselves or your estates ; and I am persuaded that Colonel Mosheim, Major Laureal, and Captain Champain will feel equally indignant with ourselves at so gross a misrepresentation of the motives which guided us on those expeditions. And be assured, my good sir, it affords me great satisfaction to have it in my power to enable you thus publicly to contradict insinuations suggested solely to poison the public mind. With respect to the sentiments of the inhabitants of the Spanish Main towards you, I can say with great truth, wherever I had an opportunity of communicating with them, they expressed the highest veneration for your character, and placed the greatest confidence in your government.

I am, my dear Sir,

Yours very sincerely,

E. S. DICKSON, Captain R.N.

Colonel Picton, &c. &c.

APPENDIX, No. IV.

MY DEAR SIR,

In perusing Colonel Fullarton's publication relating to certain transactions in the Island of Trinidad during your government, I cannot, as an officer who then held a considerable time the command of one of his Majesty's sloops on that station, help expressing that indignation I must naturally feel at the very malicious aspersions with which that gentleman has thought proper to stigmatize the conduct of the naval officers during that period.

The reasons for which he has introduced in his work this calumny, of predatory excursions being undertaken for private purposes, and particularly to obtain negroes for the governor of Trinidad's estates, is foreign to the purpose; but so serious an imputation cannot be passed over in silence; indeed, it behoves every one against whom this accusation is brought to vindicate himself; and as that is the sole object of this address, you will make that use of it you may deem most advisable to that end.

Mr. Fullarton must know that every atom of what he has above asserted respecting the navy is, *as I now declare it to be, perfectly false.* Though the ships and vessels of war were under the command of Captain E. S. Dickson, we were both on service on the Spanish Main, but not for the purpose of committing depredations. We had a more laudable object, in searching for and destroying a cowardly foe, still numerous in the West Indies;—brigands who were harbouring in the Spanish Main, and taking every opportunity of committing depredations on the island of Trinidad; and, but for the excellent look-out upon their plans, much mischief might have ensued to the colony: and on no other account have I received any other orders respecting this service, nor were any slaves or cattle taken by me as asserted; if they were, my present declaration would fall to the ground, as a reference to the ship's journals would establish the point as well as living testimony. I believe, my dear sir, you had at that time no landed property in the island; and if you had, I am convinced, from our long acquaintance, and your well-established honest integrity, you are one of the last, I should conceive, who could have admitted a thought of stocking your lands by such means. Captain Dickson, Major Mosheim, and myself must spurn at these base insinuations. With long and faithful regard to your eminent services and faithful friendship,

I am, my dear Sir,

Your most assured friend,

WILLIAM CHAMPAIN, Captain R.N.

Jason, Woolwich, December 28th, 1804.
　To Colonel Picton, &c. &c.

APPENDIX, No. V.

London, October 1st, 1805.

SIR,

Having had the honour of serving under your command in the Island of Trinidad in the years 1798 and 1799,—periods the most critical, during which your vigilance, activity, and wise measures preserved that valuable colony,—I could not help reading with the utmost astonishment and surprise, " A Statement of Letters and Documents respecting the Affairs of Trinidad, &c. &c." I must declare the same in one particular instance to be " a statement of the most base and malicious falsehood ;" and firmly persuade myself that, after a just and candid investigation, the whole will appear in its true merits; as having been brought forward purposely to create amongst an ignorant public an unfavourable impression concerning your acts of government, which unquestionably will stand the most rigid ordeal.

I allude to number 83,—Colonel Fullarton's answer to Colonel Picton's address, page 172,—where it is said, " The various expeditions against Guiria, Point-à-Pierre, and Carussano, on the river Guarapuchy, were merely predatory enterprises to procure mules and cattle, and to punish individuals who had incurred Colonel Picton's resentment." Also page 11, in a note: " The chief object of these expeditions was to plunder cattle from the unoffending inhabitants for his own emolument."

I have been the officer whom you ordered to embark with a detachment of an hundred men, " to disperse several armed bodies collected and assembling on the opposite coasts of the Gulf, at Guiria, the River Guarapuchy, &c. &c."

I sailed on board of his Majesty's ship Invincible, Captain Cayley, in company with his Majesty's sloop Zephyr, Captain Champain; my instructions ordering me to disperse all armed bodies along the coast assembled for the purpose of invasion, and of preventing Spanish launches to proceed to Port of Spain; enjoined the strictest attention to order and discipline, and to cultivate the good will of the inhabitants along the coast.' And I do hereby most solemnly declare, that not the least act of depredation or irregularity has been committed by this expedition, which effected several landings along the coast. The first disembarkation, which took place at Guiria, was made with all necessary precautions, not knowing what resistance we should meet with: Captain Cayley was even so obliging as to order a party of marines to proceed with me on shore. Finding, however, the enemy dispersed, and the inhabitants coming in crowds to receive us as friends, the troops were re-embarked the very same evening, and in our subsequent visits on shore we were only attended by small parties of about fifteen or twenty men.

This, therefore, sir, was no predatory enterprise; on the contrary, it was undertaken, *as all others*, for the protection of a very valuable trade with the Spanish Main, and for the security of the Island of Trinidad.

I forbear saying more, regretting much the worthy

captain then commanding his Majesty's ship Invincible being dead, and therefore not to be referred to on the occasion. I am convinced that the respectable naval officers under whose protection, assistance, and direction these expeditions did sail,—Captain Champain, Captain Dickson, &c.; Major Laureal, of the 12th West India regiment; Captain Frauchessin, of Sir Charles Green's light infantry volunteers,—will all concur with me in declaring it " a base and malicious falsehood," when it is asserted that their chief object was plunder and depredation.

I have the honour to be, with the greatest respect,

Sir,

Your very faithful and obedient servant,

Ls. MOSHEIM, Lieut.-Col.

Colonel Thomas Picton, &c. &c.
21, Edward Street.

APPENDIX, No. VI.

Lewes, 27th October 1812

SIR,

I take the liberty of addressing this letter to you, in the hope that you will at least forgive the intrusion, and allow me to detail a few introductory particulars before I presume to express my wishes.

Anticipating that my regiment (in General Hill's division) was not likely to be actively employed, I obtained leave to serve at the siege of Badajoz as an acting engineer; and on the night of the storming that city, I had the honour of conducting the third division of the army, under your auspicious command, to the point of escalade at the castle. I naturally felt considerable anxiety at the weight of the charge, when in the open space where none had before trod; although I was particularly acquainted with everything from the trenches to and about the castle,—and no delay occurred. You will, sir, I presume, recollect, that on your arrival at the mill-dam, (where streams of fire opened on you,) the forlorn-hope and others stopped the way, and some men had fallen in the water: I rushed through the crowd, and found the ladders left on the railing in the ditch, and this barrier unbroken. In this extremity, I cried out, " Down with the paling !" and with my own hands, aided by a few men, I made the opening at which you entered. At the wall, you know, sir, the fire was terrific—the men were amazed ; but I succeeded in getting the ladders erected, although three broke, and I fear a brigade-major, who laboured hard, was hurt by their fall. In applying myself, for example, to a ladder the men had abandoned, a ball lodged in the upper part of my thigh, and caused a compound fracture, and I fell on a man who had just dropped at my side. I remained till the afternoon of the next day amidst expiring brother sufferers, and being confined one hundred and thirty days to my bed, my sufferings were very severe: but I was greatly consoled by the approbation of Majors Squires and Burgoyne of the Engineers, and particularly by their assurance of your commendation.

I returned last month on sick leave ; and am, thank God ! much recovered.

His Royal Highness the Commander-in-chief some time since promised me promotion for my length of service and former wounds at Corunna; I therefore trust my exertions at Badajoz will add to my claims ; and as I intend to lay my case before his Royal Highness, I beg leave most earnestly to solicit you to honour me with your approbation, which will ensure my promotion.

I have the honour to be, Sir,

Your most obedient humble servant,

E. MAC CARTHY, Lieut. 50th Reg.

To Lieutenant-general Picton, &c.

General Picton made immediate application to the Commander-in-chief, for the promotion of this deserving officer, and he was within a few days appointed to a company.

APPENDIX, No. VII.

ACCOUNT OF THE CEREMONY OF LAYING THE FOUNDATION
STONE OF THE MONUMENT IN HONOUR OF SIR THOMAS
PICTON AT CARMARTHEN.

This long-expected and interesting ceremony took place before a great concourse of spectators, estimated at ten thousand persons. Early in the morning and the preceding evening a vast concourse of company kept pouring into the town to witness the proceedings of the day; and we can with confidence and truth assert, that a more numerous and respectable procession, or a more imposing ceremony, was never witnessed in this town by the oldest inhabitant. As the hour appointed for organising the procession approached, vast numbers of elegantly-dressed females were to be observed bending their steps towards the spot intended for the erection of the monument, who, as they arrived, were ushered by the steward, Mr. G. Goode, into the seats raised for their accommodation. The cavalry moved on to the ground under the command of the Honourable George Rice Trevor, M.P. and took their station, lining the road near the depôt. A little before twelve o'clock, the mayor and corporation of Carmarthen, the committee of the Carmarthen Cymreigyddion Society, visiters, &c. moved in procession from the Town-hall, preceded by a band of music, to the Ivy-bush Hotel, where they were joined by the

Provincial Grand Lodge for South Wales, and the other lodges and members of the honourable fraternity in masonic order; and the whole proceeded to the site of the stone, entering the ground on the right hand, passing round in front of the seats, in order to afford those who had previously taken their places an opportunity of seeing the whole procession, and retiring through the other entrance on the left hand. When the head of the procession reached the principal entrance the second time, the lines were opened, the original order of the procession was reversed, and entered the ground in the following order :—

Provincial Grand Tyler, with a drawn sword.

Band of Music.

Two P. G. Stewards, with wands.

P. G. Sword-bearer.

P. G. Steward, with a wand.   { Standard of the P. G. Lodge. }   P. G. Steward, with a wand.

Right Worshipful the Provincial Grand Master for South Wales.

Deputy P. G. Master, with a square.

P. G. Steward, with a wand.   { Volume of the Sacred Law, with the square and compasses, on a velvet cushion. }   P. G. Steward, with a wand.

Senior P. G. Warden, with the level.

Junior P. G. Warden, with the plummet.

Sir W. C. De Crespigny, P. G. Master for Hampshire.

P. G. Chaplain.

P. G. Treasurer, with the coins and inscriptions.

P. G. Registrar.

P. G. Secretary, with the book of Constitutions.

P. G. Director of Ceremonies.

P. G. Superintendent of Works, with the silver trowel and plan of elevation.

P. G. Organist.

A Master Mason, with the mallet.

After which the following lodges, arranged in masonic order, and preceded by their respective banners.

The Glamorgan of Cardiff, No. 50.

The Union of Carmarthen, No. 192.

The Indefatigable and Beaufort of Swansea, No. 427.

The Cambrian of Neath, No. 726.

The St. David's, or Loyal George the Fourth's, of Mitford, No. 728.

Brethren, not members of any lodge present.

Peace Officers.

Union Flag.

Drums and Fifes.

Staff of the Carmarthenshire Militia.

Lords Lieutenants for the counties of Pembroke, Carmarthen, and Cardigan.

Visiters of distinction.

The Standard of the Corporation.

The Mayor and Corporation of Carmarthen in their robes, preceded by the Mace and Sword-bearers.

Clergymen in their Canonicals.

Banner of the Cymreigyddion Society.

Committee of the Cymreigyddion Society.

Union Flag.

Subscribers and Gentlemen connected with the undertaking.

Peace Officers.

The several parties comprising the procession having been conducted by the steward to the stations respectively assigned them, and the regalia of the Grand Lodge being placed on a table provided for the purpose, the grand master and his officers took their station on a platform erected for their reception on the east side of the stone; the Right Honourable Lady Dynevor being on the west, and the several lodges with their officers and banners in front, forming a square, the band playing a masonic air. By command of the deputy grand master, the stone was raised about four feet, and the mortar spread on the base by Mr. Mainwaring, the architect. The Right Honourable Lady Dynevor, supported by Sir Christopher Cole, grand master for South Wales, and Sir W. C. De

Crespigny, grand master for Hampshire, then descended to the stone, when the grand treasurer, by command of the grand master, deposited the coins, &c. which were enclosed in a glass hermetically sealed, and consisted of all the gold, silver, and copper British coins of the present reign, together with the Waterloo medal of the late Sir Thomas Picton, and covered them with a plate bearing the following inscription :·

This,
The first stone of the Column
Erected to the memory of our gallant countryman
Lieutenant-general Sir THOMAS PICTON,
(Knight Grand Cross of the Bath, and of several foreign orders,)
Who, after serving his king and country
In several campaigns,
Died gloriously at the battle of Waterloo,
Was laid
By the Right Honourable Frances Baroness Dynevor,
Assisted by
Sir Christopher Cole, (Knight Commander
Of the Bath, Captain in the Royal Navy of Britain, Member
Of Parliament for the County of Glamorgan,
And Provincial Grand Master of
Masons for South Wales,)
On the 16th day of August 1825.

The upper part of the stone was then lowered slowly to its destined position, the band playing solemn music.

After which the Rev. John Davies of Llandovery, provincial grand chaplain for South Wales, invoked the blessing of the Great Architect of the Universe in the following words:—" O Almighty and Eternal God, by whom the foundations of the earth were laid, and the curtains of the heavens were spread, and upon whom dependeth the success of everything we take in hand; we, thy humble creatures, implore Thee to bless and countenance this our present undertaking, that, as it is begun in order, it may be carried on in⸱ harmony, and finally be crowned with success, through Jesus Christ our Lord.   Amen."

The grand master then proved that the stone was properly adjusted, by the application of the plumb, rule, level, and square, which were successively delivered to him by the junior and senior grand wardens and deputy grand master.   The mallet was then delivered to the grand master, who handed it to Lady Dynevor, with which her ladyship struck the stone three times, the band playing ' God save the King,' amidst the enthusiastic applause of the assembled spectators, and a salute of twenty-one guns from the depôt.

The scene at this moment was peculiarly imposing. Every person present uncovered as it were instinctively, one common sentiment seeming to pervade the assembled thousands ; every face was lighted up with enthusiasm, and every voice exerted to cheer the commencement of an undertaking which will transmit to posterity the heroic achievements of one of the ablest and bravest generals that ever graced the military annals of this or any other country.

The plan and elevation of the column were then presented by the grand superintendent of works to the grand master for his inspection, with which he expressed his approbation, and delivered them to the architect for his guidance, and also the implements of operative masonry, desiring him to erect the structure conformably to the same. Lady Dynevor was reconducted to the platform prepared for her at the west end of the area ; and the grand master resumed his station with the Grand Lodge at the eastern end of the stone, the band playing a national air.

The grand master then addressed the mayor and corporation, noblemen, clergy, and gentry present, as follows:—

" Gentlemen,—I beg leave to congratulate you on the ceremony which has just taken place, preparatory to the erecting a monument to the memory of that gallant and distinguished officer the late Sir Thomas Picton ; and you will allow me now to assure you, that I have had the sincerest gratification, as provincial grand master of masonry for South Wales, in finding myself in a situation to lend my humble aid to the business of this day. I am perfectly aware that on this subject I have a wide field for observation ; but I must throw myself upon the indulgence and kind-heartedness of those who hear me, and at once confess my total inability to render even common justice to the eminent merits of this gallant officer, whose loss we have so long deplored : and it might perhaps be justly considered presumption in so humble an individual as myself to attempt to utter anything like a detailed panegyric or eulogium on the character of that great officer whose memory we have met this day to do honour to. But, gentlemen, it has happened to me in the performance of my professional duties, many years ago, whilst serving in a distant quarter of the globe, to be called under the notice of that distinguished character, when he held a situation of high trust and responsibility as governor of one of the West India Islands ; and I had frequent opportunities of witnessing the activity, ability, and rigid principle, which marked his conduct in this high situation: and I left the Island of Trinidad with impressions of respect and admiration which time can never efface.

" Gentlemen,—if these were'my feelings, it was with
a degree of disgust that I will not attempt to describe,
that I found by the public prints not long afterwards,
when serving on a still more distant station, that a
most violent persecution existed against the conduct
and character of this honest and upright public servant,
which ended in a criminal prosecution. But this disgust was soon followed by a corresponding feeling of
exultation, when, supported alone by the firmness of
his own mind, by the integrity of his own principles,
he was enabled to throw back tenfold upon his accusers
that odium which they had vainly endeavoured to affix
to his character.

" It is impossible for me to quit this part of the life
of Sir Thomas Picton without mentioning a circumstance which may not have come to the knowledge of
many that hear me, and which, I am sure, will be considered as redounding as much to his honour as any of
those more brilliant events which accompanied the latter part of his glorious life. At the time he was under
the circumstances I have mentioned, the respectable
and well-disposed inhabitants of the Island of Trinidad
entered into and realized a subscription which amounted to a large sum of money, and which they transmit-
ted to their late governor, as a proof of their respect
and devoted attachment, to enable him the more easily
to meet the expenses of the prosecution, which, unhap-
pily in this country, often press as heavily upon the
innocent as the guilty. A dreadful fire had, about
this time, consumed nearly the whole of the town at
the principal sea-port on the island, and the inhabitants, by this visitation of Providence, were reduced to
a state of the greatest misery and distress. With a

feeling of generosity and magnanimity which can never be too much admired, the whole of this sum was remitted back to the island for the relief of their necessities. And be it remembered, that there must have been many in the number of sufferers who had been unfriendly to him under his difficulties; but, with true Christian charity, on this occasion he drew no distinction between friend and foe.

" Gentlemen,—after the most honourable public acquittal, a short time placed him on a wider scene of action, for which he had been prepared by the best military education in his youth; and in that very quarter, the West India Islands, he soon gave an earnest of that harvest of glory which he afterwards reaped on so many fields of battle on the continent of Europe. I now approach a period of this great officer's life with a feeling of diffidence and incapacity, which entirely prevents my making an attempt to give any detailed account of his distinguished services during the war in Spain and Portugal. And, gentlemen, his actions are too deeply engraved on the hearts of those to whom I address myself, to make it necessary for me to refer more particularly to that period of his career: it is sufficient for me to say, that there is not a volume—scarcely a page of history of the Peninsular war, that does not teem with the heroic exploits of Sir Thomas Picton; and it is known that he returned from that war with the admiration of his fellow-soldiers, together with the admiration and gratitude of his countrymen.

" If I feel difficulties in touching upon the exploits of Sir Thomas Picton in the Peninsular war, how much must these difficulties be increased when I look upon the circumstances of his glorious death on the field of Waterloo! Perhaps the finest compliment ever paid to a military talent was paid by the greatest captain of the age, when he offered a prominent command to this distinguished soldier in that army which their great captain was about to lead to the Continent, to give confidence to Europe, and to give the final blow to the arrogant ambition and inordinate lust of dominion of the greatest conqueror, but the greatest despot, that this world ever produced. It is known that the fall of this hero was accompanied by a desperate and new example in military tactics; and that, at the head of a body of infantry, he attacked at the point of the bayonet, and defeated, what had been until that day considered the finest cavalry in Europe; and no British heart can do otherwise than give the meed to his memory, of having devoted himself to death for the glory and safety of his country.

" Long may that stone continue as a memorial of the eminent abilities, the undaunted courage, the brilliant heroism, of this lamented general! Long may it remain as a proof that, in possessing these qualities, he found the best reward that a Briton can receive in this world,—the ardent admiration and generous gratitude of his fellow-countrymen !"

Immense cheering followed the close of this speech, which was also repeatedly applauded during its delivery.

INDEX.

A.

Abercromby, Sir Ralph, appointed commander-in-chief in the West Indies, i. 23 ; his friendly reception of Major Picton, 24 ; directs his forces against St. Lucia, 25 ; orders an assault to be made against Morne Chabot, 26 ; passage from the orders issued by him, 31 ; recommends Major Picton to the lieutenant-colonelcy of the 56th regiment, 32 ; arranges with Major Nicholls an expedition against Grenada, *ib.* ; proceeds to attack the island of St. Vincent, *ib.* ; accompanies Colonel Picton to Martinique, from thence to England, 33 ; returns to the West Indies, accompanied by Colonel Picton, 34 ; makes arrangements with Admiral Harvey for the expedition against Trinidad, *ib.* ; appoints Colonel Picton governor of Trinidad, 36 ; his instructions for the management of the island, 37 ; instructions from his Majesty's government to him, 46 ; Colonel Picton's letter to him, 80.

Achard, Lagar, Esq. one of the witnesses at General Picton's second trial, i. 220.

Addington, Mr. Gen. Picton's letter to, i. 112.

" Adventures of the Rifle Brigade," ii. 77 *n.* 374.

Albuera, battle of, ii. 25 ; passage from Colonel Napier's, description of, 26.

Albuquerque, Duke de, defends Cadiz on his own responsibility, i. 254.

Aldea de Ponte, desperate conflict at, ii. 48.

Alhandra, hills of, i. 363.

Almeida, fall of, i. 302.

Alvarado, Vicar-general, gives a cer-

tificate of Luise Calderon's baptism, i. 170.

Angeles, Josef Maria, curate of the Catholic church, i. 169; found guilty of perjury, 170.

Angoulême, Duc d', his entry into Bordeaux, ii. 312.

" Annals of the Peninsular Campaign," extracts from, i. 259. 395 ; ii. 228. 278.

B.

Badajoz, cantonment around broken up, i. 256 ; fortress of, invested by the British, ii. 83 ; attack made on Fort Picurina, 84 ; taken, 88 ; outline of the siege of, 89 ; the castle taken by General Picton, 120 ; surrender of the garrison to the British, 127;

Batty, Capt. his account of Soult's attack upon the left wing of the allied army, ii. 274.

Beckwith, Col. assists in the engagement of Sabugal, ii. 6 ; his perilous situation, 7 ; Lord Wellington's remark respecting his bravery, 9.

Begorrat, Senor Hilariot, official communication from him to Governor Picton, i. 163.

Belvidere, Conde de, his army beaten at Estremadura, i. 244.

Bentinck, Lord William, supersedes Sir John Murray in the command in Catalonia, ii. 236 ; resigns the command, *ib.*

Beresford, Marshal, lays siege to Badajoz, ii. 24; compelled to give battle to Soult at Albuera, 25 ; his judgment at the battle of Albuera, *ib.* ; wounded at the battle of Salamanca, 171 ; left wing under him commenced the attack at the battle of Orthes, 301 ; his critical situation at the battle of Tou-

THE END.

LONDON :
PRINTED BY SAMUEL BENTLEY,
Dorset Street, Fleet Street.

ND - #0037 - 010824 - C0 - 229/152/51 - PB - 9780282375119 - Gloss Lamination